The Story of Christianity

VOLUME II

The Reformation to the Present Day

REVISED AND UPDATED

Justo L. González

HarperOne

An Imprint of HarperCollins*Publishers*

HarperOne

THE STORY OF CHRISTIANITY VOLUME II: *The Reformation to the Present Day.* Revised and Updated. Copyright © 2010 by Justo L. González. All rights reserved. Printed in the United States of America. No part of this book may be used or reproduced in any manner whatsoever without written permission except in the case of brief quotations embodied in critical articles and reviews. For information, address HarperCollins Publishers, 10 East 53rd Street, New York, NY 10022.

HarperCollins books may be purchased for educational, business, or sales promotional use. For information, please write: Special Markets Department, HarperCollins Publishers, 10 East 53rd Street, New York, NY 10022.

HarperCollins Web site: http://www.harpercollins.com
HarperCollins®, ® and HarperCollins™
are trademarks of HarperCollins

SECOND EDITION
Designed by Level C

Library of Congress Cataloging-in-Publication Data is available upon request.

ISBN 978–0–06–185589–4

11 12 13 14 15   RRD   10 9 8 7 6 5 4 3 2 1

To Catherine

Contents

PART I

THE
REFORMATION

CHRONOLOGY

Popes	Emperors	Castile	Aragon	France	England	Scotland	Events
		Isabella (1474–1504)	Ferdinand (1479–1516)		Henry VII (1485–1509)	James IV (1488–1513)	Columbus in America (1492)
Alexander VI (1492–1503)	Maximilian I (1493–1519)	Joanna the Mad (1504–1516)		Louis XII (1498–1515)	Henry VII (1509–1547)	James V (1513–1542)	
Pius III (1503)							
Julius II (1503–1513)							

Popes	Emperors	Spain	France	England	Scotland	Events
Leo X (1513–1521)						
			Francis I (1515–1547)			Erasmus' New Testament (1515)
		Charles I (1516–1556)				Luther: Ninety-five These (1517)
	Charles V (1519–1556)					Diet of Worms (1521)
Adrian VI (1522–1523)						Loyola at Manresa (1522)
Clement VII (1523–1524)						
						Peasants' War (1524–1525)
						Vienna besieged by Turks (1529)

Popes	Emperors	Spain	France	England	Scotland	Events
						Marburg Colloquy (1529)
						Augsburg Confession (1530)
Paul III (1534–1549)						†Zwingli (1531)
						England breaks with Rome (1534)
						Fall of Münster (1535)
						Calvin's *Institutes* (1536)
						Jesuits approved by pope (1540)
					Mary Stuart (1542–1567)	
						Council of Trent (1545–1563)
			Henry II (1547–1559)	Edward VI (1547–1553)		† Luther (1546)
Julius III (1550–1555)						

Popes	Emperors	Spain	France	England	Scotland	Events
Marcellus II (1555)				Mary Tudor (1553–1558)		Peace of Augsburg (1555)
Paul IV (1555–1559)		Philip II (1556–1598)				†Ignatius Loyola (1556)
	Ferdinand I (1558–1564)					
Pius IV (1559–1565)			Francis II (1559–1560)	Elizabeth I (1558–1603)		Calvin's *Institutes*, final edition (1559)
			Charles IX (1560–1574)			†Menno Simons (1561) Wars of religion in France (1562)
	Maximilian II (1564–1576)					†Calvin (1564)
Pius V (1566–1572)					James VI (1567–1625)	Uprising in the Netherlands (1566)

Popes	Emperors	Spain	France	England	Scotland	Events
Gregory XIII (1572–1585)						Massacre of St. Bartholomew's day (1572)
						†Knox (1572)
	Rudolph II (1576–1612)		Henry III (1574–1589)			Pacification of Ghent (1576)
						†William the Silent (1584)
Sixtus V (1585–1590)						†Mary Stuart (1587)
			Henry IV (1589–1610)			
Urban VII (1590)						
Gregory XIV (1590–1591)						
Innocent IX (1591)						
Clement VIII (1592–1605)		Philip III (1598–1621)				Edict of Nantes (1598)

I

The Call for Reformation

The dissolution is such, that the souls entrusted to the clergy receive great damage, for we are told that the majority of the clergy are living in open concubinage, and that if our justice intervenes in order to punish them, they revolt and create a scandal, and that they despise our justice to the point that they arm themselves against it.

ISABELLA OF CASTILE, ON NOVEMBER 20, 1500

As the fifteenth century came to a close, it was clear that the church was in need of profound reformation, and that many longed for it. The decline and corruption of the papacy was well known. After its residence in Avignon, where it had served as a tool of French interests, the papacy had been further weakened by the Great Schism, which divided Western Europe in its allegiance to two—and even three—popes. At times, the various claimants to the papal see seemed equally unworthy. Then, almost as soon as the schism was healed, the papacy fell into the hands of men who were more moved by the glories of the Renaissance than by the message of the cross. Through war, intrigue, bribery, and licentiousness, these popes sought to restore and even to outdo the glories of ancient Rome. As a result, while most people still believed in the supreme authority of the Roman see, many found it difficult to reconcile their faith in the papacy with their distrust for its actual occupants.

Corruption, however, was not limited to the leadership in Rome. The councils that had been convened as a means to reform and to end the Great Schism were able to end the schism, but not to bring about the needed reformation. Furthermore, even in ending the schism the conciliar movement showed its own flaws, for there were soon two rival councils—just as before there had been two or even three rival popes, and conciliarism had failed miserably in the task of bringing about the much-needed reform. One of the reasons for such failure was that several of the bishops sitting in the councils were themselves among those who profited from the existing corruption. Thus, while the hopeful conciliarist reformers issued anathemas and decrees against absenteeism, pluralism, and simony—the practice of buying and selling ecclesiastical positions—many who sat on the councils were guilty of such practices, and were not ready to give them up.

Such corrupt leadership set the tone for most of the lesser clergy and the monastics. While clerical celibacy was the law of the church, there were many who broke it openly; and bishops and local priests alike—and even some popes—flaunted their illegitimate children. The ancient monastic discipline was increasingly relaxed as convents and monasteries became centers of leisurely living. Monarchs and the high nobility often provided for their illegitimate offspring by having them named abbots and abbesses, with no regard for their monastic vocation or lack of it. The commitment to learning for which monastic houses had been famous also declined, and the educational requirements for the local clergy fell to practically nil.

The conciliar movement had waned, and with it also the hope that a general council of the church could produce the much-needed reformation. A sign of this was the Fifth Lateran Council, which was convoked by Pope Julius II, supposedly in order to reform the church, but in truth in an effort to regain the political control the papacy had been losing. The council convened in 1512, and by the time it disbanded in 1517 it had achieved little beyond decreeing an extraordinary taxation to span the next three years—theoretically, in order to raise funds for a new crusade—reaffirming the authority of the pope in the face of French attempts to limit such authority, and insisting on the power and dignity of bishops and other prelates. It should be noted that the council adjourned in March of 1517, a few months before the beginning of the Protestant Reformation.

In such circumstances, even the many priests and monastics who wished to be faithful to their calling found this to be exceedingly difficult. How could one practice asceticism and contemplation in a monastery that had become a house of leisure and a meeting place for fashionable soirées? How could a priest resist corruption in his parish, when he himself had been forced to buy his position? How could the laity trust a sacrament of penance administered by a member of the clergy who seemed to have no sense of the enormity of sin? The religious conscience of Europe was divided within itself, torn between trust in a church that had been its spiritual mother for generations, and the patent failures of that church.

But it was not only at the moral level that the church seemed to be in need of reformation. Some among the more thoughtful Christians were becoming convinced that the teachings of the church had also gone astray. The fall of Constantinople, half a century earlier, had flooded Western Europe, and Italy in particular, with scholars whose views were different from those that were common in the West. The manuscripts these scholars brought with them alerted Western scholars to the many changes and interpolations that had taken place in the copying and recopying of ancient texts. New philosophical outlooks were also introduced. Greek became more commonly known among Western scholars, who could now compare the Greek text of the New Testament with the commonly used Latin Vulgate. From such quarters came the conviction that it was necessary to return to the sources of the Christian faith, and that this would result in a reformation of existing doctrine and practice.

Although most who held such views were by no means radical, their call for a return to the sources tended to confirm the earlier appeals by reformers such as Wycliffe and Huss. The desire for a reformation in the doctrine of the church did not seem so out of place if it were true that such doctrine had changed through the centuries, straying from the New Testament. The many followers of those earlier reformers still had in England, Bohemia, and other areas now felt encouraged by scholarship which, while not agreeing with them on their more radical claims, confirmed their basic tenet: that it was necessary to return to the sources of Christianity, particularly through the study of Scripture.

To this was added the discontent of the masses, which earlier had found expression in apocalyptic movements like the one led by Hans Böhm. The economic conditions of the masses, far from improving, had worsened in the preceding decades. The peasants in particular were increasingly exploited by the landowners. While some monastic houses and church leaders still practiced acts of charity, most of the poor no longer had the sense that the church was their defender. On the contrary, the ostentatiousness of prelates, their power as landowners, and their support of increasing inequality were seen by many as a betrayal of the poor, and eventually as a sign that the Antichrist had gained possession of the church. The ferment brewing in such quarters periodically broke out in peasant revolts, apocalyptic visions, and calls for a new order.

Meanwhile, the ancient feudal system was coming to an end. First France, and then England and Spain, saw the development of powerful monarchies that forced the nobility to serve the ends of the nation as a whole. The sovereigns of such states felt the need to limit and control the power of the prelates, many of whom were also feudal rulers of vast areas. As France had earlier led in the suppression of the Templars, Spain now felt compelled to bring the ancient military orders, such as Calatrava and Santiago, under royal supremacy; and to that end King Ferdinand was made their grand master. Areas that did not enjoy the same unity, such as the Netherlands and Germany, seethed with nationalist discontent and dreams of union and independence. Latin, which earlier had been a common bond for much of Western Europe, was increasingly limited to ecclesiastical and scholarly circles, while the various vernacular languages came to be regarded as equally respectable. Indeed, the fifteenth and sixteenth centuries were the formative period for most of the literary languages of Western Europe. Nationalism, which had begun to develop centuries earlier, found expression in

The Convento de Santo Domingo, in Avila, served as the headquarters for Torquemada's inquisitorial activities.

these languages, and soon became the order of the day, both in those nations that had achieved political unity and in those that still fretted under feudal disunion and foreign dominance. Such sentiments in turn undermined the ancient dream of "one flock under one shepherd," which now appeared to many as little more than an excuse for foreign intervention.

In some areas, the growing power of the monarchs, the divergent opinions and ideas in a time of intellectual unrest, and frustration with the actual life of the church, led to an increase in the powers and activities of the Inquisition. Already in the Middle Ages it was not uncommon for bishops to act as inquisitors, investigating the theological opinions of their flocks, seeking to correct those whose views were considered heretical, and severely punishing the teachers and leaders who espoused those views. But in the fifteenth century, particularly in Spain, the powers and activity of the Inquisition rose to new heights. The Inquisition, normally under papal authority and in the later Middle Ages used mostly as a tool of papal policy, was placed by the pope under the authority of Ferdinand and Isabella. The Dominican friar Tomás de Torquemada, who was known for his uncompromising love for orthodoxy, was appointed to head the Inquisition in Castile, and his name has become famous for the zeal with which he persecuted those whom he

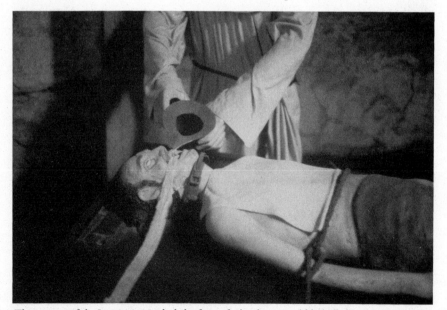

The tortures of the Inquisition included a form of what later would be called "water-boarding."

considered heretics. These were mostly Jews who had been converted under duress, and who were now accused of "Judaizing."

As we shall see, at that time there was a concerted effort to reform the church on the part of Queen Isabella and her confessor Francisco Jiménez de Cisneros. During Isabella's reign, and with the firm encouragement of Jiménez, the pressure on Jews and "Judaizing" Christians became increasingly severe. Finally, in 1492, it was decreed that all Jews must either accept baptism or leave all territories under Isabella and Ferdinand. Most refused to be baptized, even though it meant exile and the loss of most of their possessions. Although exact figures are not available, it seems that approximately two hundred thousand Spaniards of the Jewish faith were thus condemned to exile—which in many cases led to death, capture by pirates, and other such misfortunes.

Shortly before the promulgation of the royal decree against Jews, Granada had fallen to Castilian arms. This was the last Moorish stronghold in the peninsula, and the terms of surrender included freedom for the Muslims to continue practicing their religion. But soon Jiménez and his representatives were seeking the forced conversion of the Moors, who saw no alternative but rebellion. This was drowned in blood. But resistance continued, and eventually it was decreed that all Moors had to choose between baptism and exile. When it became clear that there would be a massive exodus, a new edict was issued, forbidding the Moors from leaving the country, and forcing baptism on them. After such unwilling conversions, the Inquisition was kept busy tracking down those who persisted in their Muslim beliefs and practices. Jiménez, who had been made Inquisitor General, took this task to heart. In 1516, after the death of both Ferdinand and Isabella, he was also made regent, and sought to use his power to force the "converted" Moors to abandon their traditional garb and other customs. In this he failed, and again the kingdom was shaken by rebellion and bloodshed.

Then came the Protestant Reformation and the "discovery" of the New World, and both led to broader actions by the Inquisition. As we shall see, in Europe this was part of the Catholic Reformation, which used the Inquisition as one of its tools to prevent the spread of Protestantism. In the New World, the powers of the Inquisition were eventually employed also to prevent and punish interlopers from other European nations.

The means of torture used during the Inquisition, and the manner in which it was exploited for political reasons as well as for personal gain and vengeance,

An old world was passing away, and a new one was being born to take its place. In this illustration from one of Galileo's works, he is depicted as discussing the universe with Ptolemy and Copernicus.

are well known, and their memory would long survive as a prime example of the dangers and consequences of religious extremism and obscurantism.

While it does not justify it, the context within which the Inquisition took place must be understood, including other momentous events that were changing Western Europe's worldview and creating an atmosphere of both expectation and uncertainty. New worlds were being discovered beyond the Western horizon. Travel to the Far East was becoming increasingly common. The flat earth around which the sun and the stars revolved became a relic of the past. Great advances were being made in medicine, mathematics, and physics. And all this was made readily available to scholars in various areas by means of the printing press, which was coming into its own precisely at that time.

An old world was passing away, and a new one was being born. It was unavoidable that the church too would feel the impact of the new times and that, just as new ways of being human were emerging, new ways of being Christian would also emerge. Exactly how this was to be done, however, was open to debate. Some sought to reform the old church from within, while others lost all hope for such reformation, and openly broke with the papacy. In an age of such turmoil, many sincere Christians went through profound soul searching that eventually led them to conclusions and positions they could not have predicted. Others, equally sincere and devout, came to opposite conclusions. The resulting disagreements and conflict marked the entire age that we now call the Reformation of the sixteenth century.

As the Middle Ages drew to a close, many advocates of reform were convinced that the greatest ill of the church was the obscurantism of what soon would be called the *Dark Ages*. The printing press, the influx of Byzantine scholars, and the rediscovery of the artistic and literary legacies of antiquity gave credence to the hope that the furtherance of scholarship and education would produce the much-needed reformation of the church. If at some point in the past centuries practices had been introduced that were contrary to original Christian teaching, it seemed reasonable to surmise that a return to the sources of Christianity—both biblical and patristic—would do away with such practices.

This was the program of the humanist reformers. In this context, the term *humanist* does not refer primarily to those who value human nature above all else, but rather to those who devote themselves to the "humanities," seeking to restore the literary glories of antiquity. The humanists of the sixteenth century differed greatly from one another, but all agreed in their love of classical letters. Long before the Protestant Reformation broke out, there was a large network of humanists who carried a vast correspondence among themselves and who hoped that their work would result in the reformation of the church. Their acknowledged leader, respected by many and known as the *Prince of Humanists*, was Desiderius Erasmus of Rotterdam.

Erasmus was the illegitimate offspring of a priest and a physician's daughter, and throughout his life felt burdened by his humble origins. Reared in the midst of the bustling commercial activity of Holland, his

Erasmus, the "prince of humanists," as Albrecht Dürer saw him in 1526. The Greek words affirm that the works of Erasmus himself convey a better portrait than Dürer's.

opinions came to reflect the common values of the bourgeoisie: tolerance, moderation, stability, and so forth. He studied some scholastic theology, but soon came to despise its excessive subtlety and seemingly idle curiosity. He then decided to turn his attention to classical literature, which was enjoying a revival of interest. In a later visit to England, he became part of a circle of humanists interested in the reformation of the church, and these introduced him to the study of Scripture and of early Christian literature, which he saw as captive to the scholastics. It was at that time that he decided to perfect his rudimentary knowledge of Greek, which he soon mastered. Meanwhile, he published the *Enchiridion militis Christiani—Dagger* (or *Handbook) of the Christian Soldier.* There, using military metaphors, he expounded on what he took to be the Christian life, and the resources available to the "soldier of Christ."

As a young man, Erasmus had studied under the Brethren of the Common Life, and their "modern devotion" had had a profound impact on him. Now, combining the humanist spirit to that devotion, he came to describe Christianity as above all a decent, moderate, and balanced life. The commandments of Jesus he saw as similar to the best precepts of Stoicism and Platonism: Their purpose is to subject passion to the rule of reason. This is to be achieved through a fairly ascetic discipline, although this discipline must not be confused with monasticism. The monastic withdraws from the common life of the world; the true "soldier of Christ" trains for practical and daily life in the midst of human affairs. What the church needs, in order to be reformed, is for Christians to practice this discipline, and to abandon the vices of the pagans. In this reference to pagan vices, Erasmus had in mind the evil example set by the popes of the Renaissance, who had preferred comparison with Jupiter or with Julius Caesar than with Jesus or St. Peter. He therefore rejected the pomp and the quest for earthly glories that characterized much of the life of the church in his time, and called for a lifestyle of greater simplicity. This did not mean, however, a mere revival of the monastic spirit. He had much to say against monks and monasteries, which had become havens of idleness and ignorance. But he also rejected the monastic ideal as based on the unacceptable distinction between the precepts of Jesus, which all must obey, and his "counsels of perfection," addressed to monastics in particular. Such distinction, while encouraging some to radical obedience, implied that common Christians were somehow not also "soldiers of Christ," called to complete obedience.

Erasmus viewed such obedience as more important than doctrine. He did believe that doctrines were significant, and he held to traditional Christian orthodoxy on matters such as the incarnation and the Trinity. But he insisted that righteousness was more important than orthodoxy, and he frequently attacked friars who were capable of subtle theological discussions but whose lives were scandalous.

On the other hand, the true Christian life is one of inwardness. Profoundly influenced by Platonism—and by ancient Christian writers who had suffered the same influence—Erasmus was convinced that the Christian struggle was an inner one. While outward means, such as the sacraments, were important and should not be discarded, their significance was in their inner meaning, in the message they conveyed to the secret heart of the believer. As he would say of baptism, "what good is it to be outwardly sprinkled with holy water, if one is filthy within?"

In short, what Erasmus sought was the reformation of customs, the practice of decency and moderation, an inner devotion shaped by learning and meditation, and a church that encouraged these things. Although his birth was quite humble, he eventually won the admiration of scholars throughout Europe who shared similar hopes, and whose mouthpiece he became. Among his admirers were many in the nobility and even some crowned heads. His followers served as secretaries and mentors in some of the most powerful courts in Europe. The reformation he advocated seemed about to take place.

Then the Protestant Reformation broke out. Spirits were inflamed. Tolerance and moderation became increasingly difficult. It was no longer a matter of reforming customs, or of clarifying some aspects of Christian theology that might have gone astray, but rather of radically shifting some of the fundamental premises of traditional Christianity. Partisans on both sides sought the support of Erasmus, who preferred to stay out of a conflict in which passion seemed to have replaced reason. Eventually, he broke with Luther and his followers, as we shall see later on. But still he refused to support the Catholics in their attacks against the Protestants. To the very end, he had admirers in both camps but very few followers. From his study, while others called for inquisitorial intolerance, he continued calling for tolerance and moderation, for a reformation after the humanist design, and for the ancient virtues of the Stoics and the Platonists. Few paid heed to him, at least during his lifetime, and he would complain, "I detest dissension, because it goes both against the teachings of Christ and against a secret inclination of nature. I doubt that either side in the dispute can be suppressed without grave loss. It is clear that many of the reforms for which Luther calls are urgently needed. My only wish is that now that I am old I be allowed to enjoy the results of my efforts. But both sides reproach me and seek to coerce me. Some claim that since I do not attack Luther I agree with him, while the Lutherans declare that I am a coward who has forsaken the gospel."[1] But centuries later, after passions had subsided, both Protestants and Catholics would agree that his was a great mind and a great heart, and that all had something to learn from him

2

Martin Luther: Pilgrimage to Reformation

> Many have taken the Christian faith to be a simple and easy matter, and have even numbered it among the virtues. This is because they have not really experienced it, nor have they tested the great strength of faith.
>
> MARTIN LUTHER

Throughout the history of Christianity, few have been the object of as much debate as Martin Luther has been. Some describe him as the ogre who destroyed the unity of the church, the wild boar that trampled the Lord's vineyard, a renegade monk who spent his life shattering the very foundations of monasticism. For others, he is the great hero through whose efforts the preaching of the pure gospel was restored, the champion of biblical truth, and the reformer of a corrupt and apostate church. In recent years, however, there has been a growing mutual understanding among Christians of different persuasions. As a result of more balanced studies of Luther, Catholics as well as Protestants have been led to amend opinions that had resulted, not from historical research, but from the heat of polemics. Now few doubt Luther's sincerity, and many Catholic historians affirm that his protest was amply justified, and that he was right on many points of doctrine. On the other hand, few Protestant historians continue to view Luther as the gigantic hero who almost single-handedly reformed Christianity, and whose sins and errors were only of minor importance.

Luther appears to have been an erudite and studious man who was also uncouth and even rude in his manner. Perhaps this helped him express his very profound theological points in a manner that found ready response

*This painting by Lucas Cranach (1526), now in the National Museum
of Stockholm, is probably the most authentic extant portrait of Luther.*

among the masses. He was sincere in his faith to the point that it became
a passion burning within him, which he could also be vulgar in expressing.
Nothing mattered to him as much as his faith and his obedience to God.
Once he became convinced that God wished him to pursue a certain course
of action, he followed it to its ultimate consequences. He was clearly not the
sort of disciple who, having put a hand to the plow, looks back. His use of
language—both Latin and German—was masterful, although he was in-

clined to underline the importance of a particular assertion by exaggerating it to the point of distortion. Once convinced of the truth of his cause, he was ready to face the most powerful lords of his time. But the very depth of his conviction, his passionate stance on truth, and his tendency to exaggerate led him to utter expressions and take positions that he or his followers would later regret.

On the other hand, much of Luther's impact was due to circumstances that he neither created nor controlled, and of whose role in the process of reformation he himself was only dimly aware. The invention of the movable type printing press gave his writings a widespread audience they otherwise would not have had—in fact, Luther was the first to make full use of the value of printing as a medium for propaganda, and to write with the printed page in mind. The growing German nationalist sentiment of which he himself partook offered unexpected but very valuable support. Many humanists who hoped for reformation, while disagreeing with many of Luther's tenets and methods, insisted that he should not be condemned without a hearing, as had happened earlier to John Huss. Political circumstances at the outset of the Reformation also prevented Luther's immediate condemnation, and by the time civil and ecclesiastic authorities were ready to intervene it was too late to quiet the storm. On studying Luther's life and work, one thing is clear: the much-needed reformation took place, not because Luther decided that it would be so, but rather because the time was ripe for it, and because the Reformer and many others with him were ready to fulfill their historical responsibility.

THE LONG QUEST

Luther was born in 1483, in Eisleben, Germany. His father, of peasant origin, had first become a miner and then the owner of several foundries. Young Martin's childhood was not a happy one. His parents were extremely severe, and many years later he would still speak bitterly of some of the punishments he had suffered. Throughout his life he was prey to periods of depression and anxiety, and some scholars suggest that this was due to the excessive austerity of his early years. His first experiences at school were no better, and he later spoke of having been whipped for not knowing his lessons. Although the importance of such early experiences ought not be exaggerated as the sole explanation for the course of Luther's life, there is no doubt that they left a deep imprint on his character.

In July 1505, when almost twenty-two years of age, Luther joined the Augustinian monastery at Erfurt. Many causes led to this decision. Two weeks earlier, in the midst of a thunderstorm, he had felt overwhelmed by the fear of death and hell, and he had promised St. Anne that he would become a monk. According to his own later explanation, it was his harsh upbringing that led him to the monastery. His father had planned for him a career in law, and had not spared efforts so that he could have the necessary education. But Luther had no desire to become a lawyer, and therefore it is possible that Luther, though not entirely aware of his motives, was interposing a monastic vocation between his father's plans and his own inclinations. Upon hearing of his son's decision, the older Luther was incensed, and took his own good time in forgiving what appeared to him as a betrayal of his lofty goals for his son. Ultimately, however, Luther was led to the monastery by a concern for his own salvation. The theme of salvation and damnation permeated the atmosphere in which he lived. The present life was little more than a preparation and testing for the one to come. It seemed foolish to devote oneself to gaining prestige and riches in the present, through the practice of law, to the detriment of life everlasting. Luther therefore entered the monastery as a faithful child of the church, with the clear purpose of making use of the means of salvation offered by that church, of which the surest was the monastic life of renunciation.

During the year of his novitiate, Luther was convinced that he had made a wise decision, for he felt happy and at peace with God. His superiors promptly recognized his unusual abilities, and decided that he should become a priest. Luther himself later wrote about the overwhelming experience of celebrating his first mass, when he was gripped by terror upon thinking that he was holding and offering nothing less than the very body of Christ. That feeling of terror then became increasingly frequent, for he felt unworthy of God's love, and he was not convinced that he was doing enough to be saved. God seemed to him a severe judge—much the same as his father and his teachers had been at an earlier time—who, in the final judgment, would ask for an account and find him wanting. In order to be saved from the wrath of such a God, one must make use of all the means of grace offered by the church.

But those means were not sufficient for someone as deeply religious, sincere, and passionate as Luther. Good works and the sacrament of penance were supposed to suffice for the young friar's need to be justified before God.

But they did not. Luther had an overpowering sense of his own sinfulness, and the more he sought to overcome it, the more he became aware of sin's sway over him. It is mistaken to suppose that he was not a good monk, or that his life was licentious or immoral. On the contrary, he sought to obey his monastic vows to the fullest. He would repeatedly punish his body, as recommended by the great teachers of monasticism. And he went to confession as often as possible. But such practices did not allay his fear of damnation. If sins had to be confessed to be forgiven, there was always the horrifying possibility that he might forget some sin, and thus lose the reward after which he was so diligently striving. He therefore spent hours listing and examining all his thoughts and actions, and the more he studied them the more sin he found in them. There were times when, at the very moment of leaving the confessional, he realized that there was some sin that he had not confessed. He would then grow anxious and even desperate, for sin was clearly more than conscious actions or thoughts. It was a condition, a way of being, something that went far beyond the individual sins one could confess to a priest. Thus, the very sacrament of penance, which was supposed to bring relief to his sense of sinfulness, actually exacerbated it, leaving him in a state of despair.

His spiritual advisor then recommended the reading of the great teachers of mysticism. As we have already seen, toward the end of the Middle Ages (partially as a response to the corruption of the church) there was a great up-surge in mystical piety, which offered an alternative path through which to approach God. Luther resolved to follow that path, not because he doubted the authority of the church, but because that authority, in the person of his confessor, advised him to do so.

Mysticism captivated him for a time—as monasticism had earlier. Per-haps here he would find the path to salvation. But soon that path became another blind alley. The mystics affirmed that all one had to do was to love God, and that all the rest would follow as a result of that love. This was a word of liberation for Luther, for it was no longer necessary to keep a strict account of all his sins, as he had so eagerly endeavored to do, to be rewarded only by failure and despair. But he soon discovered that loving God was not an easy matter. If God was like his father and his teachers, who had beaten him to the point of drawing blood, how could he love such a God? Eventu-ally, Luther came to the terrifying conclusion that what he felt for God was not love, but hatred!

There was no way out of such difficulties. In order to be saved, one must confess one's sins, and Luther had discovered that, in spite of his best efforts, his sin went far beyond what he could confess. If, as the mystics claimed, it sufficed to love God, this was no great help, for Luther had to acknowledge that he could not love the just God that demanded an account of all his actions.

At that point, his confessor, who was also the superior, took a bold step. Normally, one would suppose that a priest who was going through such a crisis as Luther's should not be made a pastor and teacher for others. But that was precisely what his confessor decided he should be. Centuries earlier, Jerome had found in his Hebrew studies an escape from temptation. Although Luther's problems were different from Jerome's, perhaps study, teaching, and pastoral responsibilities would have a similar effect on him. Therefore, Luther was ordered, much against his expectations, to prepare to teach Scripture at the new University of Wittenberg.

Protestant folklore has it that as a friar Luther did not know the Bible, and that it was only at the time of his conversion, or shortly before, that he began to study it. This is false. As a monk who had to follow the traditional hours of prayer, Luther knew the Psalter by heart. Besides, in 1512, after studies that included the Bible, he received his doctorate in theology.

When Luther found himself forced to prepare lectures on the Bible, he began seeing new meanings in it, along with the possibility that such meanings would provide an answer to his spiritual quest. In 1513, he began to lecture on the Psalms. Since he had spent years reciting the Psalter, always within the context of the liturgical year—which centers on the main events in the life of Christ—Luther interpreted the Psalms Christologically. When the Psalmist speaks in the first person, Luther took this to be Christ speaking about himself. Therefore, in the Psalter, Luther saw Christ undergoing trials similar to his own. This was the beginning of his great discovery. By itself, it could have led Luther to the commonly held notion that, while God the Father exacts obedience and righteousness, God the Son loves us and works for our forgiveness. But Luther had studied theology, and knew that such dichotomy within the Godhead was unacceptable. Therefore, while he found consolation in Christ's sufferings, this did not suffice to cure his anguish and despair.

The great discovery probably came in 1515, when Luther began lecturing on the Epistle to the Romans. He later declared that it was in the first chapter of that epistle that he found the solution to his difficulties. That solution did not come easily. It was not simply a matter of opening the Bible one day and reading that "the just shall live by faith." As he tells the story, the great discovery followed a long struggle and bitter anguish, for Romans 1:17 begins by declaring that, in the gospel, "the righteousness of God is revealed." According to this text, the gospel is the revelation of the righteousness—the justice—of God. But it was precisely the justice of God that Luther found unbearable. How could such a message be gospel, good news? For Luther, good news would have been that God is not just, meaning that God does not judge sinners. But, in Romans 1:17, the good news and the justice of God are indissolubly linked. Luther hated the very phrase "the justice of God," and spent day and night seeking to understand the relationship between the two parts of that single verse, which, after declaring that in the gospel "the justice of God is revealed," affirms that "the righteous shall live by faith."

The answer was surprising. Luther came to the conclusion that the "justice of God" does not refer, as he had been taught, to the punishment of sinners. It means rather that the "justice" or "righteousness" of the righteous is not their own, but God's. The "righteousness of God" is that which is given to those who live by faith. It is given, not because they are righteous, nor because they fulfill the demands of divine justice, but simply because God wishes to give it. Thus, Luther's doctrine of "justification by faith" does not mean that what God demands of us is faith, as if this were something we have to do or achieve, and which God then rewards. It means rather that both faith and justification are the work of God, a free gift to sinners. As a result of this discovery, Luther tells us, "I felt that I had been born anew and that the gates of heaven had been opened. The whole of Scripture gained a new meaning. And from that point on the phrase 'the justice of God' no longer filled me with hatred, but rather became unspeakably sweet by virtue of a great love."

THE STORM BREAKS

Although later events revealed another side to his personality, until this time Luther seems to have been quite reserved, devoted to his studies and to his spiritual struggle. His great discovery, while bringing him to a new understanding of the gospel, did not immediately lead him to protest against the church's interpretation of Christianity. On the contrary, our friar continued in his teaching and pastoral duties and, although there are indications that he taught what he had recently learned, he did not frame it in opposition to the traditional teaching of the church. Moreover, he does not seem to have been aware of the radical contradiction between his discovery and the entire penitential system that was so fundamental to accepted theology and piety.

Through quiet persuasion, Luther brought most of his colleagues at the University of Wittenberg over to his way of thinking. When he became convinced that he must challenge traditional views, he composed ninety-seven theses designed to be debated in an academic setting. He wrote these theses in Latin, the language of the academy, and in them he attacked several of the main tenets of scholastic theology. He clearly expected that their publication and debate would cause a stir, allowing him to divulge his great discovery. But, much to his surprise, the theses and the debate on them aroused little interest beyond the university itself. It seemed that the notion that the gospel was entirely other than was commonly thought, which Luther took to be of paramount importance, was received with little more than a great yawn.

Then the unexpected happened. Luther wrote another set of theses, also in Latin, with no expectation that they would have more impact than the previous ones. But someone translated them into German, and circulated them in an inexpensive edition. The result created such a stir that eventually all of Christendom was involved in its consequences. The reason for this very different reaction was that these other theses—officially titled *Ninety-Five Theses on the Power and Efficacy of Indulgences*, now commonly known as Luther's *Ninety-five Theses*—attacked the sale of indulgences and its theological presuppositions. With little awareness of what he was doing, or whom he was attacking, Luther had spoken against plans for profit designed by very powerful lords and prelates.

The particular sale of indulgences that prompted Luther's protest had been authorized by Pope Leo X, and also involved the economic and political ambitions of the powerful house of Hohenzollern, which aspired to hegemony in Germany. One of its members, Albert of Brandenburg, was already in possession of two episcopal sees, and hoped to acquire the most important archbishopric in Germany, that of Mainz. He began negotiations with Leo X, one of the worst popes in an age filled with corrupt, avaricious, and indolent popes. The result was an agreement whereby, for the sum of ten thousand ducats, Albert could have what he requested. Since this was a considerable sum, the pope also authorized Albert to announce a great sale of indulgences in his territories, on the condition that half of the proceeds would be sent to the papal coffers. Leo was concerned with the need to refurbish Rome where, as a result of the Great Schism and of the warring inclinations of some of the popes of the Renaissance, many beautiful buildings showed signs of neglect. One of his dreams was to finish building the Basilica of Saint Peter, begun earlier by Julius II, and for this he needed the funds that he hoped to receive from Albert's sale of indulgences. Thus, the refurbishment of the great basilica that is now the pride of Roman Catholicism indirectly helped foment the Protestant Reformation.

The man put in charge of the sale of indulgences in Germany was the Dominican John Tetzel, an unscrupulous man who was willing to make scandalous claims about his wares as long as such claims would help sales. Thus, for instance, Tetzel and his preachers were heard announcing that the indulgences that they sold made the sinner "cleaner than when coming out of baptism," and "cleaner than Adam before the Fall," and that "the cross of the seller of indulgences has as much power as the cross of Christ." Those who wished to buy an indulgence for a loved one who was deceased were promised that, "as soon as the coin in the coffer rings, the soul from purgatory springs."

Such claims aroused the indignation of many among the learned, who knew that Tetzel and his preachers were misrepresenting the doctrine of the church. Among humanists, who bemoaned the prevailing ignorance and superstition, Tetzel's preaching was seen as another example of the deep corruption of the church. Others who were imbued with the growing German nationalist sentiment saw Tetzel's campaign as one more instance in which Rome was fleecing the German people, exploiting their credulity in order to squander the results on feasts and luxury. But such sentiments were only quietly expressed, and the sale went on.

It was at that point that Luther nailed his famous *Ninety-five Theses* to the door of the castle church in Wittenberg. His theses, written in Latin, were not calculated to cause a great religious commotion, as he had hoped would be the case with his earlier theses. After his previous experience, he seems to have thought that such issues were important only to theologians and that his new set of theses would not be read or debated beyond academic circles. But these *Ninety-five Theses*, written with a deep sense of righteous indignation, were much more devastating than the earlier ones. While addressing fewer theological issues, they did evoke a positive response from those who

A copy of one of the indulgences against which Luther protested.

resented the exploitation of Germany by foreign interests—and by Germans such as the Hohenzollerns in connivance with those interests. Also, in concretely attacking the sale of indulgences, Luther was endangering the profits and designs of the pope and of the house of Hohenzollern. And, although his attack was relatively moderate, Luther went beyond the question of the efficacy of indulgences, and pointed to the exploitation that stood at the heart of it. According to Luther: if it is true that the pope is able to free souls from purgatory, he ought to use that power, not for trivial reasons such as the building of a church, but simply out of love, and freely (thesis 82). In truth, the pope should give his money to the poor from whom the sellers of indulgences wring their last coins, and he ought to do this even if it were to require selling the Basilica of Saint Peter (thesis 51).

Luther published his theses on the Eve of All Saints, and their impact was such that that very date, October 31, 1517, is often said to mark the beginning of the Protestant Reformation. Printers soon spread copies of the *Ninety-five Theses* throughout Germany, in both their original Latin text and in a German translation. Luther sent a copy to Albert of Brandenburg personally, with a very respectful cover letter. Albert sent both the theses and the letter to Rome, asking Pope Leo to intervene. Emperor Maximilian

The wooden doors of the Castle Church in Wittenberg, on which Luther nailed his Ninety-five Theses, were replaced by metal ones in the nineteenth century. The new doors are inscribed with the text of the famous theses.

was enraged at the impertinence of the upstart friar, and he too asked Leo to silence Luther. Meanwhile, Luther published an extensive explanation of the theses, clarifying what he had meant in those very brief propositions, but sharpening his attack on indulgences, and expounding on parts of the theological stance on which he based his protest.

The pope's response was to ask the Augustinian Order to deal with the matter, for Luther was one of its members. The Reformer was called to the order's next chapter meeting, in Heidelberg. He went in fear for his life, for he expected to be condemned and burned as a heretic. But he was surprised to find that many of his fellow friars favored his teachings, and that some of the younger ones were even enthusiastic about it. Others saw the dispute between Luther and Tetzel as one more instance of the ancient rivalry between Dominicans and Augustinians, and therefore refused to abandon their champion. Eventually, Luther was able to return to Wittenberg, strengthened by the support of his order, and encouraged by those whom he had won to his cause.

The pope then attempted a different tack. The Imperial Diet—the assembly of the princes and nobles—was scheduled to meet in Augsburg, with Emperor Maximilian presiding over it. As his legate to that gathering, Leo sent Cardinal Cajetan, a man of vast erudition whose main task was to convince the German princes to undertake a crusade against the Turks, who were threatening Western Europe, and to agree to a tax for the support of that enterprise. Fear of the Turkish threat was such that Rome was seeking reconciliation with the Hussites in Bohemia, and was even willing to accept some of the conditions they imposed. As a secondary task, Cajetan was also instructed to meet with Luther and force him to recant. If the friar proved obstinate, he was to be sent as a prisoner to Rome.

Luther's ruling prince, Frederick the Wise, elector of Saxony, secured from Emperor Maximilian a safe-conduct for Luther. The latter, however, put little trust in the imperial word, remembering that little more than a century before, under similar circumstances and in violation of an imperial safe-conduct, John Huss had been burned at Constance. But in spite of this, he went to Augsburg, convinced that he would not die unless God willed it.

The meeting with Cajetan did not go well. The cardinal refused to discuss Luther's teachings, and demanded that he simply recant. The friar, for his part, declared that he was willing to withdraw what he had said, if he could only be convinced that he was wrong. When he learned that Cajetan did not have to debate the issues at stake, because he was armed with the pope's authority to arrest him, Luther secretly left Augsburg at night and returned to Wittenberg, where he issued an appeal to a general council.

During all this time, Luther had been able to count on the protection of Frederick the Wise, Elector of Saxony and therefore the lord of Wittenberg. At this point, Frederick felt compelled to protect Luther, not because he was convinced of the truth of the friar's teachings, but simply because justice demanded that he be given a hearing and a fair trial. Above all else, Frederick wished to be known and remembered as a wise and just ruler. With that end in mind, he had founded the University of Wittenberg, where many professors supported Luther, and told him that he was by no means a heretic. At least until Luther was duly judged and condemned, Frederick would protect him from the possibility of becoming a victim of a crime such as had been committed in the burning of John Huss. Such steadfastness on the elector's part was not easy, for opposition was mounting, and the number and power of those who declared Luther to be a heretic were constantly increasing.

At that point, Maximilian's death left the imperial throne vacant. Since this was an elective honor, it was now necessary to settle on a successor to the dead emperor. The two most powerful candidates were Charles I of Spain and Francis I of France. The accession of either Charles or Francis to the imperial throne was feared by Pope Leo, whose policies would be threatened by the resulting concentration of power in a single person. Charles already had, besides Spain—rapidly becoming rich through the gold flowing from its colonial empire—vast hereditary possessions in Austria, the Low Countries— now the Netherlands, Belgium, and Luxembord—and southern Italy. Were the imperial crown to be placed on his brow, his power would be unrivaled in Western Europe. Francis of France, while not holding as much territory as Charles was also feared by Leo, for the union of the French and German crowns would place the papacy once again under the shadow of France. The pope therefore had to find another candidate worthy of support, not because of his power but by reason of his personal prestige. Given such criteria, the ideal candidate with whom the pope could oppose both Charles and Francis was Frederick the Wise of Saxony, who had earned the respect and admiration of other German princes. Were Frederick to be elected emperor, the resulting balance of power would allow Leo greater influence and independence. Therefore, even before Maximilian's death, the pope had decided to court Frederick, and to select him as his candidate for emperor.

But Frederick protected Luther, at least until the friar was properly tried and convicted. Therefore, Leo followed a policy of postponing the condemnation of Luther and seeking better relations both with the Reformer and with his protector. To seek such rapprochement, he sent Karl von Miltitz, a relative of Frederick, as his ambassador to Saxony. As a sign of special papal favor, Miltitz took with him a golden rose for Frederick. Although the pope refrained from sending a similar gift to Luther, he instructed his legate to approach the rebellious monk a conciliatory manner.

Miltitz met with Luther, who promised that he would abstain from further controversy as long as his opponents did likewise. This brought about a brief truce, which was broken by John Eck, a professor at the University of Ingolstadt who was incensed by Luther's teachings. Eck was an astute opponent, and therefore instead of attacking Luther, which would have made him appear to have broken the existing peace, he attacked Andreas Rudolph Bodenstein von Karlstadt, another professor at Wittenberg. Karlstadt had been converted to Luther's position, but he was an impetuous man who was ready to carry his new beliefs to their radical conclusions. This in itself made him more vulnerable than Luther to the charge of heresy, and therefore Eck was well advised to challenge Karlstadt to a debate. This was to take place in Leipzig, and was originally billed as a discussion, not of Luther's theses, but of Karlstadt's theology. But the questions posed for debate were clearly those raised by Luther, and therefore the Reformer declared that this was merely a subterfuge to attack him, and that he too would participate in the debate.

The event was conducted with the strict formality of an academic debate and lasted for several days. When Luther and Eck finally confronted each other, it was clear that the former had greater knowledge of Scripture, whereas the latter was more at home in canon law and medieval theology. Eck very ably maneuvered the discussion into his own field of expertise, and finally Luther felt compelled to declare that the Council of Constance had erred in condemning Huss, and that a Christian with the support of Scripture has more authority than all popes and councils against that support. That sufficed. Luther had declared himself in agreement with a heretic who had been condemned by an ecumenical council, and had even dared accuse the council itself of having erred. In spite of the strength of Luther's arguments, which bested Eck at a number of points, it was his rival who won the debate, for he had proven what he had set out to prove: that Luther was a heretic and a supporter of the teachings of Huss.

Thus began a new stage in Luther's struggle, marked by more open confrontations and greater dangers. But the Reformer and his followers had made good use of the time granted to them by political circumstances, with the result that throughout Germany, and even beyond its borders, there were increasing numbers who saw in Luther the champion of biblical faith. Events such as those that took place at the University of Ingolstadt were repeated throughout Germany. In Ingolstadt, the faculty supported the arrest and exile of one of its younger members, on the grounds that he held Lutheran views. Soon there was uproar. Argula von Grumbach, a Bavarian noblewoman who had been converted to Luther's views, and the first woman to publish Protestant treatises, came to the defense of the young professor in a blistering letter in which she showed herself more adept at theological debate than the learned faculty at Ingolstadt. In two months, there were twenty editions of her letter, which became a cause célèbre. While not always as dramatic, similar events shook practically every part of Germany.

To those who found themselves in theological agreement with Luther was added the support of many humanists and German nationalists. The former saw many points of contact between Luther's protest and the reformation that they proposed. The latter saw in him the mouthpiece of German outrage in the face of the abuses of Rome.

Bulla contra errores
Martini Lutheri
z sequacium.

The papal bull Exsurge Domine, *calling Luther a wild boar and demanding his recantation.*

A few weeks before the Leipzig Debate, Charles I of Spain had been elected emperor, and was known thereafter as Charles V. Although Charles owed a debt of gratitude to Frederick the Wise for having supported his candidacy, he was a strictly orthodox man who would not countenance heresy in his lands, and therefore his election bode ill for Luther. Frederick still supported him—the more so since he was becoming increasingly convinced that the Reformer was right. But now the pope had no reason to delay a formal condemnation that had earlier been stayed only for political considerations. In the papal bull *Exsurge Domine,* in which Leo declared that a wild boar had entered the Lord's vineyard, he ordered all books by Martin Luther to be burned; and he gave the rebellious friar, under the threat of the penalty of excommunication and the declaration of anathema, sixty days to submit to Roman authority.

The bull took a long time to reach Luther. As copies of it arrived in various German territories, there were conflicting reactions. In some places, the pope's instructions were obeyed, and there were public burnings of Luther's books. But in other places students and other supporters of Luther chose to burn the works of his opponents. When the bull finally reached Luther, he burned it publicly, together with other books that he declared to be the worst proponents of "popish doctrines." The breach was final, and there was no way to undo it.

It was still necessary to determine the attitude of the emperor and the other German lords, for without their support there was little that Leo could do to silence the Reformer. The political maneuvers that took place in this regard were too complicated to retell here. Let it suffice to say that even Charles V, a convinced Catholic, showed himself willing to use Luther as a threat when he feared that Leo was showing too much favor for his rival, Francis I of France. Eventually, after much back and forth, it was decided that Luther would appear before the Imperial Diet to be gathered at Worms in 1521.

At Worms, Luther was taken before the emperor and several of the great lords of the German Empire. The man in charge of the process showed him a number of books, and asked him if he had indeed written them. After examining them, Luther responded that such was the case, and that he had also written other books besides these. Then he was asked if he still held to what he had declared in those publications or wished to recant anything. This was a difficult moment for Luther, not so much because he feared imperial power but rather because he feared God. To dare to oppose the entire church and the emperor, whose authority had been ordained by God, was a dreadful act. Once again the friar trembled before the divine majesty, and asked for a day's time in which to consider his answer.

By the next day it was widely known that Luther was to appear before the Diet, and the hall was filled. The emperor's presence at Worms, with a corps of Spanish soldiers who showed little respect for Germans, had irritated the populace as well as many German princes. Once again, Luther was asked to recant. In the midst of a great hush, the friar answered that much of what he had written was basic Christian doctrine, held by both him and his opponents, and that therefore no one should expect him to repudiate such teaching. At some other points, he continued, his works dealt with the tyranny and injustice that the German people suffered. This too he could not recant, for such was not the purpose of the Diet, and in any case to withdraw such words would result in greater injustice. Third, in his works there were attacks against certain individuals, and points of doctrine that were at issue between him and his opponents. Perhaps, he confessed, some of these things had been said too harshly. But their truth he could not deny, unless someone could convince him that he was in error.

It was not the emperor's purpose to engage in a debate on Luther's teaching, and therefore he was asked once again, "Do you recant, or do you not?"

To this Luther responded in German, therefore setting aside the Latin of traditional theological debate: "My conscience is a prisoner of God's Word. I cannot and will not recant, for to disobey one's conscience is neither just nor safe. God help me. Amen."[2] Then, with a gesture of victory, he left the hall and returned to his quarters.

In burning the papal bull, Luther had challenged Rome. Now, at Worms, he was challenging the empire. Therefore, he had ample reason to plead: "God help me!"

3

An Uncertain Decade

Luther is now to be seen as a convicted heretic. He has twenty-one days from the fifteenth of April. After that time, no one should give him shelter. His followers also are to be condemned, and his books will be erased from human memory.

EDICT OF WORMS

EXILE, UNREST, AND REBELLION

By burning the papal bull, Luther had challenged the pope's authority. At Worms, by refusing to recant, he challenged that of the emperor. The latter had no intention of allowing a rebellious friar to question his authority, and therefore was ready to take action against Luther, in spite of the safe-conduct Frederick the Wise had obtained for the Reformer. But several powerful members of the Diet opposed such action, and Charles was forced to negotiate with them. When the Diet finally acquiesced to the emperor's wishes by promulgating the edict quoted above, Luther was nowhere to be found.

What had happened was that Frederick the Wise, aware the emperor would demand that the Diet condemn Luther, had taken steps to ensure the Reformer's safety. An armed band, following the elector's instructions, had abducted Luther and taken him to Wartburg Castle. Based on his own instructions, Frederick was not informed and thus did not know where Luther had been hidden. Many thought him dead, and there were rumors that he had been killed by order of the pope or the emperor.

Hidden at Wartburg, Luther grew a beard, sent word to some of his closest friends not to fear for him, and spent his time writing. His most significant work of this period was the German translation of the Bible. The translation of the New Testament, begun at Wartburg, was finished two years later; the Old Testament took ten years to be completed. But that work was well worth the time spent on it, for Luther's Bible, besides adding impetus to the Reformation itself, shaped the German language and national identity.

While Luther was in exile, his collaborators in Wittenberg continued the work of reformation. Foremost among these were Karlstadt (who was mentioned earlier as a participant at the Leipzig Debate) and Philipp Melanchthon. The latter was a young professor of Greek whose temperament differed substantially from Luther's but who was wholly convinced of the truth of his older colleague's teachings. Until then, the reformation Luther advocated had not been implemented in the religious life of Wittenberg. Luther's fear of God and of unwarranted innovation was such that he had hesitated to take the concrete steps that should follow from his doctrine. But now, while he was absent, several such steps were taken in rapid succession. A number of monks and nuns left their monastic communities and were married. Worship was simplified, and German was substituted for Latin. Masses for the dead were abolished, as were days of fasting and abstinence. Melanchthon also began to offer communion in both kinds—that is, to give the laity the cup as well as the host.

At first, Luther supported these changes. But soon he began to question the excesses that were taking place at Wittenberg. When Karlstadt and several of his followers began tearing down images of saints in churches, Luther recommended moderation. Then three laymen appeared at Wittenberg from neighboring Zwickau, declaring themselves prophets. They claimed that God spoke directly to them, and that they therefore had no need for Scripture. Melanchthon was at a loss as to how to respond to such claims, and asked Luther's advice. Finally, the latter decided that what was at stake was nothing less than the gospel itself, and that he must return to Wittenberg. Before taking that step, he notified Frederick the Wise of his intentions, making it clear that he was returning to Wittenberg counting not on Frederick's protection but on God's.

Although Luther was not one to take such matters into account when it was a question of obedience to God, political circumstances favored him, making it possible for Frederick to keep him hidden at the Wartburg Castle, and later allowing him to return to Wittenberg without being arrested and executed. Charles V was determined to stamp out the Lutheran "heresy." But he was threatened by more powerful enemies, and could not allow

Luther at the Diet of Worms. Bas-relief in the monument to the Reformation at Worms.

himself the luxury of alienating those among his German subjects who supported Luther. Charles's most constant rival was Francis I of France. The latter, who in earlier years had been the most influential sovereign in Europe, was not pleased at the rising star of Charles I of Spain, who now had become Charles V of the Holy Roman Empire, and who also held vast hereditary possessions that virtually surrounded France. Shortly before the Diet of Worms, the two rivals had clashed in Navarre. (As we shall see later, it was in that conflict that Ignatius Loyola received the wound that would eventually cause him to become one of the leaders of the Catholic Reformation.) From the year of the Diet (1521) until 1525, Charles was repeatedly at war with Francis. Finally, at the Battle of Pavia, the king of France was captured by imperial troops, and the conflict between the two most powerful monarchs in Western Europe seemed to have come to an end.

Meanwhile, a few months before the Diet of Worms, Leo X had died, and Charles had used his influence to see that his tutor, Adrian of Utrecht, was elected pope. The new pope, who took the name of Adrian VI and was the last non-Italian pope until the twentieth century, was eager to reform the life of the church, but would brook no deviation from traditional orthodoxy. He brought austerity of life to Rome, and began a program of reformation that he hoped would respond to the critics of the church and steal Luther's thunder. But Adrian died a year and a half after his election, and his program was abandoned. His successor, Clement VII, returned to Leo's policies, for he too was more interested in the arts and in Italian politics than in ecclesiastical matters. Soon there was serious friction between him and the emperor, and this prevented the Catholic party from taking coordinated action against the German reformers.

Charles V signed a peace treaty with his prisoner Francis, and on that basis restored him to freedom and to his throne. But the conditions to which Francis had been forced to agree were harsh, and once he was back in France he secured Clement's support against Charles. The latter was eager to destroy Lutheranism and to put an end to the Turkish menace at his Eastern borders. Given the nature of these two causes, he hoped to be able to count on the support of France and the papacy. But just as he was preparing his campaign, both Francis and Clement declared war on him.

In 1527, imperial troops, mostly Spanish and German, invaded Italy and marched on Rome. The city could not be defended, and the pope fled to the Castel Sant'Angelo, leaving the city to be sacked by the invaders. Since many of these were Lutheran, the sack of Rome took on religious overtones: God was finally punishing the Antichrist. The pope's situation was desperate when, early in 1528, a French army, with English financial support, came to his aid. The imperial troops were forced to withdraw, and would have suffered great losses had an epidemic not forced the French to abandon their pursuit. In 1529, Charles agreed to peace, first with the pope, and then with Francis.

Charles was once again preparing to take strong measures against the heretics in his German territories when the Turks, led by Suleiman, marched on Vienna, the capital of Charles's Austrian territories. The fall of Vienna would leave Germany open to Turkish attack, and therefore the emperor and his German subjects set aside their religious differences and joined in a campaign against the Turks. The defenders of Vienna were resolute, and the city stood firm until the advancing German armies forced Suleiman to withdraw.

It was then that, after a prolonged absence, Charles returned to Germany, with the clear intention of stamping out the Lutheran heresy. During the intervening years, however, several important events had taken place. In 1522 and 1523, there had been a rebellion of knights, under the leadership of Franz von Sickingen. The knightly class had seen its fortunes declining for some time and, among the landless and penniless knights, nationalist feelings ran high. Many blamed Rome for their ill fortune, and saw Luther as the champion of the German nation. Some, such as Ulrich von Hutten, were also convinced of the truth of Luther's religious teachings but felt that the Reformer was too timid. When they finally rebelled, many claimed that they were doing so in defense of the Reformation, although Luther had done nothing to encourage them. The rebels attacked Trier, but were decisively defeated by the German princes, who took the opportunity to dispossess the lesser gentry of the few lands that still remained in their hands. Sickingen died in battle, and von Hutten fled to Switzerland, where he died shortly thereafter. All this was seen by Luther and his closest colleagues as a great tragedy, proving once again that one should submit to the established authorities.

In 1524, a peasant rebellion broke out. For decades the conditions of the German peasantry had been worsening. As a result, there had been rebellions in 1476, 1491, 1498, 1503, and 1514. But none of these was as widespread or as devastating as the uprisings of 1524 and 1525. One of the elements making these rebellions particularly virulent was that they took on religious overtones, for many among the peasantry believed that the teachings of the reformers supported their economic demands. Although Luther himself refused to extend the application of his teachings to the political realm in terms of revolution, there were others who disagreed with him on that point. Foremost among these was Thomas Müntzer, a native of Zwickau, whose early teachings were similar to those of the "prophets" from his village who created such a stir in Wittenberg. Müntzer claimed that what was most important was not the written word of Scripture but the present revelation of the Spirit. In his case, such spiritualist doctrine had political consequences, for he felt that those who had been born again via the Spirit should join in a theocratic community to bring about the Kingdom of God. Luther had forced Müntzer out of Saxony, for he feared the consequences of his teachings. But the fiery preacher returned and joined the peasant rebellion.

Even apart from Müntzer's participation, this uprising had a measure of religious inspiration. In their *Twelve Articles*, the peasants made both economic and religious demands. They sought to base their claims on the authority of Scripture, and concluded by declaring that, if any of their demands was shown to be contrary to Scripture, it would be withdrawn.

Therefore, although Luther himself could not see any relationship between his doctrines and the rebellion, the peasants themselves did see such relationship.

In any case, Luther was at a loss as to what his attitude should be. Possibly his difficulties were related to his doctrine of the two kingdoms (see Chapter 4). When he first read the *Twelve Articles*, he addressed the princes, telling them that what was demanded of them in the articles was just, for the peasants were sorely oppressed. But when the uprising broke out, and the peasants took up arms, Luther tried to persuade them to follow a more peaceful course, and finally called on the princes to suppress the movement. Later, when the rebellion was drowned in blood, he urged the victorious princes to be merciful. But his words were not heeded, and it is said that more than a hundred thousand peasants were killed.

These events had fateful consequences for the Reformation. Catholic princes blamed Lutheranism for the rebellion, and from that time even the most moderate among them took measures against the spread of heresy in their territories. Vast numbers of peasants, convinced that Luther had betrayed them, either returned to the old faith or became Anabaptists (see Chapter 6).

Although the peasant rebellion occupied much of his time, there was also turmoil in Luther's personal life. Even though the law regarded such actions as crime, when a group of nuns in a nearby convent sent word that they had been convinced by Luther's arguments, and sought his help in escaping from the convent, Luther did arrange for their escape. He then had to provide for each of them by either finding a position in a household or arranging for marriage. One of the nuns, Katharina von Bora, proved reluctant to marry any of her suitors. Several of Luther's friends suggested that he ought to marry. Katharina made it clear that there were only two men she would consider as potential husbands—and one of them was Dr. Luther. At first Luther joked about it. He was also reluctant to marry because at that point he believed that it was quite possible that he would soon have to die as a martyr. But eventually he agreed to marry Katharina. Although clearly shaped by the patriarchal attitudes of the time, their marriage was quite happy. There are many hints at humor in their relationship—she complained that Luther was a slob, and he agreed that he owed much to "my lord" Katharina. He would also comment at the strangeness of waking up in the morning to find a pair of pigtails on his pillow. They had six children, and they worked jointly at providing a home for them as well as for a number of orphans and students. Luther would say that his family was like a "small church," and would rejoice in being part of it. Out of these experiences, and out of the life of the family, came the famous *Table Talks* that his students compiled and published and which are one of the best avenues for insight into him as a man. His efforts to educate his children as well as others have been cited as a forerunner of public education. Furthermore, Luther's family life became the model that many devout Germans would follow for generations.

Katharina Von Bora

But while Luther was learning how to be a husband and a father, Germany was undergoing ever greater turmoil, and Catholic moderates throughout Europe were forced to choose sides between Luther and his opponents. The most famous of the humanists, Erasmus, had looked with favor on the early stages of the Lutheran movement but did not find the resultant discord much to his liking. He found controversy and dissension most repugnant, and would have preferred to stay out of the debate. But he was too famous to be allowed such a luxury and eventually was forced to take a stand. Although he had frequently criticized the ignorance and corruption of the clergy, he had never advocated a radical reformation in theology, and therefore, when forced to speak out, he was bound to take the side of Luther's adversaries.

Still, Erasmus preferred to choose his own field of battle. Therefore, instead of attacking Luther on such issues as justification by faith, the mass as a sacrifice, or the authority of the pope, he raised the issue of free will. Luther had been led to affirm the doctrine of predestination both because it was a corollary of justification by faith as a free gift of God, and because he found it amply supported by the authority of Paul and Augustine. It was on this point that Erasmus attacked him, publishing a treatise on free will.

Luther responded by thanking Erasmus for having shown the wisdom to focus his attention on a fundamental issue and not on peripheral matters such as the sale of indulgences, the relics of the saints, and so on. But then he went on to defend his position with characteristic vehemence. As he saw matters, the notion of free will as held by pagan philosophers and by the moralists of his time did not take into account the enormous power of sin. Sin is such that we are powerless to be rid of it. Only by divine intervention can we be justified and freed from the power of evil. And even then we continue to be sinners. Therefore, when it comes to serving God, our much-vaunted free will can do nothing of itself. It is only by God's initiative—by divine predestination—that we are justified.

The controversy between Luther and Erasmus led many humanists to abandon the Lutheran cause. A few, such as Philipp Melanchthon, continued their staunch support of Luther while maintaining cordial relations with Erasmus and his friends. But these were by no means the majority, and therefore the controversy over predestination and free will marked the end of all hope for close collaboration between Lutherans and humanists.

THE DIETS OF THE EMPIRE

While all this was taking place, and in the emperor's absence, it was necessary to govern the empire. Since Charles V had left the country almost immediately after the Diet of Worms, and since that diet's edict against Luther had been the result of imperial pressure, nothing was done to enforce the decree against the reformer. When the Imperial Diet met again at Nuremberg, in 1523, it adopted a policy of tolerance toward Lutheranism, in spite of the protests of the legates of both pope and emperor.

In 1526, when Charles was engaged in his struggles with Francis I of France and Pope Clement VII, the Diet of Spire formally withdrew the Edict of Worms, and granted each of the many German states the freedom to choose its own religious allegiance. Austria and many of the southern territories of Germany opted for Catholicism, while others began implementing the Lutheran Reformation. Germany had thus become a religious mosaic.

In 1529, the Second Diet of Spire took a different tack. At that point there was renewed threat of imperial intervention, and princes who until then had been fairly moderate joined the ranks of the staunch Catholics. The result was that the Edict of Worms was reaffirmed. This prompted the Lutheran princes to present a formal protest, thus receiving the name of "Protestants."

Charles V finally returned to Germany in 1530, in order to attend the Diet of Augsburg. At Worms, the emperor had refused to listen to Luther's arguments. But now, in view of the turn of events, he requested an orderly exposition of the points at issue. This document, whose main author was

Philipp Melanchthon, is now known as the *Augsburg Confession*—and for a long time Lutherans commonly referred to themselves as "Christians of the *Augsburg Confession*." When first drawn, it spoke only for the Protestants of Saxony. But other princes and leaders also signed it, and thus it was the instrument whereby most Protestants presented a united front before the emperor (although there were two other minority statements that disagreed on several points with Melanchthon's document). When the signatories of the *Augsburg Confession* refused to abandon their faith, the emperor was enraged and ordered that they must recant by April of the following year, or suffer the consequences.

The survival of Protestantism was threatened. If the emperor joined his hereditary resources from Austria, Spain, and other lands to those of the Catholic German princes, he would easily crush any Protestant prince who refused to recant. The Protestant princes decided that their only hope was to offer a common front. After long hesitation, Luther agreed that it was licit to take up arms in self-defense against the emperor. The Protestant territories

Emperor Charles V listening to the Augsburg Confession *while the rulers who signed it stand around him, each identified by his coat of arms. The scenes in the background represent various Lutheran services. Note that in Communion the people are receiving both the bread and the wine, and that blood flows from Christ's side into the chalice.*

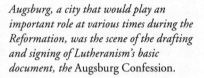

Augsburg, a city that would play an important role at various times during the Reformation, was the scene of the drafting and signing of Lutheranism's basic document, the Augsburg Confession.

then joined in the League of Schmalkalden, whose purpose was to resist the imperial edict if Charles sought to impose it by force of arms.

Both sides were making ready for long and cruel war when international events once more forced Charles to postpone action. Francis of France was again preparing for war, and the Turks were planning to avenge their earlier failure at the walls of Vienna. To counteract such powerful enemies, Charles needed a united Germany. These circumstances demanded negotiation rather than war, and finally Protestants and Catholics agreed to the Peace of Nuremberg, signed in 1532. This stipulated that Protestants would be allowed to practice their faith, but could not seek to extend it to other territories. The imperial Edict of Augsburg was suspended and, in return, the Protestants offered the emperor their support against the Turks. They also promised not to go beyond what they had declared to be their faith in the *Augsburg Confession*. Once more, political circumstances favored Protestantism, for it continued advancing into new territories in spite of the agreement of Nuremberg.

4

Luther's Theology

The friends of the cross affirm that the cross is good and that works
are bad, for through the cross works are undone and the old Adam,
whose strength is in works, is crucified.

MARTIN LUTHER

At this point in the life of Luther, we must pause to consider his theology, the driving force that would determine much of the rest of his
life. By 1521, when he appeared before the Diet of Worms, Luther had come
to the main theological conclusions that would characterize the whole of
his thought. After that time, he would primarily expand and elaborate on
the main points that had led him to his position at Worms. Therefore, this
seems to be the best point in our narrative at which to pause and discuss the
basic themes of Luther's theology. Earlier, while telling of his personal quest
for salvation, we spoke of the doctrine of justification by faith. But this was
by no means the totality of Luther's theology.

THE WORD OF GOD

As is commonly known, Luther sought to make the Word of God the
starting point and the final authority for his theology. As a professor of
Scripture, the Bible was for him of paramount importance, and it was in it
that he found an answer to his anguished quest for salvation. But this does
not mean that he was a rigid biblicist, for what he understood the "Word of
God" to be was more than the words written in the Bible.

In its primary sense, the Word of God is none other than God. This is
supported by the first verses of the Gospel of John, where it is written that
"in the beginning was the Word, and the Word was with God, and the
Word was God." The Bible itself declares that, strictly speaking, the Word

of God is none other than God the Son, the Second Person of the Trinity, the Word who was made flesh and dwelt among us. Therefore, when God speaks, we are not simply given information; also, and above all, God acts. This is what is meant in the book of Genesis, where the Word of God is a creating force: "God said, let there be . . . and there was." When God speaks, that which is uttered is also created. God's Word, besides telling us something, creates something in us and in all creation. That creative and powerful Word is Christ, whose incarnation is both God's greatest revelation and God's greatest action. In Jesus, God was revealed to us. And also in Jesus, God overcame the powers of evil that had held us in subjection. God's revelation is also God's victory.

Given this biblical understanding of the Word of God, what makes the Bible the Word of God is not that it is infallible, nor that it can serve as a source of authority for theological and religious debate. The Bible is the Word of God because in it Jesus, the Word incarnate, comes to us. Any who read the Bible and somehow do not find Jesus in it, have not encountered the Word of God. This was the reason why Luther, while insisting on the final authority of Scripture, could make deprecating comments about parts of it. The Epistle of James, for instance, seemed to him "pure straw," because he could not find the gospel in it, but only a series of rules of conduct. The book of Revelation also caused him difficulty. Although he was not ready to delete such books from the canon, he openly confessed that it was difficult for him to see Jesus Christ in them, and that therefore they were of little value to him.

This notion of the Word of God as Jesus Christ himself allowed Luther to respond to one of the main objections Catholics raised to his doctrine of the authority of Scripture above the church. They argued that, since it was the church that had determined which books should be included in the canon of Scripture, it was clear that the church had authority over the Bible. Luther responded that it was neither the church that had made the Bible, nor the Bible that had made the church, but the gospel, Jesus Christ, that had made both the Bible and the church. Final authority rests neither in the church nor in the Bible, but in the gospel, in the message of Jesus Christ, who is the Word of God incarnate. Since Scripture gives a more trustworthy witness to that gospel than the pope's corrupt church, or even the best in Christian tradition, the Bible has authority over church, pope, and tradition. This is so, even though it is also true that in the early centuries of Christianity it was

Luther's Bible was a formative document for German identity, shaping both its religion and its language.

the church that recognized the gospel in certain books, and not in others, and thus determined the actual content of the Bible.

THE THEOLOGY OF THE CROSS

Luther had been formed in the tradition of late medieval theology, which had profound doubts about the ability of reason to investigate or to prove matters of faith. Even so, he agreed with most traditional theology that it is possible to know something about God by purely rational or natural means. Such knowledge includes the fact that God exists, and allows us to distinguish between good and evil. The pagan philosophers of antiquity had this knowledge, and it is clear from the laws of ancient Rome that they were able to distinguish between good and evil. Furthermore, the philosophers were able to conclude that there is a single Supreme Being from which all things draw their existence.

But all this is not the true knowledge of God. As Luther would say, one does not get to know God by speculation, like one can get to the roof by climbing a ladder. All human efforts to climb to heaven, and thus to know God, are futile. Such efforts are what Luther calls "a theology of glory." This theology seeks to know the divine being in itself, in its own glory, while ignoring the enormous distance between God and humans. In the final analysis, a theology of glory seeks God in those things that humans consider most valuable and praiseworthy, and that is why it is so concerned with the power of God, the glory of God, and the goodness of God. But this is little more than creating God after our own image, and we deceive ourselves into believing that God's nature is what we would like it to be.

The fact of the matter is that the God of revelation is very different from the God of a theology of glory. God's highest self-disclosure takes place in the cross of Christ, and therefore Luther proposes, instead of a theology of glory, a "theology of the cross." Such theology seeks God, not where we choose, nor as we would like God to be, but in the divine revelation of the cross. There God is seen in weakness, in suffering, as a stumbling block. This means that God acts in a radically different way than we would expect. In the cross, God destroys our preconceived notions of divine glory. When we know God in the cross, we must set aside our previous knowledge of God, that is, all that we thought we knew by means of reason or of the inner voice of conscience. What we now know of God is very different from the easily assumed knowledge of a theology of glory.

LAW AND GOSPEL

It is in the divine revelation that God is truly known. But in that revelation God is made manifest in two ways: law and gospel. This does not mean simply that the law is first, and then the gospel. Nor does it mean that the Old Testament is law, and the New Testament is gospel. This is a misunderstanding that eventually led many Lutherans to consider Judaism and Jews as great enemies of the Christian faith, for they supposedly emphasized law, while Christianity is a matter of grace. It is true that Luther shared many—though not all—of the prejudices of his time against Jews. But for Luther, God is revealed in law and gospel in both the Old Testament and the New. The contrast between law and gospel shows that God's revelation is both a word of judgment and a word of grace. The two always come together, and one cannot hear the word of grace without hearing also the word of judgment.

The doctrine of justification by faith, the message of God's forgiveness, does not imply that God is indifferent to sin. It is not simply that God forgives us because after all our sin is not of great consequence. On the contrary, God is holy, and sin is repugnant to the divine holiness. When God speaks, we are overwhelmed by the contrast between such holiness and our own sin. That is what Luther means by the Word of God as law.

But God also speaks a word of forgiveness—a forgiveness so tied up with the divine holiness that sometimes the same word is both judgment and grace. That forgiveness is the gospel, made all the more joyful and overpowering because the judgment of the law is so crushing. This gospel does not contradict or obliterate the law. God's forgiveness does not deny the gravity of our sin. It is precisely that gravity that makes the gospel such surprising good news.

When we hear that word of pardon, however, the character of the law changes for us. What earlier seemed an unbearable weight now becomes bearable and even sweet. Commenting on the Gospel of John, Luther declares:

> At an earlier time there was no pleasure in the law for me. But now I find that the law is good and tasty, that it has been given to me so that I might live, and now I find my pleasure in it. Earlier, it told me what I ought to do. Now I begin to adapt myself to it. And for this I worship, praise, and serve God.[3]

This constant dialectic between law and gospel means that a Christian is at one and the same time both sinful and justified—in an oft-quoted phrase: *simul justus et peccator*. The sinner does not cease to be such upon being justified. On the contrary, upon being justified one discovers how deeply sinful one is. Justification is not the absence of sin but the fact that God declares us to be just, even while we are still sinners. The indissoluble bond between gospel and law is paralleled by our own Christian life as both sinners and justified believers.

THE CHURCH AND SACRAMENTS

Contrary to common belief, Luther was neither an individualist nor a rationalist. During the nineteenth century, when both rationalism and individualism seemed to be the wave of the future, some historians sought to depict Luther as the forerunner of such currents. This was frequently tied to an effort to show that Germany was the mother of modern civilization, of the use of reason, and of individual freedom. In such interpretations, Luther became the great national hero of Germany, the founder of modernity.

But all this is far removed from historical truth. The fact of the matter is that Luther was far from being a rationalist. His frequent references to reason as "dirty" or "a whore"—which reflect his upbringing in late medieval theology—should suffice to prove this point. As to his supposed individualism, this was more characteristic of the Italian leaders of the Renaissance than of the German Reformer; and, in any case, Luther attached too much importance to the church to be classified as a true individualist.

In spite of his protest against commonly accepted doctrine, and despite his rebellion against the authorities of the Roman church, Luther was convinced that the church was an essential element of the Christian message. His theology was not that of an individual in direct communion with God, but rather of a Christian life to be lived within a community of believers, and this community he frequently called "mother church."

While it is true that all Christians, by virtue of their baptism, are priests, this does not mean—as some later interpreters have said—that one is self-sufficient to approach God for oneself. There is a direct communion with God that all Christians can and should enjoy. But there is also an organic reality within which all communion with God takes place, and that reality is the church. To be priests does not mean primarily that we are our own individual priests, but rather that as part of the priestly people of God we are priests for the entire community of belief, and that they are priests for us—while all of us, as the believing community, are priests for the world. Rather than setting aside the need for the community of the church, the doctrine of the universal priesthood of believers strengthens it. It is true that access to God is no longer controlled by a hierarchical priesthood. But we still stand in need of the community of believers, the body of Christ, in which each member is a priest for the rest, and feeds the rest. Without such nourishment, an isolated member cannot live.

In that community, all have a place or a vocation, and all occupations—as long as they are honest and godly—are equally valuable before the eyes of God. The monastic life is no holier or worthier than the life of a ruler or of a cobbler, for all contribute to God's designs and order. With this assertion, which is usually called "the sanctity of the common life," Luther opened the way for the modern sense of vocation—although, being a man of his time, he generally felt that each one's calling was generally determined by birth. It would be in the next generation, with Calvin and his contemporaries, that a sense of vocation providing opportunities to move into new walks of life would come to the foreground.

Within the life of that church, the Word of God comes to us in the sacraments. For a rite to be a true sacrament, it must have been instituted by Christ, and it must be a physical sign of the promise of the gospel. Applying such criteria, Luther comes to the conclusion that there are only two sacraments: baptism and communion. Other rites and ceremonies that are commonly called sacraments, although perhaps beneficial, ought not to be considered sacraments of the gospel—although for a time Luther did consider the possibility of declaring penance to also be a sacrament.

Baptism is first of all a sign of the believer's death and resurrection with Jesus Christ. But it is much more than a sign, for by its power we are made members of the body of Christ. Baptism and faith are closely tied, for the rite itself without faith is not valid. But this does not mean that one must have faith before being baptized, or that infants born in the church but as yet incapable of faith ought not to be baptized. To come to such a conclusion, Luther declares, would be to fall into the error of believing faith to be a human work, something we must do, and not a free gift of God. In salvation, the initiative is always God's, and this is precisely what the church proclaims in baptizing infants who are incapable of understanding what is taking place. Furthermore, baptism is not only the beginning of the Christian life but also the foundation and the context in which the entire life of the believer takes place. Baptism is valid, not only when it is received but throughout life. That is why we are told that Luther himself, when he felt sorely tried, was wont to exclaim, "I am baptized." In his own baptism lay the strength to resist the powers of evil.

Communion is the other Christian sacrament. Luther rejected a great deal of commonly accepted doctrine regarding communion. He was particularly opposed to the celebration of private masses, to the understanding of communion as a repetition of the sacrifice of Calvary, to the notion that there are "merits" in simply attending mass, to the doctrine of transubstantiation, and to the "reservation" of the sacrament—the claim that the body of Christ remains present in the bread even after the celebration of communion is over. But, in spite of his opposition to what he saw as the misuse and misinterpretation of communion, he continued to attach great importance to the sacrament itself, and to the presence of Christ in it. While insisting on the need for the preached Word, he retained the Word made visible in communion as the center of Christian worship.

The question of the manner in which Christ is present in communion gave rise to long debates, not only with Catholics, but also among Protestants. Luther categorically rejected the doctrine of transubstantiation, which he saw as unduly tied to Aristotelian—and therefore pagan—metaphysics. Also, the manner in which the doctrine of transubstantiation had been used had tied it to the theory that the mass was a meritorious sacrifice, and this ran contrary to justification by faith.

On the other hand, Luther was not ready to reduce communion to a mere sign or symbol of spiritual realities. He took Jesus' words at the institution of the sacrament as very clear and undeniable proof of his physical presence at the sacrament: "this is my body." Therefore, Luther felt compelled to affirm that in communion one truly and literally partakes of the body of Christ. This need not imply, as with transubstantiation, that the bread and wine become body and blood. The bread is still bread, and the wine is still wine. But now the body and blood of the Lord are also with them, and the believer is nourished by that body and that blood through the very act of eating the bread and drinking the wine. Although later interpreters have commonly used the term *consubstantiation* to describe Luther's doctrine of the presence of Christ in communion in contrast to Roman Catholic *transubstantiation*, Luther never used such metaphysical terms, but would speak of the presence of the body of Christ in, with, under, around, and behind the bread and wine.

Not all who opposed traditional doctrine agreed with Luther on these points, and this soon gave rise to conflicts among leaders of the Reformation. Karlstadt, Luther's colleague at the University of Wittenberg who debated Eck at Leipzig, claimed that the presence of Christ in communion was merely symbolic, and that when Jesus said "this is my body" he was pointing to himself and not the bread. Ulrich Zwingli (who is discussed in Chapter 5) held similar views although with better arguments. As we shall see, when they met at Marburg in 1529, this was the one point on which they could not agree. Eventually, the question of how Christ is present in communion became one of the main points at issue in the debates between Lutherans and Reformed.

THE TWO KINGDOMS

Before concluding this brief overview of Luther's theology, a word must be said regarding the relationship between church and state. According to Luther, God has established two kingdoms: one under the law, and the other under the gospel. The state must operate under the law, and its main purpose is to set limits to human sin and its consequences. Without the state, sin would lead to chaos and destruction. Believers, on the other hand, belong to the other kingdom, which is under the gospel. This means that Christians ought not to expect the state to be ruled by the gospel, nor to support orthodoxy by persecuting heretics. Furthermore, there is no reason why Christians should require that the state be ruled by fellow believers in order to obey them. Rulers, as such, must follow the law, and not the gospel. In the kingdom of the gospel, civil authorities have no power. In that which refers to this second kingdom, Christians are not subject to the state, and owe it no allegiance. But one must always remember that believers are at once justified and sinners; therefore, as people who are still sinners, we are under the authority of the state.

In concrete terms, this meant that true faith should not seek to impose itself by means of civil authority, but only through the power of the Word. In the complex realities of power and politics, however, such principles were difficult to follow. Luther repeatedly rejected offers of help from the princes who had embraced his cause, and yet found himself being helped by them. When those who had embraced the Reformation were threatened by Catho-

REGNVM SATANAE ET PAPAE.
2. THESS. 2.

This Lutheran caricature shows the bitterness of the struggle between Catholics and Protestants. Note the pope sitting on his throne at the very mouth of Hades, and the devils crowning him.

lic armies, Luther hesitated on a proper response, but eventually agreed with the Lutheran princes that they were justified in going to war in self-defense. Similarly, in the case of the peasants' revolt, Luther held that the peasants were being treated unjustly, but that as Christians they still had no right to revolt. Over the centuries, Luther's understanding of the relationship between the church and the civil order has repeatedly affected the manner in which his followers have dealt with oppressive or unjust governments, which has not been as radical as has been the case with those of the Reformed (or Calvinist) tradition.

Luther was not a pacifist. Being subject to the law, the state can take up arms when circumstances and justice so demand. When the Turks threatened to overrun Christendom, Luther advised his followers to take up arms. And when he became convinced that certain movements, such as the peasant uprisings and Anabaptism (see Chapter 6), were subversive, he declared that civil authorities were under obligation to crush them. He had serious doubts regarding the traditional understanding of the relationship between church and state. But his own doctrine of the two kingdoms, on which he sought to base his actions in the political arena, was difficult to apply to concrete situations.

5

Ulrich Zwingli and the Swiss Reformation

If the inner man is such that he finds his delight in the law of God because he has been created in the divine image in order to have communion with Him, it follows that there will be no law or word which will delight that inner man more than the Word of God.

ULRICH ZWINGLI

Humanism and nationalism, both contributing factors to the Lutheran Reformation even against Luther's intentions, became conscious elements of the reformation Zwingli led in Switzerland.

ZWINGLI'S PILGRIMAGE

Ulrich Zwingli was born in a small Swiss village in January 1484, less than two months after Luther. After learning his first letters from an uncle, he studied in Basel and Bern, where humanism was thriving. He then went to the University of Vienna, and again studied in Basel. After receiving a Master of Arts degree in 1506, he became a priest in the Swiss village of Glarus. There he continued his humanistic studies, and became proficient in Greek. This combination of priestly duties with humanistic studies was exceptional, for records show that many parish priests in Switzerland at that time were ignorant, and that some had never even read the entire New Testament. In contrast, when Erasmus published his Greek New Testament, Zwingli made a copy of it which he carried with him in order to memorize as much of it as possible.

Zwingli was not only a pastor and a scholar, but also a patriot. At that time large contingents of Swiss mercenaries were being hired by various

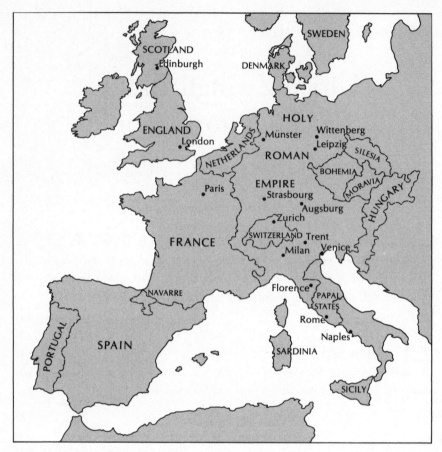

Europe at the Time of the Reformation.

warring factions, to the point that this had become an important source
of income for the Swiss cantons. In 1512, and again in 1515, Zwingli went
on Italian campaigns with mercenary soldiers from his district. The first
expedition was successful, and the young priest saw his parishioners brutally
looting the conquered region. The outcome of the second was the opposite,
and he now had occasion to see the impact of war on the defeated. This
convinced him that one of the great evils of Switzerland was that mercenary
service destroyed the moral fiber of society—or, as he would say, that the
Swiss were selling blood for gold.

After spending ten years at Glarus, Zwingli was made a priest of an abbey
to which many went on pilgrimage. He soon drew attention to himself by

Ulrich Zwingli, the reformer of Zurich, reached his theological conclusions quite independently from Luther, and by an entirely different route.

preaching against the notion that exercises such as pilgrimages could avail for salvation, and declaring that he found nothing in the New Testament in support of such practices. His fame grew to the point that in 1518 he was transferred to Zürich. By that time he had reached conclusions similar to those of Luther. His route to such conclusions had not been the anguished quest of the German Reformer, but rather the study of Scripture according to the method of the humanists, and his zealous outrage against the superstition that passed for Christianity, against the exploitation of the people by some leaders of the church, and against mercenary service.

Zwingli's preaching, devotion, and learning soon won him the respect of his parishioners in Zürich. In 1519, the city suffered a plague that killed over a quarter of the population, and infected Zwingli as he tended to his flock; he barely survived. When a seller of indulgences arrived, Zwingli convinced the government that he should be expelled from the city before he could peddle his wares.

Then Francis I of France, who was at war with Charles V, requested mercenary contingents from the Swiss Confederation, and all cantons sent their soldiers—except Zürich. The pope, an ally of Francis, insisted that Zürich had an obligation to the papacy, and prevailed on the government to send mercenary soldiers to serve under Francis. That incident directed Zwingli's attention to the abuses of the papacy, and his attacks against superstition and the unjust use of power became more sharply focused on the papacy.

This was the time when Luther was creating a stir in Germany, daring to oppose the emperor's will at the Diet of Worms. Now Zwingli's enemies spread the word that his teachings were the same as those of the German heretic. Later, Zwingli would declare that, even before having heard of Luther's teachings, he had come to similar conclusions through his study of the Bible. Thus, Zwingli's reformation was not a direct result of Luther's; rather, it was a parallel movement that soon established links with its counterpart in Germany. In any case, by 1522, the year after the Diet of Worms, Zwingli was ready to undertake the great task of reformation, and the Council of Government of Zürich was ready to support him in this endeavor.

THE BREAK WITH ROME

Zürich was under the ecclesiastical jurisdiction of the bishop of Constance, who expressed concern over what was taking place in Zürich. In 1522, when Zwingli preached against the laws of fasting and abstinence, and some of his parishioners gathered to eat sausages during Lent, the suffragan bishop of Constance accused the preacher before the Council of Government. But Zwingli defended his preaching on the basis of Scripture, and he was allowed to continue preaching. Shortly thereafter he expanded the scope of his attacks on traditional Christianity by declaring that priestly celibacy was not biblical, and further declaring that those who commanded it did not follow their own injunctions. He and ten other priests had written to the pope requesting permission to marry. When his petition was denied, he secretly married the widow Anna Reinhart, who would be a faithful companion and supporter the rest of his life. Pope Adrian VI, who was aware of the need to reform the church but was not willing to go as far as Luther and Zwingli demanded, made him tempting offers. But Zwingli refused, insisting on the scriptural base for the reforms he advocated. This led the Council of Government to call for a debate between Zwingli and a representative of the bishop.

At the appointed time, several hundred spectators gathered. Zwingli expounded on several theses, and defended them on the basis of Scripture. The bishop's representative refused to respond to him, declaring that a general council would gather soon, and at that time, all the matters currently being debated would be settled. When he was asked to try to show that Zwingli was wrong, he again refused to do so. Therefore, the council decided that, since no one had refuted Zwingli's teachings, he was free to continue preaching. This decision marked Zürich's final break with the bishopric of Constance, and therefore with Rome.

From that point on, Zürich's reformation marched apace, with the support of the Council of Government. Zwingli's main goal was to restore biblical faith and practice. But in the exact content of this program he differed from Luther, for while the German was willing to retain all traditional uses that did not contradict the Bible, the Swiss insisted that all that had no explicit scriptural support must be rejected. This led him, for instance, to suppress the use of organs in church, for such instruments—as well as the violin, which he played expertly—were not found in the Bible. But he also banned music and other practices that do appear in the Bible, on the grounds that nothing should be allowed to lead the mind away from the central task of hearing the Word of God. Even communion should not be celebrated too frequently, for it could detract from the Word, and therefore Zwingli preferred that it be celebrated only four times a year, and that people remain seated as they partook.

Rapid changes took place in Zürich under Zwingli's direction. Communion in both kinds—the bread and the cup—was offered to the laity. Many priests, former monks, and nuns were married. General public education, with no class distinctions, became the norm. And many took it upon themselves to spread Zwingli's ideas to other Swiss cantons.

The Swiss Confederation was not a centralized state, but rather a complex mosaic of different states, each with its own laws and government, that had come together in order to achieve a number of common goals, particularly independence from the German Empire. Within that mosaic, some cantons became Protestant, while others continued in their obedience to Rome and its hierarchy. Religious disagreement, added to other causes of friction, made civil war seem inevitable.

The Catholic cantons took steps to seek an alliance with Charles V, and Zwingli recommended that the Protestant cantons take the military initiative before it was too late. But authorities in the Protestant areas were not willing to be the first to resort to arms. When Zürich finally decided that it was time to go to war, the other Protestant cantons disagreed. Against Zwingli's advice, economic measures were taken against the Catholic cantons, which the Swiss Protestants accused of treason for having joined the cause of Charles V, of the hated house of Hapsburg.

In October of 1531, the five Catholic cantons joined in a surprise attack on Zürich. The defenders hardly had time to prepare for combat, for they did not know that they were at war until they saw the enemy's banners. Zwingli marched out with the first soldiers, hoping to resist long enough to allow the rest of the army to organize to defend the city. In Kappel, the Catholic cantons defeated the army of Zürich, and Zwingli was killed after the battle by a mercenary captain who found him among the wounded. His body was then quartered and burned, amidst much rejoicing by the victors.

The First Peace of Kappel was signed a little more than a month later. The Protestants agreed to cover the expenses of the recent military actions and, in return, each canton would have the freedom to make its own choice in matters of religion. From that time, Protestantism was firmly established in several Swiss cantons, while others remained Catholic. The movement of population from one canton to another, seeking freedom for the practice of religion, soon made some cantons staunchly Protestant, and others Catholic. In Zürich itself, Zwingli's mantle fell to Heinrich Bullinger, a disciple and companion of Zwingli who would continue providing leadership for almost another half century, until his own death in 1575.

ZWINGLI'S THEOLOGY

Since Zwingli's theology coincided with Luther's on many points, it shall suffice here to show the main points of contrast between the two reformers. The main difference between them resulted from the paths that each followed. While Luther's was that of a tormented soul that finally found solace in the biblical message of justification by faith, Zwingli's was that of the humanist who studied Scripture because it was the source of Christian

Finding himself in agreement with Luther on many points, Zwingli studied the writings of the German reformer. The marginal notes on this copy of one of Luther's works are in Zwingli's handwriting.

faith, and humanism encouraged such return to the sources. This in turn meant that Zwingli had a more positive view of the power of reason than did Luther.

A good example of this difference is the manner in which each dealt with the doctrine of predestination. They agreed that predestination was scriptural, and that it was necessary to affirm it as the basis for the doctrine of justification by grace alone. For Luther, the doctrine of predestination was the expression and the result of his experience of knowing himself powerless before his own sin, and therefore finding himself forced to declare that his salvation was not his own work, but God's. In contrast, Zwingli saw predestination as the logical consequence of the nature of God. For the Swiss reformer, the main argument in favor of predestination was that, since God is both omnipotent and omniscient, God knows and determines all things beforehand. Luther would not employ such arguments, but would be content with declaring that predestination is necessary because human beings are incapable a doing anything for their own salvation. He would probably have rejected Zwingli's arguments as the result of reason, and not of biblical revelation nor of the experience of the gospel.

Zwingli's view of original Christianity had been colored by a particular tradition of whose influence he was not fully aware: the long history of a Neoplatonic interpretation of Christianity that had made its way into Christian theology through the influence of Justin, Origen, Augustine, Dionysius the Areopagite, and others. One element in that tradition is a tendency to undervalue matter, and to contrast it with spiritual reality. This was one of the reasons why Zwingli insisted on a simple form of worship, one that would not lead the believer to the material through excessive use of the senses. Luther, on the other hand, saw the material, not as an obstacle, but as an aid to spiritual life.

The consequences of these diverging views were evident in the two reformers' understanding of sacraments, particularly the eucharist. While Luther held that an inner divine action took place when the outer human action was performed, Zwingli refused to grant such efficacy to the sacraments, for this would limit the freedom of the Spirit. For him, the material elements, and the physical actions that accompany them, can be no more than signs or symbols of spiritual reality. In the case of communion, Zwingli held that the presence of Christ in the elements is symbolic, and that the effectiveness of the sacrament is in the faith of those who partake of it. Baptism, however, presented greater difficulties. Zwingli was not willing to abandon infant baptism—an action that would have undermined his view that church and state are coextensive. But, if the efficacy of the sacrament is merely symbolic, why perform it on those who cannot perceive the symbol? It was this inner tension in Zwingli's theology that would be laid bare in Zürich by the first Anabaptists (see Chapter 6).

Their diverging views on the sacraments were important for both Zwingli and Luther, for they were part and parcel of the rest of their theology. Therefore, when political circumstances led Landgrave Philip of Hesse to try to bring together the German and Swiss reformers, the question of how Christ is present at communion proved to be an insurmountable obstacle. This took place in 1529, when under the bidding of Philip the main leaders of the reformation gathered at Marburg: Luther and Melanchthon from Wittenberg, Bucer from Strasbourg, Oecolampadius from Basel, and Zwingli from Zürich. On fourteen out of fifteen issues there was agreement, but not on the meaning and efficacy of communion. Perhaps even there an agreement could have been reached, had Melanchthon not reminded Luther that a compromise with Zwingli on this point would further alienate Catholic Germans whom Luther and his companions still hoped to win for their cause. Some time later, when the break with Catholics was clearly irreversible, Melanchthon himself reached an agreement with the reformers from Switzerland and Strasbourg.

In any case, there is no doubt that the phrase attributed to Luther at the Colloquy of Marburg, "we are not of the same spirit," correctly summarizes the situation. Their differences regarding communion were not an unimportant detail in the whole of their theologies, but were rather the result of their divergent views on the relation between matter and spirit, and therefore on the nature of God's revelation.

These and other differences between Luther and Zwingli would give rise to two Protestant traditions, the Lutheran and the Reformed, that would differ particularly on the matter of the Lord's presence in the eucharist. While eventually the Reformed tradition would claim Calvin as its foundational theologian, there would still be much in it that bore Zwingli's imprint. On the matter of the eucharist, many Reformed would hold to Zwingli's views rather than to Calvin's (see Chapter 7). And the many cases in which the Reformed have taken up armed rebellion as a matter of righteousness and justice—for instance, in the Netherlands, Scotland, England, and the United States—have echoed Zwingli's preaching and attitudes as both a reformer and a patriot.

6

The Radical Reformation

Now everybody hopes to be saved by a superficial faith, without the fruits of faith, without the baptism of trial and tribulation, without love or hope, and without truly Christian practice.

CONRAD GREBEL

Both Luther and Zwingli were convinced that over the course of centuries Christianity had ceased to be what it was in the New Testament. Luther sought to cleanse it from all that contradicted Scripture. Zwingli went further, holding that only that which had a scriptural foundation should be believed and practiced. But soon there were others who pointed out that Zwingli did not carry such ideas to their logical conclusion.

THE FIRST ANABAPTISTS

According to these critics, Zwingli and Luther forgot that in the New Testament there is a marked contrast between the church and the society surrounding it. The result was persecution, since Roman society could not tolerate primitive Christianity. Therefore, the compromise between church and state that took place as a result of Constantine's conversion was in itself a betrayal of primitive Christianity. In order to be truly obedient to Scripture, the reformation begun by Luther must go much further than was allowed by the Reformer. The church must not be confused with the rest of society. The essential difference between the two is that, while one becomes a member of a society merely by being born into it, and through no decision on one's own part, one cannot belong to the true church without a personal decision to that effect. In consequence, infant baptism must be rejected, for it takes for granted that one becomes a Christian by being born into a supposedly Christian society. This obscures the need for a personal decision that stands at the very heart of the Christian faith. The resultant community of faith is then responsible for disciplining its own members, whose purity of life must be a witness to the gospel—a purity that cannot be guaranteed nor enforced by the civil government. This was the one point at which some of the more moderate reformers sought to follow the Anabaptist lead, for first Martin Bucer in Strasbourg and then John Calvin in Geneva insisted on the right and obligation of the church to discipline its members, and not leave such matters to the state.

Most of these radical reformers also held that pacifism is an essential element in Christianity. The Sermon on the Mount must be obeyed literally, and any who object saying that this is impossible simply show their lack of faith. Christians ought not to take up arms to defend themselves, nor to defend their country, even if the Turks threaten it. As was to be expected, such teachings were not well received in Austria and Germany, where the Turks were a constant threat, nor in Zürich and the other Protestant areas of

The city of Zurich, where Zwingli had led the movement for reformation, was also the birthplace of one of the many Anabaptist groups.

Switzerland, where there was always the danger that Protestantism would be crushed by Catholic armies.

These ideas circulated in various seemingly disconnected parts of Europe, including some Catholic countries. But it was in Zürich that they first received public attention. In that city, there was a group of believers who urged Zwingli to undertake a more radical reformation. These people, who called themselves the *brethren*, insisted on the need to found a congregation of true believers, in contrast with the multitudes who called themselves *Christian* simply because they had been born in a Christian country and had been baptized as infants.

When it finally became apparent that Zwingli would not follow that course of action, some of the "brethren" decided that it was time to found such a congregation. George Blaurock, a former priest, asked another of the brethren, Conrad Grebel, to baptize him. On January 21, 1525, at the fountain that stood in the city square in Zürich, Grebel baptized Blaurock, who then did the same for several others. At that time they did not baptize by immersion, for their main concern was not the manner in which the rite was administered but rather the need for faith before receiving baptism. Later, as they sought to conform to the New Testament, they began baptizing by immersion.

Their enemies soon began calling them *anabaptists*, which means *rebaptizers*. Such a name was not quite accurate, for the supposed *rebaptizers* did not hold that one should be *re*baptized, but rather that infant baptism was not valid, and therefore the first real baptism takes place when one receives the rite after having made a public confession of faith. In any case, history knows them as *Anabaptists*, a title which has lost its earlier pejorative connotation.

The Anabaptist movement drew great opposition from Catholics as well as from other Protestants. Although that opposition was usually couched in theological considerations, in fact Anabaptists were persecuted because they were considered subversive. In spite of their radical views on other matters, both Luther and Zwingli accepted the notion that church and state must live side by side, supporting each other, and both refrained from any interpretation of the gospel that would make it a threat to the established social order. The Anabaptists, without seeking to do so, did threaten the social order. Their extreme pacifism was unacceptable to those in charge of maintaining social and political order, particularly amidst the upheavals of the sixteenth century.

Also, by insisting on emphasizing the contrast between the church and civil society, the Anabaptists implied that the power structures within civil society should not be adopted by the church. Even though Luther's original goals did not intend it, Lutheranism was now supported by the princes who had embraced it, and such princes enjoyed great authority in matters both civil and ecclesiastic. In Zwingli's Zürich, the Council of Government had the final word in religious matters. And the same was true in Catholic lands, where medieval traditions prevailed. This certainly did not preclude repeated clashes between church and state. But there was at least a body of common presuppositions that provided the framework for the solution of such conflicts. All this the Anabaptists undid with their insistence on the church as a voluntary community, totally distinct from the civil community. Furthermore, many Anabaptists were radical egalitarians. In most of their groups, women had the same rights as men; and, at least in theory, the poor and the ignorant were as important as the rich and the learned.

In this, the Anabaptist movement proved to be a significant forerunner of the modern spirit of religious tolerance. Because the church was not coextensive with the state, the latter had no authority to determine the religion of its subjects. On rare occasions (when they took possession of the city of Münster, for example), some of the more extreme Anabaptists abandoned this principle, but most Anabaptists would hold to it, and would thus leave a significant though indirect imprint on modernity.

It was partly as an attempt to curb extremism among their ranks that a number of Anabaptist leaders met in Schleitheim, Switzerland, in 1527—barely two years after the beginning of the movement—and issued the *Confession of Schleitheim*, a brief document that expounded on the seven fundamental practices and principles held by most Anabaptists. The first such principle was that baptism should only be administered to those who have repented and amended their lives, and who believed in Christ. Over against this, infant baptism is the worst of all the "abominations of the Pope." The second principle had to do with discipline, or the "ban," which was to be applied to those who refuse to amend their lives after two private and one public admonitions, who should then be banned from the communion table. The third is that communion—which is done in remembrance of the broken body and the shed blood of Christ—was not to be offered to those who were not baptized—as adults—for in communion all true believers are made into one bread. Fourth, true believers must separate themselves from all that is not united with God and Christ, for all of it is abomination. Indeed, all creatures are either good or bad, and believers must shun the latter. The fifth outlines the duties of pastors. Finally, the sixth and seventh principles of the *Confession of Schleitheim* rejects the use of "the sword"— meaning all forms of war or violence—as well as the giving of oaths, and spells out that this means that true believers must not participate in any activity connected with either the sword or oaths—meaning war, civil service, oaths to rulers or magistrates, and so on.

All this appeared highly subversive, and therefore Anabaptists had to face severe persecution. This was one of the reasons why the *Confession of Schleitheim* was issued. In 1525, two years before the *Confession*, the Catholic areas of Switzerland began condemning them to death. The following year, the Council of Government of Zürich followed suit. In a few months, persecution spread to the rest of Switzerland. In Germany there was no uniform policy, for each state followed its own course, generally applying to Anabaptists various ancient laws against heretics. In 1528, Charles V ordered that they be put to death on the basis of an ancient Roman law, directed against the Donatists, that established the death penalty for all guilty of rebaptizing. The Diet of Spire of 1529—the same in which the Lutheran princes protested and were first called *Protestants*—approved the imperial decree against Anabaptists. The only German prince who followed his conscience and refused to apply the edict was Philip I, Landgrave of Hesse. In some areas, including Luther's Electoral Saxony, Anabaptists were accused both of heresy and of sedition. Since one was a religious offense, and the other a crime, both ecclesiastical and civil courts had jurisdiction over those accused of being Anabaptist.

The martyrs were many—probably more than those who died during the three centuries of persecution preceding Constantine. The manner of their death varied from region to region, and even from case to case. With ironic cruelty, many were drowned. Others were burned to death, as had become customary with heretics centuries earlier. Some were tortured to death, or drawn and quartered. The stories of heroism in such difficult circumstances would fill several volumes. And still, the more fiercely it was persecuted, the more the movement grew.

With cruel irony, many Anabaptists were drowned. The drowning of Maria von Monjon, in 1552, is the subject of this engraving by Jan Luiken.

THE REVOLUTIONARY ANABAPTISTS

Many of the first leaders of the movement were scholars, and almost all were pacifists. But soon that first generation succumbed to persecution. The movement then became increasingly radical, and became an expression of the popular resentment that had earlier resulted in peasant rebellions. The original pacifism was then forgotten, and hopes of violent revolution took its place.

Even before the heyday of Anabaptism, Thomas Müntzer had brought together some of its tenets with the peasants' hopes for social justice. He joined the revolt, and as a result was executed in 1525, just over four months after the first Anabaptist baptisms in Zürich. Now many Anabaptists did likewise. One of them was Melchior Hoffman, a leather-dresser who had been first a Lutheran and then a Zwinglian before becoming an Anabaptist. In Strasbourg, where a measure of tolerance had allowed Anabaptism to become relatively strong, Hoffman began announcing that the Day of the Lord was near. His preaching inflamed the multitudes, which flocked to Strasbourg in the hope that the New Jerusalem would become a reality there. Hoffman himself announced that he would be imprisoned for six months, and that then the end would come. He also rejected the initial

Anabaptist pacifism on the grounds that, as the end approached, it would become necessary for the children of God to take up arms against the children of darkness. When he was imprisoned, thus fulfilling the first half of his prediction, even more people went to Strasbourg, there to await a sign from heaven that the time had come to take up arms. But the growing number of Anabaptists in the city provoked authorities to take repressive measures, and in any case Hoffman was still in prison after the predicted day of the Second Coming.

Then someone suggested that the New Jerusalem would not be established in Strasbourg but rather in Münster. In that city, the existing balance of power between Catholics and Protestants had forced a measure of tolerance, and therefore Anabaptists were not persecuted. The visionaries went there, as did many others whom intolerable oppression had led to despair. The Kingdom would come soon. It would come in Münster. And then the poor would receive the earth as their inheritance.

Soon the number of Anabaptists in Münster was such that they took over the city. Their leaders were John Matthys, a Dutch baker, and his main disciple, John of Leiden. Abandoning the Anabaptist principle of religious tolerance, one of their first acts was to expel the Catholics from the city. The bishop, forced to leave his see, gathered an army and laid siege to the New Jerusalem. Meanwhile, inside the city, there was a growing insistence that everything must conform to the Bible. Moderate Protestants were also expelled. Sculptures, paintings, and all sorts of items connected with traditional belief and worship were destroyed. Outside the city, the bishop killed every Anabaptist who fell into his hands. The defenders, seeing their situation worsen daily as food became increasingly scarce, became more emotional. There were daily claims of visions and revelations. In a military sortie against the bishop, John Matthys was killed, and John of Leiden became the leader of the besieged city. As a result of the prolonged war, and of the constant exodus of males, there were now many more women than men. As a remedy, John of Leiden decreed the practice of polygamy, following the example of the patriarchs of the Old Testament.

Although the besieged suffered increasing deprivation, the bishop lacked the funds to keep an army in the field. John of Leiden then led his followers in what seemed a successful sortie, and they in response proclaimed him king of the New Jerusalem. But shortly after these events some of the inhabitants of the city, tired of the excesses of the visionaries, opened the gates to the bishop. The king of the New Jerusalem was captured and exhibited throughout the area, jointly with his two principal lieutenants. Then they were tortured and executed. Thus ended the primary outburst of revolutionary Anabaptism. Melchior Hoffman, forgotten by most, continued to serve his sentence in prison, very likely until his death. For generations, in the Church of St. Lambert in Münster, visitors could see the three cages in which the king of the New Jerusalem and his two aides had been exhibited.

THE LATER ANABAPTISTS

The fall of Münster put an end to revolutionary Anabaptism. Soon the explanation given for the tragedy of Münster was the abandonment of pacifism. Like the first Anabaptists, the new leaders of the movement held that the reason why Christians are not willing to follow the precepts of the Sermon on the Mount is not that such precepts are impossible to obey but rather that they require great faith. Those who possess such faith will practice the love that Jesus taught, leaving the consequences in God's hands.

The principal figure in this new generation was Menno Simons, a Dutch Catholic priest who was led to reconsider the matter of infant baptism by the martyrdom of an Anabaptist in 1531. Five years later, in 1536—the same year that John of Leiden and his cohorts were executed—Menno left his position as a parish priest and embraced Anabaptism. He joined a Dutch Anabaptist fellowship, and eventually his followers came to be called *Mennonites*. Although the Mennonites suffered the same persecution as other Anabaptists, Menno Simons survived, and spent years traveling through Holland and northern Germany preaching his faith and encouraging his followers. He also wrote a vast number of treatises, of which *Foundations of the Christian Doctrine*, published in 1539, became the most influential. He was convinced that pacifism was an essential part of true Christianity, and therefore refused to have anything to do with the revolutionary Anabaptists. He also felt that Christians ought not to offer any oaths whatsoever, and that they should not occupy positions requiring them. But they should obey civil authorities, as long as what is required of them is not contrary to Scripture. Baptism—which he performed by pouring water over the head—should be administered only to adults who confess their faith publicly. Neither that rite nor communion confer grace, but rather are outward signs of what takes place inwardly between God and the believer. Finally, following Jesus' example, Menno and his followers practiced footwashing.

*Menno Simons, who became an Anabaptist in 1536, was soon one
of the movement's most famous leaders. His staunch pacifism was
characteristic of most later Anabaptists.*

In spite of their refusal to participate in subversive acts, Mennonites
were considered subversive by many governments because they would not
take oaths or offer military service. For this reason they were scattered
throughout Eastern Europe, particularly Russia. Later, others left for North
America, where they were offered religious tolerance. But in both Russia
and North America they encountered difficulties, for in both cases the state
required that they serve in the armed forces—a requirement later waived in
the Unites States and other countries. Thus, in the nineteenth and twenti-

eth centuries many Mennonites immigrated to South America, where there were still territories where they could live in relative isolation from the rest of society. By the twentieth century, Mennonites were the main branch of the old Anabaptist movement of the sixteenth century, and they still insisted on their pacifist stance. But persecution appeared to be chiefly a matter of the past, and Mennonites had gained an honored place in society through their social service.

7

John Calvin

Let us beware lest our words and thoughts go beyond what the Word of God tells us. . . . We must leave to God His own knowledge, . . . and conceive Him as He makes Himself known to us, without attempting to discover anything about His nature apart from His Word.

JOHN CALVIN

Without any doubt, the most important systematizer of Protestant theology in the sixteenth century was John Calvin. While Luther was the daring trailblazer of the movement, Calvin was the careful thinker who bound the various Protestant doctrines into a cohesive whole. Also, Luther's tortured quest for salvation and his joyous discovery of justification by faith were such that they always dominated his theology. Calvin, as a theologian of the second generation, did not allow the doctrine of justification to eclipse the rest of Christian theology, and therefore was able to pay more attention to several aspects of Christian faith which Luther had virtually ignored—in particular, the doctrine of sanctification.

CALVIN'S EARLY CAREER

Calvin was born in the small town of Noyon, in France, on July 10, 1509. By that time, Luther had delivered his first lectures at the University of Wittenberg. Calvin's father was part of the rising middle class of Noyon, and served as secretary to the bishop and procurator of the cathedral chapter. Through such connections, he obtained for young John the income from two minor ecclesiastical posts, to defray his expenses as a student.

Making use of such resources, and hoping for an ecclesiastical career, young Calvin studied in Paris, where he became acquainted with humanism as well as with the conservative reaction against it. The theological discussion that was then taking place made him familiar with the doctrines of Wycliffe, Huss, and Luther. But, as he later declared, "I was stubbornly tied to the superstitions of the papacy."[3] In 1528, he received the degree of Master of Arts. His father, who apparently had fallen out with the bishop and lost his influence in Noyon, then decided that his son should abandon theology and pursue a career in law. With that end in mind, Calvin studied in Orleans and Bourges, under two of the most famous jurists of the time, Pierre de l'Estoile and Andrea Alciati. The former followed the traditional methods for the study and interpretation of law, whereas the latter was an elegant humanist with a reputation for being somewhat pompous. When controversy arose between the two, Calvin took the side of de l'Estoile. This serves as an indication that, at the very time he was most profoundly imbued in the spirit of humanism, Calvin felt no admiration for the vacuous elegance that characterized some of the most famous humanists.

THE INSTITUTES

When his father died, Calvin returned to Paris to finish his interrupted studies in theology, and eventually to join the Protestant cause. How Calvin arrived at his break with Rome, or the exact date this took place, is not known. In contrast to Luther, Calvin wrote little about the inner state of his soul. It seems likely that through the influence of some members of his circle of humanists, and through his study of Scripture and early Christian times, he came to the conclusion that he must leave the Roman communion and follow the route of Protestantism.

In 1534, he returned to Noyon and gave up the ecclesiastical posts his father had secured for him, although they were his main source of funds. Whether by that time he had decided to abandon the Catholic Church, or this was only one more step in his spiritual pilgrimage to reformation, it is impossible to ascertain. The fact is that in October of that year Francis I, who until then had shown relative tolerance toward Protestants, changed his policy, and in January 1535 Calvin went into exile in Switzerland, in the Protestant city of Basel.

He felt called to spend his time in study and literary labors. What he sought was not to become one of the leaders of the Reformation, but rather to settle in a calm environment where he could study Scripture and write about his faith. Shortly before arriving at Basel, he had written a short treatise on the state of the souls of the dead before the resurrection. What he

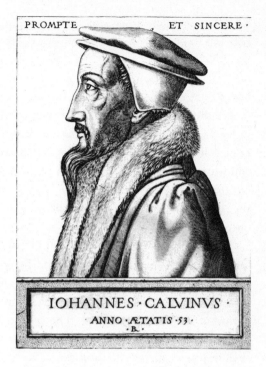

PROMPTE ET SINCERE ·

IOHANNES · CALVINVS ·
ANNO · ÆTATIS · 53 ·
· B ·

*John Calvin, who spent most of his
career in Geneva, was without doubt
the most important systematizer of
Protestant theology in the sixteenth
century.*

now hoped to do was to write other such treatises, to help clarify the faith of
the church in those confused times.

His main project on this score was a short summary of the Christian
faith from a Protestant viewpoint. Until then, most Protestant literature,
drawn by the urgency of polemics, had dealt exclusively with the points at
issue, and had said little regarding other basic doctrines such as the Trinity,
the incarnation, and so on. Calvin proposed to fill this vacuum with a short
manual that he called the *Institutes of the Christian Religion.*

The first edition of the *Institutes* appeared in Basel in 1536 and was a
book of 516 pages. It was small in format so that it would fit easily into the
wide pockets that were then in use, which would therefore allow for discreet
circulation throughout France. It had only six chapters. The first four dealt
with the Law, the Creed, the Lord's Prayer, and the sacraments. The last
two, more polemical in tone, summarized the Protestant position regarding
the "false sacraments" of Rome, and Christian freedom.

The book enjoyed immediate and surprising success. The first edition,
which was in Latin and therefore could be read in several countries, sold out
in nine months. From that point on, Calvin continued working on successive editions of the *Institutes,* and these grew in volume through the years.

The controversies of the time, the opinions of various groups that Calvin believed to be in error, and the practical needs of the church contributed to the growth of the work; thus, in order to follow Calvin's theological development and the various controversies in which he was involved, it would suffice to compare the successive editions of the *Institutes*.

Another edition appeared in Strasbourg, also in Latin, in 1539. In Geneva, in 1541, Calvin published the first French edition, which became a classic of French literature. From that point on, editions were paired, a French one appearing immediately after one in Latin, as follows: 1543 and 1545, 1550 and 1551, 1559 and 1560. Since the Latin and French editions of 1559 and 1560 were the last to appear during Calvin's lifetime, they constitute the definitive text of the *Institutes*.

That definitive text is far removed from the small handbook on the Christian faith that Calvin published in 1536, for the six chapters of that early edition had become four books containing a total of eighty chapters. The first book treats of God and revelation, as well as of creation and the nature of the human creature. The second is concerned with God as Redeemer, and how this is made known to us, first in the Old Testament and then in Jesus Christ. The third shows how, through the Spirit, we can share in the grace of Jesus Christ, and the fruits this produces. Finally, the fourth book deals with the "external means" of that sharing, that is, the church and the sacraments. The entire work shows a profound knowledge, not only of Scripture, but also of ancient Christian literature—particularly the works of Augustine—and of the theological controversies of the sixteenth century. There is no doubt that this was the high point of Protestant systematic theology at the time of the Reformation.

THE REFORMER OF GENEVA

Calvin had no intention of following the active lifestyle of the many Protestants who, in various parts of Europe, had become leaders of the Reformation. Although he respected and admired them, he was convinced that his gifts were not those of the pastor or the leader, but rather those of the scholar and author. After a short visit to Ferrara, and another to France, he decided to settle in Strasbourg, where the Protestant cause was victorious, and where there was theological and literary activity that offered the proper milieu for the work he proposed to do.

But the direct route to Strasbourg was closed by military operations, and

Calvin had to make a detour through Geneva. Conditions there were difficult. Some time earlier, the Protestant city of Bern had sent missionaries to Geneva. These missionaries had gained the support of a small nucleus of educated laity who ardently desired the reformation of the church, and also of a powerful sector of the bourgeoisie whose goal it was to avoid certain economic and political restrictions that a break with Rome would abolish. The clergy, apparently with little instruction and even less conviction, had simply obeyed the orders of the government of Geneva when it decreed that the mass was abolished, and that the city was now Protestant. All this had taken place just a few months before Calvin's arrival in Geneva, and therefore the Bern missionaries, whose leader was William Farel, now found themselves at the helm of the religious life of the city, and sorely lacking in personnel.

Calvin arrived in Geneva firm in his intention to stop there no longer than a day before continuing his journey to Strasbourg. But someone told Farel that the author of the now famous *Institutes*—published only four months earlier—was in town, and the result was an unforgettable interview that Calvin himself later recorded. Farel, who "burned with a marvelous zeal for the advancement of the gospel," presented Calvin with several reasons why his presence was needed in Geneva. Calvin listened respectfully to the other man, some fifteen years older. But he refused to heed Farel's plea, telling him that he had planned certain studies, and that these would not be possible in the confused situation Farel was describing. When the latter had exhausted his arguments, and failed to convince the young theologian, he appealed to their common Lord, and challenged Calvin with a dire threat: "May God condemn your repose, and the calm you seek for study, if before such a great need you withdraw, and refuse your succor and help." Calvin continues his report: "These words shocked and broke me, and I desisted from the journey I had begun."[4] Thus began his career as the Reformer of Geneva.

Although at first Calvin agreed to no more than lending his aid to the Protestant leaders of the city, particularly to Farel, soon his theological insight, his legal training, and his reforming zeal made him the central figure in the religious life of the city. Farel, who until then had been the leader of the Protestant cause, gladly became Calvin's main collaborator and support. But not all were ready to follow the path of reformation that Calvin and Farel laid out. As soon as the two pastors began insisting that the decision to reform the church be taken seriously, many of the bourgeoisie who had encouraged the break with Rome began demurring, while they circulated rumors in other Protestant cities regarding the supposed errors of the Gene-van reformers. The conflict finally came to a head on the matter of church discipline and the right to excommunicate. Calvin insisted that, if religious life was to conform to the principles of reformation, it was necessary to excommunicate unrepentant sinners. The government, then in the hands of the bourgeoisie, refused to allow this, claiming that it was unwarranted rigorism and a usurpation of government authority. The final result was that Calvin, who insisted on his position, was banned from the city. Farel, who was invited to remain, preferred to join his friend in exile rather than serve as an instrument for the bourgeois in their quest for a religion with many liberties and no obligations.

Calvin saw this as the God-given opportunity to return to the life of writing and scholarship he had projected, and therefore completed his long-interrupted journey to Strasbourg. But once again peace eluded him. There was in the city a large community of exiles who had left France for reason of their faith, and Martin Bucer, the leader of the reformation in Strasbourg, insisted that Calvin should be their pastor. During this sojourn in Stras-bourg he had long conversations with Bucer, who became his mentor and profoundly influenced Calvin's theology and his understanding of pastoral ministry. It was in the context of these responsibilities that Calvin produced a French liturgy, as well as French translations of several psalms and other hymns, to be sung by the exiled French community. While in Strasbourg, Calvin also prepared the second edition of the *Institutes*—now much ex-panded, and showing signs of Bucer's influence—and he married Idelette de Bure, a widow with whom he was very happy until her death in 1549.

The three years Calvin spent in Strasbourg, from 1538 to 1541, were prob-ably the happiest and most peaceful of his life. But in spite of this he regret-ted being prevented from continuing his work with the church in Geneva, for which he still felt deep concern. Therefore, when circumstances changed in the Swiss city, and the new government invited him to return, Calvin agreed without hesitation.

Calvin returned to Geneva in 1541, and one of his first concerns was the preparation of a series of *Ecclesiastical Ordinances* that the government approved with some modifications. By this action, the government of the church in Geneva was placed primarily in the hands of the Consistory, whose members were the pastors and twelve lay "elders." Since there were

The chair in Saint Peter's Cathedral in Geneva from which Calvin conducted much of his teaching.

five pastors, the lay elders held the majority of the positions in the Consistory. But in spite of this, Calvin's personal authority was such that the Consistory usually followed his advice.

The *Ordinances* organized the ministry of the church into four orders which Calvin thought reflected the practice of the New Testament. In this fourfold distribution of responsibilities, the pastors were in charge of the ministry of the Word and the sacraments. The teachers, or doctors, were responsible for the education of the entire community of faith—children as well as adults. The elders would supervise the religious life of their neighborhoods, admonishing those who sinned and, if they would not mend their ways, reporting them to the Consistory. And the deacons were in charge of the social services of the church.

During the next twelve years, the Consistory and the government of the city clashed repeatedly, for the ecclesiastical body, following Calvin's promptings, sought to regulate the customs of the citizens—who were also the members of the church—with a severity not always matched by the government. By 1553, the opposition had again come to power, and Calvin's political position was precarious.

It was then that the famous process against Michael Servetus took place. Servetus was a Spanish physician whose physiological studies had made a significant contribution to medical science. But he was also the author of a number of theological treatises in which he argued that the union of church and state after Constantine's conversion was in truth a great apostasy, and that the Council of Nicea, in promulgating the doctrine of the Trinity, had offended God. He had recently escaped from the prisons of the Catholic Inquisition in France, where he was being tried for heresy, and was passing through Geneva when he was recognized. He was arrested, and Calvin prepared a list of thirty-eight accusations against him. Some in Geneva who opposed Calvin took up Servetus's cause, arguing that he had been accused of heresy by Catholics, and therefore that he should be seen as an ally. But the government of the city asked the advice of the various Protestant cantons of Switzerland, and all agreed that Servetus was a heretic, not only by Catholic standards, but also by Protestant ones. This put an end to the opposition, and Servetus was burned to death—although Calvin had argued in favor of a less cruel death by beheading.

Servetus's death was severely criticized, especially by Sebastian Castello, whom Calvin had earlier expelled from Geneva for having interpreted the Song of Songs as a poem of erotic love. Ever since, the burning of Servetus—a noted physician—has become a symbol of the rigid dogmatism of Calvin's Geneva. Undoubtedly, there are grounds for harsh judgment on the proceedings, and particularly on Calvin's role in them. But one should also remember that at that time all over Europe both Protestants and Catholics were acting in similar fashion against those whom they considered heretics. Servetus himself was condemned by the French Inquisition, which had not burned him only because he had escaped.

After Servetus's execution, Calvin's authority in Geneva had no rival. This was especially true since the theologians of all the other Protestant cantons had supported him, while his opponents had found themselves in the difficult position of defending a heretic who had been condemned by both Catholics and Protestants.

In 1559, Calvin saw the fulfillment of one of his fondest dreams in the opening of the Genevan Academy, under the direction of Theodore Beza—who would eventually succeed him as theological leader of the city. In that academy, the youth of Geneva were educated according to Calvinist principles. But its student body also included many from various other parts of Europe, who later returned to their native lands taking Calvinism with them.

As he saw his end approach, Calvin prepared his will and bid farewell to his closest associates. Farel, who had taken the responsibility of leading the

Reformation in nearby Neuchâtel, paid his friend a last visit. Calvin died on May 27, 1564.

CALVIN AND CALVINISM

During Calvin's lifetime, the main issue dividing Protestants—except for the Anabaptists, whom other Protestants considered heretics—was the manner of the presence of Christ in communion. This was the main point of conflict between Luther and Zwingli at the Colloquy of Marburg. On this point, Calvin followed the lead of his friend Martin Bucer, the reformer of Strasbourg, who took an intermediate position between Luther and Zwingli. Calvin affirmed that the presence of Christ in communion is real, although spiritual. This means that such presence is not merely symbolic, nor is communion a mere devotional exercise; rather, there is in it a true divine action for the church that partakes of the sacrament. On the other hand, this does not mean that the body of Christ descends from heaven, nor that it can be present in several altars at the same time, as Luther claimed. Rather, in the act of communion, by the power of the Holy Spirit, believers are taken to heaven and share with Christ in a foretaste of the heavenly banquet.

In 1526, Bucer, Luther, and others had reached the *Wittenberg Concord*, which made room for both Luther's and Bucer's views. In 1549, Bucer, Calvin, the main Swiss Protestant theologians, and several others from southern Germany, signed the *Zürich Consensus*, a similar document. Also, Luther had been pleased with the publication of Calvin's *Institutes*. Therefore, the difference between Calvin and Luther on the presence of Christ in communion should not have been an insurmountable obstacle to Protestant unity.

But the followers of the great teachers were less flexible than their masters. In 1552, Joachim Westphal, a Lutheran, published a treatise against Calvin in which he declared that Calvinist views were surreptitiously making their way into traditionally Lutheran territories, and offered himself as the champion of Luther's views on communion. On their part, some Calvinists accused Lutherans of being practically Catholic in their views on communion. By then Luther had died, and Melanchthon refused to attack Calvin, as Westphal demanded. But the net result was a growing distance between those who followed Luther and those who accepted the *Zürich Consensus*, who were then called *Reformed* in contraposition to *Lutherans*.

Therefore, during this early period the main characteristic of Calvinist or Reformed theology was not its doctrine of predestination—on which the

Reformed generally agreed with Lutherans. What actually distinguished the Calvinists from the Lutherans was their understanding of communion. It was in the following century, as we shall see as our story unfolds (Chapter 20) that predestination came to be seen as the hallmark of Calvinism.

In any case, due partly to the influence of the Genevan Academy, and partly to the *Institutes,* Calvin's theological influence was soon felt in various other parts of Europe. Eventually, a number of churches appeared—in the Netherlands, Scotland, Hungary, England, France, and so forth—that followed the teaching of the Genevan reformer, and are now known as *Reformed* or *Calvinistic*. Significantly, in most of these countries Calvinism was joined with a zeal for reforming society that did not exist in Lutheran lands, for Calvinists were convinced that it was their duty to make the civil government conform to the law of God. Thus, one of the most lasting consequences of Calvinism—and one that Calvin most likely would never have imagined—was a series of revolutions that opened the way for the modern world.

8

The Reformation in Great Britain

The universall defection, whereof Saint Paul did prophesy, is easy to
be espyed as well in religion as in manners. The corruption of life is
evident, and religion is not measured with the playne Worde of God,
but by custome, consuetude, will, consent, and determination of men.

JOHN KNOX

Until early in the seventeenth century, Great Britain was divided between the house of Tudor in England, and the Stuart kingdom of
Scotland. The two houses were related by blood, and eventually the two
kingdoms would be united. But during the sixteenth century their relationship was one of enmity and open warfare, and therefore the Reformation
followed a different course in each of them. For this reason, in the present
chapter we shall deal first with the Reformation in England, and then turn
to the Scottish Reformation.

HENRY VIII

The sixteenth century opened with Scotland an ally of France, England an
ally of Spain. The hostility between the two great kingdoms on the Continent was reflected in the hostility between the two British kingdoms. In
order to strengthen his ties with Spain, Henry VII of England arranged for
the marriage of his son and heir, Arthur, to Catherine of Aragon, a daughter
of Ferdinand and Isabella of Spain—and therefore an aunt of Charles V.
The wedding took place amid great celebrations when the bride was fifteen
years old, and it should have sealed the friendship between England and
Spain. But Arthur died four months later, and Spain then proposed a union
between the young widow and her deceased husband's younger brother,
Henry, who was now heir to the English throne. The king of England, eager

to retain both the friendship of Spain and the widow's dowry, agreed to the marriage. Since canon law prohibited a man's marriage to his brother's widow, the English representatives in Rome obtained a papal dispensation, and as soon as young Henry was old enough he was married to Catherine.

It was not a happy marriage. In spite of papal dispensation, there was some doubt as to whether the pope had the power to grant dispensation from the principle that a man should not marry his brother's widow. This in turn meant that the legality of the marriage itself was also in doubt. The failure of Henry and Catherine to produce a male heir—their only surviving child was Princess Mary Tudor—could be interpreted as a sign of divine wrath. The nation had recently suffered the bloodletting of a war of succession, and therefore it seemed imperative that the king have a male heir. But after several years of marriage it was clear that such an heir would not result from Henry's union to Catherine.

Several solutions were proposed. Henry himself suggested that his bastard son, whom he had made duke of Richmond, be declared legitimate, and made his heir. But such an arrangement would require papal action, and the pope refused to take a step that would alienate Spain. The cardinal who was in charge of these negotiations then suggested that Henry arrange the marriage of Mary with his bastard son. But King Henry felt that marrying Mary to her own half-brother would only compound the original error of his marrying his brother's widow. His own solution was to request that Rome annul his own union with Catherine, thus leaving him free to marry a queen with the potential to bear him the necessary heir. It appears that at the time of his first petition of annulment, Henry was not yet enamored of Anne Boleyn, and that he was initially moved by reasons of state rather than of the heart.

Such annulments were not uncommon, for popes would grant them for various reasons. In this particular case, the argument was that, in spite of the papal dispensation, the marriage between Henry and his brother's widow was not licit, and that therefore it had never been a true marriage. But other factors completely unrelated to canon law were much more weighty. The main consideration was that Catherine was the aunt of Charles V, who at that time had the pope virtually under his thumb, and who had received a plea from his aunt to save her from the dishonor of having her marriage declared illegitimate. The pope, Clement VII, could not invalidate Henry's marriage to Catherine without alienating Charles V. He prolonged the matter as long as possible, and his representatives even suggested that Henry,

Henry VIII, earlier known for his defense of Catholicism against Luther, and in no way a supporter of Protestant doctrine, led the Church of England in its break with Rome.

instead of repudiating his first wife, secretly take a second one. But this was no solution, for the king needed a publicly acknowledged heir. Thomas Cranmer, the king's main advisor in religious matters, suggested that he consult the main Catholic universities. The most prestigious of these—Paris, Orleans, Toulouse, Oxford, Cambridge, and even those in Italy—declared that Henry's marriage to Catherine was not valid.

From that point on, Henry VIII followed a policy that would eventually lead to a break with Rome. Ancient laws forbidding appeals to Rome were reenacted, putting the clergy more directly under the king's authority. He also toyed with the idea of retaining funds that normally went to Rome. By threatening to do so, he forced the pope to name Cranmer archbishop of Canterbury. His conflicts with the papacy did not mean, however, that he felt the least sympathy for Protestantism. In fact, a few years earlier he had published a treatise against Luther that had been acclaimed by Pope Leo X, who conferred on him the title of "defender of the faith" as a result of it. As Henry saw matters, what was needed was not a reformation like the one taking place on the Continent, but rather a restoration of the rights of the crown against undue papal intervention.

But Lutheran ideas, joined now with what still remained of Wycliffe's, were circulating in England, and those who held to them generally rejoiced in the growing distance between their sovereign and the papacy. Wycliffe's program of reformation included the creation of a national church under the direction of civil authorities, and Henry's policies were inexorably leading in that direction. Such was also the hope of Cranmer, who envisioned a reformation of the church under royal authority.

The final break took place in 1534, when Parliament, following the dictates of the king, enacted a series of laws forbidding the payment of annates and other such contributions to Rome, ruling that Henry's marriage to Catherine was not a true marriage, that therefore Mary was not the legitimate heir to the throne and, finally, that the king was the "supreme head of the Church of England." In order to enforce this last decision, Parliament also declared that any who dared call the king a schismatic or a heretic would be considered guilty of treason.

The most notable figure opposing these laws was Sir Thomas More, who had been chancellor of the kingdom and a personal friend of Henry VIII. He refused to swear loyalty to the king as head of the church, and for that reason was imprisoned. There he was visited by one of his daughters, for whom he had secured an excellent humanistic education. She tried to convince him to recant and accept the king's authority over the church, and to that end she listed the names of the many respectable and admired people who had done so. It is said that Thomas More's answer was: "I never intend to pin my conscience to another man's back." At his trial, the ex-chancellor defended his position, saying that he had never denied that the king was the head of the church but had only refused to affirm it, and that one cannot be condemned for not having said something. But after he had been condemned to death he openly declared that, in order to clear his conscience, he wished it to be clear that he did not believe that a layman such as the king

Thomas More was the most famous of the opponents of Henry's religious policy, and he paid for it with his life.

could be the head of the church, nor that any human being had the authority to change the laws of the church. Five days later, he was executed in the Tower of London, after declaring that he died "the king's good servant, but God's first." In 1935, four hundred years after his death, Thomas More's name was added to the official list of saints of the Roman Catholic Church.

Up until then, what had taken place was little more than a schism, with no attempt at reformation, and with no more doctrinal content than was necessary to justify the schism itself. But there were many in England who felt the need for a thorough reformation, and who saw the events of their time as an opportunity to achieve it. Typical of this attitude was Cranmer, who supported the king's policies in the hope that they would lead to further and deeper changes.

Henry VIII was essentially conservative on religious matters. He seems to have been a firm believer in most of the traditional teachings of the church, although there is no doubt that his main motivation was political. Therefore, during his reign the laws having to do with religion wavered according to changing political considerations.

Naturally, as soon as he was made head of the church, Henry declared his marriage to Catherine void, and regularized his secret marriage to Anne Boleyn that had already taken place. Anne gave him no male heir, but only a daughter, Elizabeth, and eventually she was accused of adultery and condemned to death. The king then married Jane Seymour, who finally bore him a male heir—the future Edward VI. After Jane's death, Henry tried to utilize his fourth marriage to establish an alliance with German Lutherans, for he felt threatened by both Charles V and Francis I of France. For that reason, he married Anne of Cleves, a sister-in-law of the leading Protestant prince, John Frederick of Saxony. But when it became apparent that the Lutherans insisted on their doctrinal positions even though Henry was opposed to them, and that Charles V and Francis I could not agree on a common policy against England, Henry divorced his fourth wife, and ordered that the man who had arranged it be beheaded. The new queen, Catherine Howard, supported the conservative position, and therefore the king's fifth marriage opened a period of difficulties for the advocates of reformation. Henry reached an agreement with Charles V for a joint invasion of France. Since he no longer had to fear the emperor, who had become his ally, he broke all negotiations with German Lutheran leaders. In England, he took steps to make the church conform as much as possible to Roman Catholicism, except in the matter of obedience to the pope. He also refused to restore monasteries, which he had suppressed and confiscated under pretense of reformation, and whose properties he had no intention of returning. But Catherine Howard fell into disgrace and was beheaded, and Charles V, for his own reasons, broke off his alliance with England. The next and last wife of Henry VIII, Catherine Parr, was a supporter of reformation, and the position of those who opposed it was precarious when the king died, early in 1547.

During all the years of Henry's reign, at times with the king's support and at times against his wishes, ideas of reformation had spread throughout the nation. Cranmer had ordered that the Bible be translated into

English, and by royal decree a great English Bible had been placed in every church, at a place where all could read it. (Interestingly, the impact of the different translations of the time may still be seen in the Lord's Prayer as it is said throughout the English-speaking world, where some say "trespasses" following William Tyndale's translation, and others "debts" following Myles Coverdale's.) The English Bible was a powerful weapon in the hands of the advocates of reform, who went from place to place drawing attention to those passages in Scripture that supported their teachings and their goals. The suppression of monasteries deprived the conservative wing of its staunchest allies. And the humanists, who were both numerous and powerful, saw in the royal policies an opportunity to achieve a reformation without what they considered to be the excesses of German Protestants. The net result was that at the time of Henry's death the advocates of reformation had ample support throughout the kingdom.

EDWARD VI

Henry had decided, and Parliament had agreed, that he would be succeeded by his only male heir, Edward, and then by his two daughters Mary and Elizabeth, in the order of their birth. Edward was a sickly young man who lived only six years after his father's death. The first three years of Edward's reign, under the regency of the duke of Somerset, were a period of great advances for the cause of the reformers. The cup in communion was restored to the laity, members of the clergy were allowed to marry, and images were withdrawn from the churches. But the most important religious achievement of Somerset's regency was the publication of the *Book of Common Prayer,* whose main author was Cranmer and which, for the first time, gave the English people a liturgy in their own language.

After Somerset's regency, the post fell to the duke of Northumberland, a man of lesser principles than his predecessor, but who for reasons of expediency continued the policies of reformation. During his regency a revised edition of the *Book of Common Prayer* was published. The Zwinglian tendency of this new edition is apparent when one compares the words the minister is to say in offering the bread to the communicants. The earlier version reads: "The body of our Lord Jesus Christ which was given for thee, preserve thy body and soul unto everlasting life." The new edition reads: "Take and eat this in remembrance that Christ died for thee, and feed on him in thy heart by faith with thanksgiving." While the first edition could be understood either in a Catholic or in a Lutheran sense, the second clearly drew its inspiration from Zwingli and those who held similar positions. This difference between the two books was an indication of the direction in which things were moving in England. The leaders of the reformist party, who were increasingly inclined toward Reformed theology, had reasons to hope that their cause would win without great opposition.

MARY TUDOR

When Edward VI died, the crown went to his half-sister Mary, the daughter of Henry VIII and Catherine of Aragon. Mary had always been a Catholic, for in her experience the movement of reformation had begun with her own dishonor in her youth, when she had been declared an illegitimate child. Furthermore, if Henry had been correct in proclaiming himself head of the church and his marriage to Catherine null and void, Mary was a bastard, and her right to succession could be cast into doubt. Therefore, for reasons both of conviction and of political necessity, Mary was committed to the goal of restoring Roman Catholicism in England. In this task she had the powerful support of her cousin Charles V, and also of a number of conservative bishops who had been deposed during the two previous reigns. But she knew that she must move with caution, so during the first months of her reign she took the time to consolidate her position within England, while she strengthened her ties with the Catholic house of Hapsburg by marrying her cousin Philip of Spain—later Philip II.

As soon as she felt herself secure on the throne, however, Mary began a series of increasingly repressive measures against Protestants. Late in 1554, England officially returned to obedience to the pope. Most of what had been done during the reigns of Henry and Edward was now undone. The feast days of the saints were restored. Married clergy were ordered to set their wives aside. Finally, open persecution of Protestant leaders became the policy of the kingdom. Almost three hundred of them were burned, while countless others were imprisoned or went into exile. For these reasons, the queen acquired the name by which she is known to this day: Bloody Mary.

In 1563, five years after Mary's death, the suffering of Protestants under her reign was highlighted in John Foxe's *Book of Martyrs*. Foxe had begun writing his book long before Mary's reign, and originally conceived his work as a tribute to martyrs of all time. But as news of what was taking place in England under Queen Mary reached him in exile in Strasbourg, the focus of

Mary Tudor, nicknamed by the Protestants "Bloody Mary," restored Catholicism, and during her reign most of the Protestant leaders who did not go into exile were condemned to death.

the book shifted, giving much more emphasis to the more recent English Protestant martyrs. This new focus may be seen in the full title of the book, *Actes and Monuments of these Latter and Perillous Dayes, Touching Matters of the Church.* The book's impact was greatly strengthened by numerous woodcuts depicting sundry and cruel martyrdoms. In part, thanks to those woodcuts, it soon became standard fare in the education of children, particularly among Puritans, and thus contributed to a long-lasting animosity against Catholics and their faith.

The most illustrious of the martyrs during Mary's reign was Cranmer. Since he was archbishop of Canterbury, his case was sent to Rome, where he was condemned as a heretic and burned in effigy. But the queen's goal was to force the figurehead of the reformist party to recant, thus achieving a moral victory over the Protestants. To that end, he was forced to watch from his prison the execution of two of his main supporters, close associates in his work of reformation, Bishops Hugh Latimer and Nicholas Ridley. Eventually, Cranmer did sign a recantation. To this day historians debate whether he did this out of fear of the pyre, or rather because he had always declared that he would obey his sovereigns. In all likelihood, he did not know his exact motives himself. The fact is that he did recant in writing, and that in spite of this he was condemned to death, as an example to any would-be followers. Arrangements were then made for a public recantation before his death. The archbishop was taken to the Church of St. Mary, where a wooden platform had been set up, and after the sermon he was given the opportunity to recant. He began by speaking of his sins and his weakness, and all expected him to conclude by declaring that he had sinned in leaving the Church of Rome. But he surprised his tormentors by withdrawing his words of recantation:

> They were written contrary to the truth which I thought in my heart, and written for fear of death, to save my life if it might be. . . . And forasmuch as I have written many things contrary to what I believe in my heart, my hand shall first be punished; for if I may come to the fire it shall first be burned. As for the Pope, I refuse him, for Christ's enemy and antichrist, with all his false doctrine.

That last act of valor of the elderly man—who did in fact hold his hand in the fire until it was charred—caused his earlier wavering to be forgotten, and Protestants considered Cranmer the great hero of their cause. Heartened by his example, many insisted on spreading Protestant teachings, and it became increasingly clear that Mary would have to take even harsher measures if Protestantism was to be eradicated.

ELIZABETH

Mary died late in 1558, and was succeeded by her half-sister Elizabeth, the daughter of Henry VIII and Anne Boleyn. Charles V had repeatedly suggested that Mary have her half-sister executed, but the Bloody Queen had not dared go that far, and now her policies were undone by her predessesor. This was also the time when many who had left the kingdom for religious reasons returned to their homeland, bringing with them Zwinglian and Calvinist ideas they had learned on the Continent. Just as Mary had been a Catholic both out of conviction and out of political necessity, Elizabeth was a Protestant for similar reasons. If the head of the church in England was the pope, and not the king, it followed that the marriage of Henry VIII with Catherine of Aragon was valid, and that Elizabeth, born from Anne Boleyn while Catherine still lived, was illegitimate. Paul IV, who was then pope, indicated that he was ready to declare Elizabeth a legitimate daughter of Henry, as long as she continued in the Roman communion. But Elizabeth did not even notify him of her elevation to the throne, and recalled the English ambassador to Rome. Although much more politically inclined than Mary, she had been brought up to believe that her father had done right in proclaiming himself head of the Church of England, and she would not waver in that conviction.

Elizabeth was not a Protestant extremist. Her ideal was a church whose practices were uniform, thus uniting the kingdom in common worship, but in which there would also be great latitude for varying opinions. Within that church, there would be no place for either Roman Catholicism or extreme Protestantism. But any moderate form of Protestantism would be acceptable, as long as it participated in the common worship of the Church of England.

Elizabeth's religious policy found expression and support in a new edition of the *Book of Common Prayer*. As an indication of her policy of theological inclusiveness, the new book combined the two different formulas that the earlier versions ordered ministers to use in the distribution of the bread. The new text read as follows:

> The body of our Lord Jesus Christ which was given for thee, preserve thy body and soul unto everlasting life. Take and eat this in remembrance that Christ died for thee and feed on Him in thy heart by faith with thanksgiving.

Naturally, the purpose of this double formula was to accommodate the divergent opinions of those who believed that communion was simply an act of remembrance, and those who insisted that in it one really partook of the body of Christ.

The same policy may be seen in the *Thirty-nine Articles*, promulgated in 1562 in order to serve as doctrinal foundation for the Church of England. In them several Catholic doctrines and practices are explicitly rejected, but there is no attempt to choose among the various Protestant views. On the contrary, the articles seek to achieve a *via media* in which all but Roman Catholics and the most doctrinaire Protestants could participate. Ever since that time, this has been one of the main characteristics of the Anglican Communion—that is, the Church of England and those religions derived from it.

During Elizabeth's reign Catholicism continued a precarious existence in England. Some Catholics took up the cause of Mary Stuart, the queen of Scotland who had been forced into exile in England and whose career we shall follow in the next section of this chapter. Were Elizabeth to be declared illegitimate, Mary Stuart would gain the English throne. Therefore, she was the focal point of several conspiracies by Catholics, whom the pope had declared free from any obligation of obedience to Elizabeth. Exiled Catholic leaders declared that Elizabeth was a heretical usurper, and plotted her downfall and the elevation of Mary Stuart to the throne of England. Meanwhile, graduates of Catholic seminaries in exile secretly returned to England, where they risked their lives taking sacraments to the faithful. It was difficult to distinguish between secret meetings for forbidden worship, and conspiracies against the queen and her government. Infiltrated priests and Catholics who conspired against the queen were equally captured and put to death. There was abundant proof of conspiracies against the queen's life and most of these centered on the hope of crowning Mary Stuart. Whether or not Mary herself inspired such conspiracies is not clear. But in the end she was involved in them and Elizabeth, after much hesitation, ordered that her cousin be put to death.

The total number of those executed for religious reasons during Elizabeth's reign was approximately equal to those who died under her half-sister Mary Tudor—although it should be remembered that Elizabeth's reign was almost ten times as long as Mary's. In any case, toward the end of Elizabeth's life, Catholics were indicating that they were ready to distinguish between their religious obedience to the pope and their political and civil loyalty to the queen. It was on the basis of this distinction that they would eventually be allowed to practice their religion openly.

It was also toward the end of Elizabeth's reign that the Puritans began to grow in number. They were called *Puritans* because, inspired by Calvinist ideas, they insisted on the need to restore the pure practices and doctrines of the New Testament. Since it was at a later time that they became a driving force in English religious life, we shall postpone our discussion of them until another chapter in our story (see Chapter 18).

THE REFORMATION IN SCOTLAND

The kingdom of Scotland, to the north of England, had traditionally followed the policy of seeking the support of France against the English, who frequently invaded its territories. But in the sixteenth century the country was divided between those who supported that traditional policy, and those who held that circumstances had changed, and that it was in the nation's best interest to establish closer ties with England. The advocates of the new policy gained a major victory in 1502, when James IV of Scotland married Margaret Tudor, a daughter of Henry VII of England. Therefore, when Henry VIII became king of England, there was hope that the two kingdoms could finally live in peace with each other. James V, the son of James IV and Margaret Tudor, was Henry's nephew, and the latter sought even closer ties by offering James the hand of his daughter Mary. But Scotland decided to return to its traditional alliance with France, and to that end James married the French Mary of Guise. From that point on, the two British kingdoms followed opposite courses, particularly in matters affecting the reformation of the church and relations with the papacy.

While these events were taking place, Protestantism had been making its way into Scotland. Since a much earlier date, the doctrines of the Lollards and the Hussites had found followers in the country, and it had been impossible to uproot them. Now Protestantism found fertile soil among those who held to such doctrines. Many Scots who had studied in Germany returned to their homeland, taking with them the ideas and writings of Luther and other reformers. The Scottish Parliament issued laws against those writings, and against those who sought to spread Protestant teachings. The year 1528 saw the first martyrdom of one of these itinerant preachers, and after that time ever-increasing numbers were executed. But it was all in vain. In spite of persecution, the new doctrines continued gaining adherents. The spread of Protestantism was particularly noticeable among the nobility, who resented the growing power of the crown and the loss of many of their ancient privileges, and among university students, who constantly read and circulated the smuggled books of Protestant authors.

When James V died in 1542, the heir to the throne was his infant daughter Mary Stuart, and this led to a power struggle. Henry VIII sought to

These letters mark the spot where Patrick Hamilton, who had read the works of Luther while on the Continent, was burned at the stake, thus becoming the first martyr of the Scottish Reformation.

marry the infant queen to his son and heir, Edward—a plan supported by the Protestant Scottish nobles, who were also Anglophiles. The Catholics, Francophiles, wished to see Mary sent to France for her education and married to a French prince. In this they succeeded, thus foiling Henry's plans.

On their part, a group of Protestant conspirators took the castle of St. Andrew, and killed the Protestant archbishop. The government, torn by inner conflict, could do little. An army was sent to capture and punish the rebels, but after a short siege the troops were withdrawn, and Protestants throughout the kingdom began considering St. Andrew's the bastion of their faith.

It was then that John Knox entered the scene. Little is known of the early years of this fiery reformer, who soon became the leader of Scottish Protestantism. Born in or about 1515, he studied theology, and was ordained a priest before 1540. He then became a tutor to the sons of two noblemen who conspired to take St. Andrew's, and he had also been in contact with George Wishart—a famous Protestant preacher who had died for his faith. When the conspirators took possession of St. Andrew's, he was ordered to take his young charges to the castle. Although he planned to leave for Germany after delivering the young boys and to devote some time to the study of Protestant theology, once he arrived at St. Andrew's, he found himself inextricably involved in the events that were shaking the nation. Against his own will, he was made preacher of the Protestant community, and from that time he was the main spokesman for the cause of reformation in Scotland.

The Protestants holed up in St. Andrew's were able to hold out because both England and France were going through difficult times and could not intervene in Scottish affairs. But as soon as France found itself free to send reinforcements to Scotland, the government sent a strong army to storm the castle, and the Protestants had to surrender. Although this was in violation of the terms of surrender, Knox and several others were condemned to the galleys, where the future reformer spent nineteen months in cruel labor. He was finally released thanks to the intervention of England, where Edward VI now ruled, and where Knox later became a pastor.

That English interlude ended when the death of Edward placed Mary Tudor on the English throne, and persecution broke out against Protestantism. Knox then went to Switzerland, where he was able to spend some time in Geneva with Calvin, and in Zürich with Bullinger, Zwingli's successor. He also visited Scotland on two occasions, seeking to strengthen the resolve of the Protestant community.

Meanwhile, important events were taking place in Scotland. Young Mary Stuart had been sent to France, where she enjoyed the protection of her relatives in the house of Guise. Her mother, also of that family, remained in Scotland as regent. In April 1558, Mary married the heir to the French throne, who slightly more than a year later was crowned Francis II. Thus Mary, sixteen years old, was both queen consort of France and titular queen of Scotland. But such titles and honors were not enough, for she also claimed to be the legitimate queen of England. Mary Tudor had died in 1558, and had been succeeded by her half-sister Elizabeth. But if Elizabeth was illegitimate, as Catholics claimed, the throne belonged to Mary Stuart, great-granddaughter of Henry VII. Therefore, upon Mary Tudor's death, Mary Stuart took the title of queen of England, which made her the avowed enemy of her cousin Elizabeth. In Scotland, the queen mother Mary of Guise ruled as regent. Her pro-Catholic policies forced Protestant leaders to unite and, late in 1557, they made a solemn covenant. Since they promised to serve "the very blessed Word of God, and His congregation," they were known as *Lords of the Congregation*. They were aware that their cause was similar to that of English Protestants, and established ties with them. The regent ordered increased persecution against the "heretics," but they persisted in their position, and in 1558 organized themselves into a church. Shortly before that, they had written to Switzerland, asking Knox to return to Scotland.

In exile, Knox had written a virulent attack against the women who then reigned in Europe: the regent of Scotland, Mary Tudor in England, and Catherine de Medici in France. His work, *The First Blast of the Trumpet against the Monstrous Regiment of Women,* was poorly timed, for it had scarcely been circulated in England when Mary Tudor died and was succeeded by Elizabeth. Although the book was written against her now dead half-sister, Elizabeth resented much of what it said, for its arguments based on anti-feminine prejudice could just as easily apply to her. This hindered the natural alliance that should have developed between Elizabeth and John Knox, whose repeated retractions did not suffice to appease the English queen.

Events were not working in favor of the Scottish Protestants. The regent requested troops from France in order to crush the Lords of the Congregation. The latter did achieve some victories over the invaders. But their army, lacking in material resources, could not remain in the field for long. They sent repeated appeals to England, arguing that, if the Catholics were able to crush the Protestant rebellion in Scotland, and that kingdom was thus in the hands of the Catholic faction, and closely tied to France, Elizabeth's crown would be endangered. Knox, who had returned shortly before these events, sustained the Protestants with his sermons and the force of his conviction. Finally, early in 1560, Elizabeth decided to send troops to Scotland. The English army joined the Scottish Protestants, and a long war seemed inevitable. But then the regent died, and the French decided that it was time to sue for peace. As a result, both the French and the English withdrew their troops.

As soon as the immediate danger was past, however, disputes began between Knox and the lords, who until then had supported the cause of reformation. Although other reasons were adduced, at bottom the conflict was economic. The lords sought possession of the riches of the church, while Knox and his supporters wished to employ those resources for establishing a system of universal education, to lighten the load of the poor, and for the support of the church.

In the midst of such struggles, the nobles decided to invite Mary Stuart to return to Scotland and claim the throne she had inherited from her father. Mary had hoped to remain in France as queen of that country, but the death of her husband had deprived her of that honor, and therefore she agreed to the Scottish request. She arrived in Scotland in 1561. Although she had never been popular, at first she was content to follow the advice of her bastard half-brother James Stuart, earl of Moray, a Protestant leader who prevented her from immediately alienating the other Protestant lords.

Knox himself seems to have been convinced that a clash with the queen was inevitable, and on this she probably agreed with him. From the time of her arrival, Mary insisted on having mass celebrated in her private chapel, and the fiery reformer began preaching against the "idolatry" of the "new Jezebel." The two had a number of increasingly tempestuous interviews. But the lords, content with the existing situation, did not follow the preacher in his extremism.

The growing tension with the queen, and with some of the Protestant lords, did not prevent Knox and his followers from organizing the Reformed Church of Scotland, whose polity was similar to later Presbyterianism. In each church, elders were elected, as was a minister, although the latter could not be installed before being examined by the other ministers. The pillars of the new church were the *Book of Discipline,* the *Book of Common Order,* and the *Scots Confession.*

In the end, Mary Stuart caused her own downfall. She had always dreamed of sitting on the throne of England, and in pursuit of that dream she lost first her own throne and then her life. In order to strengthen her claim to the English throne, she married her cousin Henry Stuart, Lord Darnley, who also had a distant claim to it. Moray objected to this marriage and to Mary's agreement with Spain to uproot Protestantism in her own country, and when his objections went unheeded he rebelled. Mary then called upon James Hepburn, Lord Bothwell, an able military leader who defeated Moray and forced him to seek refuge in London. Encouraged by this victory, Mary declared that she would soon sit on the throne in London.

Having lost Moray's counsel, Mary's policies became increasingly unwise. She decided that she had made a mistake in marrying Darnley, and let her feelings be known to Bothwell and others. Shortly thereafter, Darnley was murdered, and the main suspect was Bothwell. He was legally exonerated in a trial in which no witnesses for the prosecution were allowed. But this did little to allay suspicion, particularly since Mary married Bothwell a few months later.

The Scottish lords hated Bothwell, and they soon rebelled. When the queen sought to quell the rebellion, she discovered that her troops were not willing to support her cause, and she found herself in the hands of the lords. These convinced her that they had proof of her participation in Darnley's death, and gave her the choice of either abdicating or being tried for murder. She abdicated in favor of her one-year-old son James VI, whom she had had with Darnley, and Moray returned from England as regent of Scotland. Mary managed to escape and raise an army in support of her cause. But she was defeated by Moray's troops, and her only recourse was to flee to England and seek refuge under her hated cousin Elizabeth.

Romantic imagination has woven many a tale around Mary's captivity and death, making her a martyr in the hands of a cruel and ambitious cousin. The truth is that Elizabeth received her with greater courtesy than could be expected for someone who had so long declared her illegitimate in an effort to take possession of her crown. Although she was a prisoner in the sense that she was not allowed to leave the castle of her residence, there were strict orders that she should be treated as a queen, and she was allowed to choose her own body of thirty servants. But she was the hub of many a conspiracy, most of which included the death of Elizabeth, who was the main obstacle in her path to the English throne and to the restoration of Catholicism in England. Another common element of most of these conspiracies was the invasion of England by Spanish troops in support of Mary's cause. When the third such conspiracy was discovered, with clear proof that Mary was, if not the instigator of the plot, at least a willing participant, she was tried and condemned to death. When she was finally taken before the executioner, she faced death with royal dignity.

In Scotland, Mary's exile did not put an end to disputes among the various parties. Knox supported the regency of Moray. But there was still significant opposition when the reformer suffered an attack of paralysis and had to withdraw from active life. When he heard of the St. Bartholomew's Day Massacre of Protestants in France—of which we shall say more in Chapter 11—he made a last effort to return to the pulpit, where he told his fellow Scots that they must continue their struggle, lest they suffer a similar fate. He died a few days after this last sermon. By then, it was becoming apparent that Scotland had been won by the Reformed tradition.

9

Further Developments within Lutheranism

A Christian ruler may and must defend his subjects against every higher authority that seeks to force them to deny the Word of God and practice idolatry.

MAGDEBURG CONFESSION (1550)

THE WAR OF SCHMALKALDEN

The peace of Nuremberg, signed in 1532, allowed Protestants the free exercise of their faith in their own territories but prohibited any further expansion of Protestantism. It seems that Charles V thus hoped to contain the advance of Lutheran heresy until he could gather the resources necessary to eliminate it. But such a policy was doomed to failure for, in spite of the stipulations of Nuremberg, Protestantism continued its expansion.

The political situation in Germany was extremely complex and fluid. Although Charles was emperor, many interests hampered full exercise of his authority. Even apart from religious matters, there were many who feared the growing power of the house of Hapsburg, which Charles headed. Some of these were Catholic princes who suspected that Charles would use his opposition to Lutheranism for the aggrandizement of his house, and thus they were not willing to commit fully to the anti-Protestant crusade Charles hoped to organize. Furthermore, one of the most powerful princes blocking the house of Hapsburg was Philip of Hesse, who was also the leader of the League of Schmalkalden. For these reasons, the emperor could not stop the expansion of Protestantism into lands in which it should not have been permitted according to the terms agreed on at Nuremberg.

In 1534, Philip of Hesse wrested the duchy of Württemberg from the Catholics, who had taken possession of it. After diplomatic maneuvers assured him that other Catholic princes would not intervene, Philip invaded the duchy and recalled its exiled duke, who then declared himself for Protestantism. The population of the duchy had already given signs of inclination toward Lutheranism and soon took up the religious allegiance of its restored prince.

Another severe blow for German Catholicism was the death of Duke George of Saxony, in 1539. Saxony comprised two separate territories, Ducal Saxony and Electoral Saxony. The latter, under the rule of Frederick the Wise, had been the cradle of Lutheranism. But Ducal Saxony had resisted the new faith, and Duke George had been one of the most bitter enemies of Luther and his followers. At his death, his brother and successor, Henry, declared himself a Protestant, and Luther was invited to preach in the capital, Leipzig, where years earlier he had debated Eck.

In the same year of the death of Duke George of Saxony, Brandenburg also became Protestant, and there was even talk that the three ecclesiastical electors, the archbishops of Trier, Cologne, and Mainz, were considering embracing the Protestant faith. This would give Protestants a clear majority in the electoral college of seven magnates—four lay princes and three archbishops—whose task it would be to choose the next emperor.

Charles's hands were tied, for he was involved in too many conflicts spread across distant parts of the world, and all he could do was encourage the Catholic princes to form an alliance to rival the League of Schmalkalden. This was the League of Nuremberg, founded in 1539. Faced by political realities, Charles also turned to a more conciliatory policy, seeking a rapprochement between Catholics and Protestants. Under this new policy, several dialogues took place but with little or no result. Meanwhile, the League of Schmalkalden took over the territories of Henry of Brunswick, the emperor's staunchest ally in northern Germany, and the area became Protestant. Several bishops who were also feudal lords, realizing that the majority of the people in their dioceses leaned toward Lutheranism, turned their possessions into secular states, made themselves into hereditary lords, and declared for Protestantism. Naturally, in such moves there was a great deal of personal ambition. But the fact remained that Protestantism seemed on the verge of overrunning all of Germany, and that for more than ten years the emperor and the pope saw their power and influence diminish.

Shortly thereafter, however, Protestantism would suffer several severe blows. The first of these was the bigamy of Philip of Hesse. This prince, the leader of the League of Schmalkalden, was a sincere man, firmly committed to the Protestant cause. His conscience, however, was deeply troubled because for years he had had no marital life with his wife, and he found it impossible to remain celibate. He was no libertine, but rather a man tormented by his sexual appetites, and by the guilt that he felt at their illicit satisfaction. He consulted the main Protestant theologians, and Luther, Melanchthon, and Bucer—the reformer of Strasbourg—agreed that the Bible did not forbid polygamy, and that Philip could take a second wife without setting the first aside. It was necessary, however, for this to be done in secret, for although polygamy was not a crime in God's eyes, it was such in the eyes of civil law. This Philip did, and when the secret became public the ensuing scandal put both Philip and his theological advisors in an extremely difficult position. Besides the enormous loss of moral authority these events implied, they also weakened the League of Schmalkalden, for many of its members objected to Philip's continuing leadership.

The second blow was the refusal of Duke Maurice of Saxony to join the league. While declaring himself a Protestant, he insisted on carrying out his own independent policy. When Charles explained that he was not opposing Protestantism, but only the rebellion of the Lutheran princes, and promised him special consideration, Maurice decided to believe the emperor, and to take his side against the League of Schmalkalden.

The third blow was Luther's death, in 1546. Although he had lost much prestige as a result of the peasant's rebellion and the bigamy of Philip of Hesse, Luther was still the only figure who could unite Protestants under a single banner. His death, shortly after the discovery of Philip's bigamy, left the Protestant party headless both politically and spiritually.

But the most severe blow came from the emperor, who was finally free to turn his attention to Germany, and was eager to avenge the obstinate rebelliousness of the Protestant princes and the humiliations he had suffered because of them. Profiting from the disarray in the Protestant ranks, and with the support of Duke Maurice, Charles invaded Germany and captured both Philip of Hesse and John Frederick, the son and successor of Frederick the Wise.

THE INTERIM

In spite of his military victory, the emperor knew that it was too late to impose his will on religious matters, and therefore was content with promulgating the *Augsburg Interim*, written by a joint commission of Catholic and Protestant theologians. By the emperor's command, all Germans were to obey this *Interim*, so called because it was to be the law of the land until a General Council could be convened to decide on the issues in debate. (The Council of Trent had begun its sessions three years earlier, in 1545; but the pope and the emperor were at odds, and therefore the latter refused to accept that council as valid.) Charles hoped to reform the church in Germany, as was already being done in Spain since the reign of his grandmother Isabella—that is, by prosecuting abuse and corruption, encouraging piety and learning, and disallowing any doctrinal divergence. By means of the Interim, he hoped to gain the time necessary to set in motion such a reformation.

But neither Catholics nor Protestants were gratified by this attempt to legislate on matters of conscience. There was general resistance to the Interim. Several Protestant theologians flatly refused to obey it. Those at Wittenberg, led by Melanchthon, finally agreed to a modified version, the *Leipzig Interim*. But even this was not acceptable to the majority of Lutherans, who accused Melanchthon and his followers of cowardice. The latter responded by arguing that it was necessary to distinguish between the essential and the peripheral—the *adiaphora*—and that they had made concessions in peripheral matters in order to be able to continue preaching and practicing the essential.

In any case, Charles was unable to exploit the advantages gained by the War of Schmalkalden. Many German princes, among them several Catholics, protested against the ill treatment received by Philip of Hesse and John Frederick of Saxony. There were rumors that in order to capture Philip, Charles had made use of means that sullied his honor. The Protestant princes, sharply divided before the war, were drawn together by their opposition to the Interim. Both the pope and the king of France resented Charles's successes and made diplomatic maneuvers to hamper him.

Soon the Protestant princes were conspiring against Charles V. Maurice of Saxony, discontent with the emperor's rewards for his betrayal of the Protestant cause, and fearing the growing power of the house of Hapsburg, joined the conspiracy, which sent an embassy to the king of France in order to secure his support. When rebellion finally broke out, the armies of King

Emperor Charles V, who was also Charles I of Spain, was firmly convinced of the need to stamp out Protestantism, but various political necessities repeatedly stayed his hand.

Henry II of France invaded Charles's possessions beyond the Rhine. The troops on whose loyalty the emperor could depend were not sufficient to wage combat, and therefore Charles was forced to flee. Even this was not easy, for Maurice of Saxony had taken possession of several strategic places, and Charles was nearly taken prisoner. After his escape, Charles instructed his armies to retake Metz, which the French had taken. But the French repulsed the attack, and the Protestant princes continued in open revolt. Toward the end of his career, it must have appeared to Charles that his German policy was an almost complete failure.

Charles had increasingly delegated German affairs to his brother Ferdinand, who finally agreed with the rebellious princes to the Peace of Passau. By the terms of this agreement, Philip of Hesse and John Frederick of Saxony were freed, and freedom of religion was granted throughout the empire. This freedom, however, had a number of limitations. It did not mean that all subjects were free to choose their own religion, but rather that local rulers could make that decision for themselves and for their subjects— the principle of *cuius regio, eius religio*—and that the emperor would not insist on the return of the Protestant princes to Catholicism. Also, the freedom this treaty granted applied only to those who held either to traditional Catholicism or to the Confession of Augsburg. Anabaptists and Reformed were not included in its provisions.

In part, his failure in Germany led Charles to relinquish his power and seek the peace of the monastery. In 1555, he began to rid himself of his territories. In favor of his son Philip he abdicated first the Low Countries and then his Italian possessions and the throne of Spain. The following year, he formally resigned as emperor and withdrew to the monastery of St. Yuste, in Spain, where he still surrounded himself with imperial pomp, and continued serving as an advisor to his son Philip II of Spain. He died two years later, in September 1558.

The new emperor, Ferdinand I, abandoned his brother's religious policy, and was so tolerant that some Catholics feared that he had secretly become a Protestant. Under his rule, and that of his successor Maximilian II, Protestantism continued expanding to new areas, which included Austria itself, the main hereditary possession of the Hapsburgs. The resulting tensions with Catholic leaders repeatedly broke out in minor political and military clashes. Finally, in the next century, these led to the Thirty Years' War, to which we shall return later.

SCANDINAVIAN LUTHERANISM

While all this was taking place in Germany, Luther's impact was also being felt in neighboring Scandinavia. But, while in Germany the Reformation and the ensuing struggles divided the country and helped the high nobility assert its power over against the monarchy, in Scandinavia the Reformation had the opposite effect. There monarchs took up the Reformation as their cause, and its triumph was also theirs.

In theory, Denmark, Norway, and Sweden were a united kingdom. But in truth the king ruled only Denmark, where he resided. His power in Norway was limited, and in Sweden it was nil, where the powerful house of Sture, with the title of regents, held sway. Even in Denmark itself, royal authority was limited by the power of the aristocracy and of the ecclesiastical hierarchy, who staunchly defended their ancient privileges against every encroachment on the king's part. Since the crown was elective, at the time of each election the magnates, both civil and ecclesiastic, wrung new concessions from those who would be elected. The people, oppressed by great secular and ecclesiastical lords, could do nothing but pay ever-increasing taxes and obey laws designed for the protection of the powerful.

When the Reformation broke out in Germany, the Scandinavian throne was occupied by Christian II, who was married to Charles V's sister Isabella. Since the Swedes would not allow him effective power in their land, he appealed to his brother-in-law and to other princes, and with largely foreign troops moved into Sweden and had himself crowned at Stockholm. Although he had vowed to spare the lives of his Swedish enemies, a few days after his coronation he ordered what came to be known as the Massacre of Stockholm, in which the nation's leading aristocrats and ecclesiastics were murdered.

The Massacre of Stockholm caused grave resentment, not only in Sweden, but also in Norway and even in Denmark. Magnates throughout Christian's territories feared that, after destroying Swedish aristocracy, the king would turn on them. Christian claimed that he sought to free the people of Sweden from the oppression of its own aristocracy. But the treacherous means by which he had disposed of his enemies, and the intense ecclesiastical propaganda against him, soon lost him any popularity he might have garnered.

Christian then tried to use the Reformation as a tool for his own ends. Shortly before these events, the first Lutheran preachers had made their way into Denmark, and the people seemed ready to lend them an attentive ear. But again this policy failed, for it exacerbated the prelates' enmity toward the king, at a time when most Protestants preferred to keep their distance from the instigator of the Massacre of Stockholm. Eventually, rebellion broke out, and Christian was forced to flee. He returned eight years later, now with the support of several Catholic rulers from other parts of Europe. He landed in Norway and declared himself the champion of Catholicism. But his uncle and successor, Frederick I, defeated and imprisoned him. He remained in prison the rest of his days—for twenty-seven years.

Frederick I was a Protestant, and by that time many of the people and the nobility were of similar persuasion. But, at the time of his election, the new king promised that he would neither attack Catholicism nor use his authority to favor Protestantism. He realized that it was better to be the true king of a smaller kingdom than the fictitious ruler of a large one, and therefore gave up all claim to the Swedish crown, and allowed Norway to elect its own king. The Norwegians then elected him, and thus Frederick was able to retain part of the older Scandinavian union without having to resort to his nephew's tyrannical methods. Being able to concentrate on the affairs of Denmark and Norway, he took steps to consolidate the power of the crown in those two kingdoms. In religious matters, he kept the vows he had taken at the time of his election. But Protestantism, allowed free rein, made rapid gains. In 1527, it was officially recognized and granted toleration, and by the time of Frederick's death in 1533 most of his subjects were Protestants.

At that point there was an attempt to impose a Catholic king on the land by means of foreign intervention. But the pretender was defeated, and the new ruler was Christian III, a convinced Lutheran who had been present at the Diet of Worms and who greatly admired Luther both for his doctrines and for his courage. He promptly took measures in support of Protestantism and limiting the power of bishops. He requested from Luther teachers to help him in the work of reformation. Eventually, the entire Danish church subscribed to the Confession of Augsburg.

Meanwhile, events in Sweden were following a similar course. When Christian II sought to impose his authority on that country, among his prisoners was a young Swede by the name of Gustavus Erikson, better known as Gustavus Vasa. The young man escaped and, from his refuge overseas, sought to curb the power of Christian. When he learned of the Massacre of Stockholm, in which several of his relatives were killed, he secretly returned to his homeland. Working as a journeyman, and living among the people, he confirmed the popular sentiment against Danish occupation. He then proclaimed a national rebellion, and took up arms with a disorganized band of followers from among the common people. As victory followed victory, and one daring feat of arms followed another, his name became legendary. In 1521, the rebels named him regent of the kingdom, and, two years later, king. A few months after this last proclamation, he entered Stockholm in triumph, and there he was received with shouts of acclamation.

But the royal title carried little authority, for the nobility and the prelates insisted on their ancient privileges. The new king followed a subtle policy of dividing his enemies. At first his harsher measures were directed against the bishops. In every case, he distinguished between the powerful who incited rebellion and their followers. When two rebellious bishops were defeated, captured, and condemned to death, the king pardoned all their followers, declaring that they had been misguided. Thus, he drove a wedge between clergy and nobility, and between both of these groups and the majority of the population. The same year as the bishops' rebellion, he convened a national assembly that was attended, not only by prelates and nobles, but also by some from among the bourgeoisie and even the peasantry. When the clergy and the nobility banded together to thwart the king's program of reforms, he simply resigned, declaring that Sweden was not ready for a true king. Three days later, threatened by chaos, the assembly agreed to recall the king and to curb the power of the prelates.

The result of that national assembly, and of Gustavus Vasa's victory, was that the higher clergy lost its political power. From that point on, Lutheran influence was on the rise, and Protestant beliefs were usually joined to royalist convictions. Gustavus Vasa was not a man of profound religious conviction. But by the time he died, in 1560, Sweden was a Protestant country, with a Lutheran ecclesiastical hierarchy, and the monarchy had ceased to be elective in order to become hereditary.

10

The Reformation in the Low Countries

Let it be known that each of us has two arms, and that if hunger makes it necessary we shall eat one to have the strength to fight with the other.

A PROTESTANT DEFENDER AT THE SIEGE OF LEIDEN

In the Low Countries, as in the rest of Europe, Protestantism gained adherents from a very early time. In 1523, in Antwerp, the first two Protestant martyrs were burned. From that point on, there are clear indications that Protestantism made headway in various areas. But political circumstances were such that this advance of Protestantism soon became involved in the long and bitter struggle for independence.

THE POLITICAL SITUATION

Near the mouth of the Rhine River, there was a group of territories jointly known as the Seventeen Provinces, roughly comprising what are today the Netherlands, Belgium, and Luxembourg. These various territories were under the lordship of the house of Hapsburg, and therefore Charles V had inherited them from his father, Philip the Fair. Since Charles had been born and raised in the region, he was well-liked by its inhabitants, and under his rule the Seventeen Provinces grew closer together.

Such political unity, however, was partly fictitious. Although Charles V encouraged the development of common institutions, throughout his reign each territory retained many of its ancient privileges and particular forms of government. Cultural unity was also lacking, for between the French-speaking south and the Dutch-speaking north there was an area where

Flemish was the common language. The ecclesiastical situation was even more complex, for the jurisdiction of the various bishops did not coincide with political divisions, and some areas were part of bishoprics whose sees were beyond the borders of the Seventeen Provinces.

When Charles V, in a ceremony held at Brussels in 1555, placed the Seventeen Provinces under the rule of his son Philip, he expected the latter to continue his policies. This was precisely what Philip attempted. But what his father had begun was not easy to continue. The Seventeen Provinces regarded Charles as Flemish, and that was indeed the language in which he always felt most at ease. Philip, on the other hand, had been raised in Spain, and both his language and his outlook were Spanish. In 1556, having received from his father the crown of Spain, he became Philip II, and he made it clear that to him the most important of his possessions was Spain. The Low Countries were put at the service of Spain and her interests. This in turn provoked the resentment of leaders in the Seventeen Provinces, who tenaciously opposed Philip's efforts to complete the unification of the area, and to treat it as part of the hereditary possessions of the Spanish crown.

PROTESTANT PREACHING

Even before the Protestant Reformation broke out, in the Low Countries there had been a strong movement of reformation. This was the birthplace of the Brethren of the Common Life, and of the greatest of humanist reformers, Erasmus of Rotterdam. One of the characteristic themes of the Brethren of the Common Life was the need to read Scripture, not only in Latin, but also in the native language of the people. Therefore, the Protestant Reformation found in the Low Countries fertile ground for its preaching.

Soon Lutheran preachers entered the region, gaining a large number of converts. Then the Anabaptists, particularly those who followed the teachings of Melchior Hoffman, made great headway. It is noteworthy that the leaders of the New Jerusalem in Münster were natives of the Low Countries. While Münster held, many of their countrymen sought to join them, but were intercepted and killed by imperial troops. Then there were several unsuccessful attempts by Anabaptists to gain possession of various cities in the Seventeen Provinces themselves. Finally, there was a great influx of Calvinist preachers from Geneva, France, and southern Germany. Eventually, these Calvinist preachers would be the most successful, and Calvinism would become the main form of Protestantism in the region.

Charles V took stern measures against the spread of Protestantism in these lands. He issued several edicts against Protestantism, and in particular against Anabaptists. The frequency with which such edicts succeeded one another is proof of their failure to stem the tide of Protestant teaching and conversions. Tens of thousands died for their faith. The leaders were burned, their followers beheaded, and many women were buried alive. But, in spite of such cruel punishments, Protestantism continued its advance. There are indications that toward the end of Charles's reign there was a growing tide of opposition to his religious policies. But Charles was a popular ruler, and in any case most of the people were still convinced that Protestants were heretics who amply deserved their punishment.

Philip, who had never been popular in the Low Countries, prompted even greater enmity through a combination of folly, obstinacy, and hypocrisy. When he decided to return to Spain, and to leave the Provinces under the regency of his half-sister Margaret of Parma, he sought to strengthen her authority by quartering Spanish troops in the Low Countries. Such troops had to be supported by the resources of the land. Friction and clashes soon developed between the Spanish soldiers and the native inhabitants of the area, who questioned the need for the presence of foreign troops. Since there was no war requiring their presence, the only possible explanation was that Philip doubted the loyalty of his subjects.

To this was added the appointment of new bishops who were given inquisitorial powers. Undoubtedly, the church in the Seventeen Provinces was in need of reorganization; but Philip's timing and manner were not wise. Part of the rationale offered for the reorganization of the church was the need to stamp out heresy. Since the inhabitants of the Low Countries knew that in Spain the Inquisition had become an instrument of torture in the hands of royal policy, they feared that the king intended to do the same in their country.

Even worse, Philip and the regent paid scant attention to their most loyal subjects. William, Prince of Orange (who had been a close friend of Charles V) and the Count of Egmont (who had rendered outstanding military service) were made members of the Council of State. But they were not consulted on matters of importance, which were decided by the regent and her foreign advisors. Most hated of such advisors was Bishop Granvelle, whom the natives of the Low Countries blamed for every injustice and humiliation they suffered. After repeated protests, the king recalled Granvelle. But it soon

William, Prince of Orange, led the rebellion of the Seventeen Provinces.

became apparent that the deposed bishop had done no more than obey his master's instructions, and that the offensive policies and practices had been dictated by the king himself.

In order to argue their cause, the leaders of the Seventeen Provinces sent the Count of Egmont to Spain. Philip received him with honors and promised a radical change in policy. Egmont returned to his homeland, pleased with the assurances he had received. But he was bitterly disappointed when he opened before the council the sealed letter Philip had given him, and it clearly contradicted what the king had promised. At the same time, Philip sent instructions to Margaret that the decrees of the Council of Trent against Protestantism be enacted, and that all who opposed them should be put to death.

The royal orders caused a great stir. The leaders and magistrates of the Seventeen Provinces were not ready to execute the vast number of their fellow citizens for whom the king decreed the death penalty. In response to Philip's commands, several hundred leaders of the nobility and the bourgeoisie joined in a petition to the regent that such policies not be implemented. Margaret received them, and was showing signs of agitation when one of her courtiers intervened, telling her that she ought not to heed nor fear "those beggars."

THE BEGGARS

The moniker captured the imagination of the patriots. Since their oppressors called them *beggars*, that was the name they would adopt. The leather bag of a beggar became the banner of rebellion. Under that symbol the movement, until then limited to the nobility and the bourgeoisie, took root among the entire population. The standard of rebellion was flaunted everywhere, and the authorities were at a loss as to how to respond.

Before reaching the field of battle, the movement took on religious overtones. There were frequent outdoor meetings in which Protestantism and opposition to the authorities were preached under the protection of armed Beggars. For fear of greater disturbances, the regent's troops allowed such meetings. Then there were bands of iconoclasts who invaded churches, overturned altars, and destroyed images and other symbols of the old religion. When such a band invaded a church, no one intervened, for many rejoiced secretly while others marveled that heaven did not destroy those who committed such sacrilege.

Finally, the Council of State had to appeal to William of Orange, whose advice it had frequently chided. With the same loyalty with which he had served Charles, and risking his life, William intervened. Thanks to his pleas, and to others who supported him, violence abated, and the iconoclastic wave ceased. This was accomplished, however, only after the council suspended the Inquisition and allowed a limited freedom of worship. On their part, the Beggars promised to refrain from action as long as the government did not seek to impose the Inquisition and other forms of oppression.

But Philip was not a king to be swayed by his subjects' opposition. He had declared, with vehement sincerity, that he had no desire to be the "lord of heretics." The old principle that there was no need to keep faith with the unfaithful applied in this situation. While he promised to abide by the agreements reached in the Provinces, and to pardon the rebels, he was raising an army with which to force his will and faith on the Low Countries. William of Orange, who was aware of the king's duplicity, advised his friends, particularly the counts of Egmont and Horn, to join in armed resistance. But they put their trust in the king's promises, and William withdrew to his possessions in Germany.

The storm arrived swiftly. Early in 1567, the duke of Alba invaded the country with an army of Spanish and Italian troops. The king had given him such powers that the regent became a figurehead, and Alba was the true ruler. His mission was to drown all rebellion and heresy in blood. One of his first steps was to organize a Council of Disturbances, which the people soon dubbed the "Council of Blood." This court was not bound by any legal requirements for, as Alba explained to Philip, legality would allow only for the conviction of those whose crimes were proven, whereas in this case "matters of state" demanded more drastic measures. Protestants were condemned for their heresy, and Catholics for not having been sufficiently firm in resisting heresy. Even to express doubt as to the authority of the Council of Disturbances was high treason. The same charge of high treason was brought against any who had opposed the reorganization of the church, or who had declared that the provinces had rights and privileges that the king could not overturn. So numerous were those put to death under such ordinances that chroniclers of the time speak of the stench in the air, and of hundreds of bodies hanging from trees along the wayside. The counts of Egmont and Horn, who had remained in their lands with candid trust and loyalty, were arrested and brought to trial. Since William of Orange was not available, Alba captured his fifteen-year-old son, Philip William, and sent him to Spain. William responded by investing all his financial resources in raising an army, mostly German, with which he invaded the Low Countries. But Alba defeated him repeatedly and, in retaliation, ordered the execution of Egmont and Horn.

Alba seemed to be in full command of the situation when the rebels received support from an unexpected quarter. Orange had granted privateer licenses to a few sailors, in the hope that they would harass Alba's communications with Spain. These *Beggars of the Sea*, at first little more than pirates, achieved a measure of organization, and Philip's naval forces could not contain them. For some time, Elizabeth of England gave them support, most significantly by allowing them to sell their prizes in English ports. Eventually, Spain pressured her to change this policy. But by then the Beggars of the Sea were too strong to be easily suppressed. In a brilliant maneuver, they captured the city of Brill and, after that, their ongoing success made them a legend and inspired the patriots who resisted on land. Several cities declared themselves in favor of William of Orange, who once again invaded the provinces, this time with French support. But the French also were dealing in treachery, and William was approaching Brussels when he learned of the Massacre of St. Bartholomew's Day—to which we shall return in the next chapter—and this put an end to all possible collaboration between Protestants and the French crown. Lacking in funds and in any form of military support, William was forced to disband his troops, who were mostly mercenary soldiers.

Alba's vengeance was terrible. His armies took city after city, and repeatedly broke the terms of surrender. Prisoners were killed for no other reason than revenge, and several cities that had resisted were put to the torch. Women, children, and the elderly were indiscriminately killed along with the rebels. Soon every rebel stronghold was in Alba's hands.

It was only on the sea that the rebels remained strong. The Beggars continually defeated the Spanish, and even captured their admiral. This in turn made it very difficult for Alba to receive supplies and funds for his troops, who therefore began showing signs of mutiny. Tired of the long struggle, and bitter because Spain did not send him the resources he required, Alba asked to be appointed elsewhere.

The new Spanish general, Luis de Zúñiga y Requesens, had the wisdom to exploit the religious differences among the rebels. He sought a separate peace with the Catholics of the southern provinces, thus driving a wedge between them and the Protestants, who were most numerous in the north. Up until that point, the religious question had been only one element among many in what was really a national rebellion against foreign rule. William of Orange, the leader of the uprising, had been a liberal Catholic at least until his exile in Germany, and it was only in 1573 that he declared himself a Calvinist. But Requesens's policies underscored the religious element of the struggle, thus neutralizing the Catholic provinces of the south.

The Protestant cause was therefore desperate while its armies were repeatedly and roundly defeated. Its only hope seemed to be in the Beggars of the Sea. The crisis came at the Siege of Leiden, an important trading center that had declared itself for Protestantism, and which the Spanish had surrounded. An army sent by William of Orange to break the siege was defeated by the Spanish, and in that battle two of William's brothers were killed. All was lost when William, whose enemies called him *William the Silent* or *the Sly*, suggested that the dikes be opened, thus flooding the land around Leiden. This implied the destruction of many years of hard work, and the loss of a great deal of arable land. But the citizens agreed. In spite of an incredible shortage of food, the besieged continued their resistance during the four months that it took the sea to reach Leiden. Riding in on the flood, the Beggars of the Sea also arrived, shouting that they would rather be Turkish than Popish. Lacking naval support, the Spanish were forced to abandon the siege.

At that moment, Requesens died. His troops, having neither chief nor pay, mutinied, and set about sacking the cities of the south, which were easier prey than those of the north. This served to reunite the inhabitants of the Seventeen Provinces, who, in 1576, agreed to the *Pacification of Ghent*. This was an alliance among the various provinces, making it clear that what was at stake was national freedom and not religious differences. This agreement was hailed by William of Orange, who had repeatedly argued that religious dogmatism and sectarian intolerance were an obstacle to the unity and freedom of the provinces.

The next governor was Don Juan de Austria, an illegitimate son of Charles V, and therefore a half-brother of Philip II. Although he was one of the most admired military heroes in Christendom, for his defeat of the Turks at the Battle of Lepanto, he was not allowed to enter Brussels until he had agreed to the stipulations of the *Pacification of Ghent*. But Philip II would not give up the struggle. A new army was sent into the region, and once again the southern provinces abandoned the struggle. Then the northern provinces, against the advice of William of Orange, formed a separate league for the defense of their faith and freedom.

The struggle dragged on for years. Though masters of the southern provinces, the Spanish could not conquer those of the north. In 1580, Philip II issued a proclamation promising a reward of twenty-five thousand crowns and a title of nobility to anyone who would kill William the Silent. The latter and his followers responded with a formal declaration that they were independent of all royal authority. But three years later, after several unsuccessful attempts by other parties, an assassin on a quest for the reward was able to kill William. (Once again, Philip proved untrue to his word, at first refusing to pay any reward and then paying only a portion of it.) Philip had hoped that William's death would put an end to the rebellion. But William's son Maurice, then only nineteen years old, proved to be a better general than his father, and led his troops in several victorious campaigns.

In 1607, almost a decade after the death of Philip II, Spain decided that her losses in this struggle were not worth the effort and cost of continuing the war, and a truce was signed. By then, the vast majority of the population in the northern provinces was Calvinist, and many in the north equated their Calvinist faith with their nationalist loyalty, while the southern provinces remained Catholic. Eventually, religious, economic, and cultural differences would lead to the formation of three countries, one Protestant—the Netherlands—and two Catholic—Belgium and Luxembourg.

II

Protestantism in France

O Lord, we cry to you: Will you allow such crimes to be committed
at the expense of your honor?

ETIENNE DE MAISONFLEUR

A t the dawn of the sixteenth century, no other nation in Western Europe
had achieved the degree of national unity and centralization that France
had attained. Yet, during the course of that century, few nations were also as
bitterly divided. This was due to the continuing conflict between Protestants
and Catholics, which in France led to long, internecine warfare.

SHIFTING ROYAL POLICIES

At the beginning of the reformation, France was ruled by Francis I, the last
great king of the house of Valois. His religious policy was always ambiguous
and hesitant, for he had no desire to see Protestantism enter his territories
and divide them, but he encouraged its spread in Germany, where it was a
thorn in the flesh of his rival Charles V. Thus, although Francis never lent
his support to French Protestants, his attitude toward them varied according to the dictates of political expediency. When he sought closer ties with
the German Protestants in order to weaken Charles V, he was constrained
to allow a measure of freedom to those in his own lands who were of the
same persuasion. But, at other times, Protestants were persecuted as vigorously as they were in other Catholic countries. In spite of such fluctuations,
Protestantism gained many adherents in France, particularly among the
learned and the nobility. Those very fluctuations, granting periods of respite
followed by severe persecution, led many French Protestants into exile—
John Calvin among them. From neighboring cities such as Geneva and

Catherine de Medici was the dominant figure in France during the reign of her three sons, Francis II, Charles IX, and Henry III.

Strasbourg, these exiles followed events in their homeland, and were ready to intervene whenever possible.

Meanwhile, in the neighboring kingdom of Navarre—between France and Spain—Francis's sister Margaret of Angouleme, who was married to King Henry of Navarre, encouraged the reform movement. She was a scholarly woman who had supported the French humanist reformers while she was still living in France. Now she offered sanctuary in her court to French Protestant exiles who were fleeing her brother's territories. From Navarre, and from cities just across the French border such as Strasbourg and Geneva, Protestant books were constantly smuggled into France. But in spite of this, there is no record of Protestant churches in France until much later, in 1555.

Francis I died in 1547, and was succeeded by his son Henry II, who continued his father's policies, although his opposition to Protestantism was more constant and cruel. In spite of persecution, it was during Henry's reign that the first Protestant church, was formally organized, following the rules set forth by the exiled John Calvin. Four years later, when the first national synod gathered, there were churches scattered throughout the nation. That assembly, meeting secretly near Paris, approved a *Confession of Faith* and a *Discipline* for the new church.

Shortly after that gathering, Henry II died of wounds received during a tournament. He left four sons, three of whom would successively inherit the throne—Francis II, Charles IX, and Henry III—and three daughters, among them Margaret of Valois, who would be queen of France after her brothers' death. Their mother was Catherine de Medici, an ambitious woman who sought to rule through her children.

Catherine's projects, however, were hindered by the leaders of the house of Guise. That family, from Lorraine, had become prominent during the reign of Francis I. Francis of Guise and his brother Charles, cardinal of Lorraine, had been the main advisors of Henry II. And now, since young Francis II was not interested in matters of state, these two brothers ruled in his name, but their power was resented by the older nobility, and particularly by the *Princes of the Blood*, that is, the king's closest relatives.

Among these Princes of the Blood were Antoine de Bourbon and his brother Louis de Condé. The former had married Jane d'Albret, a daughter of Margaret of Navarre who had followed her mother's religious inclinations and become a Calvinist. Her husband, Antoine, and her brother-in-law Louis then accepted her religion, and thus Protestantism made headway among the highest nobility of the kingdom. Since the house of Guise was staunchly Catholic, and sought to stamp out Protestantism, their struggle with the Bourbons soon took religious overtones. Then a plot was discovered, the Conspiracy of Amboise, whose goal was to take possession of the king and separate him from the Guises. Although the plot was not strictly religious in motivation, most of the conspirators were *Huguenots*—a name of uncertain origin given to French Protestants. Among those implicated, and imprisoned by the Guises, was Louis de Condé. This in turn caused grave misgivings among the nobility, both Catholic and Protestant, who feared that the imprisonment, trial, and conviction of a Prince of the Blood would be a severe blow to their ancient privileges.

At that point Francis II died unexpectedly. Catherine de Medici quickly intervened and took the title of regent for her ten-year-old son, Charles IX. Since she had been repeatedly humiliated and thwarted by the Guises, one of her first actions was to free Condé and join the Huguenots in their efforts to limit the power of the house of Lorraine—as the Guises were also called. By that time, Protestants in France were numerous; there were some two thousand Huguenot churches. Therefore, for reasons of policy rather than conviction, Catherine cultivated the Protestants. Those who were in prison were freed, with a mild admonition to abandon heresy. She then convened a colloquy of Protestant and Catholic theologians that gathered at Poissy in order to seek an agreement. This failed, as was to be expected. But in 1562 the regent issued the Edict of St. Germain, which granted Huguenots freedom to practice their religion, but forbade their owning places of worship, gathering in synods without a previous permit, collecting funds, supporting an army, and so on. Thus, all that the Huguenots were granted was the right to gather for worship, as long as this took place outside cities, at daytime, and without arms. Catherine hoped by these measures to gain the favor of Protestants, while limiting any political or military power they might have. She wished to make the Huguenots a threat to the house of Lorraine, but not to the unity of the nation or the power of the throne.

The Guises refused to obey this edict, hoping thus to undermine Catherine's authority. Slightly more than two months after the proclamation of the edict, the two Guise brothers, with two hundred armed noblemen, surrounded the stable where a group of Huguenots were worshiping in the village of Vassy, and slew as many as they could.

The Massacre of Vassy resulted in the first of a long series of religious wars that ravaged France. Protestant mobs attacked Catholic Churches, overturning their altars and their images, and sometimes attacking priests and monks. Catholic mobs, sometimes led by priests, ransacked the churches and homes of Protestants, whom they often slaughtered. After several skirmishes, each side raised an army and took the field—the Catholics under the leadership of the duke of Guise, and the Protestants under Admiral Gaspard de Coligny. The Catholics won the majority of the battles, but their general was assassinated by a Protestant nobleman; and exactly a year after the Massacre of Vassy the two sides agreed to a truce that granted the Huguenots a measure of tolerance. But this was not a lasting peace, for there were two other religious wars between 1567 and 1570.

THE MASSACRE OF ST. BARTHOLOMEW'S DAY

After prolonged wars, the peace of 1570 offered the promise of lasting peace. Catherine de Medici seemed willing to make concessions to the Protestants, hoping they would help her in her power struggle against the Guises. In 1571, Coligny appeared in court, and he made such a favorable impression on the young king that the latter called him "my father." There were also plans for a marriage between Catherine's daughter Margaret Valois and the Protestant prince Henry Bourbon, Antoine's son. All bode well for the Huguenots, who after long struggles were now able to appear freely at court.

But beneath sweet appearances lurked other intentions. The new duke of Guise, Henry, was convinced that his father's death had been ordered by Coligny, and was eager for revenge. Catherine herself began to fear the growing influence of the Protestant admiral who had won the king's trust and admiration. Thus developed a plot to rid themselves of the admiral— one of the most upright figures of those turbulent times.

The main Huguenot leaders had come to Paris for the wedding of Henry Bourbon, by then king of Navarre, and the French king's sister Margaret Valois. The ceremony took place, amid great rejoicing and signs of reconciliation, on August 18. The Protestant nobles were lulled into overconfidence by their friendly reception and by the king's obvious good will. Then, as Coligny was returning to his lodgings from the Louvre, then the royal palace, someone shot at him from a building owned by the Guise family. He lost one finger on his right hand, and his left arm was also wounded. But the attempt on his life had failed.

The Huguenot leaders, incensed at such a breach of the king's hospitality, demanded justice. Charles IX took the investigation seriously, and uncovered evidence that the shot had been fired from an arquebus belonging to the duke of Guise, and that the assassin had fled on a horse from Catherine's stables. Some even suspected that the king's brother, Henry of Anjou—later Henry III—was part of the conspiracy. The indignant king banned the Guises from court, while inquiries continued.

The conspirators then took drastic measures. Apparently Catherine convinced Charles that there was a vast Huguenot plot to wrest the throne from him, and that its leader was Coligny. The king, who had never shown great strength of conviction, believed what he was told, and thus the stage was set for the massacre of Protestants. The king convened his main counselors— except those who were Protestant—and on the evening of August 23 it was decided that they would take drastic measures.

The following day was St. Bartholomew's Day, August 24, 1572. With the approval of both Charles IX and Catherine de Medici, the duke of Guise met with those in charge of keeping order in Paris and gave them detailed instructions, including what dwelling each would attack, and who their victims were to be. He took personal charge of the death of Coligny, who was still convalescing. The admiral was taken by surprise in his bedchamber, and his attackers inflicted several wounds. While he was still alive, he was thrown out the window to the duke who waited below, and it is said that the duke kicked and killed him. Then his body was horribly mutilated, and what was left was hanged from the gibbet at Montfaucon.

Altogether, about two thousand Huguenots met a similar fate. Even at the royal palace, the Louvre, blood ran down the stairs as some thirty members of the Bourbon guard were slaughtered. The two Protestant princes of the blood, Louis de Condé and Henry Bourbon—the latter king of Navarre and now Charles's brother-in-law—were dragged before the French king, where they saved their lives by denying their faith.

The massacre in Paris signaled the beginning of similar events in the provinces. The duke of Guise had given orders that Protestant leaders in every corner of the kingdom were to be killed. A few upright magistrates

The Massacre of St. Bartholomew's Day, and the events leading to it, are depicted in this woodcut. From the building on the left, a man fires at Coligny. At the top right, Coligny is attacked while in bed and then thrown out the window. Other scenes of terror appear in the rest of the picture. On the top left, the king is at play while all this takes place.

refused to obey, declaring that they were neither executioners nor murderers. But most did obey, and mobs went beyond the duke's order, ransacking Protestant homes and killing entire families. The number of victims reached into the tens of thousands.

The news spread throughout Europe. As has been said, William of Orange, who was marching on Brussels with an army he had raised with French support (and who later married one of Coligny's daughters) felt compelled to disband his troops and abandon the campaign. In England, Elizabeth dressed in mourning. Emperor Maximilian II, although a faithful Catholic, expressed horror at the news. But in Rome and Madrid the reaction was different. Pope Gregory XIII, while declaring that he deplored the bloodshed, ordered that a *Te Deum*—a hymn of Thanksgiving—be sung in celebration of the occurrences on night of St. Bartholomew, and that the same be done every year in memory of such glorious deeds. Spanish chroniclers affirm that Philip II smiled in public for the first time when he received the news of the massacre, and that he too ordered the singing of a *Te Deum* and other celebrations.

THE WAR OF THE THREE HENRYS

In spite of the many casualties, Protestantism itself had not been stamped out. Lacking in military leaders as a result of the massacre, the Huguenots made themselves strong in La Rochelle and Montauban, cities that had been granted to them by an earlier peace treaty. They declared themselves ready to fight, not only the house of Guise, but also the king himself, whom they now declared to be a traitor and a murderer. Many Catholics, tired of internecine warfare and bloodshed, and convinced that a policy of tolerance was necessary, offered their support. As for Charles IX, it was apparent that he was unable to rule, and the country lived in near chaos until his death in 1574.

The crown then passed to his brother Henry of Anjou—Henry III—one of the authors of the massacre. His mother, Catherine de Medici, had arranged to have him elected king of Poland, where he now ruled. But when he received news of his brother's death he rushed to Paris to claim the French throne, without even bothering to abdicate the Polish one. Like his mother, Henry had no other convictions than those necessary to take and hold power. Therefore, when he decided that it was to his advantage, he made peace with the Protestant rebels, who were granted freedom of worship, except in Paris.

The more belligerent Catholics, led by the duke of Guise, reacted vigorously. With Spanish support, they declared war on the Huguenots. Eventually Henry III joined them, and thus began another war of religion—the eighth in a seemingly endless series—that bled the country and solved nothing, for the Huguenots were too weak to defeat the Catholics, and the latter were not strong enough to stamp out Protestantism.

Then events took an unexpected turn. Since Henry III had no direct heir, the legal succession to the throne now belonged to Henry Bourbon, king of Navarre. This prince, who had been a prisoner in Paris after the Massacre of St. Bartholomew's Day, had managed to escape in 1576. He then changed his religion for a fourth time—and not the last—declaring himself a Protestant. Although the Huguenots did not find his licentiousness (and that of his wife) to their liking, he had become the center of Protestant resistance. Therefore, as conditions now stood, the legal heir to the crown was a Protestant.

This the Catholic party could not tolerate, and therefore they put forward Henry of Guise as the rightful heir to the throne. A document was supposedly unearthed in Lorraine, showing that the house of Guise was descended from Charlemagne, and that therefore its right to the crown superseded the claims of the Bourbons and even of the Valois, whose last king was Henry III.

Thus three parties resulted, each headed by a different Henry. The legitimate king, Henry III, was the least worthy and able of the three. The Catholic pretender, Henry of Guise, based his claims on a document that was clearly spurious. The Protestant chief, Henry Bourbon, did not claim the throne itself but only his right to inherit it.

The war dragged on until Henry of Guise took Paris and had himself proclaimed king. Then Henry III had recourse to the same methods Henry of Guise had earlier employed against the Protestants. Two days before Christmas 1588, by the king's order, Henry of Guise was murdered at the same place where sixteen years earlier he had issued instructions for the Massacre of St. Barthlomew's Day.

This did not put an end to Catholic opposition, however. Very few were ready to trust a king who had repeatedly made use of political assassination. The Catholic rebels simply found new leaders and continued fighting. Soon the king's situation was desperate, and he had no alternative but to flee from Paris and seek refuge in the camp of his erstwhile rival, Henry Bourbon, who at least acknowledged him as the legitimate king.

Henry Bourbon received the king with due respect and granted him asylum, but would not let him determine the policies to be followed. This awkward situation, however, did not last long, for a fanatical Dominican friar, convinced that the king was a tyrant and that in such circumstances regicide was licit, entered the Protestant camp, and killed the king.

The death of Henry III did not end the war. Henry Bourbon, who was now clearly the legitimate heir, took the name of Henry IV. But French Catholics were not ready to have a Protestant king. In Spain, Philip II was planning to seize the opportunity to make himself master of France. The

A service in the Calvinist church in Lyons, in 1564, shows the centrality of the pulpit and of preaching in the Reformed tradition.

pope declared that Henry Bourbon's claim to the throne was not valid. For these reasons, the war continued for four more years. Finally, Henry IV decided that the throne would never be his unless he became a Catholic, and therefore once again he changed his religion. Although he probably never said the words attributed to him, "Paris is well worth a mass," they clearly express his sentiments. The year after this fifth conversion, the new king entered Paris, and ended several decades of religious wars.

Although he had become a Catholic, Henry IV did not forget his former comrades in arms. On the contrary, he showed them such loyalty and favor that the more recalcitrant Catholics claimed that he was still a heretic. Finally, on April 13, 1598, he issued the Edict of Nantes, granting the Huguenots freedom of worship in all places where they had had churches by the previous year, except in Paris. He also guaranteed their security by granting them all the fortified towns they had held in 1597.

In spite of his inconstant religious convictions and the licentiousness of his personal life, Henry IV ruled the nation wisely. During his reign the country prospered, and soon he was respected by many of his former foes. But religious hatred and prejudice had not entirely disappeared, and Henry himself fell victim to them in 1610, when his life was ended by a Catholic fanatic who was convinced that the king was still a Protestant heretic, and that God would be served by his death.

12

The Catholic Reformation

On the Cross there hangs the Lord
of Heaven and earth
And amid the stress of war
Peace comes to birth.

ST. TERESA (TR. E. ALLISON PEERS)

T he Protestant movement did not encompass all the strong and varied currents of reformation that were sweeping Europe. Well before Luther's protest, there were many who longed for an ecclesiastical reformation, and who worked toward it. This was particularly true in Spain where, under Queen Isabella and Cardinal Francisco Jiménez de Cisneros, the Catholic Reformation was well under way when Luther was still a young boy.

THE REFORMATION OF SPANISH CATHOLICISM

When Isabella inherited the crown of Castile in 1474, the church in her land was in urgent need of reformation. As in the rest of Europe, many prelates were also great lords, more given to war and intrigue than to the spiritual welfare of the faithful. Most of the lower clergy were insufficiently trained, to the point that many were able to do no more than recite the mass. As in other parts of Europe, monasticism was at low ebb, and some of the larger convents and monasteries had become fashionable places of retreat for the illegitimate children of royalty and nobility.

Isabella was determined to reform the church, and to that end began by securing from the papacy the right to name those who were to fill high ecclesiastical posts. Her husband Ferdinand, the king of neighboring Aragon, obtained similar rights for his territories. But their motivations were very different. Isabella was interested in having the authority to reform the

church, whereas Ferdinand saw in the naming of prelates an important political prerogative that would strengthen the crown. Thus, while Isabella was
energetically seeking the best candidates to fill vacant posts, Ferdinand filled
the vacant archbishopric of Saragossa, his capital, by naming to that post his
illegitimate son, who was then six years old.

If Isabella found no support for her program of reformation in her husband Ferdinand, the same was not true of her confessor, Francisco Jiménez
de Cisneros. He was an austere Franciscan who had spent ten years in prison
for refusing to participate in the corrupt practices of his time. While in
prison, he had studied Hebrew and Chaldean, for he was imbued with the
scholarly interests of the humanists. Finally, through the recommendation of
the reformist bishop of Toledo—who had been chosen by Isabella—he was
made confessor to the queen. When the archbishop died, Isabella took the
steps necessary to have Jiménez named to the vacant see, the most important in the kingdom. Jiménez refused, and the queen obtained from Pope
Alexander VI—who was anything but a reformer—a papal bull ordering the
reluctant friar to accept.

*Isabella, the great queen of
Castile, was a champion of
reformation long before Luther's
protest. Her program did
not include the reformation
of doctrine, however, as did
Luther's.*

The queen and the archbishop set about the reformation of convents and monasteries. They personally visited the most important monastic houses, and those best known for their laxity, calling all to renewed obedience to their monastic vows, reproving those who showed little improvement, and, in some cases, severely punishing those who resisted their entreaties. Protests were sent to Rome. But the pope, while not a reformer, was a politician who understood the need to humor the reformist queen. As a result, her hand was further strengthened, and even the most corrupt among the prelates of her kingdom had to take steps to reform the church.

Jiménez's scholarship, most particularly his great interest in Scripture, was an important element in Isabella's program of reformation. She was convinced that both the church and her kingdom were in need of learned leadership, and therefore encouraged studies. She herself was a scholar, and surrounded herself with an impressive array of intellectual men and women. With Ferdinand's support, she encouraged the printing of books, and soon there were printing presses in all the major cities of their kingdoms. In all these projects, Jiménez was an important ally. But his two most significant contributions were the founding of the University of Alcala and the publication of the *Complutensian Polyglot*. The University of Alcala, a few miles from Madrid, soon counted among its alumni several of the most prominent figures in Spanish religious and literary life—Cervantes and Loyola among them. The *Complutensian Polyglot*—named after *Complutum*, the Latin name for *Alcala*—was a great multilingual edition of the Bible prepared by the best scholars available: three converts from Judaism prepared the Hebrew text, a Cretan and two Spanish scholars were chiefly responsible for the Greek, and the best Latin scholars in Spain worked on the text of the Vulgate. All these appeared in parallel columns, and the entire work comprised six volumes (the Old Testament in four, the New in the fifth, and a thorough discussion of Hebrew, Chaldean, and Greek grammar in the sixth). Although the work was finished in 1517, it was not officially published until 1520. It is said that when the work was completed, Jiménez rejoiced over "this edition of the Bible that, at this critical time, opens the sacred sources of our religion, from which will flow a much purer theology than any derived from less direct sources." Such a clear affirmation of the superiority of Scripture over tradition, had it been made a few years later, would have led to accusations of "Lutheran heresy."

The scholarly interests of Jiménez and Isabella, however, did not lead to tolerance. Studies were to be encouraged as long as they contributed to the reformation of customs and morals, but doctrinal deviation would be severely punished. Thus, Cardinal Jiménez, the scholar who directed the *Complutensián Polyglot,* the patron of books and learning, the reformer of the life of the church, was also the grand inquisitor who would brook no diversity or doctrinal deviation. In this he was typical of most of the Catholic Reformation, which sought to purify the church through austerity, devotion, and scholarship, but at the same time insisted on strict adherence to traditional dogma. Most of the saints and sages of the Catholic Reformation, like Isabella, were pure, devout, and intolerant.

POLEMICS AGAINST PROTESTANTISM

Although the Catholic Reformation had begun earlier, the advent of Protestantism gave it a new character. It was no longer a matter of the need to reform the church out of an inner necessity, but also an attempt to respond to those who included doctrine among the things to be reformed. Especially in those regions where Protestantism was a real threat, Catholic reformers felt compelled to respond with both a reformation of custom and a defense of traditional doctrine.

IACOBVS LATOMVS.

Ædificat Latomus multa & præclara difertus
  Diſponenſque manu conſtruit artifici.
Qui loca quæſierit fidei bene commoda noſtræ
  Flla petat, doctus quæ poſuit Latomus.

                          C₂

James Latomus was one of many Catholic scholars who opposed Luther and his views.

Some of these Catholic leaders were scholars, while others feared that the humanist program posed as great a threat as Protestantism. John Eck, the theologian who debated Luther and Karlstadt at Leipzig, was also a conscientious pastor and a scholar who in 1537 published his own German translation of the Bible. On the other hand, James Latomus, rector of the University of Louvain, attacked both Protestants and humanists, arguing that in order to understand Scripture it sufficed only to read it in Latin, in the light of the tradition of the church, and that the study of Greek and Hebrew was useless. Eventually, however, it became clear that scholarship was necessary to refute Protestant teachings; and thus appeared a host of theologians and scholars who devoted their efforts to counter Protestant arguments. Foremost among these were Robert Bellarmine and Caesar Baronius.

Bellarmine was the main systematizer of Catholic theological arguments against Protestant claims. For twelve years, beginning in 1576, he held in Rome the newly founded Chair of Polemics, and toward the end of his tenure there he began publishing his great work, *On the Controversies of the Christian Faith,* which he completed in 1593. This became the classical

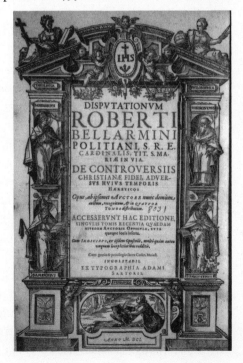

Robert Bellarmine provided what would become the primary Catholic arguments against Protestantism for centuries.

source of arguments against Protestantism. In fact, to this day most of the arguments used by conservative Catholics in their polemics against Protestantism are drawn from Bellarmine's work. Bellarmine was also one of the participants in the trial of Galileo, which concluded that the notion that the earth moves around the sun is heretical.

Caesar Baronius, on the other hand, was a great Catholic historian. A group of scholars at the University of Magdeburg had begun publishing a vast history of the church in which they sought to show how Roman Catholicism had deviated from original Christianity. Since this work—never completed—devoted a volume to each century, it became generally known as *The Centuries of Magdeburg*. In answer to them, Baronius wrote his *Ecclesiastical Annals*. It was not until late in the seventeenth century, with the publication in 1696 of Gottfried Arnold's *True Picture of the First Christians*, and, in 1699, of his *Nonpartisan History of the Church and of Heretics*, that an attempt was made at producing a church history that looked at the past objectively, rather than simply justifying the historian's positions—and even then, Arnold's Pietist inclinations may be seen in the manner in which he understands the history of the church.

NEW ORDERS

Although it is true that monastic life had reached low ebb at the outset of the Reformation, it is also true that there were still many in convents and monasteries who took their vows seriously, and who bemoaned the sad state of monastic life. During the sixteenth century, such longings came to fruition in the reformation of the old orders, as Isabella and Jiménez had advocated, and in the founding of new ones. Among these new orders, some sought to renew the ancient strict observance of monastic vows, whereas others were shaped to respond to the new conditions of the sixteenth century. The most noteworthy new order of the first type was that of the Discalced Carmelites, founded by St. Teresa. Meanwhile, the Jesuits, under the leadership of Ignatius Loyola, were foremost among the orders that hoped to respond to the new times with new solutions.

Teresa spent most of her youth in Avila, an ancient walled city perched high in the plateaus of Castile. Her grandfather was a converted Jew who had moved with his family to Avila after having been shamed by the Inquisition in his native Toledo. She had felt attracted to the monastic life from an early age, although she later declared that she also feared it. When she finally

Many students of Teresa's mysticism believe that the walls of Avila, where she lived, inspired Teresa to think of the soul as an "inner castle."

joined the Carmelite convent of the Incarnation, just outside Avila, she did so against her father's wishes. There, her wit and charm made her so popular that it became a fad for the aristocracy of the city to visit and exchange pleasantries with her. But she herself was unhappy with this easy style of monasticism, and spent as much time as possible reading books of devotion.

She was dismayed when the Inquisition published a list of forbidden books that included most of her favorites. She then had a vision in which Jesus told her: "Fear not, for I shall be to you like an open book." From then on, such visions became increasingly frequent. This led her into a prolonged inner struggle, for she had no way of determining whether the visions were genuine or, in her words, "it was a demon." Her confessors, whom she changed repeatedly, were of little help. One even told her to exorcise the visions with an obscene sign—a thing she could never bring herself to do. Finally, with the help of some learned friars, she came to the conviction that her visions were genuine.

She then felt called, again by a vision, to leave the convent and found another one nearby, in order to follow the monastic life with more rigor there. Overcoming great opposition from the bishop as well as from other nuns and from the aristocracy of the city, she managed to found her little convent. But this was not enough, for her visions called her to found similar houses throughout Spain. Her enemies accused her of being a gadabout. But she won the respect of bishops and royalty, and eventually the order she founded spread throughout Spain and its possessions. Since her nuns wore sandals instead of shoes, they became generally known as the Discalced (or Barefoot) Carmelites.

She was joined in her efforts by John of the Cross—later known as St. John of the Cross—a man so short that, when she met him, St. Teresa is said to have quipped, "Lord, I asked you for a monk and you sent me half of one." The two became close friends and collaborators and,

"Santa Teresa de Jesús" as depicted in Avila by Carmelite sculptor Jesús de Santa Teresa.

through John's work, Teresa's reform resulted in the male branch of the Discalced Carmelites. Thus, Teresa is the only woman in the history of the church to have founded monastic orders for both women and men.

While deeply involved in all the administrative matters related to the convents she founded, Teresa also spent time in mystical contemplation, which often led to visions or to ecstasy. Her many works on the subject have become classics of mystical devotion and, in 1970, Pope Paul VI added her name to the official list of "Doctors of the Church"—an honor she shares with one other woman, St. Catherine of Siena, and also with St. John of the Cross.

While Teresa's reformation was directed at the monastic life and the stricter observance of the ancient rule of the Carmelites, the one led by St. Ignatius Loyola that had begun a few years earlier, was intended to respond to the outward challenges the times posed for the church. Ignatius was the scion of an ancient aristocratic family and had hoped to attain glory through a military career. These dreams were shattered when, at the siege of Pamplona in Navarre, he suffered a wound that caused him to limp for the rest of his life. While still bedridden, and prey to both excruciating pain and bitter disappointment, he turned to the reading of devotional books. This led to a vision he later retold, referring to himself in the third person:

> Lying awake one night, he clearly saw the image of Our Lady with the Holy Child Jesus, and with that vision he received remarkable consolation for a long time, and was left with such repugnance for his former life, and especially for things of the flesh, that it seemed like all the images that had been painted on his soul were erased.[5]

Loyola then went on pilgrimage to the hermitage of Montserrat, where, in a rite reminiscent of the ancient orders of chivalry, he devoted himself to the service of his Lady, the Virgin, and confessed

Monument to St. John of the Cross in Avila.

all his sins. Then he withdrew to Manresa, where he intended to live as a hermit. But this did not suffice to calm his spirit, tormented—as Luther's had been earlier—by a profound sense of his own sin. His account of those days is strikingly similar to Luther's:

> At that point he came to have much travail with scruples, for, although the general confession he had made at Montserrat had been done with great diligence and in writing, [. . .] it still seemed to him that there were some things that he had not confessed. And this caused him great affliction because, even having confessed those other things, he was not at peace.

Then [...] the confessor ordered him not to confess anything of the past, but only those things that were very clear to him. But to him all these things were very clear, and therefore this order was of no benefit to him, and he was still in great travail. [...]

When he had such thoughts, very often the temptation came to him with great force, to jump from a big hole in his room, next to the place where he prayed. But then, acknowledging that to kill himself would be a sin, he would cry out, "Lord, I shall do naught to offend thee."[6]

Such were the torments the future founder of the Jesuits suffered until he came to know the grace of God. He does not tell how this happened. But he does say that "from that day on he was free of those scruples, being certain that our Lord had wished to free him by His mercy."[7]

At this point, however, the parallel between Luther and Loyola diverges, for while the German friar set out on a path that would eventually lead to an open break with the Catholic Church, the Spaniard took an opposite tack. From then on he devoted his life, no longer to the monastic quest for his own salvation, but now to the service of the church and its mission. Hoping to become a missionary to the Turks, he first went to the Holy Land, which for centuries had exerted a mysterious attraction on the European soul. But the Franciscans who were already working there feared the complications the fiery Spaniard could create, and forced him to leave. He then decided that he must learn theology in order to better serve God. By then a mature man, he studied beside younger students at the universities of Barcelona, Alcala, Salamanca, and Paris. Soon a small band gathered around him, drawn by his fervent faith and enthusiasm. Finally, in 1534, he returned to Montserrat with his small band, and there all made solemn vows of poverty, chastity, and obedience to the pope.

The initial purpose of the new order was to work among the Turks in the Holy Land. But by the time Pope Paul III gave it his formal approval, in 1540, the threat of Protestantism was such that the Society of Jesus—commonly known as the Jesuits—came to be one of the main instruments of the Catholic offensive against Protestantism. The Jesuits, however, did not set aside their original missionary commitment, and soon hundreds of them were laboring in the Far East and the New World. As a response to Protestantism, the Society of Jesus was a powerful weapon in the hands of a reformed papacy. Their organization, patterned after the military, enabled

St. Ignatius of Loyola was probably the most influential leader in the Catholic Reformation.

them to respond rapidly and efficiently to various challenges and opportunities. Many of them were also scholars who contributed their knowledge to the polemic against Protestantism.

PAPAL REFORMATION

When Luther nailed his theses on the Wittenberg door, the papacy was in the hands of Leo X, who was more interested in embellishing the city of Rome, and in furthering the interests of the house of Medici, than in religious matters. Therefore, even those who remained loyal Catholics had little hope that the necessary reformation would come from Rome. While some called on lay rulers to put the church's house in order, others revived the earlier conciliarist ideas, calling for a council to discuss both the issues posed by Luther and his followers, and to develop a program for putting an end to corruption and abuse within the church.

The brief pontificate of Adrian VI offered some hope of reformation. He was a man of lofty ideals who did indeed wish to reform the church. But the intrigues of the curia thwarted most of his projects, which in any case were cut short by his unexpected death. The next pope, Clement VII, was a cousin of Leo X, and his policies were similar to those of his kinsman. Although he did succeed in his plans for the beautification of Rome, his pontificate was disastrous for the Roman church, for it was during his time that England declared itself independent of papal authority, and the troops of Charles V sacked Rome. Paul III, who succeeded Clement, remained an ambiguous figure. He seemed to trust astrology more than theology, and his papacy, like those of his predecessors, was tainted by nepotism: his son was made duke of Parma and Piacenza, and his teenage grandsons were made cardinals. He too wished to make Rome the wealthiest center of Renaissance art, and for that reason continued the systems of exploitation whereby the papacy sought to collect funds from all nations in Europe. But he was also a reforming pope. He was the one who gave official recognition to the Jesuits and began employing them in missions and in polemics against Protestantism. In 1536, he appointed a distinguished commission of cardinals and bishops to report to him on the need and proposed means of reformation. Their report somehow reached the hands of the enemies of the papacy, and gave Protestants abundant ammunition for their campaign against "Popery." Paul himself, having realized that a significant portion of his income was derived from practices that his own commission had declared corrupt, decided that it was best to leave matters as they were. He did, however, convoke the council for which so many had been clamoring. It began its sessions at Trent in 1545. The next pope, Julius III, possessed all the vices of his predecessor, and few of his virtues. Once again nepotism became the order of the day, and the Roman court became a center of games and festivities, in imitation of other courts in Europe. Then Marcellus II, a man with a firm commitment to reformation, became pope. But his sudden death put an end to his pontificate.

Finally, in 1555, Cardinal Giampietro Carafa was elected pope, and took the name of Paul IV. He had been a member of the commission appointed earlier by Paul III, and as soon as he became pope he set out to correct the evils that that commission had decried. He was an austere, virtually rigid man, and he tended to equate the need for reformation with strict uniformity in all matters. Under his leadership, the activity of the Inquisition increased to the point of terror; and the *Index of Forbidden Books,* published under his direction, included some of the best Catholic literature. But in spite of this Paul IV deserves credit for having cleansed the Roman curia, and for having placed the papacy at the head of the Catholic Reformation. In varying ways and degrees, his was the policy followed by his successors for several generations.

THE COUNCIL OF TRENT

The reader will remember that Luther and several other reformers repeatedly appealed to a universal council. During the early years of the Reformation, however, the popes opposed the convocation of such an assembly, for they feared a rebirth of the conciliarist movement, which had claimed supremacy over the papacy. Therefore, it was only during the reign of Paul III, when the breach between Protestants and Catholics became permanent, that Rome gave serious consideration to the possibility of calling a universal council. After many difficult and complicated negotiations, it was decided that the council would meet at Trent in December 1545. Charles V had insisted that the council meet in his territories, and that was why they selected Trent, an imperial city in northern Italy. Even so, it was attended by few prelates—thirty-one in the first session, and two hundred and thirteen in the last.

Until then, most of the great councils had dealt with a few problems, or with a particular doctrine considered heretical. But the issues posed by Protestantism were of such magnitude, and the church was in such need of reformation, that the council was not content with condemning Protestantism. Instead, it felt compelled to discuss every item of theology that the Protestant Reformation had questioned, and to issue a number of decrees for the reformation of the church. Linking uniformity with orthodoxy, the council also took measures regulating the life and worship of the church.

The Council of Trent, considered by the Roman Catholic Church the nineteenth ecumenical council, had a checkered history. When relations between Pope Paul III and the emperor grew tense, the pope moved the gathering to the papal states. But the emperor ordered his bishops to

The Council of Trent, considered by the Roman Catholic Church the nineteenth ecumenical council, responded to the various issues raised by the Reformation and set the tone for Roman Catholicism for the next four centuries.

remain at Trent, with the result that the council was suspended in 1547. It was reconvened in 1551, and suspended again the following year. In 1555, Paul IV became pope. Although he wished to continue the work of reformation begun by the council, he feared the excessive influence of the Spaniards in the assembly, and therefore refrained from reconvening it. Finally, in 1562, during the pontificate of the next pope, Pius IV, the council gathered again, completing its work, in 1563. Therefore, although in theory the council lasted from 1545 to 1563, during most of that time it was in recess.

The decrees of the Council of Trent are too numerous to list here. As measures of reformation, it ordered bishops to reside in their sees, condemned pluralism (the holding of several ecclesiastic offices simultaneously), listed and defined the obligations of the clergy, regulated the use of such things as relics and indulgences, and ordered the founding of seminaries for the training of the ministry (until that time, there had been no generally accepted regulations or educational requirements for ordination). It also promoted the study of Thomas Aquinas, making his the dominant theology in the Catholic Church. On the other hand, it took measures against Protestantism. In this vein, it declared that the Latin translation of the Bible, the Vulgate, would be authoritative in matters of dogma; that tradition has an authority parallel to that of Scripture; that there are seven sacraments; that the mass is a true sacrifice that can be offered for the benefit of the deceased; that com-

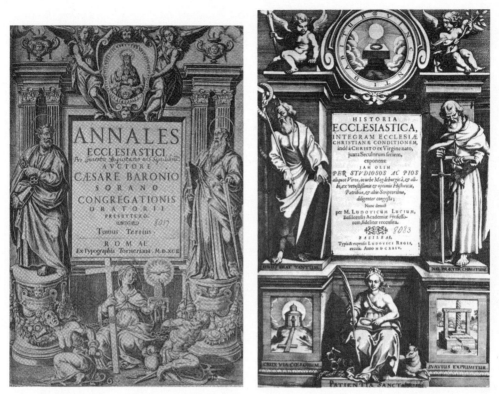

The debate between Catholics and Protestants forced both to look again at the entire history of the church. On the Catholic side, Baronius came to be known as the father of church history. His Protestant counterparts were the authors of the Centuries of Magdeburg.

munion in both kinds—that is, with the laity receiving both the bread and the wine—is not necessary; that justification is based on good works done through the collaboration between grace and the believer; and so forth.

In spite of its checkered history, of the scant number of prelates who attended it, and of the resistance of many sovereigns who would not allow its decrees to be published in their territories, the Council of Trent marked the birth of the modern Catholic Church. This was not exactly the same as the medieval church against which Luther protested, for it bore the marks of a reaction against Protestantism. During the next four centuries, that reaction would be such that the Roman Church refused to concede that many of the elements of the Protestant Reformation that the Council of Trent had rejected did have deep roots in Christian tradition. It would be much later, in the twentieth century, that the Catholic Church would finally be able to set its own agenda for reformation apart from a reaction to Protestantism.

13

Protestantism at the Edges

In the name of the Vaudois Churches of the Alps, of Dauphiné, and of Piedmont . . . we here promise, our hands on the Bible, and in the presence of God, that all our valleys shall courageously sustain each other in matters of religion. . . . We promise to maintain the Bible, whole and without admixture, according to the usage of the true apostolic church, persevering in the holy religion, though it be at peril of life.

WALDENSIAN DECLARATION, 1561

During the sixteenth century, Catholics, Lutherans, Reformed, and Anglicans, all took for granted that a state must have a single religion to which all its subjects must adhere. While the Anabaptists—except for extreme groups such as those who established the New Jerusalem at Münster—did not hold to this opinion, their very refusal to become a state religion meant that the tolerance they advocated was seldom granted by any state. As we have seen in following the story of Lutheranism in Germany, peace was only attained by deciding that some states would be Lutheran and some Catholic—once again, the principle of *cujus regis eius religio*. The tragic story of the wars of religion in France, and of their aftermath, is a prime example of the consequences of the notion that a state could have but one religion. Even the Edict of Nantes, whereby those wars ended, guaranteed the survival of Protestantism by granting it a number of cities that would be Protestant, while the rest of the nation would remain Catholic.

But it is not easy to legislate on matters of religion, and therefore in every land there were those who disagreed with the faith espoused by the government. We have already noted the struggles in England and in France, both

The monastery of Santiponce, at the outskirts of Seville, was one of the main centers from which Protestantism spread in Spain.

of which resulted in dire conditions for those who followed a different faith than their governments—Catholics in England, and Protestants in France. While it is impossible to follow the history of the brave souls, both Catholic and Protestant, who remained firm in their convictions in spite of governmental pressure and even persecution, the story of Christianity in sixteenth-century Europe would be incomplete without acknowledging at least some of their struggles and their contributions.

SPAIN

Before the outbreak of the Protestant Reformation, there were many who hoped that Spain would take the lead in the long-overdue reformation of the church. As we have noted, Isabella and Cardinal Jiménez de Cisneros had implemented a vast program of religious reformation—including the renewal in biblical studies that took place in connection with the Complutensian Polyglot Bible. There were also in Spain many humanists—some of them in high positions—who looked to a reformation such as that which Erasmus proposed.

But then, as a result of the Protestant Reformation, things changed. At the Diet of Worms, an upstart German monk by the name of Martin Luther had dared confront Emperor Charles V, who was also King Charles I of

The first edition of Casiodoro de Reina's translation of the Bible is known as La Biblia del Oso *because the illustration on the first page is of a bear eating honey.*

Spain, and the house of Austria, became the champion of opposition to Lutheranism and all that seemed to approach it. The Spanish Inquisition, previously directed mostly at those accused of "Judaizing" or of witchcraft, now turned its attention to those whose call for reformation could be dubbed "Lutheranism." A number of the leading humanists fled to lands where they could enjoy greater freedom. Others simply turned to their literary studies, and let religious matters follow their own course.

Yet the Inquisition was not able to put a stop to all "Lutheran contagion." This was particularly true in Valladolid and Seville, where repeated autos-da-fe punished those who were convicted of Lutheranism. Unbeknownst to the officers of the Inquisition, a Jeronimite monastery in Santiponce, a few miles outside of Seville, became a center of reformation to which Bibles and Protestant books were smuggled in barrels supposedly containing oil or wine. When the smuggler was captured and burned, and word arrived that the Inquisition had wind of the goings-on in the monastery, twelve of the monks decided to flee, and to meet a year later in Geneva. Their personal adventures were quite a saga, but eventually they did meet in Geneva. One of them became pastor of the Spanish-speaking community in Geneva. Another, Casiodoro de Reina, devoted the rest of his life to translating the Bible into Spanish, and after many vicissitudes did publish a translation that has won general praise as a masterpiece of Spanish literature (1569). Some years later, another of the twelve, Cipriano de Valera, revised this version, which is now known as the Reina-Valera Bible. Meanwhile, in their old monastery in Santiponce, as well as throughout the region of Seville, the Inquisition continued cleansing the church of all trace of "Lutheranism"—so called by the inquisitors, although in fact most of them were Calvinists or simply Erasmians who continued hoping for reformation along humanist lines. Still, studies in the twentieth century would seem to indicate that the Inquisition was not totally successful, and that even in Santiponce itself some remnants of the movement continued existing for some time.

ITALY

In the most inaccessible valleys among the Alps, and in lesser numbers in other regions of Italy and southern France, the ancient community begun by Peter Waldo in the twelfth century (see Vol. I, Chapter 32), continued a secluded and threatened existence. Repeatedly attacked by armies seeking to suppress their "heresy," they had long stood firm in their mountain strongholds, which they successfully defended against all invaders. But by the early sixteenth century the movement seemed to have lost impetus as repeated threats and persecutions sought to suppress them. Many of them felt that the price they paid for disagreeing with Rome was too high, and increasing numbers were returning to Catholicism.

Then strange rumors arrived. It was said that in other lands a great movement of reformation had begun, and that this movement was making impressive progress. An emissary sent to inquire about these rumors returned in 1526 declaring that they were indeed true, that in Germany, Switzerland, France, and even more distant regions, a reformation was afoot, and that many of the doctrines of the reformers agreed with what the Waldensians had held for centuries. Further delegations met with some of the leading reformers—Oecolampadius and Bucer among others—who received them enthusiastically and affirmed most of their doctrines, while also suggesting some points at which those doctrines could be brought into closer accord with Scripture. In 1532, the Waldensians gathered in a synod representing, as they said, "the pastors and heads of families of the valleys of Piedmont," and after some discussion adopted what amounted to the main tenets of the Protestant Reformation, thus becoming the oldest Protestant church—existing more that three centuries before the Reformation itself!

This did not make things easier for the Waldensians. Their fellow believers in southern France, whose lands were more vulnerable than the valleys in the Alps, were invaded and practically exterminated—most of the survivors fled for refuge in the Alps. Then a series of edicts ensued, first forbidding attendance at Protestant worship, and then commanding attendance at mass. Once again, the more accessible regions of the Piedmont were devastated, and greater numbers of Waldensians sought refuge in more secluded areas in the Alps. Meanwhile, the Waldensian communities that had developed earlier in Calabria, in southern Italy, were exterminated.

Seeing that the Waldensians in the Alps remained steadfast in their faith, large armies encouraged and supported by the pope, by the duke of Savoy, and by other powerful lords repeatedly invaded the area, only to be defeated and even routed by the defenders. On one occasion, six men with firearms held back an entire army at a narrow pass while others climbed the mountains above. When rocks began raining on them, the invading soldiers panicked, and the entire army was routed. When peace was finally attained for an extended period, plague broke out decimating the population. The devastation was such that only two pastors survived. As their replacements came from outside—mainly from the Reformed areas of Switzerland— closer ties developed between the Waldensians and the Reformed. Still their woes would not end, for in 1655 all Waldensians living in what is now northern Italy were commanded under penalty of death to quit their lands within three days, selling them to good Catholics and moving to less desirable places. That same year the Marquis of Pianeza, charged with exterminating the Waldensians, marched at the head of an army; but, convinced that were he to invade the Alps his army would suffer the same fate as all earlier invaders, he then offered peace to the Waldensians. Since the latter had always insisted that they would make war only to defend themselves, they now admitted Pianeza's soldiers into their homes, providing them food and shelter from the cold, and allowing them to move into some of the most secluded valleys. Then, two days later, at a prearranged signal, the supposedly peaceful guests turned on their hosts, killing men, women and children—a victory which they then celebrated with a *Te Deum*.

Still the Waldensians resisted, and still they believed their enemies would make peace with them. Louis XIV of France, known among other things for ordering the expulsion of all Huguenots from France, demanded that the duke of Savoy do likewise with his Waldensian subjects. Finally, large numbers of Waldensians abandoned their mountain homes and went to life in exile in Geneva and other Protestant areas, but others insisted on remaining on their ancestral lands, where they were constantly menaced by renewed invasions and violence. It was not until the revolution of 1848, and the promulgation of the constitution for the kingdom of Piedmont—which would eventually unify Italy—that the Waldensians and other dissident groups were finally granted freedom of worship.

Even then, life would not be easy for the Waldensians. In 1850 famine broke out. It soon became apparent that their alpine valleys, long overexploited and now overpopulated, could no longer sustain the population. After much debate, the first of many Waldensian contingents left for the recently formed Republic of Uruguay. There—and later in Argentina—they settled and flourished, taking the leadership in promoting agricultural innovation. In 1975, the two Waldensian communities, one on each side of the Atlantic, made it clear that they were still one church by deciding that they would be governed by a single synod which would normally hold two sessions, one in the Americas in February, and the other in Europe in August.

Although the Waldensian saga has occupied much of our attention here, theirs was not the only Protestant presence in Italy. Among many others, Juan de Valdés and Bernardino Ochino deserve special mention. Valdés was a Spanish Erasmian of Protestant inclinations who was forced to leave Spain and seek refuge in Italy in 1531, when it became clear that Charles V was determined to extirpate Protestantism from Spain. Settling in Naples, he gathered around himself a group of followers and colleagues who devoted themselves to devotion and to Bible study, who did not seek to make their views public, and who were fairly moderate in their Protestant leanings. Among the members of this group was Giulia Gonzaga, a woman of such fame that at one point in her life the Sultan in Constantinople sought to have her kidnapped. But it was another member of this group, Bernardino Ochino, a famous and pious preacher who twice had been elected general of the Capuchins, who openly embraced and taught Protestant principles. When threatened by the Inquisition, he fled to Geneva. From that point on, his life was a series of wanderings, both geographical and doctrinal. He moved first to Geneva, then to Basel, Augsburg, Strasbourg, London, and finally Zürich. Doctrinally, he became ever more radical, eventually rejecting the doctrine of the Trinity and defending polygamy—for which reason he had to leave Zürich and continue wandering until he died of the plague in 1564.

HUNGARY

At the beginning of the Protestant Reformation, Hungary was ruled by the rather ineffectual King Louis II, who was ten years old at his accession to the throne in 1516. In 1526, the Ottoman Turks defeated the Hungarians and killed their king. The leaders among the Hungarian nobility then elected Ferdinand of Hapsburg to occupy the vacant throne, but others of strong nationalist sentiments named Janus II Zapolya (also knows as John Sigismund) as their king. After complex conflicts and negotiations, Hungary was partly under Hapsburg, but mostly under Ottoman, rule. As elsewhere, the Hapsburgs supported Catholicism, and took every possible measure to prevent what they considered to be the Protestant contagion. But theirs was only the western edge of Hungary, for the rest of the nation was ruled by the Ottomans. Transylvania (or Royal Hungary) enjoyed a measure of autonomy, and eventually King Sigismund, seeing that religious division weakened the nation, declared, "That is enough theology," and decided that four forms of Christianity would have equal standing: Roman Catholicism, Lutheranism, the Reformed tradition coming from Switzerland, and Unitarianism—which we shall encounter again as we look at the Reformation in Poland. However, most of Hungary was occupied by the Ottomans, whose policy with regard to Christianity was to promote divisions among Christians, most of the time putting Catholicism at a disadvantage—until Protestantism grew strong, at which time the policy was reversed. The pressure on Catholicism was such that in the period between 1500 and 1606 the number of Franciscans in the land was reduced from fifteen hundred to thirty.

Lutheranism reached Hungary at an early date, and had to live under these conditions. There is evidence that Luther's ninety-five theses were circulating in Hungary barely a year after their posting. By 1523, the Hungarian Diet under Hapsburg rule ordered that Lutherans be burned to prevent the spread of their nefarious teachings. A few years later, Zwingli's teachings entered the scene, and similar measures were taken against them. Even though Ottoman rule was harsh, and atrocities were committed against all Christians, it was in the territories occupied by the Ottomans that Protestantism grew most rapidly. Since Hungarians were suffering under a highly centralized rule, they preferred the Reformed tradition to the Lutheran, for the latter seemed too hierarchical, while the Swiss form of church government, in which pastors and laity shared authority, was closer to what the Hungarians wanted in both church and civil government. Also, this decentralized form of government made it more difficult for Ottoman authorities to exert pressure on the leaders of the church. (While such pressure was often religiously inspired, it also was a means for corrupt authorities to extort money from Christians. There are records indicating that the Ottoman authorities would accept the appointment of a parish priest on the condition that the congregation promise to pay if the priest was arrested for any reason. Needless to say, such priests were often arrested, and were freed only when a bribe was paid.)

Both the Hapsburgs and the Ottomans took measures to prevent the spread of unwanted teachings by means of the printing press. Already in 1483—long before the Reformation—the sultan had issued a decree condemning printers to having their hands cut off. Now Ferdinand I issued a similar ruling against unauthorized printers—except that, instead of having their hands amputated, they were to be drowned! Even so, Protestant books circulated, often produced in clandestine presses that were constantly moving from place to place, and sometimes smuggled in barrels purporting to hold merchandise—much as was being done at the same time in Spain. One result of this was the proliferation of publications in the vernacular, culminating in the publication of the Karoly Bible in 1590 and the Vizsoly Bible in 1607, which played in Hungarian a role similar to that of Luther's Bible in German. It was estimated that by 1600 as many as four out of five Hungarians were Protestant.

Then conditions changed. Early in the seventeenth century, Ottoman power was waning, and Transylvania, supported by Hungarian nationalist sentiments, clashed with the Hapsburgs. At first Transylvania gained the upper hand, and the conflict was settled by the treaty of Vienna, which granted equal rights to both Catholics and Protestants. But then the Thirty Years' War—in which Transylvania opposed the Hapsburgs and their allies—brought greater devastation to the country. Even after the end of the Thirty Years' War, the tripartite conflict among the Hapsburgs, Royal Hungary and the Ottomans continued. In the end, the Hapsburgs gained the upper hand, and the peace of Karlowitz in 1699 gave them control over practically all of Hungary—a control they retained until 1918. In Hungary, as elsewhere, the Hapsburgs imposed strong anti-Protestant measures, and eventually the country became predominantly Catholic; but still the Reformed Church of Hungary had a strong and continued presence in the country—as did also the Socinian Unitarians.

POLAND

At the time when Luther posted his ninety-five theses, there was already in western Poland a growing number of Hussites who had fled difficult circumstances in Bohemia. Then Luther's writings and teachings made their way into Poland, brought mostly by students from Wittenberg. The Poles, however, had long been in conflict with the Germans, and distrusted anything coming from such a source. For that reason, although Lutheranism did spread, its growth was relatively slow. It was when Calvinism made its way into the country that Protestantism began making headway, for here was a form of Protestantism that was not tainted by German origins. The king at the time was Sigismund I (1501–1548), who strongly opposed all Protestant doctrine. But by the middle of the century Calvinism enjoyed a measure of support from King Sigismund II (1548–1572), who even corresponded with Calvin.

The leader of the Calvinist movement in Poland, Jan Laski (or Johannes a Lasco, 1499–1560), was a nobleman who maintained correspondence with a wide circle with people of reforming inclinations, including Melanchthon and Erasmus—whose library he purchased. Temporarily exiled from Poland for his Calvinist inclinations, he was called back by some among the nobility who favored Calvinism. Besides gaining converts to Calvinism, Laski translated the Bible into Polish, and worked for a rapprochement between Calvinists and Lutherans—an effort that culminated in a consensus at the synod of Sendomir in 1570, ten years after Laski's death.

In general, the Polish government followed a policy of greater religious tolerance than most of Europe. As a result, a large number of people—mostly Jews and Christians of heterodox persuasions—sought refuge there. Among these was Faustus Socinius (1539–1604), whose uncle Laelius Socinius (1525–1562) had run afoul of several leaders in the Protestant Reformation for his anti-Trinitarian doctrines. Faustus Socinius embraced his uncle's teachings, denying the essential divinity of Jesus, and eventually sought refuge first in Transylvania and then (1579) in Poland, where he joined others who shared his convictions in denying the doctrine of the Trinity— hence the name of *Unitarians*. His views were expressed and defended in the *Racovian Catechism*, written by two of his followers and published in 1605. This document, greatly admired among Unitarians, affirms and argues that only the Father is God, that Jesus is not divine, but purely human, and that the Holy Spirit is just a way of referring to God's power and presence.

Throughout most of the sixteenth century, and well into the seventeenth, the Protestant faith as affirmed at the Synod of Sendomir had a growing number of followers—as did also Socinian Unitarianism. But as the national identity of Poland developed in contradistinction and opposition to Russian Orthodox to their east, and the German Lutherans to their west, and as both Russia and Germany repeatedly sought to occupy Polish territory, that identity became increasingly Roman Catholic, so that by the twentieth century Poland was one of the most Catholic nations in Europe.

The brief survey of these four nations at the edge of the Protestant Reformation should suffice to show that Protestantism made a significant impact, not only in those countries that became Protestant, but also in the rest of Europe. Furthermore, one may also conclude that this was also true for Eastern Orthodoxy, for—as we shall see in Chapter 30—in 1629 the patriarch of Constantinople, Cyril Lukaris, published a Protestant *Confession of Faith*, and early in the eighteenth century Feofan Prokopovic (1681–1736), Russian Orthodox archbishop of Novgorod, argued that the Russian Orthodoxy would profit from Protestant influences.

14

A Convulsed Age

A mighty fortress is our God,
A bulwark never failing;
Our helper He amidst the flood
Of mortal ills prevailing.

MARTIN LUTHER

The sixteenth century was a pivotal period in the entire history of Christianity. The turning points had been set in motion in the previous century, with the Fall of Constantinople to the Turks in 1453 and the "discovery" of America in 1492. Until that time, Christianity had been generally hemmed in by Muslims to the south and east—with the notable exception of Russian Christianity, which continued to expand eastward as the power of the czars also expanded—and by the Atlantic Ocean to the west. When Christians thought of the world-wide mission of the church, they thought almost exclusively in terms of the conversion of Muslims. And when they thought of challenges to the faith, this too they did in terms of the challenges of Islam. This world view seemed to be corroborated by the Fall of Constantinople and the advance of Turkish power, which seemed the greatest menace to the survival of Christianity itself.

Yet in the course of a century, things changed radically. Toward the east and south, the challenge of Islam was seemingly countered by the completion of the Spanish Reconquista in 1492, by the failure of the Turkish armies to take Vienna in 1529, and by the Battle of Lepanto in 1571, in which the joined navies of Spain, Venice, and the papal states, under the leadership of Don Juan de Austria, dealt a crushing defeat to the Turkish navy, which until then had been the dominant force in the eastern Mediterranean.

At the same time, the Atlantic ceased to be a barrier to the expansion of Western civilization, and of Christianity with it. Sailing westward, the Spanish conquered lands enormously larger than Spain itself, and in those lands established the Roman Catholic faith. Sailing south around Africa, the Portuguese established trading colonies and missions in the Far East. Islam, which once seemed the greatest barrier to Christian expansion, now saw its heartland hemmed in by the increasing economic and military might of Western powers. Eventually, many of the traditional Muslim lands in North Africa and in western Asia would become European colonies. When they finally gained their independence in the twentieth century, and particularly as oil revenues enriched them, some of these very lands would become centers of a militant and anti-Western Islamic reaction.

Meanwhile, in the lands far across the Atlantic, and in others in Sub-Saharan Africa and in the Far East, Christianity was establishing firm footholds, and centuries later these too would become centers of vitality and mission, precisely at a time when Christianity was losing ground in Western Europe.

As is usually the case, those who lived at the time did not fully comprehend the enormous consequences of the events they witnessed. Even after the voyages of Columbus, the pope felt confident that he could avoid conflicts between Spain and Portugal by decreeing that one should sail west and the other east—with the predictable but unexpected result that they would eventually collide in the Philippines. Luther continued to use the term "Turks" to refer to people who were neither Christian nor Jewish. Except in Spain and Portugal, the lands most affected—and enriched—by the colonial enterprise, few gave much thought to what Amerigo Vespuci declared to be a *New World*. Even in Spain, King Ferdinand, and his grandson Charles V, were more concerned with the politics of the Mediterranean than with the promises of the Atlantic.

But there were other momentous changes that the entire population of Europe did experience. In those very years of the sixteenth century when these vast geopolitical changes were taking place, the towering edifice of medieval Christianity collapsed. Salvaging what it could from the debacle, the Council of Trent set the tone for modern Catholicism, while several Protestant confessions arose amid the ruins. The ancient ideal of a single church, with the pope as its visible head, which had never been current in the East, now lost its power in the West as well. From that point on, Western Christianity was divided among various traditions that reflected great cultural and theological differences.

At the dawning of the sixteenth century, in spite of the corruption that prevailed in many quarters, and of the many voices clamoring for reformation, there was general agreement among Christians that the church was in essence one, and that its unity must be seen in its structure and hierarchy. Indeed, all the main figures of the Protestant Reformation began by holding such an understanding of the church, and very few came to the place where they completely rejected it. Most of the major Protestant leaders did believe that the unity of the church was essential to its nature, and that therefore, although it was temporarily necessary to break that unity in order to be faithful to the Word of God, that their very faithfulness demanded that all possible efforts be made to regain the lost unity.

The early sixteenth century also took for granted, as did the preceding Middle Ages, that the existence and survival of a state demanded religious agreement among its subjects. That notion, which Christians had rejected when they constituted a minority in the Roman Empire, became prevalent a few decades after the conversion of Constantine. All who lived in a Christian state must be Christian, and faithful children of the church. The only possible exceptions were Jews and, in some areas of Spain, Muslims. But such exceptions were seen as anomalies, and did not protect the followers of those religions from civil disenfranchisement and repeated persecution.

This view of national unity linked with religious uniformity was at the root of the many wars of religion that shook both the sixteenth and the seventeenth centuries. Eventually, in some areas sooner than in others, the conclusion was reached that religious agreement was not necessary for the security of the state, or that, although desirable, its price was too high. This happened, for instance, in France, where the Edict of Nantes recognized the failure of the previous policy requiring all the king's subjects to fit a single religious mold. In the Low Countries, for different political reasons, leaders such as William the Silent also denied the need for religious uniformity. Thus began a long process whose consequences would prove enormous, as one after another the various European states—even those that still had an official church—came to adopt policies of religious tolerance. This eventually led to the more modern idea of the lay state—that is, a state with no religious connections—that was decried by some churches and hailed by others. (We shall return to these developments later in our narrative.)

During the sixteenth century the church, traditionally symbolized by the ark, was tossed by violent storms.

The sixteenth century also witnessed the collapse of the ancient dream of political unity under the empire. The last emperor who, even in a limited way, could harbor such illusions was Charles V. After him, the so-called emperors were little more than kings of Germany and even there their power was limited.

Finally, the conciliarist hope for reformation was also shaken. For several decades, the Protestant reformers hoped that a universal council would prove them right and set the pope's house in order. But exactly the opposite took place. The papacy managed to achieve its own reformation without the help of a council and, by the time the Council of Trent finally assembled, it was clear that it would not be a truly international and ecumenical tribunal but rather a tool in the hands of the papacy.

Devout Christians, both Protestant and Catholic, whose lot it was to live in the sixteenth century saw many of the old certainties crumble around them. Even the discoveries and conquests that were taking place in the New World, Africa, and Asia posed questions that could not be answered within the old parameters. The medieval foundations—the papacy, the empire, tradition—were no longer solid. As Galileo affirmed, the earth itself was not a fixed point of reference. Social and political commotions were frequent. The ancient feudal system was making way for the early stages of capitalism.

Such was the time of Luther, Erasmus, Calvin, Knox, Loyola, Menno Simons, and the other great reformers. But in the midst of what could have appeared chaotic, these reformers stood firm on their faith in the power of the Word of God. That Word, which had created the world out of nothing, was certainly capable of producing the reformation the entire church needed, and to which the Protestant movement remained a preamble. Luther and Calvin, for instance, always insisted that the power of the Word was such that, as long as the Roman Catholic Church continued reading it, and even though the pope and his advisors might refuse to listen to it, there was always in the Roman communion a "vestige of the church," and they therefore awaited the day when the ancient church would once again hearken to the Word, and reforms such as they advocated would take place.

Thus, two cataclysmic events dominated the history of Christianity in the sixteenth century: the Reformation and the colonization of vast new lands—the latter aided by the temporary lull in the perceived threat of Islam at Christendom's Eastern borders. Most church historians have paid more attention to the first of these than to the second. But the truth is that to this day it is impossible to tell which of these two will ultimately have had a greater impact on the future history of Christianity.

Suggested Readings

Paul Althaus. *The Theology of Martin Luther*. Philadelphia: Fortress, 1966.

Paul Ayris and David Selwyn. *Thomas Cranmer: Churchman and Scholar*. Woodbridge [UK]: Boydell Press, 1999.

Roland H. Bainton. *Here I Stand: A Life of Martin Luther*. Nashville: Abingdon, 1950.

Ernest Belfort Bax. *Rise and Fall of the Anabaptists*. New York: American Scholar Publications, 1966.

Gordon Donaldson. *The Scottish Reformation*. Cambridge: University Press, 1960.

Justo L. González. *A History of Christian Thought*. Vol. 3. Nashville: Abingdon, 1975.

P. E. Hughes. *Theology of the English Reformers*. London: Hodder & Stoughton, 1965.

Franklin H. Littell. *The Free Church*. Boston: Starr King, 1957.

Geddes Macgregor. *The Thundering Scot: A Portrait of John Knox*. London: Macmillan & Co., 1958.

Clyde L. Manschreck. *Melanchthon: The Quiet Reformer*. Nashville: Abingdon, 1958.

Martin Marty. *Martin Luther*. New York: Penguin Books, 2004.

John C. Olin. *The Catholic Reformation: Savonarola to Ignatius Loyola*. New York: Harper & Row, 1969.

H. J. Selderhuis, ed. *The Calvin Handbook*. Grand Rapids: Wm. B. Eerdmans. 2009.

W. Peter Stephens. *Zwingli: An Introduction to His Thought*. Oxford [UK]: Clarendon Press, 1994.

George Stroup. *Calvin*. Nashville: Abingdon, 2009.

Thomas Worcester, ed. *The Cambridge Companion to the Jesuits*. Cambridge [UK]: Cambridge University Press, 2008.

A. D. Wright. *The Counter-Reformation: Catholic Europe and the Non-Christian World*. Burlington, VT: Ashgate, 2005.

PART II

ORTHODOXY, RATIONALISM, AND PIETISM

CHRONOLOGY

Popes	Emperors	Spain	France	England	Events
Clement VIII (1592–1605)	Rudolf II (1576–1612)	Philip III (1598–1621)	Henry IV (1589–1610)	Elizabeth I (1558–1603)	
				James I (1603–1625)	Gunpowder plot (1605)
Leo XI (1605)					
Paul V (1605–1621)					Founding of Jamestown (1607)
					Evangelical Union in Germany (1608)
					Catholic League in Germany (1609)
			Louis XIII (1610–1643)		
	Matthias (1612–1619)				
					Synod of Dort (1618–1619)
					Thirty Years' War (1618–1648)

Mayflower pilgrims (1620)

Ferdinand II (1619–1637)

Gregory XV (1621–1623)
Urban VIII (1623–1644)

Philip IV (1621–1665)

Richelieu's government (1624–1642)

Charles I (1625–1649)

Siege of La Rochelle (1627–1628)
Treaty of Lübeck (1629)
Puritan migration to New World (1630–1642)
†Gustavus Adolphus (1632)
Founding of Providence (1636)
Descartes's *Discourse in Method* (1637)

Ferdinand III (1637–1657)

Anne Hutchinson in Rhode Island (1638)
Long Parliament (1640)
Civil War in England (1642)

Louis XIV (1643–1715)

Innocent X (1644–1655)

Charles I prisoner of Parliament (1647)
Treaty of Westphalia (1648)
Charles I beheaded (1649)

Interregnum (1649–1660)

Cromwell's Protectorate (1653–1658)

Alexander VII (1655–1667)

Quakers persecuted in Massachusetts (1656)

Leopold I (1658–1705)

Charles II (1660–1685)

Popes	Emperors	Spain	France	England	Events
		Charles II (1665–1700)			British take New Amsterdam (1664)
Clement IX (1667–1669)					
Clement X (1670–1676)					
Innocent XI (1676–1689)					King Philip's War (1675–1676)
					Spener's *Pia Desideria* (1675)
					Bunyan's *Pilgrim's Progress* (1678)
					Founding of Pennsylvania (1681)
				James II (1685–1688)	Revocation of Edict of Nantes (1685)
Alexander VIII (1689–1691)				William III	Tolerance in England (1689)
				(1689–1702)	Locke's *Essay* (1690)
Innocent XII (1691–1700)				and Mary II	†George Fox (1691)
				(1689–1694)	
Clement XI (1700–1721)		Philip V (1700–1746)			
				Anne (1702–1714)	
	Joseph I (1705–1711)				
	Charles VI (1711–1740)		Louis XV (1715–1774)	George I (1714–1727)	
Innocent XIII (1721–1724)					
Benedict XIII (1724–1730)					
				George II (1727–1760)	†Francke (1727)
Clement XII (1730–1740)					Founding of Georgia (1733)

Events

Wesley in Georgia (1736)
Wesley's Aldersgate experience (1738)

†Zinzendorf (1760)

Captain Cook's voyages (1768–1779)

†Swedenborg (1772)

War of Independence, USA (1775–1783)
†Voltaire (1778)
Kant's *Critique of Pure Reason* (1781)
Methodist Episcopal Church, USA (1784)
Tolerance in France (1787)

Taking of the Bastille (1789)

Louis XVI executed (1792)

England

George III (1760–1820)

France

Louis XVI (1774–1792)

Republic

Spain

Ferdinand VI (1746–1759)

Charles III (1759–1788)

Charles IV (1788–1808)

Empire

Charles VII (1742–1745)
Francis I (1745–1765)

Joseph II (1765–1790)

Leopold II (1790–1792)
Francis II (1792–1806)

Popes

Benedict XIV (1740–1758)

Clement XIII (1758–1769)

Clement XIV (1769–1774)

Pius VI (1775–1799)

15

An Age of Dogma and Doubt

Our most holy religion is founded on Faith, not on reason; and it
is a sure method of exposing it to put it to such a trial as it is, by no
means, fitted to endure.

DAVID HUME

The sixteenth century had been a period of enormous religious vitality which swept up Protestants and Catholics, theologians and rulers, the high and the low. On either side of the religious struggles of the time, there were those who were convinced that their purpose was religious. Charles V on the Catholic side, and Frederick the Wise on the Protestant, knew of no higher interest than the cause of God's truth as they saw it, and subordinated their political and personal ambitions to that cause. Luther and Loyola lived through years of intense anguish before reaching the conclusions and establishing the attitudes for which they are famous. Their actions, and those of their immediate followers, bore the stamp of those profound religious experiences. Even Henry VIII, whose character few would praise, seems to have convinced himself that his actions in matters of religion were guided by a sincere attempt to serve God. Therefore, the bitter words and even violent actions with which Christians of one persuasion attacked those of another were partly due to the strength of their convictions, and to the overwhelming experiences that formed the basis of their confessions of faith.

But, as years went by, there was an increasing number who did not share the enthusiasm—and often not even the convictions—of earlier generations. Eventually, even some who were involved in wars of religion gave signs that political and personal considerations were paramount. Typical was the case of Henry IV of France, who repeatedly changed his religion in order to save his life or to achieve his political goals. When he finally attained the throne, his policy of limited religious tolerance was one of the pillars on which he built modern France.

During the seventeenth and eighteenth centuries, many followed Henry's example. The Thirty Years' War, to which we shall turn in the next chapter, had consequences in Germany similar to those of the earlier wars of religion in France. More and more, German princes and their ministers made use of religion in order to further their political programs. This hindered the political unity of Germany at a time when nationalist sentiment was on the rise, and therefore many Germans came to the conclusion that doctrinal disagreements should not lead to war, and that religious tolerance was a wiser policy.

Partially as a result of all this, and partially as a result of new scientific discoveries, rationalism took hold of Europe. Why be concerned about details of Christian doctrine that produce nothing but quarrels and prejudice, if natural reason, a faculty common to all human beings, can answer the fundamental questions regarding God and human nature? Would it not be much more profitable to construct a "natural religion" on that basis, and to leave to the credulous and fanatical, all that can only claim revealed authority? Hence, the seventeenth and eighteenth centuries were characterized by doubts regarding the traditional dogmas of both Protestantism and Roman Catholicism.

On the other hand, there were others whose zeal for true doctrine was no less than Luther's, Calvin's, or Loyola's. But this was no longer the time of great theological discoveries, leading up unknown paths. Theologians in the seventeenth and eighteenth centuries zealously defended the teachings of the great figures of the sixteen, but without the fresh creativity of that earlier generation. Their style became increasingly rigid, cold, and academic. Their goal was no longer to be entirely open to the Word of God but rather to uphold and clarify what others had said before them. Dogma was often substituted for faith, and orthodoxy for love. Reformed, Lutheran, and Catholic alike developed orthodoxies to which one had to either adhere strictly or be counted out of the fold of the faithful.

Not all, however, were content with such orthodoxies. The rationalist option has already been mentioned. Others whose beliefs were not accepted in their native country migrated to new lands. Some sought an alternative by emphasizing the spiritual dimension of the gospel, sometimes ignoring or even denying its relation to physical and political realities. Still others—

Of Enuie.

{ Where Gods word preached is in place : vnto the people willingly :
Woe be to them that would deface : for if such ceafe, the Stones will crie.

¶The fignification.

*H*E which preacheth in the pulpit, fignifieth godly zeale, &
a furtherer of the gofpel : and the two which are plucking
him out of his place, are the enemies of Gods word, threat-
ning by fire to cófume the profeffors of the fame : and that
company which fitteth ftill, are *Nullifidians*, fuch as are of no
religion, not regarding any doctrine, fo they may bee quiet
to liue after their owne willes and mindes.

*In this Puritan drawing, a preacher
is being pulled from the pulpit by two
"enemies of God's word."*

the Methodists in England, and the Pietists on the Continent—organized groups of believers who, while not severing their ties with the established churches, sought to cultivate a more intense and personal faith and piety.

From all this follows the outline of this portion of our narrative. We shall deal first with the great religious wars that took place in Germany (Chapter 16), France (Chapter 17), and England (Chapter 18). We shall then turn to the development of orthodoxy within Roman Catholicism (Chapter 19), Lutheranism (Chapter 20), and the Reformed or Calvinist tradition (Chapter 21). Chapter 22 will deal with rationalism. In Chapter 23 we shall look at those who sought refuge in a spiritualist interpretation of the gospel. German Pietism and English Methodism will be the subject of Chapter 24. And, at the end of this section, in Chapter 25, we shall look at those who decided to seek an alternative in the new colonies beyond the Atlantic.

16

The Thirty Years' War

Where, alas, shall we have the liberty to appear before the Lord in His own house, without our lives being thereby endangered?

A PROTESTANT PREACHER IN 1638

The Peace of Augsburg, which put an end to religious wars in Germany in the sixteenth century, could not last. It stipulated that princes or rulers, both Catholic and Protestant, would be free to determine the religion of their territories, and their subjects who wished to do so could migrate to lands where the official religion coincided with their own. This agreement, however, included no Protestants but those who subscribed to the Confession of Augsburg; and therefore all others, including Calvinists, were still considered heretics and subject to persecution. Since the freedom to choose their religion was granted only to rulers, many of their subjects were restless and unhappy. Finally, the Peace of Augsburg included the "ecclesiastical reservation," which guaranteed that territories ruled by bishops would remain Catholic even if their bishops became Protestant. For all these reasons, the peace achieved at Augsburg was at best an armistice that would hold only as long as each side felt unable to take military action against the other.

THE STORM GATHERS

Rudolf II, who had become emperor in 1576, was not trusted by Protestants, for he had been educated in Spain under the Jesuits, and it was said that they still determined many of his policies. He was able to reign in relative peace for thirty years, for he was a weak ruler whose policies favoring of Catholicism were often ignored. Then, in 1606, there were riots in the imperial city of Donauwörth. This city, on the border of staunchly Catholic Bavaria, had opted for Protestantism and, by 1606, the only Catholic nucleus remaining in it was a monastery where residents were allowed the free exercise of their religion but only within the monastery itself. But now the monks, perhaps encouraged by the emperor's favor, went out in procession, and the people went at them with clubs and stones, forcing them to withdraw to the monastery. Such incidents were not uncommon at the time, and usually ended with a word of admonition to both sides. In this case, however, more drastic action was taken. More than a year after the event, Duke Maximilian of Bavaria, who felt called to stamp out Protestantism, appeared at Donauwörth with a substantial army and set about forcing the conversion of the citizens to Catholicism.

The reaction was not slow in coming. Early in 1608, Protestants banded together in an Evangelical Union. A year later, their opponents organized the Catholic League. The Union, however, did not include all Protestants; therefore, if war were to break out, it was clear that the Catholic League would have little trouble crushing the Evangelical Union.

Meanwhile, in nearby Bohemia, events were also leading to a confrontation. This was the land of the ancient Hussites, who had aligned themselves with Reformed Protestantism, and to whom were now added large numbers of German Calvinist immigrants which made the majority of the population heretical in Catholic eyes. Rebellion threatened, and Rudolf's bungling forced him to abdicate. His brother and successor, Matthias, fared no better. His cousin Ferdinand, whom he appointed king of Bohemia, was a staunch Catholic who soon won the distrust of his subjects. When the Royal Council in Prague refused to listen to their objections to the king's policies, the Bohemian Protestants revolted and threw two of the king's advisors out the window—who were not badly hurt because they fell onto a pile of garbage. This episode, known as the Defenestration of Prague, sparked the Thirty Years' War, probably the bloodiest and most devastating European war prior to the twentieth century.

THE COURSE OF THE WAR

The Bohemians then called upon Frederick, elector of the Palatinate, to be their king. The Palatinate, although separated from Bohemia by Catholic Bavaria and other territories, was mostly Reformed, and therefore seemed a natural ally to the Bohemians. Rebellion soon spread east of Bohemia to the neighboring provinces of Silesia and Moravia. Meanwhile, Matthias had died, and his cousin, now Emperor Ferdinand II, called on Maximilian of

The Defenestration of Prague marked the beginning of the Thirty Years' War.

Bavaria and the Catholic League to invade Bohemia. This they did, and dealt the rebels such a crushing blow that they were forced to surrender. Frederick was deposed from both the throne of Bohemia and his hereditary lands in the Palatinate. Bohemia was restored to the same King Ferdinand whom the rebels had repudiated, and Maximilian received the Palatinate as a reward for his services. In both areas Protestants found themselves under persecution. Several of their leaders were executed, and those with property suffered its confiscation. In Bohemia, it was decreed that by Easter of 1626 any who were not ready to become Catholic must leave the country. These and similar measures caused such devastation that, over the thirty years the war lasted, the population of Bohemia declined by an estimated four-fifths.

The successes of Maximilian caused grave consternation among Protestant powers. To this were added dynastic considerations, for the house of Hapsburg—which ruled in Spain and had also held the imperial dignity since the time of Charles V—was feared by other ruling houses. Therefore, late in 1625, England, the Netherlands, and Denmark joined in a Protestant

League that proposed to invade Germany and restore Frederick—who was a son-in-law of James I of England—to his lands in the Palatinate. They also had the support of several German Protestant princes, and even of a few Catholics who feared the growing power of the Hapsburgs. Meanwhile, Ferdinand II, not content to trust his empire to the sole defense of Maximilian and the Catholic League, resolved to raise his own army, which he placed under the command of Albert of Wallenstein. Therefore, when Christian IV of Denmark invaded Germany, he had to contend with two armies, Maximilian's and Wallenstein's. Marches and battles once again ravaged German soil, until Ferdinand II and Christian IV agreed to the Treaty of Lübeck. The Danes withdrew from Germany, having achieved nothing of great consequence besides bringing further suffering to a land already ravaged by war. Thousands of forced conversions to Catholicism followed.

Then help arrived from another quarter. In 1611, when he was only seventeen years of age, Gustavus Adolphus had inherited the Swedish throne. This was a poor inheritance, for the Danes then held much of Sweden, and the land was divided among several factions, none of which showed great respect for the crown. But the young king proved an able ruler who slowly reunited his subjects and expelled the Danish invaders. As his power grew, he increasingly turned his attention to the threat of Hapsburgs attempting to gain possession of Swedish lands on the Baltic Sea. Since Gustavus Adolphus was also a staunch Lutheran who bewailed the events that were taking place in Bohemia and Germany, he felt compelled to intervene with the double purpose of defending the Protestants and defeating the ambitions of the Hapsburgs.

Ferdinand II had disbanded Wallenstein's army, whose leader he feared, and he based his power on the support of the Catholic League. In 1630, when Gustavus Adolphus invaded Germany, the army facing Ferdinand II in the name of the emperor in truth belonged to the Catholic League. At first the Swedes found little support among German Protestants, who feared the emperor's wrath and in any case did not trust the Swedish invader. But Gustavus Adolphus was a very able general whose repeated victories soon became legendary. His soldiers, in contrast to all the armies that had marched in this protracted war, treated the native population with kindness and respect. While the Swedes were clearly Protestant, they did not force the conversion of Catholics in the areas they conquered. Repeatedly, Gustavus Adolphus made it clear that he did not seek to dismember Germany for

Wallenstein, accused by his enemies of being overly ambitious, was one of the ablest generals of his time.

Swedish profit. When France offered him financial support in his campaign against the Hapsburgs, he accepted it on the condition that it be understood that not a single village in German territory would become French. Eventually, several powerful German Protestant princes came to his support. The Catholic League besieged Magdeburg, hoping that the Swedes would rush to its rescue and fall into the trap that had been laid for them. But Gustavus Adolphus saw through their plans, and continued his campaign as he had outlined it. The League then took Magdeburg, whose citizens they massacred, and then marched on to do battle with the Swedes. In the fields near Leipzig, the League was roundly defeated, and Gustavus Adolphus sent some of his German allies to invade Bohemia while he marched into southern Germany and threatened Bavaria, the very heart of the Catholic League.

By then several Catholic leaders were suing for peace, and many were willing to agree to the terms imposed by the Swedish king: religious tolerance for both Catholics and Protestants, the restoration of its ancient rights to the kingdom of Bohemia, the return of the Palatinate to Frederick, and the expulsion of the Jesuits from the empire.

Since the Catholic League had failed him, Ferdinand II once again called on Wallenstein, who came to his succor only after having been promised vast rewards. Wallenstein attacked the Protestants who had taken Prague, and forced them to withdraw. Then he joined the remnants of the Catholic League's army, and marched to do battle with the Swedes. They met on the fields of Lützen, where Wallenstein's army was crushed, but Gustavus Adolphus was killed.

The war then degenerated into skirmishes, banditry, and protracted negotiations. The Swedish government was ready for peace; but for their officers and troops, who had spent years in the field, war had become a way of life. Wallenstein secretly negotiated with the Swedish, the French, and the German Protestants. The emperor received word of this, and Wallenstein and several of his officers were murdered, although it is not certain that this was done by Ferdinand's direct order. The Spanish Hapsburgs sent an army to support their cousins in Germany. The French then became bolder in their support of the Protestants, even though France was then ruled by a cardinal of the Roman Catholic Church. Meanwhile, it was the people who suffered in this war the religious motivations of which were by then nearly forgotten, and which had become little more than an excuse for a power struggle.

THE PEACE OF WESTPHALIA

Eventually, even the most bloodthirsty tired of war and destruction. Ferdinand II had died in 1637, and his son and successor Ferdinand III, although a sincere Catholic, did not share his father's intolerance. Germans bemoaned seeing their land invaded by foreign troops in support of both sides. Sweden was ready to withdraw its army. France knew that the time had come when the greatest concessions could be obtained. Therefore, after long and complicated negotiations, the Peace of Westphalia, signed in 1648, put an end to the conflict that came to be known as the Thirty Years' War.

France and Sweden profited the most from the war, for the former expanded its borders to the Rhine, while the latter received vast lands on the Baltic and the North Sea. Since both France and Sweden wished it, German

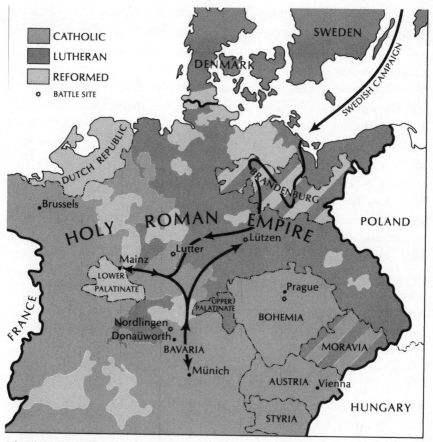

The Thirty Years' War

princes were given greater powers, to the detriment of imperial authority. In religious matters, it was agreed that all—princes as well as their subjects—would be free to follow their own religion, as long as they were Catholics, Lutherans, or Reformed. (Once again, Anabaptists, whom many considered subversive, were excluded.) Buildings and institutions were to revert to the ownership of the religious confessions that had held them in the year 1624. And a general amnesty was granted to all who during the war had rebelled against their masters—except in the hereditary possessions of the Hapsburgs.

These were the immediate results of that long and cruel war. But there were other consequences that, although not mentioned in the peace agreement, were no less significant. The principles of tolerance of the Peace of Westphalia were not born out of a deeper understanding of Christian love, but rather out of a growing indifference to religion accompanied by the feeling, even among those of deep religious commitments, that such commitments should remain private, and not be carried into civil and political life. The war had amply shown the atrocities that resulted from attempting to settle religious matters by force of arms. In the end, nothing had been resolved. Perhaps rulers should not allow their decisions to be guided by religious or confessional considerations, but rather by their own self-interest, or by the interests of their subjects. Thus, the modern secular state began to develop, as did doubt regarding matters that previous generations had taken for granted. On what grounds did theologians dare to affirm that they were correct, and that others were mistaken? Could any doctrine be true that produced the atrocities of the Thirty Years' War? Was there not a more tolerant, more profound, and even more Christian way to serve God than simply following the dictates of orthodoxy, be it Catholic or Protestant? These were some of the questions posed by the seventeenth and eighteenth centuries, partly as a result of the Thirty Years' War and other similar events.

17

The Church of the Desert

A spirit of sanctification, of power . . . and above all of martyrdom,
while teaching us to die each day in our inner being . . . also prepares
and disposes us to offer our lives with courage in the torture chamber
and on the gallows, if Divine Providence calls us to it.

ANTOINE COURT

The assassination of Henry IV by the fanatical Ravaillac, on May 14,
1610, caused great misgivings among French Protestants. Although
Henry had declared himself a Catholic for reasons of political convenience,
he had proven a faithful friend to his former companions of religion and
arms, whose freedom and lives he protected by the Edict of Nantes. They
knew that many of their former enemies deplored the peace and tolerance
that the deceased king had brought about, and would now seek to undo
his policies. Since the new king, Louis XIII, was only eight years old, the
government was in the hands of the king's mother, Marie de Medici—the
second wife of Henry IV—who felt the need to allay mistrust by confirming
the Edict of Nantes. On the basis of that action, the following general assembly of the French Huguenots swore fidelity to the new king.

But Marie gathered around herself a coterie of Italian advisors who understood neither the conditions in France, nor the pain and blood that had
been the price for the existing state of affairs. They followed a policy of close
collaboration with the Hapsburgs, and particularly with the Spanish branch
of that house, which was known for its uncompromising Catholicism and its
hatred of Protestantism. The young king was married to the Spanish princess Anne of Austria, and his sister, Isabella, to the future Philip IV of Spain.
This provoked several Huguenot uprisings that achieved no more than the
death of their leaders and the loss of a number of Protestant strongholds.

Although he was a cardinal of the Roman Church, Richelieu did not allow religious considerations to affect his policies and was quite ready to support Protestantism in his enemies' lands, if only to embarrass them.

Toward 1622, while Marie de Medici was losing her power, Cardinal Armand de Richelieu was a rising star in the French court. Within two years, he had become the king's most trusted advisor. He was a wily politician whose main goals were the aggrandizement of the French crown and of his own personal power. Although he was a cardinal of the Church of Rome, his religious policy was not based on theological or confessional considerations, but rather on calculations of convenience. Thus, since he was convinced that the main enemies of the French Bourbons were the Hapsburgs, his interventions in the Thirty Years' War—consisting mostly of undercover financial support—were in favor of the Protestants and against the Catholic emperor. The same political considerations, however, led Richelieu to an entirely different religious policy in France. He had no qualms about dividing Germany by supporting the Protestant party against the emperor. But in France the Huguenot party must be destroyed, for it was a cyst within the state. Again, what most concerned Richelieu was not that the Huguenots were Protestant heretics, but rather that Henry IV, in order to guarantee their security, had granted them several fortified cities, and these allowed the Huguenots to declare themselves faithful servants of the crown while retaining the ability to rebel and resist if their rights were violated. Richelieu's centralizing policies could not tolerate the existence of such independent power within the French state.

Richelieu's efforts to dissolve the Protestant cyst led to armed action in the Siege of La Rochelle, the main Huguenot stronghold. The siege lasted a year, during which the defenders courageously resisted the pick of the French army. When the city finally surrendered, of its twenty-five thousand inhabitants there remained only fifteen hundred famished and feeble survivors. The fortifications of the city were razed and Catholic mass was celebrated in all its churches. On hearing of this, several other Protestant cities took up arms against the king. But none of them was able to offer as staunch a defense as had La Rochelle, and in many of them the king's troops followed a policy of extermination.

However, what caused Richelieu grave concern was not the existence of Protestants in France, nor the continuation of their life of worship, but simply the political power they enjoyed. Therefore, once their fortified cities were taken in 1629, he issued an edict of toleration for Protestants, in both religious and civil matters. Without their military strongholds, the Huguenots were no longer a threat to the crown, and Richelieu had no intention of bleeding the country and weakening its economy in a protracted civil war. Having dealt with Protestant political and military power, the cardinal turned his attention to undoing the Hapsburgs; thus, during the last years of Richelieu's government, the Huguenots enjoyed relative peace.

Richelieu's death, in 1642, was followed by that of the king the following year. The new king, Louis XIV, was then five years old, and his mother and regent, Anne of Austria, entrusted affairs of state to Cardinal Jules Mazarin, a former collaborator of Richelieu who continued the policies of his predecessor. For several decades after the fall of La Rochelle and the other Protestant cities, French Protestants enjoyed religious tolerance. Although Mazarin's government was marked by repeated conspiracies and rebellions, Protestants were generally not involved in them, and their numbers grew among all social classes. In the countryside there were many Protestants, both among peasants and among rural nobility. And in the cities Huguenot intellectuals were accepted into the most distinguished salons.

Louis XIV was twenty-three years old when Mazarin died, and he refused to name a successor to the cardinal. The king, who came to be called "the Sun King," would allow no one to overshadow him. For that reason he also clashed with the pope, who sought to intervene in French affairs. Against the centralizing efforts of the papacy of his time, Louis proclaimed and defended the "liberties of the Gallican church"—to which we shall return in

Mazarin, Richelieu's successor, changed very few of the policies followed
by the great cardinal.

chapter 19. But, for exactly the same reasons, he had no patience with heretics or dissidents of any sort, and therefore took strong measures to stamp
out French Protestantism.

The king's measures to achieve the *reunion*—as conversion to Catholicism was called—of Protestants were diverse, and grew sterner with the
passage of time. First there were attempts of persuasion and mild pressure.
Then the king practically offered to buy conversions. The argument was that
Protestant pastors who became Catholic lost their livelihood, and that those
from among the laity who did likewise lost their clients or other means of
support. Therefore, as a means of balancing such losses, money was offered
to any who would convert. But that policy was not successful, and then the
king had to resort to more severe measures. When, in 1684, France enjoyed
a brief respite from the constant wars in which the Sun King involved the
nation, the army was used to force the "reunion" of French Protestants. This
policy of violence enjoyed great success, for in some areas tens of thousands
were forcibly converted to Catholicism.

Finally, in 1685, the king issued the Edict of Fontainebleau, abolishing the provisions of the Edict of Nantes, and making it illegal to be a Protestant in France. A mass exodus immediately ensued, for French Huguenots fled to Switzerland, Germany, England, the Netherlands, and North America. Since many of these refugees were artisans and merchants, their departure represented a great economic loss to France—to the point, that it has been suggested, that the economic disruption caused by the Edict of Fontainebleau was one of the causes leading to the French Revolution.

Officially, there were no more Protestants in France after the Edict of Fontainebleau. In truth, however, many who had been outwardly converted held fast to their previous beliefs, and managed to continue gathering for the celebration of Protestant worship. For many of them, such gatherings were made all the more necessary inasmuch as they bore a heavy burden on their conscience for having denied their faith. Lacking church buildings, they turned to the open fields, or to clearings in the woods. In such places, under cover of night, and all over the country, tens and even hundreds of believers came together periodically to listen to the Word, confess their sins, and break bread. The secret of such gatherings was zealously guarded, and seldom were the agents of the government able to discover the appointed time and place. When they did gain intelligence on such meetings, they waited until all had arrived, and then fell upon the worshipers and arrested them. The men were sent off to row in the galleys, and the women were imprisoned for the rest of their days. Pastors were executed, and children were placed in foster families to be reared as Catholics. In spite of this, the movement continued; and the king's agents were unable to stamp out the *Christians of the desert*, as the Huguenots now called themselves.

As often happens in such cases, the movement then developed a radical and visionary wing, claiming that the end of the world was at hand. From his exile in Rotterdam, Pastor Pierre Jurieu published a study of the book of Revelation in which he showed that its prophecies were being fulfilled, and that the final victory would take place in 1689. Encouraged by such announcements, some of the Protestants in France became more audacious, and as a result many were killed or condemned to the galleys. But prophetic visions and mystical experiences abounded, and increasing numbers were willing to die for a cause about to be vindicated by God. Some heard voices. Others spoke while in trance. All this made it easier for the authorities to find the recalcitrant Protestants, who were then cruelly tortured. But very few were made to utter the fateful words, "I reunite"—that is, I return to the Catholic Church.

Then this prophetic spirit turned to armed rebellion. This was no longer led by Protestant nobles, as in the earlier wars of religion. The new army "of the desert" was formed mostly by peasants. These peasants still plowed, sowed, and harvested, but during the rest of the time they gathered in armed bands that attacked royal troops. Before marching out they read Scripture, and in the field of battle they sang psalms. Although these rebels never numbered more than a few hundred, they kept an army of twenty-five thousand men fully occupied. For reasons not altogether clear, the rebels came to be known as *camisards*. Since conventional warfare was unable to put the rebels down, the army followed a policy of razing the areas where the camisards operated. About five hundred villages and hamlets were thus destroyed. But this only served to engross the ranks of the rebels, now reinforced by many who had been left homeless. This struggle continued for many years. By making promises that were not kept, the king's officials were able to stop the rebellion in some areas. But resistance continued until 1709, when the last camisard leaders were captured and executed. By then, their resistance had become legendary in Protestant countries, although no one had given the camisards any significant aid. In 1710, the English finally decided to support them. But by then it was too late, for the last sparks of rebellion had been snuffed out.

Meanwhile, a different group had come to the foreground among French Protestants. These other leaders did not trust apocalyptic visions—which, in any case, had failed to come true—and advocated a return to the Reformed tradition, with worship centered on the clear and careful exposition of Scripture. The outstanding leader of this group was Antoine Court, who in 1715 organized the first synod of the French Reformed Church. Following Calvin and Beza's teachings, Court advised his followers that civil authorities should be obeyed in all matters, except when they demanded something that was contrary to the Word of God, and this became the official policy of the newly organized church. Ten days after the meeting of that first synod, Louis XIV died, and was succeeded by his five-year-old great-grandson Louis XV. But the death of the Sun King brought no respite to the persecuted Huguenots, for the new government, under the regency of Philippe d'Orleans, continued the religious policies of the previous reign. In spite of this, Court and his followers persisted on the course they had set for themselves. When one of his pastors was imprisoned, Court ordered his followers to refrain from violence as a means to save the man from death. In 1726, a seminary in exile was founded in Lausanne, Switzerland. French candidates for the ministry attended it before returning to their own country, and thus the French Reformed Church began developing a cadre of preachers who were well-versed in Scripture and theology. In 1729, Court himself moved to Lausanne, where he became the mentor to an entire generation of clandestine preachers. Although now living in exile, Court visited France repeatedly, encouraging and directing the affairs of the Reformed Church. By the time of his death in 1767, at eighty-three years of age, Reformed Protestantism was firmly rooted in France. But persecution continued until 1787, when the grandson and successor of Louis XV, Louis XVI, finally decreed religious tolerance. During that long period of persecution, thousands of men had been sent to the galleys, and a like number of women had been condemned to life-imprisonment, while only a handful had uttered the words, "I reunite." Two pastors had denied their faith, but countless others had died for their unwillingness to recant. The "church of the desert" had survived.

That struggle, like the Thirty Years' War in Germany, produced in many people a profound distrust of dogma and dogmatism. Among them was Voltaire, who defended the Protestant cause, not because he felt any sympathy for it, but rather because he considered intolerance to be both absurd and immoral. During those years of persecution and resistance, of horror and glory, the minds were shaped that would later espouse the ideals of the French Revolution.

18

The Puritan Revolution

The civil magistrate may not assume to himself the administration
of the Word and Sacraments . . . yet he hath authority, and it is his
duty to take order, that unity and peace be preserved in the Church,
that the truth of God be kept pure and entire, that all blasphemies
and heresies be suppressed, all corruptions and abuses in worship and
discipline prevented or reformed, and all the ordinances of God duly
settled, administered, and observed.

WESTMINSTER CONFESSION

In discussing the Reformation in England, we have seen that Queen Elizabeth followed an intermediate course between those conservatives who
sought to retain as much as possible of ancient practice and belief, and the
Calvinist Protestants who believed that the entire life and structure of
the church ought to adjust to what they saw as the biblical norm. During
the queen's lifetime, that delicate balance was maintained; but the tensions
inherent in the situation surfaced repeatedly, and only the strong and decisive intervention of the queen and her ministers was able to restrain them.

JAMES I

When Elizabeth died in 1603 she left no direct heir, but declared her legitimate successor to be James, the son of Mary Stuart, who was already king
of Scotland. The transition took place without major difficulties, and thus
the house of Stuart came to reign over England. The new king—James I of
England, but James VI of Scotland—did not find the government of England an easy matter. The English always considered him a foreigner. His
plans for the union of the two kingdoms—which eventually came about—
won him enemies in both Scotland and England. Elizabeth's measures in

favor of trade were bearing fruit, and therefore the merchant class, which resented the king's policies in support of the nobility and his favorites, was becoming increasingly powerful. But James's greatest conflicts were with those Protestants who thought that the Reformation had not progressed sufficiently far enough in England, and that this was due to the policies of the sovereigns and their advisors. Since neighboring Scotland, from whence the new king had originated, had moved further along the road of reformation, English Calvinists felt that the time was ripe for similar changes in their own land.

These more radical Protestants were not organized in a single group, nor did they agree on all matters, and therefore it is difficult to describe them in general terms. They were given the name *Puritans* because they insisted on the need to *purify* the Church through a return to biblical religion. They opposed many of the traditional elements of worship that the Church of England had retained, such as the use of the cross, certain priestly garments, and the celebration of communion on an altar—whether there ought to be a table or an altar, and where this was to be placed, implied varying interpretations of the meaning of communion and led to long and bitter controversy. They also insisted on the need for a sober life, guided by the commandments of Scripture, and lacking in luxury and ostentation. Since a great deal of the worship of the Church of England appeared to them as needlessly elaborate, this caused further objection to that worship. Many insisted on the need to keep the Lord's Day, devoting it exclusively to religious exercises and to the practice of charity. They also rejected the *Book of Common Prayer* and the use of written prayers in general, declaring that such prayers led to insincerity, so that even the Lord's Prayer, rather than a set of words to be repeated, was to be used as a model for prayer. They were not absolutely opposed to the use of alcohol, for most of them drank moderately, but they were very critical of drunkenness, particularly among ministers of the Church of England. They were also very critical of all that they considered licentious—and this included the theater, not only because immorality was often depicted, but also because of the apparent duplicity implicit in acting.

Many Puritans were opposed to bishops. They argued that the episcopacy, at least as it existed in their time, was a later invention, not to be found in the Bible; and that the church ought to look to Scripture as its constitution not only in matters of doctrine, but also in things having to do with its organization and governance. The more moderate among the

Puritans simply declared that in the Bible one could find several forms of church government, and that therefore the episcopacy, although perhaps good and useful, was not a matter "of divine right." Others insisted that the New Testament church was ruled by "presbyters," that is, by elders, and that a truly biblical church ought to be so ruled. Still others affirmed that each congregation ought to be independent of all others, and were dubbed "Independents."

The Baptists arose mostly among these independents. One of their early leaders was John Smyth (1554–1612), an Anglican priest who decided that Anglicanism had not gone far enough in the process of reformation and established an independent—and therefore illegal—congregation. As this congregation grew, Smyth and his followers decided to flee to Amsterdam. There he continued his study of the Bible, and came to the point of refusing to use translations of the Bible in worship, for only the original text had absolute authority. At church, he would read Scripture in Hebrew or Greek, and translate the text as he preached. Partly through his study of Scripture, and partly through contact with the Mennonites—whose pacifism and refusal to take oaths he adopted—he eventually became convinced that infant baptism is not valid, and therefore proceeded first to baptize himself with a bucket and a ladle, by pouring water over his head, and then to baptize his followers—for which his critics dubbed him "the self-baptizer."

The flight of Smyth and his congregation to Amsterdam had been financed by a well-to-do lawyer, Thomas Helwys, who broke ranks with Smyth over the issues of absolute pacifism and the taking of oaths—which Helwys, as a lawyer, considered fundamental to social order. Helwys and his followers then returned to England, where in 1611 they founded the first Baptist Church in the land.

Eventually, there was disagreement among Baptists over matters similar to those that divided the strict Calvinists and the Arminians (see Chapter 21). Those who took the Arminian position came to be known as General Baptists, for they believed that salvation was generally available to all, in contrast to the "Particular Baptists," who held that only the predestined would be saved.

Meanwhile, the official church was following a parallel but opposite course. Elizabeth's balance had been achieved by establishing a church whose theology was moderately Calvinist, while retaining in its worship and governance all that did not clearly and directly contradict its new theology.

But this Elizabethan settlement was difficult to maintain. In order to defend traditional elements in worship, some began to abandon Calvinist theology. Among the leading theologians of the Church of England there was such appreciation for the beauty of worship as it was then practiced that there was little effort to make it conform to such outside requirements as theology or biblical exegesis. Soon Puritans began to fear that a vast movement was afoot to return to "Romanism."

All these elements were already present below the surface when James inherited Elizabeth's crown. From that point on, conflicts that had been latent for a long time would surface with increasing violence. The Puritans did not trust the new king, whose mother was none other than Mary Stuart. In truth, James did not favor the Catholics, who had hoped to gain major concessions from him, and were repeatedly disappointed. His ideal was an absolute monarchy such as existed in France. In Scotland, his Presbyterian subjects had not allowed him to reign with the freedom he wished—and was convinced kings deserved—and therefore in England he sought to strengthen the episcopacy as a means to increase his own power. As he is said to have declared, "Without bishops, there is no king"—in other words, the monarchical structure of the state was to be supported by the monarchical structure of the church.

James's personal character did little to increase his prestige. He was a homosexual at a time when there were great prejudices against homosexuality, and his favorites enjoyed unmerited privileges and power in his court and in his government. While insisting on his right to be an absolute monarch, he wavered between stubborn rigidity and weak flexibility. Although he managed his finances honestly, he was prodigal in spending for superfluous matters, and important projects were hindered for lack of funds. His liberality in granting titles and honors to his friends offended many who had served the crown for a lifetime with little or no reward.

James tried to follow a religious policy similar to that of Elizabeth. Only the Anabaptists were systematically persecuted, for their egalitarian ideas horrified the king. Catholics were seen as loyal to the pope, and therefore as potential traitors. But if the pope was willing to acknowledge James's right to the throne, and to condemn regicide—which some extreme Catholics proposed as a solution to England's religious troubles—the king was willing to tolerate Catholics in his kingdoms. Presbyterians, whom the king had come to hate in Scotland, were tolerated in England, and James even

James I of England, who was also James VI of Scotland, was convinced that the alliance between the crown and the episcopacy was absolutely necessary; he therefore abhorred the Presbyterian form of government advocated by many Puritans.

granted them some minor concessions. But the one thing that he would not abandon was the episcopal system of government, for he was convinced—and rightly so—that the bishops were among the most committed and useful supporters of the crown.

The tension between the prelates of the official church and the Puritans grew during James's reign. In 1604, Richard Bancroft, archbishop of Canterbury, had a series of canons approved in which it was affirmed that episcopal hierarchy was an institution of divine origin, and that without it there could be no true church. This implied a rejection of the many Protestant churches on the Continent that had no bishops, and therefore Puritans saw in it a step toward breaking Protestant ties in order to reintroduce Catholicism in England. Besides this, several other canons approved on the archbishop's insistence were clearly directed against Puritans.

Parliament was in session, for James had been compelled to call it in order to approve new taxes. The lower chamber, or House of Commons, included many Puritans who now joined with others in an appeal to the king against Bancroft's canons. James called a conference that gathered at Hampton Court, over which he presided. When one of the Puritans made passing reference to a "presbytery," the king declared that there could be no closer connection between the monarchy and a presbytery than that between God and the Devil. All attempts at conciliation failed, and the only result of that meeting was the new translation of the Bible that appeared in 1611, generally known as the King James Version. Since this was produced at the high point of the English language, it—as well as the *Book of Common Prayer*—became a classic that profoundly influenced later English literature.

That was the beginning of a growing enmity between the House of Commons and the more conservative of the bishops. The latter joined the king in affirming that bishops as well as kings rule by divine right. In 1606, a new series of canons, more clearly anti-Puritan, was approved by church authorities. Parliament responded by attacking, not the king or the archbishop, but the more vulnerable of their defenders. Eventually, during the next reign, this growing tension would lead to civil war.

Meanwhile, late in 1605, what was called the *Gunpowder Plot* was discovered. A repressive law against Catholics had been issued the previous year, on the pretext that they were loyal to the pope rather than to the king. It seems that its real purpose was to collect funds, for the authorities used it mostly to impose heavy fines and to confiscate property. In any case, some Catholics decided that it was necessary to be rid of the king. One of them rented a property whose underground storage extended below Parliament's meeting place. The plan was to fill several wine barrels with gunpowder, set them directly under the meeting room, and blow them up while the king was opening the next session of Parliament. This would kill both the king and the Puritans who now sat in Parliament. But the plot was discovered, and the main conspirators, as well as several whose participation in the plot was never proven, were executed. In some areas, Catholics were hunted down. James himself seems to have attempted to distinguish between the guilty and those who were simply Catholic. But he did take the opportunity to impose more fines and confiscations. Soon thousands of Catholics were in prison.

After the first years of his reign, James tried to rule without convening Parliament. But the authorization of that body was required in order to impose new taxes, and therefore, in 1614, when his financial situation was desperate, James decided to convoke a meeting of Parliament. When the new elections resulted in a House of Commons that was even more intractable than the previous one, James dissolved it and tried to manage with only those tariffs that he had the authority to impose. He was also compelled to borrow from the bishops and the nobility. Then the Thirty Years' War broke out. The deposed elector of the Palatine and King of Bohemia, Frederick, was James's son-in-law. But James did not offer him support, and many English Protestants began declaring that he was a coward and a traitor, while he retorted that he could not intervene in the war for lack of funds. Finally, in 1621, the king called Parliament once again, hoping that the Puritans in the House of Commons would agree to new taxes with the proviso that some of the additional revenue would go to support of German Protestants. But then it was learned that the king was planning to marry his son and heir to a Spanish princess. Such an alliance with the Hapsburgs was an abomination before the eyes of the Puritans in Parliament, who approved some minor taxes and then insisted on presenting their grievances before the king. The latter responded by dissolving the assembly and arresting several of its leaders. The marriage plans were then abandoned for other reasons, and in 1624 James once again called a meeting of Parliament, only to dissolve it anew without obtaining the funds he required. Shortly thereafter, the king died, and was succeeded by his son Charles.

CHARLES I

The new king was as convinced as his father had been of the need for a centralized and powerful monarchy, and therefore he too clashed with Parliament. The Puritans were suspicious of the king's intentions for, after the failed negotiations with Spain, Charles had married a sister of King Louis XIII of France. The negotiations leading to this marriage had included concessions to English Catholics, and it was also agreed that the new queen and her court would be free to continue their religious observances. Many Puritans saw in this a restoration of idolatry, and complained that apostasy had now entered the royal household. Soon some were comparing the queen with Jezebel, although still only in private circles.

Charles inherited his father's conflicts with Parliament, and these came to a head in the trial of Richard Montague, a proponent of the divine right of kings and an enemy of both Puritanism and the parliamentary system. He had published several books on these subjects, and finally, after the publication of one that was particularly offensive to Parliament, the House of Commons brought him to trial and condemned him to a fine and imprisonment. King Charles saved his supporter by making him his personal chaplain, and thus exempt from the authority of Parliament. Talk then began of retaliating by accusing the duke of Buckingham, a minister of the crown, of high treason. The king then dissolved the assembly, and resolved to reign without Parliament. This, however, was not possible, for the king needed funds that only Parliament could vote in. But the king was exasperated, and took ever harsher measures. When the archbishop of Canterbury sought to mediate the situation, the king practically deprived him of his powers, and transferred them to a commission presided over by William Laud, one of the most bitter opponents of Puritanism. Repeatedly, Charles convened Parliament, only to dissolve it when the House of Commons insisted on dealing with their grievances before voting on funding. Charles rewarded those among the Commons who supported him by making them lords, thus further depriving himself of what little support he had in the lower chamber. Even the lords began turning against the king, begrudging the honors granted to commoners who had done little more than support him in parliamentary debate. When, in 1629, Charles dissolved the third Parliament of his reign, he was resolved to rule by himself, and it was only eleven years later that he finally felt constrained to convene Parliament anew.

Those eleven years of personal rule brought prosperity to the higher classes. But the rise in prices was much more rapid than the rise in wages, and therefore the majority of the population felt economically oppressed while the powerful grew richer. In order to obtain the funds he required, Charles made ever greater concessions to the aristocracy, who in turn oppressed the poor. Although the king did show some interest in the plight of the poor and took some measures to improve their situation, the fact was that the social and political order caused more suffering than the king's weak measures could alleviate. Increasingly, and particularly in industrial areas, the king and the bishops, who gave his cause religious sanction, were seen as enemies of the people. The Puritans, who attacked the excesses of the crown and of the bishops and the luxury and idolatry of the "new Jezebel," were rapidly gaining popular support.

In 1633, William Laud was made archbishop of Canterbury. He was enamored with the beauty and stateliness of Anglican worship, and a firm believer in the need for religious uniformity for the good of the state. His measures against the Puritans were both harsh and cruel, including death warrants and orders of mutilation. Enthused by such zealous support, Charles gave Laud full powers in Scotland, on whose Presbyterian church the archbishop tried to impose the Anglican liturgy. This resulted in a riot that soon grew into a rebellion. When the General Assembly of the Church of Scotland tried to limit the power of bishops, the king's agents declared it dissolved. But the Assembly refused to obey the royal command, and responded by abolishing the episcopacy and reorganizing the Church of Scotland on a Presbyterian basis.

This made war inevitable. The king had neither a sufficiently large army nor the funds to keep one in the field, and turned for support to his Irish subjects, who had strong Catholic sentiments, hoping that the queen's Catholic faith would encourage them to come to his aid. This brought Scottish Calvinists and English Puritans closer together. In 1640, Charles called a meeting of Parliament hoping to obtain funds for his war against the Scottish rebels. But it soon became clear that many in the Commons had less sympathy for the king than for his enemies, and Charles dissolved the assembly—thereafter called the *Short Parliament*. Encouraged by this turn of events, the Scots invaded English territory, and the king's troops fled in disorder. Once again, Charles was forced to convene Parliament. Thus began the *Long Parliament*, which would be of great importance to the history of England.

THE LONG PARLIAMENT

The years immediately preceding the first meeting of the Long Parliament had been marred by economic difficulties. Social and economic upheavals, which until then had affected the poor and the proletariat almost exclusively, now began having a negative impact on the bourgeoisie. Therefore, the majority of those elected to the House of Commons of the new Parliament represented those who were discontent with the king's policies, if not for religious motives, then for others of an economic nature. Since many of the nobility had joined the bourgeoisie by investing in mercantile enterprises, many in the House of Lords were willing to join the Commons in limiting the king's power. Thus, the new Parliament proved even more intractable than the previous one. The king had convened it so that it could vote the necessary funds for raising an army and expelling the Scottish rebels from English territory. But the members of Parliament knew that their power resided precisely in the threat of the rebels, and were therefore in no hurry to deal with that issue. First, they adopted a series of measures against those who, in recent years, had sought to destroy Puritanism. Those of Archbishop Laud's victims who were still alive were set free, and an indemnization was paid for their suffering. Lord Strafford, one of the king's

Charles I continued his father's policies and eventually lost both his throne and his life.

most loyal ministers, was brought to trial before Parliament and condemned to death, while the king did little or nothing to save him.

Then Parliament took steps to ensure that its measures would have permanent value. In May 1641, it passed a law establishing that the assembly could not be dissolved by the king without its own agreement. Although that law deprived him of an important prerogative, the king did not oppose it, but rather hoped that his problems would be solved by a series of complicated intrigues. When Parliament finally began discussing the matter of funds to deal with the Scottish rebels, it was discovered that the king had been negotiating with the invaders, hoping to undo the power of Parliament. A Catholic rebellion in Ireland was also said to have been instigated by the queen, supposedly to embarrass Parliament and force it to grant funds to the king for his armies. The sovereigns' duplicity, whether real or fictitious, drew the more radical Protestants into a closer alliance with those whose goal was to limit the power of the crown.

The bishops, as members of the House of Lords, were Charles's main supporters in Parliament. But the House of Commons began instituting proceedings against some of the bishops, and when the accused tried to attend Parliament the people of London rioted and barred them from the Assembly. Encouraged by these events, the more radical members of the House of Commons announced their plans to bring the queen to trial for her supposed participation in the events leading to rebellion in Ireland. Such extreme measures provoked a reaction against the Puritans. Many in the House of Lords were convinced that the time had come to restore order. Time was on the king's side. But he did not have the patience to wait for events to present him with victory, and therefore he hastily accused the leaders of the Commons before the House of Lords. The lords, fearing that some day he might take similar action against them, rejected the accusation. Then the king ordered the arrest of the accused, and Parliament refused to surrender them. The following day, a military contingent sent by Charles to arrest those whom he had accused found that Parliament had the support of the people of London, who refused to allow the arrest of the accused. Having lost his capital, the king withdrew to his palaces, Hampton Court and Windsor. Meanwhile, in London, the leader of the rebellious Parliament, John Pym, ruled as a "king without a crown." The Commons then proposed a law excluding the bishops from the House of Lords. The higher chamber agreed, the king did not object, and the prelates were therefore expelled. Thus began a process that would progressively exclude from Parliament those opposed to Puritanism, giving the assembly an ever-more-radical bent. Parliament then ordered that a militia be recruited. Since such troops would fall under Parliament's command, the king decided that the time had come for decisive action. He gathered the troops loyal to him, and prepared for battle against Parliament's militia. The conflicts between the throne and Parliament had finally led to civil war.

CIVIL WAR

Both sides began building up their armies. Charles found his greatest support among the nobility, while Parliament found its support among those who had most suffered in recent times. The bulk of its army came from the lower classes, to whom were added many merchants and a few noblemen. The king's strength was his cavalry, traditionally the specialty of the nobility; Parliament's was its infantry and the navy, for which trade was important. At first there were only minor skirmishes, while each party sought outside support: Parliament from the Scots, and Charles from the Catholics in Ireland. Also, threatened by civil war, the various Puritan factions drew closer together.

In its efforts to attract the Scots, Parliament took a series of measures that leaned toward Presbyterianism. Not all English Puritans agreed that this was the proper type of church government, but most rejected the episcopacy, considered the king's main ecclesiastical support. Eventually, the episcopacy was abolished—partly because the bishops supported the king, partly for theological reasons, and partly because the confiscation of the bishops' property meant that Parliament could obtain funds without creating new taxes.

Meanwhile, Parliament convoked a body of theologians to advise it on religious matters. This was the famous Westminster Assembly, which included, besides 121 ministers and thirty laymen appointed by Parliament, eight representatives from Scotland. Since the Scots had behind them the strongest army in Great Britain, their influence on the assembly was decisive. In Chapter 21 we shall dwell on the theology of the assembly, whose Confession became one of the fundamental documents of Calvinist orthodoxy. For the present, it suffices to say that, although some of its members were *independents*—that is, supporters of the congregational form of government—and others leaned toward episcopacy, the Assembly opted for the Presbyterian form of government, and recommended that Parliament adopt it for the Church of England. There were in Parliament many independents who would have preferred another form of government, but the course of war forced them to join with the Scots in a *Solemn League and Covenant* that committed them to Presbyterianism. This was finally enacted in 1644, and in the following year William Laud—by then archbishop of Canterbury—was executed by order of Parliament.

It was at this time, while Parliament was building up its army, that Oliver Cromwell came to the forefront. He was a relatively wealthy man, descended

Oliver Cromwell, at first an obscure member of Parliament, led the rebels to victory and became master of England.

from one of Henry VIII's advisors. A few years earlier he had become a Puritan, and was now an avid reader of Scripture. He was convinced that every decision, both personal and political, ought to be based on the will of God. This meant that, although he was often slow in coming to a decision, once he had set upon a course he was determined to follow it through to its final conclusions. Although he was respected by his fellow Puritans, until the time of the Civil War he was known as simply one more member of the House of Commons. However, when he became convinced that armed conflict was inevitable, Cromwell returned to his home, where he recruited a small corps of cavalry. He knew that the cavalry was the king's main weapon, and that Parliament would need a similar body. His zeal was contagious, and his small cadre became a mighty cavalry, who charged into battle singing psalms, convinced that it was waging holy war. Soon the entire army of Parliament was possessed of similar convictions, and became an irresistible force that crushed the king's army at the Battle of Naseby.

That battle was the beginning of the end for the king. The rebels captured his camp, where they found proof that he had been encouraging foreign Catholic troops to invade England. Charles then decided to negotiate with the Scots, hoping to win them with his promises. But the Scots took him prisoner and eventually turned him over to Parliament. Having thus won the war, Parliament adopted a series of Puritan measures, including ordering that the Lord's Day be reserved for religious observances, and forbidding frivolous pastimes.

But the Puritans, who had been united in their opposition to the king and his bishops, were deeply divided among themselves. The majority of Parliament by then supported the Presbyterian form of government, which would allow for a national church without bishops. But the Independents were the majority in the army. These Independents did not agree among themselves on many points. But they did agree that a national church with a Presbyterian form of government would deprive them of their freedom to obey the Bible as they understood it. Thus, tension grew between Parliament and its army. In 1646, Parliament tried without success to dissolve the army. More radical groups, such as the "Fifth Monarchy" and the "Levellers," gained ground in the army. Some of them declared that the Lord was about to return, and that it was necessary to transform the social order by establishing justice and equality. Parliament, where the merchant class still possessed significant power, responded with stricter measures against the army, which in turn responded by declaring that, since it included a wider representation of the people, it was the army, and not Parliament, that had the right to speak for the nation.

At that point, the king escaped. He then opened negotiations with the Scots, with the army, and with Parliament, making mutually contradictory promises to all three. He gained the support of the Scots, to whom he promised the establishment of Presbyterianism in both Scotland and in England. Meanwhile, he continued secret negotiation with Parliament. But the Puritan army defeated the Scots, captured the king, and began a purge of Parliament. Forty-five leaders of Parliament were arrested, and many more were prevented from attending the sessions, while others refused to attend. What now remained was rightly called by its enemies the

Rump Parliament, meaning that all that was left was the "rump" of a real parliament.

It was this Rump Parliament that then initiated proceedings against Charles, whom they accused of high treason and of having involved the country in civil war. The fourteen lords who dared appear for the meeting of the House of Lords unanimously refused to agree to such proceedings. But the Commons simply continued the trial, and Charles, who refused to defend himself on the grounds that his judges had no legal jurisdiction, was beheaded on January 30, 1649.

THE PROTECTORATE

The Scots, fearing the loss of their independence from England, rapidly acknowledged the dead king's son, Charles II, as their ruler. The Irish seized the opportunity to rebel. In England itself, the independent Puritans were splintering. Among the more radical, the "Diggers" grew strong. This was a movement that advocated a new social order in which the right to property would be universal. Such preaching threatened the merchant class, which earlier had supported Parliament in its opposition to the king. Meanwhile, the Presbyterians insisted on a national church, which the Independents saw as tyranny. In short, chaos threatened the land.

It was then that Cromwell took the reins of power. Although he had not participated in the purge of Parliament, he approved of its results and, in the name of the Rump Parliament, stamped out first the Irish Rebellion and then the royalist outbreak in Scotland. Charles II was forced to flee to the Continent. Then Cromwell decided to do what the king had been unable to do: when the Rump Parliament began discussing a law that would perpetuate its power, Cromwell appeared at the session, expelled the few remaining representatives, and locked the building. Thus, seemingly against his own will, he had become master of the nation. For some time he sought to return to some sort of representative government, but he eventually took the title of "Lord Protector." In theory, he was to rule with the help of a Parliament that would include representatives from England, Scotland, and Ireland. In truth, however, the new Parliament was mostly English, and Cromwell was the real government.

Cromwell then set out on a program of reformation of both church and state. Given the prevailing atmosphere, his religious policies were fairly tolerant. Although he was an Independent, he tried to develop a religious system with room for Presbyterians, Baptists, and even some moderate advocates of episcopacy. As a true Puritan, he also tried to reform the customs of the land through legislation regarding the Lord's Day, horse races, cockfights, theater, and so forth. His economic policies favored the middle class, to the particular detriment of the aristocracy but also, in some measure, of the poor. Among both the very wealthy and the very poor, opposition to the Protectorate increased.

Cromwell was able to retain control of the country as long as he lived. But his dreams of creating a stable republic failed. Like the kings before him, he was unable to get along with Parliament—even though his partisans forcibly kept his opponents from taking their seats, thus creating a new "rump." Since the Protectorate was obviously temporary, Cromwell was offered the royal crown, but he refused it, still hoping to create a republic. In 1658, shortly before his death, he named his son Richard as his successor. But this younger Cromwell lacked his father's ability, and resigned his post.

THE RESTORATION

The failure of the Protectorate left no alternative but the restoration of the monarchy. Under General Monck's leadership, Parliament recalled Charles II to his father's throne. This brought about a reaction against the Puritans. Although Charles at first sought to find a place for Presbyterians within the national church, the new Parliament opposed such projects, and preferred the traditional episcopacy. Thus, the new government restored both the episcopacy and the *Book of Common Prayer,* and issued laws against dissidents, for whom there was no place in the official church. Such laws, however, were unable to stamp out most of the movements that had emerged during the previous period of unrest. They continued to exist outside the law until, late in that century, toleration was decreed.

In Scotland, the consequences of the restoration were more severe. That country had become staunchly Presbyterian, and now by royal decree the episcopacy was reinstated, and the ministers of Presbyterian persuasion were deposed in favor of others who were willing to preach in support of bishops and the *Book of Common Prayer*. This resulted in riots and revolts. Archbishop James Sharp, the foremost prelate of Scotland, was murdered. This brought about intervention by the English in support of the Scottish royalists, and the Presbyterian rebellions were drowned in blood.

On his deathbed, Charles II declared himself a Catholic, thus confirming the suspicions of many of the persecuted Puritans and Scottish Presbyterians. His brother and successor, James II, resolved to restore Roman Catholicism as the official religion of his kingdoms. In England, he sought to gain the support of dissidents by decreeing religious tolerance. But the anti-Catholic sentiments among the dissidents ran so strong that they preferred no tolerance to the risk of a rebirth of Catholicism. Conditions in Scotland were much worse, for James II—James VII of Scotland—placed Catholics in positions of power, and decreed the death penalty for any who attended unauthorized worship.

After three years under James II, the English rebelled and invited William, Prince of Orange, and his wife Mary, James's daughter, to occupy the throne. William landed in 1688, and James fled to France. In Scotland his supporters held on for a few months, but by the following year William and Mary were firmly in possession of the Scottish crown as well. Their religious policy was fairly tolerant. In England, tolerance was granted to any who would subscribe to the Thirty-nine Articles of 1562, and swear loyalty to the sovereigns. Those who refused to swear, called *non-jurors*, were granted tolerance as long as they did not conspire against the sovereigns. In Scotland, Presbyterianism became the official religion of the state, and the Westminster Confession its doctrinal norm.

Even after the restoration, however, the Puritan ideal lingered on, and deeply influenced the British ethos. Its two great literary figures, John Bunyan and John Milton, long remained among the most read of English authors. Bunyan's most famous work, generally known by the abbreviated title of *Pilgrim's Progress,* became a popular book of devotion, and the subject of much meditation and discussion for generations to come. And Milton's *Paradise Lost* determined the way in which the majority of the English-speaking world read and interpreted the Bible.

19

Catholic Orthodoxy

There is sufficient light for those who wish to see, and sufficient darkness for those of the opposite disposition. Enough clarity to illumine the elect, and enough darkness to keep them humble. Sufficient darkness to blind the reprobate, and sufficient clarity to condemn them and make them inexcusable.

BLAISE PASCAL

The Council of Trent had determined Catholic orthodoxy for the next four centuries, and had also put forth an entire program of reformation. But both that orthodoxy and that reformation had opponents within Catholic ranks. First of all, the Tridentine program of reformation was based on a centralization of power in the papacy, and therefore conflicted with various governments. Second, there were prelates for whom the proposed reformation required sacrifices they were not willing to make. And, finally, there were those who feared that, in its efforts to reject Protestantism, Trent had gone too far, particularly by neglecting Augustine's doctrine of the primacy of grace in human salvation.

GALLICANISM AND OPPOSITION
TO PAPAL POWER

Although the Council of Trent had been necessary because the papacy had lacked the will and the power to respond to the challenges of the Protestant Reformation, by the end of its sessions the papacy had gained in prestige and was entrusted with great power over the entire Catholic Church. But this decision on the Council's part was not well-received in many European courts. This was a time of growing nationalism and absolute monarchs, and therefore both kings and nationalists opposed the notion of a centralized church under papal authority. Such attitudes were given the name *Gallicanism*—from *Gaul*, or ancient France—because it was in France that they became most powerful. Those who defended the authority of the pope were called *Ultramontanes*, for they looked for authority *beyond the mountains*—that is, beyond the Alps.

During the late Middle Ages, when the papacy existed under the shadow of France, the French monarchy had obtained a number of concessions from popes, mostly granting the French church a measure of autonomy. Now the French insisted on those ancient "freedoms of the Gallican church," denied by the centralizing edicts of Trent. While some of the Gallicans opposed the centralization of power in the papacy for political reasons, others did so because they were convinced that ecclesiastical authority resided in the bishops, and not in the pope. In any case, the decrees of Trent would not be valid in France until the crown had them promulgated, and this was not easily achieved. Although Henry IV, after protracted negotiations, agreed to the promulgation of the Council's decrees, the French Parliament blocked it. In 1615, five years after the assassination of Henry IV, the decrees still had not been promulgated by French civil authorities, and the French clergy, at that time dominated by the Ultramontanes, decided to do it on its own. But the very fact that it had been the French clergy who had validated the Council in their country would eventually be used as an argument by the defenders of the "Gallican freedoms."

There were similar movements in other parts of Europe. *Febronianism* was named after Justin Febronius, the pseudonymous author of a book published in 1763 under the title *The State of the Church and the Legitimate Power of the Roman Pontiff.* This argued that the church is the community of the faithful, and that the bishops, as their representatives, are to rule the church. Therefore, final authority resides in a council of the bishops, and not in the pope. Pope Clement XIII condemned Febronius's work as heretical. But its ideas continued circulating and gaining popularity. Some saw in them the possibility of reuniting Catholics and Protestants by means of a council. Others supported them because they were compatible with their own nationalism. And there were some opulent bishops, lords of vast dioceses, who supported them as a means to evade compliance with the reforms dictated by Rome.

In the imperial court at Vienna, Febronianism took a different turn. The emperor, Joseph II, was a learned and liberal-minded ruler who projected a

The enmity of the house of Bourbon led to the expulsion of the Jesuits from France and other Bourbon territories.

number of reforms in his territories. He needed the support of the church for such projects; but not of the Tridentine Church, which he considered obscurantist and intolerant. Therefore he took over the education of the clergy, closed down those monasteries he deemed too traditional, founded new churches, and in general carried forth a reformation of the church in the direction he thought best. Other rulers showed an inclination to follow the emperor's example, and the Church of Rome, which had already condemned Febronianism in 1764, also condemned Josephism in 1794. But it was not papal condemnation, but rather the French Revolution (to which we shall turn later) that put an end to this and other such movements.

Meanwhile, papal power had suffered a serious blow in the dissolution of the Jesuits. That order, founded precisely to serve as an army for the papacy, was not well regarded by the absolutist monarchs of the eighteenth century. The Jesuits' support of the intolerant policies that led to the Thirty Years' War did not help their popularity. In particular, the house of Bourbon had a profound aversion toward the Jesuits, who had consistently supported the rival house of Hapsburg. Therefore, as the power of the Bourbons waxed, and that of the Hapsburgs waned, the Jesuits found themselves in difficulty. In 1758, an attempt to assassinate Joseph I of Portugal was blamed on the Jesuits. A year later, the Society of Jesus was expelled from Portugal and its colonies, and the crown confiscated its property. In France, also under Bourbon rule, the Society was suppressed in 1764. Three years later, it was expelled from Spain and its colonies by Charles III. Then King Ferdinand IV of Naples followed the example of his father, Charles III of Spain. This led to a concerted effort by the Bourbons to rid themselves of the Jesuits, not only in their own territories, but also throughout the world. Early in 1769, the Bourbon ambassadors in Rome presented to the pope a joint resolution in which they demanded the dissolution of the Jesuits. Finally, in 1773, Pope Clement XIV ordered the Society of Jesus dissolved, thus losing one of the most powerful instruments of papal policy.

Gallicanism, Febronianism, Josephism, and the suppression of the Jesuits show that, while the popes insisted on their universal jurisdiction, in truth they were losing power and authority.

JANSENISM

The Council of Trent had categorically condemned the views of Luther and Calvin on grace and predestination; but there were many who feared that, in an extreme reaction against Protestantism, this could lead to a denial of St. Augustine's teachings. Thus arose among Catholics a series of controversies over grace and predestination.

Later in the sixteenth century, the Jesuits at the University of Salamanca, under the leadership of Luis de Molina, affirmed that predestination was based on God's foreknowledge. To this the Dominican Domingo Báñez, one of the best Catholic theologians of the time, responded that such teaching was contrary to Augustine, and therefore ought to be condemned. Each side accused the other before the Spanish Inquisition, the Jesuits declaring that the Dominicans were Calvinists, and the Dominicans claiming that the Jesuits were Pelagians. The Inquisition turned the matter over to Rome, and the popes, after long hesitation, simply decided that both accusations were false, and ordered each side to refrain from attacking the other.

Similar controversies at the University of Louvain had greater repercussions. There, Michael Baius proposed theses similar to those of Augustine, arguing that a sinful will can produce no good, and that therefore only grace, and not the human will, can produce repentance and conversion. In 1567, Pope Pius V condemned seventy-nine theses drawn from Baius's writings. The latter recanted, but continued teaching very similar doctrine. When a Jesuit theologian attacked Baius, the faculty of Louvain responded by declaring that the Jesuit was a Pelagian. Again, the popes intervened, trying to calm spirits. But Baius's theology continued circulating in Louvain and resurfaced six decades later, in 1640, in the work of Cornelius Jansenius. His book, *Augustine,* published posthumously, claimed to be no more than a study and exposition of the teachings of that great theologian on the subjects of grace and predestination. But what Jansenius found in Augustine was too similar to the doctrines of Calvin and, in 1643, his theses were condemned by Pope Urban VIII.

This, however, did not put an end to the controversy. In France, the Jansenist torch was taken up by Jean Duvergier, better known as *Saint-Cyran* because he was abbot of a house by that name, and by the nuns of the abbey of Port-Royal. The abbey of Port-Royal, under the leadership of the saintly Mother Angelique, had become a center of devotion and reformation, and Saint-Cyran was well known as a leading figure in that movement. He had been imprisoned by Richelieu, who feared that the religious zeal of these reformers would hinder his political program. Freed in 1643, the same year that the theses of his deceased friend Jansenius were condemned, Saint-Cyran became the champion of Jansenism, and its headquarters the abbey of Port-Royal. Now, however, Jansenism was less a doctrine regarding grace and predestination, and more a movement of zealous religious reform. The Jesuits had proposed the theory of *probabilism*, which meant that a probability, no matter how slight, that an action was correct made it morally acceptable. To the French Jansenists this was moral indifferentism, and instead they proposed a life of such discipline and rigor that it was said that the nuns of Port-Royal were "as pure as angels and as proud as demons."

Saint-Cyran died shortly after being freed, but the cause was taken up by Antoine Arnauld, Mother Angelique's brother, and by the philosopher Blaise Pascal. From an early age, Pascal had shown his genius, particularly in physics and mathematics. When he was thirty-one, eight years before his death, he converted to Jansenism. For him this was a profound religious experience that left its mark on the rest of his life. When the faculty of the Sorbonne condemned Arnauld, he published the first of his twenty *Provincial Letters*, purporting to be addressed to the Parisian Jesuits by an inhabitant of the provinces. Their humor and wit soon gained them wide circulation, and they were added to the index of forbidden books. For a time, it became fashionable among the intelligentsia and the aristocracy of Paris to be a Jansenist.

Then reaction set in. Louis XIV was not a king to tolerate such zeal, which could easily turn into sectarianism. The assembly of the clergy condemned the movement. The nuns of Port-Royal were disbanded. In spite of his Gallicanism, Louis XIV asked for the support of Pope Alexander III, who ordered all members of the clergy to repudiate Jansenism. But once again the pendulum swung. Alexander died, his successor proved more lenient, the nuns were allowed to return to Port-Royal, and there was even talk of making Arnauld a cardinal. This, however, was only a brief respite.

One of the ablest defenders of Jansenism was Balise Pascal, whose Provincial Letters *made the Parisian Jesuits the subject of ridicule.*

Eventually, Arnauld was forced into exile, where he died. Louis XIV became increasingly intolerant, and Pope Clement XI reiterated the condemnation of Jansenism. In 1709, the police took possession of Port-Royal and expelled the elderly nuns. Since people still flocked in pilgrimage to the abbey's cemetery, it was ordered dug up, and it is said that dogs fought over the disinterred remains. In 1713, Clement XI categorically condemned Jansenism in the bull *Unigenitus.*

Jansenism continued its existence, and even grew. By then, however, it had little to do with the teachings of Jansenius, or with the reforming zeal of Saint-Cyran and Angelique, or even with the profound religiosity of Pascal. It was rather a political and intellectual movement closely akin to Gallicanism. Some members of the lower clergy joined the movement as a protest against the opulence of their superiors. Others used it as a means of opposing undue interference of Rome in French affairs. Still others were rationalists who saw in the movement a reaction against dogmatic authority. Eventually, Jansenism disappeared, not because it had been condemned and persecuted, but rather because it had become amorphous.

QUIETISM

Another major controversy within Catholicism revolved around *Quietism.* This doctrine began with the publication in 1675 of a *Spiritual Guide* written by the Spaniard Miguel de Molinos. He was a controversial man whom some called a saint, and others a charlatan. His *Spiritual Guide,* and a later *Treatise on Daily Communion,* caused a great stir, for some accused him of heresy, while others claimed that his was the highest form of Christian devotion.

Molinos advocated total passivity before God. A believer is simply to disappear, to die, and be lost in God. Any activism, be it of the body or of the soul, must be set aside. Contemplation must be purely spiritual, having nothing to do with any physical or visible means—including the humanity of Christ. The same is true of ascetic discipline, which is another form of activism. When the soul is lost in contemplation of the divine, it must consider nothing else—not even the neighbor.

Such teaching provoked great opposition. Some argued that it was more akin to Muslim mysticism than to the doctrines of the great Christian teachers. Others pointed out that Molinism led to privatism, in which the church has no importance or authority, and in which Christians have nothing to do with political or social life. The Inquisition, asked to judge on the matter, at first supported Molinos. But many confessors protested that this teaching was leading to moral laxity among the faithful. Then rumors circulated that Molinos himself encouraged such laxity among his followers, and that his relations with the women among them were not above reproach.

In 1685, Molinos and several of his followers were arrested by papal order. In his trial before the Inquisition, he refused to defend himself, even from the most absurd accusations. His admirers declared that he was simply practicing the Quietism that he had preached. His accusers said that his silence proved his guilt. When ordered to recant, he did so with such humility that the recantation itself could be interpreted as a sign that he was still true to his beliefs. Although many demanded that he be condemned to death, Pope Innocent XI, not wishing to create a martyr for Quietism, had him imprisoned for the remaining eleven years of his life. In prison, he seems to have continued the life of quiet contemplation that he had advocated.

Quietism penetrated France, where it was taken up by the widowed Madame de Guyon and by her confessor, Father Lacombe. Both were people of profound religious inclinations, given to visions and other mystical experiences. Around them gathered a circle of believers whom they guided in their religious lives. When Madame de Guyon published a treatise, *A Short and Simple Means of Prayer,* her fame extended throughout the nation. Then she and her confessor moved to Paris, where their admirers included several women of the highest aristocracy.

But Madame de Guyon's doctrines were not above suspicion, for she carried the teachings of Molinos in a more radical direction. She eventually declared that there may be times when, in order to offer God a true sacrifice, one must commit sins one truly despises. Such affirmations, joined with her close collaboration with Lacombe, gave rise to evil rumors, and the archbishop of Paris ordered the priest put in prison, and Madame de Guyon placed in a convent. Lacombe was carried from one prison to another, until he lost his mind and died. Madame de Guyon was eventually freed through the intervention of one of the king's favorites.

It was then that Madame de Guyon met the young Bishop François Fénelon. He was won over to her teachings, although he never carried them to her extremes. Eventually, the issue of Quietism degenerated into a bitter controversy between Fénelon and one of the greatest French theologians of the time, Jacques Benigne Bossuet. The controversy dragged on, for Bossuet had the support of the king, but Fénelon was a man of admirable piety. Finally, under pressure from Louis XIV, Pope Innocent XII agreed to reject some of Fénelon's theses, although carefully declaring, not that they were wrong, but that they could lead some to error. Upon hearing of the papal decision, Fénelon responded with such humility that in the public mind Bossuet was condemned as an arrogant man who had unnecessarily humiliated a worthy colleague. Fénelon then withdrew to his pastoral duties as archbishop of Cambray, distributing all his possessions among the poor and leading such an admirable life that he was the probable model for Victor Hugo's saintly but fictitious Monseigneur Myriel, a leading figure in *Les Miserables.*

All these events and controversies show that during the seventeenth and eighteenth centuries Roman Catholicism was reorganizing itself after the crisis of the Reformation. The Council of Trent had strictly defined Catholic orthodoxy, and in theory the papacy had become the center of ecclesiastical power. In doctrinal matters, the decisions of Trent were inviolable, and therefore all theological controversy took place within the framework of Tridentine orthodoxy. But there were also strong political forces at work against the centralization of ecclesiastical power, thus giving rise to Gallicanism, Febronianism, and Josephism. That opposition to papal power would eventually weaken the Catholic Church and make it more difficult for it to respond to the challenges of the French Revolution.

20

Lutheran Orthodoxy

I am a Christian, profoundly committed to the Confession of
Augsburg in which my parents reared me. And I am also committed
to it as a result of my constantly renewed and considered reflexions,
and of a daily struggle against every sort of temptation.

PAUL GERHARDT

The reform that Luther advocated and began was doctrinal, and not
merely practical. Although he criticized the corruption that had
become common in the life of the church, that was not the main point
at issue. Luther's reformation began with a theological discovery, and he
was always convinced that correct belief was of crucial importance for the
church. This did not mean that all had to agree on all points of doctrine.
For many years, his main collaborator and closest friend was Philipp Melanchthon, who differed from him on many points. Luther himself said that
his task was cutting down the trees and removing the great boulders from
the field, and that Melanchthon was the more patient man whose task was
to plow and sow. Likewise, although later the differences between Calvin
and Luther have been underscored, when the German reformer read the
first edition of Calvin's *Institutes* he commented favorably on them. But not
all had the same mental amplitude, as became evident in the debates that
divided the next generation of Lutherans.

PHILIPPISTS AND STRICT LUTHERANS

After Luther's death, Melanchthon took his place as the main interpreter
of Lutheran theology. His systematic exposition of theology, commonly
known by the abbreviated title of *Loci theologici,* became the standard text-
book for the study of theology among Lutherans, and underwent several

*The first debates among Lutherans revolved around the teachings
of Melanchthon, whom some accused of having departed from the
teachings of the deceased reformer.*

editions, each with further revisions by its author. But there were those
who thought that Melanchthon was not a faithful exponent of the deceased
reformer's theology. The main point of contrast, at the heart of all other differences, was the humanist inclination of "Master Philip"—as Luther used
to call him. When Luther broke with Erasmus and his humanist program
of reformation, Melanchthon continued cordial relations with the illustrious
scholar. This was partly due to Melanchthon's love of peace. But it was also
due to his disagreement with Luther's radical rejection of "dirty reason." For
similar reasons Melanchthon, while affirming the doctrine of justification

by faith, insisted on the need for good works—although not as a means of salvation but as a result and witness to it.

These differences between Luther and Melanchthon, exaggerated by some after Luther's death, gave rise to the debate between Philippists and strict Lutherans. The immediate occasion for the conflict was the *Augsburg Interim*, an attempt to force Lutherans to agree to a compromise with Catholics (see Chapter 9). None of the Lutheran leaders was enthusiastic about the Interim, and most refused to sign it. But imperial pressure was great, and finally the Wittenberg theologians, headed by Melanchthon, agreed to a modified version of it—the *Leipzig Interim*. The strict Lutherans, who had firmly refused to sign the *Interim* in spite of the displeasure of the emperor, accused the Wittenberg Philippists of having forsaken several elements of Luther's teachings. Melanchthon responded by establishing a distinction between the central elements of the gospel and those that are peripheral to it. He called the latter by the Greek name *adiaphora*. The essential must not be abandoned at any cost. The adiaphora, although important, must not be confused with the essential. Therefore, in a situation such as that which the church was facing at the time, one could be justified in putting aside some of the secondary elements in order to have the freedom to continue preaching and teaching the essential. The strict Lutherans, under the leadership of Matthias Flacius, responded that, although it may well be true that there are some elements essential to the gospel, and others that are peripheral, there are circumstances that require a clear confession of faith. At such times, some elements that could otherwise be considered peripheral become symbols of the faith itself. To forsake them is to deny the faith. Those who sincerely wish to give clear witness to the faith refuse to yield even on peripheral matters, for fear that their yielding may be construed as surrender. In accepting the *Leipzig Interim*, Flacius argued, even if the Philippists had yielded only on peripheral matters, they had refused to confess their faith.

Then other issues were added to the debate. The strict Lutherans accused the Philippists of giving too much credit to human participation in salvation. Melanchthon, who had never agreed with Luther's assertions about the "enslaved will," was indeed moving to a position that granted the sinful human will greater freedom, and eventually came to speak of collaboration among the Spirit, the Word, and human will. Opposing him, the strict Lutherans emphasized the corruption of human nature as a result of sin, and Flacius even came to affirm that the very nature of the fallen humankind is corruption. At this time, the strict Lutherans also began insisting on the contrast between Luther and Calvin in their interpretations of the Lord's presence in communion, and declared that, since Melanchthon's views were akin to Calvin's, the Philippists were in truth Calvinists.

These and similar controversies eventually led to the *Formula of Concord* of 1577. On most of the issues debated, this formula took an intermediate position. However, it declared that while it is true that there are some elements that are not essential to the gospel, in times of persecution one should not abandon even these peripheral matters. Also on the matter of communion, the *Formula of Concord* upheld the view of strict Lutherans, denying any significant difference between Zwingli's position, clearly rejected by Luther at Marburg, and Calvin's. As a result, from that point on one of the characteristics of Lutheranism was its understanding of communion, expressed in terms of contrast with Calvinism.

THE TRIUMPH OF ORTHODOXY

The period before the Formula of Concord was marked by the controversies between Philippists and strict Lutherans, but the next generations set out to coordinate Luther's teachings with those of Melanchthon. This spirit was already apparent in the Formula of Concord and in its main architect, Martin Chemnitz, whose theology, while accepting many of the theses of strict Lutheranism, followed a methodology similar to Melanchthon's. For Chemnitz, the task at hand was reconciling the various positions within Lutheranism, while underscoring their differences from Catholicism as well as with other forms of Protestantism.

The theology that evolved out of this program has been called *Lutheran orthodoxy* or *Lutheran scholasticism*. Since this had its counterpart in the Reformed tradition, there is also a Calvinist or Reformed orthodoxy, to which we shall turn in the next chapter. Both were characterized by their attention to theological detail, seeking to clarify and discuss every possible subject, by their reinstatement of Aristotle as a tool in theology—which Luther had categorically rejected—and by a theological method in which words from Scripture were used as building blocks with which one could build vast theological systems. On this latter point, while Protestant scholastic theologians—Lutheran as well as Reformed—rejected rationalism, they emulated some of its methods.

This form of scholasticism dominated Lutheran thought throughout the seventeenth century and part of the eighteenth. Its main characteristic was its emphasis on systematic thought. Luther never sought to develop a system of theology. Melanchthon did write a short systematic work that soon gained wide recognition. But the theologians of Protestant scholasticism wrote vast systematic works that could be compared with the great summas of medieval scholasticism, in both their size and their careful distinctions and analyses. For instance, Johann Gerhardt's great work comprised nine volumes that by the second edition had become twenty-three. And, from 1655 to 1677, Abraham Calovius published a systematic theology in twelve volumes.

A second characteristic of Protestant scholasticism that made it similar to medieval theology was its use of Aristotle. Luther had declared that in order to be a theologian one must be rid of Aristotle. But toward the end of the sixteenth century there was a renewal of interest in Aristotelian philosophy, and soon most Lutheran theologians were seeking to build their systems on the basis of Aristotelian logic and metaphysics. Some even began using the works of their Jesuit counterparts, who were also doing theology on the basis of Aristotle. Thus, while in its content Protestant scholasticism was radically opposed to Catholicism, in its tone and methodology it was very similar to the Catholic theology of the time.

The third reason why Lutheran theology in the seventeenth century is properly called *scholastic* is that it was mostly the product of the schools. It was no longer, as in the previous century, a theology born out of the life of the church and directed toward preaching and the care of souls, but rather a theology developed in the universities, and addressed to other scholars and university professors.

Although Protestant scholasticism waned toward the end of the eighteenth century, it left two important legacies: its doctrine of scriptural inspiration, and its spirit of rigid confessionalism. Luther had never dealt specifically with the question of the inspiration of Scripture. There is no doubt that he was convinced that the Bible was inspired by God, and that this is the reason it must be the basis of every theological affirmation. But he never discussed the nature of inspiration. For him, what was important was not the text of Scripture itself, but the divine action to which that text testifies. The Word of God is Jesus Christ, and the Bible is the Word of God because it leads to him. But the scholastic Lutherans posed the question of the manner and sense in which the Bible is inspired. Most answered that the Holy Spirit both told the authors what to write and ordered them to write it.

This seemed necessary in order to refute the argument given by some Catholics that the apostles told their disciples some things in writing, and others verbally. According to the Lutheran scholastics, it does not matter whether or not the apostles verbally taught the disciples things that are not written in the Bible, for such teachings—if they did indeed exist—would not have been inspired by God as the Bible was inspired. Only what the Spirit told the apostles and prophets to write is authoritative for the church.

The other important question that the Lutheran scholastics posed about the inspiration of Scripture was the degree to which the individuality of the authors determined what they wrote. The most common answer was that the biblical authors were no more than secretaries or copyists for the Holy Spirit. They wrote down, letter by letter, what the Spirit told them. But the Spirit knew the individuality of each author and took it into account. That is the reason why the Epistles of Paul, for instance, are different from those of John. All this led to an emphasis on the literal inspiration of Scripture, even on the divine inspiration of the text as it has been transmitted through the centuries. On this point, it is noteworthy that, while Catholic theologians were arguing that the Vulgate—the ancient Latin translation of the Bible—was divinely inspired, there were Lutheran theologians who denied such inspiration, but who then affirmed that the Holy Spirit had inspired the medieval Jewish scholars who had added vowels to the Hebrew text of Scripture—for Old Testament Hebrew had no vowels.

GEORG CALIXTUS AND "SYNCRETISM"

The growing rigidity of Lutheran scholasticism was manifest in the controversy surrounding the proposals of Georg Calixtus. He was a convinced Lutheran who believed that, although Lutheran doctrine was the best interpretation of Scripture, this did not suffice to declare all others heretics or false Christians. He saw a denial of the very spirit of Christianity in the controversies of his time, particularly in the bitter attacks of Christians against other Christians. Therefore, he sought a rapprochement with believers of other confessions, although one that would not lead to the denial of his Lutheran convictions. In order to do this, he made a distinction similar to Melanchthon's between the essential and the secondary. Everything that is in Scripture has been revealed by God, and ought to be believed; but not all is of equal importance. Only that which relates to salvation is fundamental and absolutely necessary. The rest is equally true, and is also important, for

*TR PLVRIM REVEREND AMPLISS ATQ EXEL
LENTISS DN GEORGIVS CALIXTVS SS THEOL DOCT &
Profess minchia iulia Celeberr nec non Abbas Coenob Regio
Lothar Dionissum*

Rejected as a "syncretist" during his lifetime, Georg Calixtus was later hailed as a forerunner of the modern ecumenical movement.

otherwise God would not have revealed it. But it is not essential for being a Christian. There is a difference between heresy and error. The former is the denial of something that is essential for salvation. The latter is a denial of another element of revelation. Both heresy and error are evil, and should be avoided. But only heresy is of such gravity as to keep Christians from communion with one another.

How, then, does one distinguish the fundamental from the secondary? On the basis of what Calixtus calls "the consensus of the first five centuries." During those five centuries, Calixtus argued, there was a consensus among Christians. Some positions were condemned as heretical, and we ought to do likewise. But it would be folly to affirm that something that cannot be found in those first five centuries of Christian theology is essential for salvation. Such an assertion would lead to the conclusion that no one was saved during the early centuries of the life of the church!

Again, this does not mean that we are to believe only what can be found in the writings of the first five centuries. On the contrary, we should believe all that Scripture tells us. But lack of belief in something to be found in Scripture and not in the first five centuries of Christian theology is error, not heresy. The doctrine of justification by faith is a case in point. There is no doubt that this doctrine is found in Scripture. But it was not part of the common faith of the first five centuries. Therefore, although it is important, it is not to be required of all, as if any who reject it are heretics. Luther was right in affirming this doctrine, and Lutherans are also right in insisting on its truth. But this does not mean that Catholics are heretics. And the same can be said regarding the differences between Lutherans and Calvinists on the manner of the presence of Christ in communion. Although Calvinists are in error, they are not heretics.

By using these arguments, Calixtus hoped to achieve better understanding and mutual appreciation among Christians of different confessions— and for this reason he has been rightly called a forerunner of the ecumenical movement. But the defenders of Lutheran orthodoxy were not to be swayed. Abraham Calovius emphatically declared that everything that God has revealed in Scripture is absolutely necessary. Anyone who denies or rejects any part of biblical doctrine, no matter how small or seemingly insignificant, denies and rejects none other than God. Other theologians would not go that far, but would point out that, in introducing his theory of the *consensus of the first five centuries*, Calixtus had restored to tradition the authority that Luther had denied it. Soon the proposal of Calixtus came to be known as *syncretism*, falsely implying that he intended to mix elements from various confessions, or that he believed all confessions to be equally valid. It was only in Poland that Calixtus's proposal was tried out. There, King Wladyslaw IV tried to apply them by opening a dialogue between Catholics and Protestants. But his efforts came to naught, and Georg Calixtus was eventually forgotten.

It was clear that the orthodox theologians of each confession were becoming increasingly entrenched in their positions, as if only those who agreed with them on every point of doctrine properly deserved to be called Christians. Such dogmatism, while bolstering the conviction of some, also gave rise to increasing doubts about the truth of Christianity, or at least about the value of theology and doctrine.

21

Reformed Orthodoxy

Election is the immutable purpose of God whereby, before the foundation of the world, he chose, from among the entire human race, a certain number of people to be redeemed in Christ.

SYNOD OF DORT

During the seventeenth century, the Reformed tradition determined what would thereafter be its orthodoxy. This took place in two solemn assemblies whose pronouncements were seen as the most faithful expression of Calvinism: the Synod of Dort and the Westminster Assembly.

ARMINIANISM AND THE SYNOD OF DORT

Jacobus Arminius was a distinguished Dutch pastor and professor whose theological training had been thoroughly Calvinistic, and had taken place partly in Geneva, under the direction of Calvin's successor Theodore Beza. Having returned to Holland, he gained wide recognition through his preaching from an important pulpit in Amsterdam. It was due to his good name, and to his fame as a student of the Bible and theology, that the leadership of the church in Amsterdam asked him to refute the opinions of Dirck Koornhert, a theologian who rejected some aspects of Calvin's doctrine, particularly in the matter of predestination. With a view to refuting Koornhert, Arminius studied his writings and compared them with Scripture, with early Christian theology, and with the teachings of several of the major reformers. Finally, after a struggle of conscience, he reached the conclusion that Koornhert was right. Arminius became a professor at the University of Leiden in 1603, and his opinions became a matter of public debate. One of his colleagues, Francis Gomarus, was a firm believer in predestination in the strictest sense, and soon the two clashed. It was thus that Jacobus Arminius, who considered himself a true follower of Calvin, gave his name to Arminianism, the doctrine that many since then have considered the very antithesis of Calvinism.

The issue between Gomarus and Arminius was not whether there is such a thing as predestination. On that point they agreed, for both found abundant biblical references to predestination. They debated the basis on which predestination takes place. According to Arminius, predestination was based on God's foreknowledge of those who would later have faith in Jesus Christ. Gomarus, on the other hand, claimed that faith itself is the result of predestination, so that before the foundation of the world the sovereign will of God decreed who would have faith and who would not. Arminius responded that the great decree of predestination was the one by which God determined that Jesus Christ would be the mediator and redeemer of humankind. That was indeed a sovereign decree, in no way dependent on human response. But the divine decree having to do with the final destiny of each individual was based, not on the sovereign will of God, but rather on divine foreknowledge, by which God knew what each person's response would be to the offer of salvation in Jesus Christ. In almost every other matter, Arminius remained a strict Calvinist. His doctrine of the church and the sacraments, for instance, followed the general lines of Calvin. Therefore, although eventually it was his opponents who came to be known as Calvinists, the truth is that the entire controversy took place among Calvin's followers. Arminius died in 1609, but his death did not put an end to the debate, for the successor to his chair at Leiden held his opinions, and carried on the controversy with Gomarus.

Political and economic considerations were soon added to the theological issues at stake. Although the struggle for independence from Spain had been long and bitter, and independence was still not assured, there were those in the Netherlands who wished to improve relations with their former oppressor. These were mostly the merchants, who in some cities were a true oligarchy, and who stood to gain from improved trade with Spain. They were staunchly opposed by many of the clergy, who feared that such contacts with Spain would corrupt the doctrinal purity of the Dutch church. Those who did not participate in the prosperity brought about by trade—that is, the lower classes, imbued with patriotism, with Calvinism, and with resentment against the merchants—also opposed such relations. Soon the mercantile oligarchy took the side of Arminius, while their opponents supported Gomarus.

In 1610, the Arminian party issued a document or *Remonstrance*, and thereafter was commonly known as Remonstrants. The document itself contains five articles dealing with the issues under debate. The first article defines predestination in ambiguous terms, for it affirms that God determined before the foundation of the world that those would be saved who believe in Christ. We are not told whether this means, as Arminius taught, that God knew who would believe, and predestined those particular people; or simply that God determined that whoever would later come to believe would be saved—what later came to be called *the open decree of predestination*. In any case, this ambiguity is consistent with the final paragraph of the Remonstrance, which declares that this is all that is needed for salvation, and that "it is neither necessary nor useful to rise higher nor to search any deeper." In short, that needless speculation regarding the cause of the divine decree of predestination is to be rejected. The second article affirms that Jesus died for all human beings, although only believers actually receive the benefits of his passion. The third attempts to deal with the accusation of Pelagianism, leveled by Gomarus and his supporters against Arminius and his followers. (The reader will remember that Pelagianism was the doctrine that Augustine opposed, which held that humans were capable of doing good on their own.) To make clear that they were not Pelagians, the Remonstrants declared that humans can do nothing good on their own account, and that the grace of God is necessary in order to do good. But the fourth article rejects the conclusion drawn by both Augustine and Gomarus, that grace is irresistible, saying, "As to the manner in which this grace operates, it is not irresistible, for it is written that many resisted the Holy Spirit." Finally, the fifth article discusses whether or not those who have believed in Christ can fall from grace. The Gomarists argued that the power of predestination is such that those who have been predestined to faith cannot lose the grace they have received. The Remonstrants simply responded that biblical teaching on this point is not clear, and that they would need clearer scriptural proof before committing themselves in one direction or the other.

A few years later, political circumstances took a turn against the Remonstrants. Prince Maurice of Nassau—the son and heir of William of Orange—who had refrained from intervening in the debate, took the side of the Gomarists and of those who wished no contact with Spain. Johann van Oldenbarnevelt (or simply Barnevelt), the leading figure in negotiations with Spain, was imprisoned. His friend Hugo Grotius—best known for his work on international law—was also arrested. As part of this reaction against the mercantile party and the Arminians, the Dutch Estates General convoked a great ecclesiastical assembly to put an end to the debate between Gomarists and Remonstrants.

That assembly, known as the Synod of Dort, met from November 1618 to May 1619. In calling it, the Estates General was seeking the support, not only of Dutch Calvinists, but also of those in other parts of Europe. Therefore, invitations were extended to other Reformed churches, and a total of twenty-seven delegates attended from Great Britain, Switzerland, and Germany (the French Huguenots were forbidden to attend by Louis XIII). The Dutch were almost seventy, of which roughly half were ministers and professors of theology, a quarter were lay elders, and the rest were members of the Estates General. The first sessions of the synod were devoted to administrative matters, including the order that a new Dutch translation of the Bible be produced. But the main purpose of the gathering was the condemnation of Arminianism, necessary in order to end the strife that was dividing the Netherlands and to secure the support of other Reformed churches. Thus, although the synod did not approve the most extreme theses of Gomarus—who was one of its members—it did agree on the need to condemn Arminianism.

The canons of the Synod of Dort affirmed five doctrines the Remonstrants could not accept, and from that point on those five doctrines have become the hallmark of orthodox Calvinism. The first of these is the doctrine of unconditional election. This means that the election of the predestined is not based on God's foreknowledge of each one's response to the offer of salvation, but only on the inscrutable will of God. The second is limited atonement. The Remonstrants claimed that Christ had died for all humankind. Against them, the Synod of Dort declared that he died only for the elect. Third, the synod affirmed that, although there is still in fallen humans a vestige of natural light, human nature has been so corrupted that such light cannot be properly used. And this is true, not only in that which refers to the knowledge of God and to conversion, but also in things "civil and natural." The fourth basic tenet of Dort is irresistible grace. And, finally, the synod affirmed the perseverance of the saints, that is, that the elect will persevere in grace, and cannot fall from it. Although such perseverance is not the work of the believer, but of God, it should serve to give us trust in our own salvation and steadfastness in doing good, even though we see the power of sin still active in us. (It has become commonplace among English-speaking students of theology to remember these five points by thinking of the word *tulip*: *T* for total depravity, *U* for unconditional election, *L* for limited atonement, *I* for irresistible grace, and *P* for perseverance of the saints.)

Immediately after the Synod of Dort, severe measures were taken against the Remonstrants. Van Oldenbarnevelt was condemned to death, and Hugo Grotius to life imprisonment—although shortly thereafter, with his wife's help, he managed to escape by hiding in a trunk supposedly full of books. Almost a hundred Arminian ministers were ordered to leave the country, and many others were deprived of their pulpits. Those who insisted on preaching Arminianism were condemned to life imprisonment. The laity who attended Arminian services had to pay heavy fines. Teachers were also required to subscribe to the decisions of Dort. In some places, similar statements were even required of church organists—one of whom was said to have remarked that he did not know how to play the organ according to the canons of Dort.

Maurice of Nassau died in 1625, and after that time measures against the Remonstrants were less rigorous. Finally, in 1631, they were granted official tolerance. They then organized their own churches, many of which continue to this day. The major impact of Arminianism, however, did not take place through these churches, but rather through other groups and movements—particularly the Methodists—that espoused it.

THE WESTMINSTER CONFESSION

In Chapter 18 we examined the story of the events leading to the convocation of the Westminster Assembly, postponing the discussion of the theological content of the *Westminster Confession* until the present chapter, for that confession is one of the clearest and most important examples of the spirit of Calvinist orthodoxy. The *Westminster Confession* is much more detailed and extensive than the canons of Dort, for it deals with a great variety of themes. Therefore, it cannot be summarized here, and we must be content with pointing to some of the crucial sections that show the agreement of Calvinist orthodoxy in England with its counterpart as seen in the Synod of Dort.

The first chapter deals with the authority of Scripture, the "Supreme Judge" in all religious controversy. Since not all the Bible is equally clear, "the infallible rule of interpretation of Scripture is the Scripture itself." (1.9) This means that any obscure texts must be interpreted in the light of clearer ones. After discussing the doctrine of the Trinity in traditional terms, the

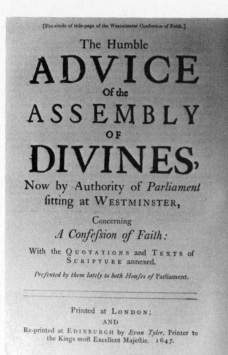

[Fac-simile of title-page of the Westminster Confession of Faith.]

The Humble

ADVICE

Of the

ASSEMBLY

OF

DIVINES,

Now by Authority of *Parliament*
fitting at WESTMINSTER,

Concerning

A Confession of Faith:

With the QUOTATIONS and TEXTS of
SCRIPTURE annexed.

Presented by them lately to both Houses of Parliament.

Printed at LONDON;
AND
Re-printed at EDINBURGH by *Evan Tyler*, Printer to
the Kings most Excellent Majestie. 1647.

The Westminster Confession became one of the foremost documents of orthodox Calvinism, particularly in English-speaking countries.

Confession moves on to the topic of God's Eternal Decree, about which it affirms that from all eternity God did "freely and unchangeably ordain whatsoever comes to pass." (3.1) Part of this decree is that some people and angels have been predestined to eternal life, and others to eternal death. Furthermore, this is in no way based on God's foreknowledge of the future actions or responses of individuals.

The *Westminster Confession* also agrees with Dort that the result of Adam's sin is "this original corruption, whereby we are utterly indisposed, disabled, and made opposite to all good, and wholly inclined to all evil." (6.4) And it also affirms limited atonement in declaring that Christ saves all those whose redemption he also acquired. After sin, human beings have lost all freedom to incline to salvation, which can only result from the "effectual calling" with which God works in the wills of the elect, "determining them to that which is good." (10.1) These elect are justified when the Holy Spirit, at the proper time, applies to them the work of Christ. Then follows sanctification which, although imperfect in this life, is inevitable. Such people "can neither totally nor finally fall away from the state of grace; but shall certainly persevere therein to the end, and be eternally saved." (17.1)

This is then followed by a long series of chapters on the matters being discussed in England at the time of the Puritan Revolution, such as the manner in which the Lord's Day is to be observed, whether or not it is lawful to swear an oath, the organization of the church, and so forth. But it is clear that the theology of the *Westminster Confession* is very similar to that of Dort, both in content and in its careful attention to strict orthodoxy. Thus, the study of the canons of Dort and of the *Westminster Confession* shows the nature of Calvinist orthodoxy in the seventeenth century—and even into the eighteenth. While claiming to be a faithful interpreter of Calvin, it tended to turn the theology of the Genevan Reformer into a strict system that Calvin himself might have had difficulty recognizing. Calvin had discovered in his own life the liberating joy of justification by the unmerited grace of God. For him, the doctrine of predestination was a means of expressing that joy and the unmerited nature of salvation. But in the hands of his followers it became a test of orthodoxy and even of divine favor. At times, they even seemed to confuse doubt regarding the doctrine of predestination with actual reprobation and consequent damnation. There was little left here of the humanist spirit of Calvin, a man who loved literature as an art and who wrote with the elegance and care of a humanist.

22

The Rationalist Option

The reasoning, simple and easy to understand, that geometricians use
to reach their most difficult demonstrations had made me think that
all that can be encompassed by human knowledge is linked in the
same fashion.

RENÉ DESCARTES

Rationalism, an attitude that reached its apex in the eighteenth and
nineteenth centuries, was characterized by its interest in the world and
by its confidence in the powers of reason. In Western Europe, there had
been a growing interest in the world of nature since the thirteenth century.
That was the time of Albert the Great and Thomas Aquinas, who reintro-
duced Aristotelian philosophy as a fundamental tool for theology. One of
the points of contrast between Aristotelianism and the Platonism that until
then had dominated theological thought was precisely that the new philosophy emphasized the importance of sense perception. This meant that the
observation of the world could lead to true and significant knowledge, and
therefore from the time of Albert the Great—who wrote not only about God
and philosophy but also about animals—there had been a growing interest
in the world of nature. The later Middle Ages, with its distrust of speculation, continued the same tendency. In a way, the art of the Renaissance, with
its appreciation for the beauty of the human body and of the world, was a
further expression of this interest. By the seventeenth century, many thought
that the goal of reason was the understanding of the world of nature.

But, parallel to that interest in the world, there appeared—mostly at the
time of the Renaissance—a growing confidence in the powers of reason.
Often, these two elements were combined in an effort to show the degree to
which the order of nature coincides with the order of reason. This may be

seen, for instance, in the work of Galileo, who was convinced that the entire natural world was a system of mathematical relations, and that the ideal of knowledge was the reduction of all phenomena to their quantitative expression. Every success of such efforts seemed to confirm the most optimistic expectations of the power of reason.

DESCARTES AND CARTESIAN RATIONALISM

These various tendencies led to the philosophy of René Descartes, whose lifetime approximately coincided with the first half of the seventeenth century (1596–1650). His philosophical system was based on a great confidence in mathematical reasoning, joined to a profound distrust of all that is not absolutely certain. He would, therefore, compare his philosophical method to geometry, a discipline that accepts only what is an undeniable axiom or has been rationally proven.

In applying that method, Descartes felt that he ought to begin with an attitude of universal doubt, thus making sure that, once he found something that could not be doubted, he could be absolutely certain of its truth. He then found that undeniable first truth in his own existence. He could doubt everything, but not that the doubting subject existed. *I think, therefore I am*—in Latin, *cogito, ergo sum*—became the starting point for his philosophy. This *I* whose existence cannot be doubted, however, is only the philosopher as a *thinking thing—res cogitans*—for the existence of his body—the *res extensa*—has not been proven and must still be doubted.

Before proving his own existence as a body, however, Descartes felt that he could prove the existence of God. He found in his mind the idea of a "more perfect being," and since his mind could not produce such an idea, which was above itself, it must have been placed there by God. Therefore, Descartes's second conclusion was that God exists. It was only then, on the basis of the existence of God, and of trust in the divine perfection, that Descartes felt free to move on to prove the existence of the world and of his own body.

Descartes was a profoundly religious man who hoped that his philosophy would be found useful by theologians. But not all agreed with him on this matter. Since it was the time of strict orthodoxies, many theologians feared the challenge of *Cartesianism*—as his philosophy was called, for his Latin name was Cartesius. The universal doubt that Descartes proposed as his starting point seemed to some no better than crass skepticism. The theological faculties of several universities declared that Aristotelianism was the philosophical system best suited to Christian theology, and there were even those who declared that Cartesianism would necessarily lead to heresy. Dismayed by such criticism, Descartes decided to leave his native France and accepted the invitation of the queen of Sweden to reside in that northern land, where he lived the rest of his days.

But there were others who were enthused by Cartesianism and saw in it the promise of a theological renewal. In France, those intellectual circles in which Jansenism was in vogue embraced Cartesianism as its philosophical counterpart. Eventually, others among the more orthodox also took up his philosophical system, and the debate regarding the value of Cartesianism continued for a long time.

The main point at which Cartesianism led to further theological and philosophical developments was the question of the relationship between spirit and matter. Descartes had affirmed that humans consist of two parts: one that thinks—*res cogitans*—and one that occupies space—*res extensa*—or, in more traditional terms, soul and body. This was perfectly acceptable to the orthodoxy of the time. The problem, however, was that Descartes had been unable to offer a satisfactory explanation of the manner in which these two relate. When the mind thinks, how are its decisions communicated to the body? When something affects the body, how is this communicated to the soul? Three main solutions were offered to this difficulty: occasionalism, monism, and preestablished harmony. Occasionalism was defended by the Flemish philosopher Arnold Geulincx and by the French priest Nicolas Malebranche. They held that the body and soul do not communicate directly, but only by divine intervention. It is God who moves the body *on occasion* of the soul's decision, and the soul *on occasion* of the body's feelings and requirements. Although the occasionalists argued that this view magnified God's greatness, their position was not generally accepted, for it seemed to blame God for all events and thoughts.

Monism—from the Greek *monos,* or *one*—was held by the Dutch Jew Benedictus (or Baruch) de Spinoza. He sought to offer an explanation of reality following a methodology similar to that of mathematics, as Descartes had suggested. He solved the problem of the communication of soul and body—and of the communication of any other substances—by denying that there is more than one substance. Thought and physical extension are not two different substances, but two attributes of a single substance, as *red* and *round* are attributes of a single apple. The same may be said about *God* and the *world*, for these are merely different attributes of the one substance which is the universe. Needless to say, these doctrines found little support among orthodox Christians, for whom belief in a God who exists apart from the world is essential.

Finally, the German philosopher and mathematician Gottfried Wilhelm Leibniz suggested "preestablished harmony." In contrast to Spinoza, Leibniz began with the existence of an infinite number of substances, absolutely independent from each other, which he called *monads*. These monads, as he said, "have no windows," that is, cannot communicate with each other. Nor does God make them communicate. Rather, from the very beginning, God has created these monads so that they may act in seeming interdependence. The manner in which soul and body communicate is very similar to that in which various clocks in a shop "communicate" among themselves: they do not. Rather, they all work according to the preestablished order set by the clockmaker. If the clockmaker was a good one, it will seem as if all the clocks communicate with one another in order to keep the same time. This solution also met a great deal of opposition for—although such was not Leibniz's intent—it seemed to imply that God had foreordained all things, both good and evil, and that there was no such thing as human freedom.

EMPIRICISM

While these philosophical developments were taking place on the Continent, in Great Britain philosophy was following a different route: *empiricism*—from a Greek word meaning *experience*. Its leading figure was Oxford professor John Locke, who in 1690 published his *Essay on Human Understanding.* He had read the works of Descartes, and agreed that the order of the world corresponded to the order of the mind. But he did not believe that there were innate ideas, which one could discover by looking into oneself. On the contrary, he held that all knowledge is derived from experience— both the "outer experience" of the senses, and the "inner experience" by which we know ourselves and the functioning of our minds. This means that the only true knowledge is that which is based on our three levels of experience: our own selves, whose existence we continually experience; those outer realities that are presently before us; and God, whose existence is proven at each moment by the existence of the self and its experiences. Apart from these three, there is no certain knowledge.

But there is another level of knowledge, that of probability, which plays an important role in human life. At this level, we do not apply the strict proofs of reason, but rather those of judgment. Judgment allows us to surmise that, since we have repeatedly experienced John's existence, it is probable that he continues to exist even when he is not before us. Judgment, although not absolutely certain, is necessary, for it is on its basis that we conduct most of our affairs in life.

Faith is assent to knowledge that is derived from revelation rather than from reason. Therefore, its knowledge, although highly probable, is never certain. Reason and judgment must be used in order to measure the degree of probability of what we are asked to believe by faith. For this reason, Locke opposed the "fanatical enthusiasm" of those who think that all they say is based on divine revelation. For the same reason, he defended religious toleration. Intolerance is born out of the muddled thinking that confuses the probable judgments of faith with the certainty of empirical reason. Besides, toleration is based on the very nature of society. The state does not have the authority to limit the freedom of its citizens in matters such as their personal religion.

In 1695, Locke published a treatise, *The Reasonableness of Christianity,* in which he claimed that Christianity is the most reasonable of religions. According to him, the core of Christianity is the existence of God and faith in Christ as the Messiah. But Locke did not believe that Christianity had added anything of importance to what could in any case have been known by the proper use of reason and judgment. In the final analysis, Christianity was little more than a very clear expression of truths and laws that others could have known by their natural faculties.

DEISM

Locke's opinions regarding religion reflected a way of thinking that was becoming widespread even before the publication of his works. Tired of the endless squabbles among the partisans of the many sects and movements that appeared in England in the seventeenth century, many sought an understanding of religion that went beyond narrow and quibbling orthodoxy. A common alternative was that of the Deists, or *freethinkers*—called *Deists* because they rejected what they considered the aberrations of the atheists, and freethinkers in contrast to those who held to the narrow limits of orthodoxy.

The first great figure of Deism was Lord Herbert of Cherbury, who held that true religion must be universal, not only in the sense of calling for the allegiance of all, but also in the sense of being a religion that is natural to all humankind. Such religion is not based on particular revelations, nor on historical events, but rather on the natural instincts of every human being. Its basic doctrines are five: the existence of God, the obligation to worship God, the ethical requirements of such worship, the need for repentance, and reward and punishment, in both this life and the one to follow. Although there may possibly be divine revelation, any doctrine claiming to stem from it must not contradict these five basic points; and in any case, since such a revelation is given only to part of humanity, there is no reason to expect all to accept it.

Shortly after the publication of Locke's *Essay*, John Toland published what would become one of the classics of Deism: *Christianity not Mysterious, or a Treatise Showing that There is Nothing in the Gospel Contrary to Reason, nor Above It, and that No Christian Doctrine Can Be Properly Called a Mystery;* and, in 1730, Matthew Tindal published *Christianity as Old as the World, or the Gospel a Republication of the Religion of Nature.* The very titles of these works suffice to show the nature of Deism, and its effort to show that whatever there is of value in Christianity coincides with "natural religion."

Deism fought on two fronts. On the one hand, it opposed the narrow dogmatism that had taken hold of most branches of Christianity. On the other, it tried to refute the easy skepticism of those who, tired of the quibbling of theologians, simply abandoned all religion. But many Christians, while not narrowly dogmatic, were uneasy with the manner in which Deism tended to discount the significance of particular historical events and revelation, for this discounted the significance of Jesus Christ. Eventually, however, the most devastating criticism of Deism came not from theologians, but from a Scottish philosopher who showed that "reason" was not as "reasonable" as Deists and other rationalists believed. His name was David Hume.

DAVID HUME AND HIS CRITIQUE OF EMPIRICISM

David Hume (1711–1776) was a man of boundless optimism who was nevertheless very pessimistic when it came to the powers of reason. His own optimism made it possible for him to be skeptical about much that the

David Hume was the man whom Kant credited with having wakened him from his "dogmatic slumber."

philosophers said, for he would not crumble even if the entire edifice of philosophy were to come tumbling down. On the contrary, he felt free to allow his intellectual curiosity to lead him wherever it would. Thus, taking as his starting point Locke's empiricism, he came to the conclusion that the scope of true knowledge was much more limited than the rationalists claimed. Indeed, a goodly part of what those philosophers thought they could affirm on the basis of observation and reason had no such basis, but was simply the result of irrational mental habits. And among such things that the mind takes for granted are such fundamental notions as those of substance and of cause and effect.

The empiricists claimed that only that knowledge which is based on experience is true. But Hume pointed out that no one has ever seen or experienced what we call *cause and effect*. We have indeed seen, for instance, that a billiard ball arrives at the place where another one is lying. Then we hear a noise and we see the first ball stop and the second one move. If we repeat this experiment several times, we get similar results. And then we say that the movement of the first ball *caused* the movement of the other one. But the truth is that we have not seen any such thing. All that we have seen is a series of phenomena, and our mind has linked them by means of the notion of cause and effect. This last step, taken by any who see a series of phenomena that are seemingly related, has no basis in empirical observation. It is rather the result of our mental habits. Therefore, according to the empiricists' definition, it is not rational knowledge.

The same can be said of the idea of substance. We say, for instance, that we see an apple. But in truth what our senses perceive is a series of attributes: form, color, weight, flavor, smell, and so forth. We also perceive that those attributes coincide in one place, and that they seem to cling together, as if something unites them. And then our mind, by one of those habits that are not truly rational, declares that all these attributes reside in a substance that we call *apple*. But, once again, we have not experienced the substance itself. Pure empirical reason does not allow us to affirm that there are such things as substances in which reside the various attributes that we perceive.

This critique of empiricist rationalism raised serious questions about Deism. If the relation of cause and effect is not truly rational, the proof that the Deists use for the existence of God, namely, that someone must have caused this world, is no longer valid. Likewise, notions such as the "soul" and "God" have little meaning if we cannot rationally speak of anything but attributes, and never of substances beyond these attributes. Even so, many felt that Hume's argument was flawed. One of these was James Reid (1710–1796), a Scotsman who in 1764 published *An Inquiry into the Human Mind on the Principles of Common Sense*. In this book, Reid argued for the value of self-evident knowledge or common sense, and for this reason his position came to be known as *common sense philosophy*. Thus, in spite of Hume's critique, Deist views such as those proposed by John Tolland more than half a century earlier did not disappear.

NEW CURRENTS IN FRANCE

Meanwhile, new currents of thought were developing in France and other areas of the Continent. The great figure of this new philosophy was François-Marie Arouet, better known under his pen name, "Voltaire." His political views led to a period of imprisonment in the Bastille, an exile in London, and several years of expatriation in Switzerland. But the more French authorities tried to suppress his teachings, the more Voltaire was admired by his fellow citizens. He was an enemy of all fanaticism. Witnessing the persecution of French Protestants during the last years of Louis XIV's reign, he was convinced that such persecution was wrong and would forever be seen as a stain on the name of the Sun King. When he read Locke's writings on political and religious tolerance, he took up that cause, and devoted his wit and his literary ability to it. But he was not convinced by the optimistic rationalism then in vogue. He commented that Cartesianism was like a good novel, in which all is credible and nothing is true. He also mocked the English Deists for claiming to know about God and the soul more than it is given to human reason to know.

Thus, Voltaire and his followers were rationalists in their own way. His satirical wit—which he also applied to himself—scoffed at all the great systems that were then fashionable. But he did believe in the use of reason as common sense, whose dictates life must follow. Furthermore, he argued that the history of humankind was no more than the history of a progressive understanding of ourselves and our institutions, and our efforts to adjust to that ever-clearer understanding. In particular, this meant progress in the understanding and safeguarding of human rights. Monarchy, although a necessary part of government, was not intended for the benefit of the sovereign, but rather for that of the subjects, whose rights all must respect and defend. By stating and divulging such ideas, Voltaire was one of the forerunners of the French Revolution.

One of Voltaire's contemporaries, Charles Louis de Secondat, Baron de Montesquieu, sought to apply the principles of reason to the theory of government. He thus came to the conclusion that a republic is a better form of government than either despotism, which is based on terror, or monarchy, whose foundation is a prejudice called *honor*. Since power corrupts, Montesquieu suggested that government should be exercised by three powers that would balance and limit each other: the legislative, the executive, and the judicial. Thus, by 1748, several decades before the American and French

Revolutions, Montesquieu was proposing some of the basic doctrines of those movements.

At about the same time, Jean Jacques Rousseau was expounding on other theories that were no less revolutionary. According to him, what we call *progress* is not really such, for what in truth has happened is that humankind has progressively departed from its natural state and fallen into artificiality. In the field of politics, this means that we must return to the original order, whose purpose was to serve the governed by safeguarding justice and freedom. Rulers are in truth employees of the people, and their task is to defend freedom and justice. In the field of religion, Rousseau held that dogmas and institutions are part of the corruption that has characterized the so-called *human progress*, and that it is necessary to return to natural religion, consisting of belief in God, the immortality of the soul, and the moral order.

Therefore, in various ways, and without agreeing on all matters, these various philosophers gave French rationalism a particular flavor, shunning the speculative flights of other rationalists, and concentrating rather on the social and political implications of reason understood as common sense. By so doing, they were preparing the way for the French Revolution.

IMMANUEL KANT

The philosophical movements of the seventeenth and eighteenth centuries led to the shattering critique of Immanuel Kant (1724–1804), one of the greatest philosophers of all time. He had been a firm believer in rationalism until, as he later declared, he was awakened from his "dogmatic slumber" by reading Hume. Cartesianism had not been able to overcome the difficulties posed by the problem of the communication of substances. Eventually, the Cartesian theory of innate ideas had led to Leibniz, for whom all ideas were innate, and there was no communication between the mind and other realities. Empiricism, on the other hand, had led to Hume's critique that, if only that knowledge is valid which is acquired through experience, there is no valid knowledge of such fundamental matters as the notion of cause and effect or the idea of substance.

In his *Critique of Pure Reason*, published in 1781, Kant proposed a radical alternative to both systems. According to him, there is no such thing as innate ideas; but there are fundamental structures of the mind, and within those structures we must place whatever data the senses provide us. Those structures are, first of all, time and space; and then twelve "categories," such as causality, existence, substance, and so forth. Time, space, and the twelve categories are not something that we perceive through the senses, rather, they are the structures that our mind has to use in order to organize the sensations that are fed to it by the senses. To make something thinkable, we must place it within the molds of our mental structures. The senses provide a chaotic multitude of sensations. It is only after the mind orders them within the structures of time, space, and the categories that they become intelligible *experiences*.

Consequently, the simplistic rationalism of previous generations is no longer possible. In knowledge, what we have is not things as they are in themselves, but rather things as our mind is able to grasp them. Therefore, there is no such thing as purely objective knowledge, and the pure rationality of Cartesians, Empiricists, and Deists is no more than an illusion.

Kant's work also meant that many of the arguments traditionally used in support of Christian doctrine were no longer valid. For instance, since existence is not a datum derived from reality, but rather one of the categories of the mind, there is no way to prove the existence of God or of the soul. Nor can we speak of an "eternity" consisting in the absence of time, since our mind cannot really conceive such a thing. On the other hand, this does not mean an absolute denial of God, the soul, or eternity. What it means is that, if such things are true, reason cannot know them, just as the eye cannot hear and the ear cannot see.

What, then, is one to say about religion? Kant dealt with this subject in several of his works—particularly in his *Critique of Practical Reason*, published in 1788, where he argues that, although pure reason cannot prove the existence of God and the soul, there is "practical reason" that has to do with the moral life, and whose procedure is different from that of pure reason. This practical reason, whose fundamental principle is to "act in such a manner that the rule for your action can be made a universal rule," does know the existence of God as the judge of all action, of the soul and its freedom as the occasion for moral action, and of life after death as the means for rewarding good and punishing evil. All this is very similar to what the Deists had said, and therefore in discussing religious matters Kant did not go much beyond them.

Kant's significance to religion and theology, however, goes far beyond his rather uninspired attempts to ground religion in morality. His philosophical work dealt a deathblow to the easy rationalism of his predecessors, and to the notion that it is possible to speak in purely rational and objective terms of matters such as the existence of God and the future life. After him, as we shall see later, theologians dealing with the relationship between faith and reason had to take his work into account. Eventually others would carry his views much further, questioning the universality and immutability of the categories of the mind, and arguing that factors such as psychology, culture, and language help shape those categories. Thus, Kant's work, which in some ways was the high point of modern philosophy, in others set the stage for the post-modern critique of the modern insistence on objectivity and universality as signs of true knowledge.

23

The Spiritualist Option

I was glad that I was commanded to turn people to that inward light, spirit, and grace, by which all might know their salvation, and their way to God; even that divine Spirit which would lead them into all Truth and which I infallibly knew would never deceive any.

GEORGE FOX

The seemingly endless debates on dogma, and the intolerance of Christians among themselves, led many to seek refuge in a purely spiritual religion. Also, excessive emphasis on correct doctrine worked in favor of the higher classes, who had greater opportunities for education. Those who did not have such opportunities, and who therefore could not discuss complicated matters of theology, were seen as children, needing someone to guide them through the intricacies of dogma in order not to fall into error. Therefore, the spiritualist movement of the seventeenth and eighteenth centuries attracted both cultured people who had little use for narrow-minded dogmatism, and others of little or no formal education who found in the movement an opportunity for expressing themselves. While some of the founders of spiritualist groups or schools were relatively unschooled, they soon counted among their ranks others of greater education and higher social standing.

Due to the nature of the spiritualist movement, its history is difficult to trace. The movement produced a multitude of currents and leaders whose followers and doctrines are so entwined that it is not always possible to distinguish among them, or to determine the originator of any particular idea. Therefore, the simplest way to grasp the nature of the movement is to turn our attention to three of its main leaders, who differ dramatically from one another: Boehme, Fox, and Swedenborg.

JAKOB BOEHME

Jakob Boehme (1575–1624) was born in Silesia, Germany. His parents were staunch Lutherans of humble means. In the midst of that pious family, young Jakob developed a deep faith; but the sermons of that time, long dissertations on theological debates, caused him to lose interest. He was fourteen years old when his father apprenticed him to a cobbler, which became his lifelong occupation. But, shortly after beginning his apprenticeship, he began having visions, and eventually his master threw him out, declaring that he wanted an apprentice, not a prophet.

Boehme then became a wandering cobbler, traveling from place to place mending shoes. In those travels he came to the conclusion that the leadership of the church had built a veritable Tower of Babel with its interminable quibbling debates. He therefore determined to cultivate his inner life, and to read all he could find on that subject. Thus he reached a series of conclusions on the nature of the world and human life, which were confirmed in visions and other spiritual experiences. But for some time he kept these convictions and experiences to himself, and was content with his life as a cobbler. When he was about twenty-five years old, he put an end to his wanderings and set up shop in the town of Goerlitz, where he was able to make a fairly comfortable living.

Although he did not feel called to preach, Boehme was convinced that God had ordered him to record his visions. The result was the book *Brilliant Dawn,* in which the seer repeatedly asserts that he is writing what God has dictated word for word, and that he is no more than a pen in the hands of God. Boehme did not publish his book, but a manuscript copy reached the local pastor, who accused him before the magistrates. Under threat of deportation, Boehme promised to teach or write no more on religious matters, and for five years kept his promise. But in 1618, compelled by new visions and by the encouragement of some of his admirers, he began writing anew. One of his followers, without his permission, published three of his works, and these also reached the pastor, who once again accused him of heresy. As a result, Boehme was forced to leave Goerlitz.

He then went to the court of the Elector of Saxony, where several theologians examined his teachings without reaching a conclusion, for they confessed themselves unable to understand exactly what he meant. Their recommendation was that Boehme be given more time to clarify his ideas. But he would not be granted that time, for he fell ill and decided to return to Goerlitz in order to die there among his friends and followers. He was fifty years old when he died.

The theologians' response—that they could not understand what he meant—was not simply a subterfuge to avoid pronouncing judgment. The truth is that Boehme's writings continue to be subject to various interpretations. In his writings, one finds an odd mixture of traditionally Christian themes with others taken from magic, alchemy, occultism, and theosophy. How all this relates is never clear, and the ambiguities are made greater by his use of daring metaphors that are never explained. What does he mean, for instance, by "the eternal womb," or by "the mother of all births"? Are these simply other names for God, or are they intended to convey something else?

In any case, in this context what is important is not the exact content of Boehme's teachings, but their basic direction. And this is very clear. It is a reaction against the cold dogmatism of theologians, and against the seemingly empty liturgy of the church. Against these, Boehme exalted the freedom of the spirit, the inner life, and direct and individual revelation. He declared, for instance, that since "the letter kills," believers ought not to guided by Scripture, but by the Holy Spirit, who inspired the biblical writers and even now inspires believers. As he said, "I have enough with the book that I am. If I have within me the Spirit of Christ, the entire Bible is in me. Why would I wish for more books? Why discuss what is outside, while not having learned what is within me?"[8]

Boehme did not have many followers during his lifetime, but his books later gained him many admirers. In England, some of these joined to form a Boehmenist movement, some followers of which clashed with the Quakers of George Fox. Thus, the spiritualist movement, born in part as a protest against the doctrinal debates of traditional theology, was eventually embroiled in similar controversies.

GEORGE FOX AND THE QUAKERS

George Fox (1624–1691) was born in a small English village in the year of Boehme's death. He too was of humble origin, and he too was a cobbler's apprentice. But at nineteen years of age, disgusted at the licentiousness of his fellow apprentices and feeling compelled by the Spirit of God, he quit his occupation and began a life of wandering and attending religious meetings of all sorts, seeking illumination from on high. He also devoted himself to the

4. George Fox Visits Swarthmoor Hall

George Fox, founder of the Quakers, or Friends, differed from other spiritualist leaders in that he paid great attention to the community of believers and to its social obligations.

study of Scripture, and it was said that he knew it by heart. Fox experienced many inner conflicts, at times despairing of finding truth, and at other times encouraged by religious experiences. Slowly, he came to the conviction that all the various sects that abounded in England were wrong, and their worship was an abomination before God.

Fox challenged much of traditional Christianity. If God does not dwell in houses made by human hands, how dare anyone call those buildings where they gather "churches"? They are in truth no more than houses with belfries. Pastors who work for a salary are not real shepherds, but "priests" and "journeymen." Hymns, orders of worship, sermons, sacraments, creeds, ministers—they are all human hindrances to the freedom of the Spirit. Over against all these things, Fox placed the "inner light." This is a seed that exists in all human beings, and is the true way we must follow in order to find God. The Calvinist doctrine of the total depravity of humanity is a denial of the love of God and of the experience of those who love God. On the contrary, there is an inner light in everyone, no matter how dim it may be. Thanks to that light, pagans can be saved as well as Christians. This light, however, must not be confused with the intellect or with conscience. It is not the "natural reason" of the Deists, nor a series of moral principles that point to God. It is rather the capability we all have to recognize and accept the presence of God. It is by it that we are able to believe and understand

Scripture. Therefore, communication with God through the inner light is previous to any communication by external means.

Although those who were close to him knew something of the fire burning within Fox, for several years he abstained from proclaiming what he was convinced he had discovered regarding the true meaning of faith and Christianity. At that time there were in England many religious sects, and Fox attended all without finding contentment in any. Finally, he felt called by the Spirit to speak out at a Baptist meeting, announcing the inner truths in which he now believed. From that point on, such urgings of the Spirit became more frequent. In gatherings of various religious groups, Fox would declare that he had been ordered by the Spirit to announce his spiritual vision of Christianity. His words were often received with contempt and hostility, and he was repeatedly thrown out of meetings, beaten, and stoned. But such incidents would not stop him, and soon thereafter he was in another "house with a belfry," interrupting the service and proclaiming his message. His followers grew rapidly in number. At first they called themselves *children of light*; but Fox preferred the name of *friends*, which would later become their official name. But those who saw that their religious enthusiasm was such that they would tremble began calling them *Quakers*, and that was the name by which they became known.

Beginning in 1652, he had the firm support of Margaret Fell, a gentlewoman who would be widowed in 1658, and would marry him in 1669. By that time she had become known as a leader in the nascent movement, who would make use of her influence as a member of the gentry in order to defend it. But political opposition to Quakerism was such that in 1664 she was arrested for supporting the movement, suffered the confiscation of all her property, and was sentenced to life imprisonment. It was after being released by order of the king that she married Fox. The rest of their lives was spent in teaching and missionary activities, repeatedly interrupted by new orders of imprisonment. George Fox died in 1691, and Margaret Fell Fox in 1702.

Since Fox and his followers believed that any structure in worship could be an obstacle to the work of the Spirit, the Friends' worship service took place in silence. Any who felt called to speak or pray aloud were free to do so. When the Spirit moved them, women had the same right to speak as men. Fox himself did not prepare to speak at such meetings, but simply allowed the Spirit to move him. There were times when many had gathered hoping to hear him speak, but he refused to do so because he did not feel moved by the Spirit. Also, the Quakers did not include in their services the traditional sacraments of baptism and communion, for they feared that physical water, bread, and wine would draw attention away from the spiritual. This was the main reason for their conflict with the Boehmenists, who continued celebrating the sacraments—although calling them *ordinances*.

Fox was aware of the danger that his emphasis on the freedom of the Spirit would lead to excessive individualism. Other movements with a similar emphasis have not lasted long, for the exercise of individual freedom has led to the dissolution of the group. Fox avoided this danger by underscoring the importance of community and love. In the Friends' meetings, decisions were not made by majority vote. If a unanimous agreement was not reached, the decision was postponed, and the meeting continued in silence until the Spirit offered a solution. If one was not received, the matter was left pending for another occasion.

There were many who disliked the teachings and practices of Fox and the Quakers. Religious leaders resented the manner in which these "fanatics" interrupted their services in order to preach or to read Scripture. The powerful felt the need to teach a lesson to these Friends, who refused to pay tithes, to swear an oath, to bow before their "betters," or to uncover their head before any but God. The Quakers argued that, since God was addressed in the familiar "Thou," no other being ought to be addressed in the more respectful "You." To many who were used to the submission of their "inferiors," all this seemed disrespectful and an intolerable insubordination.

As a result, Fox was repeatedly beaten, and he spent years in prison—as did Margaret Fell Fox. He was sent to prison for the first time for having interrupted a preacher who declared that the ultimate truth was to be found in Scripture, and arguing that this was not true, for ultimate truth was in the Spirit who had inspired Scripture. On other occasions he was accused of blasphemy, or of conspiring against the government. When the authorities offered to pardon him, he refused, declaring that he was not guilty, and that to accept a pardon for something he had not done was to lie. On another occasion, when he was serving six months for blasphemy, he was offered his freedom in exchange for service in the republican army. He refused, declaring that Christians ought not to use any weapons other than those of the Spirit, and had his sentence prolonged by an additional six months. From that point on, the Friends have been known for their staunch, unshakable convictions.

QUAAKERS VERGADERING.   FRONTI NULLA FIDES.   THE QUAKERS MEETING.

In the Quaker meetings, women as well as men were allowed to speak whenever the Spirit moved them. This brought ridicule on the Friends, as shown in this contemporary drawing.

When he was not in prison, Fox spent most of his time in Swarthmoor Hall—Margaret's home—and this became the headquarters of the Friends. The rest of the time he traveled throughout England and abroad, visiting Quaker meetings and taking his message to new areas. First he went to Scotland, where he was accused of sedition; then to Ireland; later he spent two years in the Caribbean and North America; and he also made two visits to the Continent. In all these lands he gained converts, and by the time of his death, in 1691, his followers were counted by the tens of thousands.

They too were persecuted. They were thrown in jail for vagrancy, blasphemy, inciting to riot, and refusing to pay tithes. In 1664, Charles II issued an edict forbidding unlicensed religious assemblies. Many groups continued gathering in secret. But the Quakers declared that it would be a lie to do so, and therefore simply disobeyed the royal edict. Thousands were then imprisoned, and by the time religious tolerance was granted in 1689, hundreds had died in prison.

The most famous of Fox's followers was William Penn, after whom the state of Pennsylvania is named. His father was a British admiral who tried to secure for him the best education available. While he was a student, young William became a Puritan. Then, while studying in France, he came under the influence of the Huguenots. In 1667, back in England, he became a Quaker. His father, not knowing what to do with so "fanatical" a son, threw him out of the house. Penn continued firm in his convictions, and eventually had to spend seven months in the Tower of London. It is said that at that time he sent word to the king, that the Tower was the worst of arguments to convince him, so, no matter who is right, whoever uses force to seek religious assent is necessarily wrong. Finally, thanks to the intervention of his father and other well-placed friends, he was set free. He then spent several years raising a family, traveling throughout Europe, and writing in defense of the Friends.

His arguments in defense of religious tolerance, however, were not well received. Some even said that he was secretly a Jesuit, and that his true goal was to restore to Roman Catholics the privileges they had lost. It was then that Penn conceived the idea of what he called his "holy experiment." Some friends had spoken to him about New Jersey, in North America. Since the crown owed him a significant amount of money, and was not willing to pay him in cash, Penn was able to obtain from Charles II a grant of land in what is now Pennsylvania. His purpose was to found a new colony in which there would be complete religious freedom. By then other British colonies had been founded in North America. But, with the exception of Rhode Island, all were marked by religious intolerance. In Massachusetts, the most intolerant of the colonies, Quakers were persecuted, condemned to exile, and even mutilated and executed. What Penn now proposed was a new colony in which all would be free to worship according to their own convictions. This seemed bad enough to an intolerant age. But even worse was Penn's plan to buy from the Indians the land that the crown had granted him. He was convinced that the Indians, and not the crown, were the legitimate owners of the land. And he hoped to establish such cordial relations with them that the settlers would have no need to defend themselves by force of arms. The capital of this holy experiment would be called *Philadelphia*—the city of *fraternal love*.

No matter how ill-conceived Penn's experiment might have seemed to the more "solid" British citizens, soon there were many people, not only in England, but also in other parts of Europe, willing to take part in it. Many of them were Quakers, and therefore the Friends dominated the political life of the colony for some time. But there were also settlers of many different persuasions. Under the leadership of Penn, who was the first governor of the colony, relations with the Indians were excellent, and for a long time his dream of a peaceful settlement was a reality. Much later, in 1756, another governor declared war on the Indians, and the Quakers resigned their positions in government. But the religious tolerance that was part of Penn's "holy experiment" was eventually imbedded in the U.S. Constitution, as well as in those of many other countries.

EMANUEL SWEDENBORG

George Fox was born in the year of Boehme's death; and Emanuel Swedenborg (1688–1772), was born three years before the death of Fox. Therefore, the lives of the three leaders with whom we deal in this chapter span almost the totality of the seventeenth and eighteenth centuries.

Some of Swedenborg's teachings were very similar to those of Boehme and Fox, but in other respects he was very different from them. While the other two were of humble birth, Swedenborg was born in an aristocratic Swedish family. Also in contrast to the two men, he received the best education available, for he studied at the University of Uppsala, and then spent five years traveling in England, the Netherlands, France, and Germany, always in the quest for knowledge. While Fox and Boehme showed signs of their religious restlessness from an early age, young Swedenborg was interested in scientific studies, and it was through these that he began the quest that led him to his religious convictions.

After many years of scientific inquiry, Swedenborg had a vision he said had carried him into the spiritual world, where he had been able to see eternal truths. After that vision he wrote voluminously on the true meaning of reality and of Scripture. According to him, all that exists is a reflection of the attributes of God, and therefore the visible world "corresponds" with the invisible one. The same is true of Scripture, which reflects truths that can only be known by those who have entered the spiritual world.

Swedenborg was convinced that his writings would form the beginning of a new era in the history of the world and of religion. He even claimed that what had taken place when he received his revelations was what the Bible meant when speaking of the second coming of Christ. As was to be expected, such ideas were not well received by the majority of his contemporaries, and therefore the circle of his followers was very small. He himself did not feel called to found a new church, but rather to call the existing one to a new understanding of its nature and message. But in 1784, twelve years after his death, his disciples founded the Church of the New Jerusalem, whose members were never many but which has survived into the twenty-first century. Also, early in the nineteenth century, the Swedenborgian Society was founded with the purpose of publishing and distributing his writings.

Of the three religious leaders discussed in this chapter, only Fox was able to lead and organize a vast movement. This was partly because he was convinced that a community of believers was necessary for religious life. Also, Fox and his Friends contrasted with most other spiritualists in their interest in social problems and their active participation in seeking solutions to social ills. But, apart from the case of the Quakers, the spiritualist movement was destined to have little impact on the church and on society at large, for its interest was individualistic and otherworldly. A far greater impact would be made by another movement of protest against both rationalism and cold dogmatism—a movement to which we shall now turn.

24

The Pietist Option

How many rich men are there among the Methodists (observe, there
was not one, when they were first joined together) who actually do
"deny themselves and take up their cross daily"? Who of you that are
now rich, deny yourselves just as you did when you were poor?

JOHN WESLEY

Pietism was a response to the dogmatism of the theologians and the rationalism of the philosophers, both of which it contrasted with the living
faith that is at the heart of Christianity, and to the Thirty Years' War, which
led many to see greater value in personal devotion and religious experience.
Although, in its strict sense, *Pietism* refers only to the German movement
led by Spener and Francke, in this chapter we shall deal also with the similar
movements led by Zinzendorf and Wesley.

GERMAN PIETISM: SPENER AND FRANCKE

Although many of the elements of what was later called *Pietism* were already circulating in Germany long before his time, Philip Jakob Spener
(1635–1705) has rightly been called the father of Pietism. He was born and
reared in Alsace, in an aristocratic family of deep Lutheran convictions. He
studied theology in the best Protestant universities and, after receiving his
doctorate, became a pastor in Frankfurt. Since pastors were supported by
the state, and considered government functionaries, there were many who
were content with preaching and performing the sacraments. But Spener
was convinced that his task went far beyond that, and included fostering
the personal faith of his parishioners. As a pastor in Frankfurt, he founded
groups of Bible study and devotion that he called "colleges of piety." In 1675,

five years after beginning this experiment, he published his *Pia desideria,* in which he outlined a program for the development of piety. This became the fundamental charter of Pietism.

In this book, Spener turned to the Lutheran doctrine of the universal priesthood of believers, and suggested that there be less emphasis on the differences between laity and clergy, and more on the common responsibility of all Christians. This in turn meant that there should be among the laity a more intense life of devotion and study. To attain this goal, Spener suggested small groups such as his "colleges of piety." As to pastors and theologians, he insisted that candidates should be examined to ascertain that they were "true Christians" of deep personal faith. And he also called on preachers to set aside their polemical and academic tone, for the purpose of preaching is not to show the preacher's knowledge, but rather to call believers to be obedient to the Word of God. In all this there was no attack on the doctrines of the church, for Spener was in total agreement with them. But he insisted that doctrine is not to serve as a substitute for personal faith. While it is true that theological error may have disastrous consequences for the Christian life, it is also true that those who do not go beyond dogma have scarcely penetrated the riches of Christianity. Thus, what he proposed was a new reformation—or at least the completion of what had begun in the sixteenth century and been interrupted by doctrinal debates. Soon many saw in him a new Luther, and from various parts of Germany he received letters thanking him for his inspiration and asking his advice.

All this, however, was not regarded favorably by the leaders of Lutheran orthodoxy. Although Spener did not deviate from Lutheran doctrine, he seemed to discount the fine points of doctrine that orthodoxy had clarified. And he insisted—as had Luther before him—on the need to return constantly to Scriptures and to read it with a spirit of devotion and piety. Furthermore, there was one point at which he seemed to deviate from the Lutheran tradition. Luther, concerned and overwhelmed as he was by the doctrine of justification by faith, had paid scant attention to sanctification. In the struggles of the time, he had insisted that what was important was not the manner of life of the believer, but the grace of God—for it is grace, and not personal sanctity, that justifies. Calvin and the Reformed tradition, while agreeing with Luther on justification, insisted that the God who justifies is also the One who sanctifies, and that God offers to believers the power for holiness of life. On this point, Spener and his followers were closer to Calvin than to Luther. Spener himself had been influenced by Reformed teachers, and was convinced that Lutheranism should place greater emphasis on the need for sanctification. For this reason, many orthodox Lutheran theologians declared that he was in truth a Calvinist.

Spener also made himself vulnerable by his apocalypticism. As has happened so often in difficult times, he became convinced that the prophecies of the book of Revelation were being fulfilled, and that the end was near. Since his predictions did not come true, his enemies could argue that, having erred on that point, he was probably mistaken on others as well.

In a sense, what was at stake in the controversy over Pietism was whether the Christian faith should simply serve to sanction common morality, or should rather call believers to a different sort of life. Orthodox preaching took for granted that God requires of believers nothing more than correct doctrine and a decent life. The Pietists insisted on the contrast between what society expects of its members and what God requires of the faithful. This has always been an uncomfortable challenge for a comfortable church.

Spener's greatest follower was August Hermann Francke, who was also from a well-to-do Lutheran family. His teachings were similar to Spener's—although he did not agree with the latter's interpretation of current events as those described in Revelation. Even more than Spener, he insisted on the joy of Christian life, which should be a song of praise to God. As a professor at the University of Halle, he also paid more attention to the relationship between Pietism and traditional Lutheran theology. He described his own religious experience as follows:

> Suddenly, God heard me. As easily as one turns a hand, my doubts vanished. In my heart I was certain of the grace of God in Jesus Christ. Since then I was able to call God, not only "God," but also "Father." Sadness and anxiety immediately left my heart. And I was suddenly overcome by a wave of joy, such that I praised and magnified God aloud, who had granted me such grace.[9]

This description of a religious experience, coupled with those of Wesley and others, has led to the false assumption that Pietists insisted on the need for such a personal experience. In fact, in its early stages the movement advocated a living, personal faith, and the manner or time in which one arrived at it was not of prime importance.

Thousands of Christians embraced the Pietist movement, and joined in small circles or "colleges of piety," even though some theologians accused the movement of being emotional, subjective, and even heretical. Eventually, in spite of such opposition, Pietism left its mark on the entire Lutheran tradition. And, although both Spener and Francke were Lutherans, Pietism also gained adherents among the German Reformed. The outstanding figure of Reformed Pietism was F.A. Lampe (1683–1729), whose hymns, sermons, and books did much to spread the spirit of Pietism. Lampe avoided the technical language typical of orthodoxy, and thus won a wide following among the laity, and bitter opposition from academic theologians. But Reformed orthodoxy in Germany did not have the political leverage of Lutheran orthodoxy, and therefore Reformed Pietism did not suffer the political pressures under which its Lutheran counterpart labored—at least, not until it moved into the Netherlands, where Reformed orthodoxy held sway. Later, in North America, the Great Awakening would be an indication of the degree to which Pietism was making inroads into the Reformed tradition.

However, the most significant contribution of Pietism to the story of Christianity was the birth of Protestant missions. The reformers of the sixteenth century, involved as they were in a struggle for the survival of Protestantism, paid little attention to the non-Christian world. Some even declared that modern Christians were not called to preach to other nations, since that was a commandment given exclusively to the apostles. At first, the Pietists were not interested in world missions, although they were active in meeting the needs of their fellow Christians by founding schools and institutions to serve orphans, the poor, and others in need. But in 1707 the king of Denmark, an admirer of the Pietists, decided to send missionaries to his colonies in India. He could find no one in his own possessions to undertake this task, and asked Francke at the University of Halle to send him two of his most promising disciples. These two, Bartholomaeus Ziegenbalg and Heinrich Plutschau, founded in India the mission of Tranquebar. Their letters and reports, circulated in Germany, awakened great interest among the Pietists. Soon, under Francke's direction, the University of Halle became a center for the training of missionaries. And in Denmark, with the king's support and under Pietist leadership, a school of missions was founded for training missionaries to Lapland and Greenland.

ZINZENDORF AND THE MORAVIANS

Meanwhile, Pietism had also made an impact on the young Count Nikolaus Ludwig von Zinzendorf, Spener's godson. Zinzendorf had been profoundly religious from childhood and would later declare that he had never felt separated from God, and could speak of no experience of conversion. His parents, devout Pietists, sent him to the University of Halle, where he studied under Francke. Later he also went to Wittenberg, one of the main centers of Lutheran orthodoxy, and repeatedly clashed with his teachers. After traveling to other countries, and studying law, he was married and entered the service of the court of Dresden.

It was at Dresden that Zinzendorf first met a group of Moravians who would change the course of his life. These were Hussites who had been forced to leave their native Moravia to escape persecution, and Zinzendorf offered them asylum in his lands. There they founded the community of Herrnhut, which so attracted Zinzendorf's interest that he resigned his post at Dresden and joined it. Under his direction, the Moravians became part of the local Lutheran parish. But there were tensions, for the Lutherans were unwilling to trust these foreigners imbued with Pietism.

In 1731, while in Denmark, Zinzendorf met a group of Eskimos who had been converted by the Lutheran missionary Hans Egede, and this kindled in him an interest in missions that would dominate the rest of his life. Soon the community at Herrnhut was on fire with the same zeal, and in 1732 its first missionaries left for the Caribbean. In a few years, there were also Moravian missionaries in Africa, India, South America, and North America—where they founded the communities of Bethlehem and Nazareth in Pennsylvania, and Salem in North Carolina. Thus, within a period of twenty years a movement that had begun with two hundred refugees had more missionaries overseas than had been sent out by all Protestant churches since the Protestant Reformation two centuries earlier.

Meanwhile, conflicts with Lutheran authorities in Germany did not abate. Zinzendorf himself was banned from Saxony, and traveled to North America, where he was present at the founding of the Bethlehem community in 1741. Shortly after Zinzendorf's return, peace was made between the Lutherans and the Moravians, who were acknowledged as true Lutherans. But this was only temporary. Zinzendorf himself had agreed to be made a bishop by the Moravians, who claimed to have the ancient episcopal succession of the Hussites, and this caused further tensions with the Lutherans.

Zinzendorf died at Herrnhut in 1760, and shortly thereafter his followers broke with Lutheranism. Although the Moravian church never had a large membership and soon was unable to continue sending and supporting so many missionaries, its example contributed to the great missionary awakening of the nineteenth century. But perhaps the greatest significance of the movement was its impact on John Wesley and, through him, on the entire Methodist tradition.

JOHN WESLEY AND METHODISM

Late in 1735, and early in 1736, a second Moravian contingent was sailing to the New World hoping to preach to the Indians of Georgia. On shipboard was a young Anglican priest, John Wesley by name, whom Governor Oglethorpe of Georgia had invited to serve as a pastor in Savannah. The young man had accepted, hoping to be able to preach to the Indians, about whose virtues he had unrealistic expectations. All went well during the early days of the crossing, and young Wesley learned enough German to be able to communicate with his Moravian companions. But then the weather turned against them, and the ship was soon in dire straits. The mainmast split, and panic would have overwhelmed the crew, had it not been for the unbelievable calm of the Moravians, who sang throughout the ordeal. Meanwhile, Wesley, who was also chaplain of the vessel, came to the bitter realization that he was more concerned about himself than about his fellow travelers. After the storm, the Moravians told him that they could behave so bravely because they did not fear death; and the young man began to doubt the depth of his own faith.

After reaching Savannah, Wesley asked the Moravian Gottlieb Spangenberg for advice regarding his work as a pastor and as a missionary to the Indians. In his diary, he left a record of that conversation:

> He said, "My brother, I must first ask you one or two questions. Have you the witness within yourself? Does the Spirit of God bear witness with your spirit, that you are a child of God?" I was surprised, and knew not what to answer. He observed it, and asked, "Do you know Jesus Christ?" I paused, and said, "I know he is the Saviour of the world." "True," replied he; "but do you know he has saved you?" I answered, "I hope he has died to save me." He only added, "Do you know yourself?" I said, "I do."

John Wesley, the founder of Methodism, combined the religious zeal of the Moravians with the social activism that had long characterized the Reformed tradition.

As a postscript to that conversation, the young Anglican pastor commented: "But I fear they were vain words."[10]

These experiences left him moved and confused. Wesley had always thought of himself as a good Christian. His father, Samuel Wesley, was an Anglican priest, and his mother Susanna was the daughter of another. She had been particularly careful in the religious and moral instruction of her nineteen children. When John was five, fire broke out in the parsonage. The young lad was miraculously saved, and thereafter his mother thought of him as "a brand plucked from the burning" because God had plans for him. At Oxford, he had distinguished himself both as a scholar and as a devout young man. After helping his father in the parish for some time, he had returned to Oxford, where he had joined a religious society founded by his brother Charles and a group of friends. Its members had made a covenant to lead a holy and sober life, to take communion at least once a week, to be faithful in their private devotions, to visit the prisons regularly, and to spend three hours together every afternoon, studying the Bible and books of devotion. Since he was the only ordained priest among them, and he also had exceptional gifts, John Wesley soon became the leader of that group which other students mocked as a "holy club" and—because of their methodical style of life—"methodists."

That was the story of that young priest who now, in distant Georgia, doubted the depth of his faith. As a pastor, he failed miserably, for he expected his parishioners to behave like the "holy club," and his flock expected him to be content with their attendance at worship. John's brother Charles, who was also in Georgia serving under James Oglethorpe, was disappointed with his work, and decided to return to England. But John stayed on, not because he had greater success, but because he would not give up. Then he was forced to leave under a cloud. A young woman whom he had courted had married another. Wesley, deeming the young bride frivolous, denied communion to her, and was sued for defamation. Confused and bitter, he decided to return home, which in any case seems to have been what his parishioners wanted.

Back in England, not knowing what to do, he contacted the Moravians. One of them, Peter Boehler, became his religious advisor. Wesley came to the conclusion that he lacked saving faith, and that therefore he should cease preaching. Boehler advised him to continue preaching faith until he had it, and once he had it, to continue preaching because he had it. Finally, on May 24, 1738, Wesley had the experience that changed his life:

> In the evening I went very unwillingly to a society in Aldersgate Street, where one was reading Luther's preface to the Epistle to the Romans. About a quarter before nine, while he was describing the change which God works in the heart through faith in Christ, I felt my heart strangely warmed. I felt I did trust in Christ, Christ alone for salvation: And an assurance was given me, that he had taken away *my* sins, even *mine,* and saved *me* from the law of sin and death.[11]

The methodical life of the members of the Holy Club at Oxford earned its members the moniker of "methodists."

After that experience, Wesley no longer doubted his own salvation. Furthermore, that salvation no longer consumed all his interest. Being assured of it, he could devote all his concern to the salvation of others. As a first step, he visited the Moravian community of Herrnhut. That visit, although greatly inspiring, convinced him that Moravian spirituality was ill-suited to his own temperament and involvement in social issues. Therefore, in spite of his gratitude, he decided not to become a Moravian.

While all this was taking place in Wesley's life, another former member of the "holy club," George Whitefield, had become a famous preacher. A few years earlier he had been moved by an experience similar to Wesley's at Aldersgate, and now divided his time between his parish in Georgia and preaching in England, where he had remarkable success, particularly in the industrial city of Bristol. His preaching was emotional, and when some critics objected to the manner in which he used the pulpit he began preaching in the open, as was often done in Georgia. Since he needed help in Bristol, and in any case would soon have to return to the New World, Whitefield invited Wesley to help him and take charge during his absence.

Although Wesley accepted Whitefield's invitation, the fiery preacher's methods were not entirely to his liking. He objected to preaching in the open. Much later he commented on those early days, declaring that at that time he was so convinced that God wished everything to be done in order, that he almost thought it a sin to save souls outside of church buildings. Slowly, in view of the results, he reconciled himself to that sort of preaching, although he always deplored the need for it. He was also worried about the response to his preaching. Some people would weep and loudly bemoan their sins, while others would collapse in anguish. Then they would express great joy, declaring that they felt cleansed of their evil. Wesley would have preferred more solemn proceedings. Eventually, he decided that what was taking place in such instances was a struggle between Satan and the Holy Spirit, and that he should not hinder the work of God. In any case, after the early years such extreme occurrences became less frequent.

Wesley and Whitefield worked together for some time, although slowly Wesley became the main leader of the movement. Eventually, they parted because of theological differences. Both were Calvinists in most matters; but, on the issue of predestination and free will, Wesley departed from orthodox Calvinism, preferring the Arminian position. After several debates, the two friends decided that each would follow his own path, and that they would avoid controversies—an agreement that their followers did not always keep. With the help of the Countess of Huntingdon, Whitefield organized the Calvinist Methodist Church, which was strongest in Wales.

Wesley had no interest in founding a new denomination. On the contrary, he was an Anglican minister, and throughout his life he remained such. Rather, his purpose was to awaken and cultivate the faith of the masses in the Church of England, as Pietism was doing for German Lutheranism. For that reason he avoided scheduling his preaching in conflict with the services of the Church of England, and he always took for granted that Methodist meetings would serve as preparation to attend Anglican worship and take communion in it. For him, as for most of the church through the centuries, the center of worship was communion. This he took and expected his followers to take as frequently as possible, in the official services of the Church of England.

Although the movement had no intention of becoming a separate church, it did need an organization. In Bristol, the real birthplace of the movement,

Partly through the influence of Susanna Wesley on her children, many of the early leaders of Methodism were women.

Wesley's followers were organized into *societies* that at first met in private homes and later had their own buildings. When Methodist societies grew too large for the effective care of their members, Wesley followed a friend's suggestion and divided them into *classes*, each with eleven members and a leader. These met weekly to read Scripture, pray, discuss religious matters, and collect funds. Since, in order to be a class leader, it was not necessary to be wealthy or educated, this gave significant participation to many who felt left out of the structure of the Church of England. Also, since there were classes for women, under feminine leadership, this also gave women a prominent place in Methodism.

Susanna Wesley, who had left an indelible imprint on her sons John and Charles, continued providing them with wise guidance in the early years of the movement.

The movement grew rapidly, and Wesley was forced to travel throughout the British Isles, preaching and organizing his followers. When the bishop of Bristol tried to limit his activity, telling him that his itinerant preaching perturbed the order of the parishes, Wesley responded, "The world is my parish." Those words, originally uttered in protest against a rigid ecclesiastical organization, later became the motto of the Methodist missionary enterprise. Meanwhile, however, Wesley and his young movement needed more people to share in the task of preaching. A few Anglican priests had joined the movement. Most noteworthy among them was John Wesley's brother Charles, famous for his hymns—including *O for a Thousand Tongues to Sing, Hark, the Herald Angels Sing, Christ the Lord is Risen Today*, and *Love Divine, All Loves Excelling*. It was John Wesley, however, who carried the heaviest burden, preaching several times a day and traveling thousands of miles on horseback every year, until the age of seventy.

These circumstances led to the use of lay preachers. When Wesley heard that layman Thomas Maxfield had been preaching in one of the societies in London, he planned to put a stop to it. But his mother, Susanna, asked him to hear the man before making a decision, and Maxfield so impressed Wesley that he decided that the use of lay preachers was God's answer to the movement's urgent need for preachers. These were not to take the place of the clergy, for they were not to offer communion, and this was the highest form of worship. Their function, like those of the societies, was intended to be parallel and complementary to the sacramental function of the Church of England and its ordained personnel. Among these Methodist lay preachers there were soon a number of women—which was not then possible among the ordained clergy.

With all these elements in place, Wesley organized his followers into a *Connection*. A number of societies joined to form a *circuit*, under the leadership of a *superintendent*. To aid in the administration of the Connection, Wesley began holding periodic meetings that included both the Anglican clergy who formed part of it, and the lay preachers. This eventually evolved into the Annual Conference, in which those who were to serve in each circuit were appointed—usually for a period of three years.

In this entire process, conflicts were not lacking. In the early years, there were frequent acts of violence against Methodists. Some of the clergy and the nobility resented the authority the new movement gave to people from the lower classes. Meetings were frequently interrupted by paid ruffians, and Wesley's life was occasionally in danger. Later, this opposition abated, until it eventually ceased. There were also theological conflicts. Wesley grudgingly broke with the Moravians, whose inclination to Quietism he feared and deplored.

But the most significant conflicts were with the Anglican Church, to which Wesley belonged and in which he wished to remain. Until his last days, he reprimanded Methodists who wished to break away from Anglicanism. But the breach was unavoidable. Among the Anglican authorities, some rightly saw the Methodist movement as an indication of their own shortcomings, and therefore resented it. Others felt that the Methodists' breach of order in preaching everywhere, without regard for parish boundaries, was unforgivable. Wesley himself was enough of an Anglican to bemoan the need to do this; but he felt compelled by the urge to reach people whom the church was not reaching.

A difficult legal decision came to make matters more tense. According to English law, non-Anglican worship services and church buildings were to be allowed, but they must be officially registered as such. This put the Methodists in a difficult situation, for the Church of England did not acknowledge their meetings and buildings. If they registered, this would be a tacit decla-

ration that they were not Anglicans. If they did not, they would be breaking the law. In 1787, after great hesitation, Wesley instructed his preachers
to register, and thus the first legal step was taken toward the formation of
a separate church. Three years earlier, however, Wesley had taken a step
that had more drastic theological implications. For a long time, as a serious
student of patristics, Wesley had been convinced that in the early church a
bishop was the same as a *presbyter* or *elder*. This led him to the conviction
that all ordained presbyters, including himself, had the power of ordination.
But he refrained from employing it to avoid further alienating the leadership of the Church of England. The independence of the United States,
however, posed new difficulties. During the War of Independence most
of the Anglican clergy had been Loyalists, and after independence most
of them had returned to England. This made it difficult—and sometimes
impossible—for the inhabitants of the new nation to partake in communion. The bishop of London, who supposedly still had jurisdiction over the
former colonies, refused to ordain personnel for the United States. Wesley
deplored what he took to be the unwarranted rebellion of Britain's former
colonies, both because he was a staunch supporter of the king's authority
and because he could not fathom how the rebels could claim that they were
fighting for freedom while they themselves held slaves. Even so, convinced
as he was that the celebration of communion was the very heart of Christian
worship, Wesley felt that, no matter what the political stance of people in
the colonies might be, they must not be deprived of the sacrament. Finally,
in 1784, he ordained two lay preachers as presbyters for the new country,
and made Anglican priest Thomas Coke their *superintendent*—a word that
he well knew had the same meaning as the Greek word translated as *bishop*.
Later, he ordained others to serve also in Scotland and elsewhere. In spite of
having taken these steps, Wesley continued insisting on the need to avoid
breaking with the Church of England. His brother Charles told him that the
ordination of ministers for the New World was in itself a break. In 1786, the
conference decided that, in those places where the Anglican churches hadn't
the room for the entire population, or where their priests were inept, it was
permitted to schedule Methodist gatherings in conflict with Anglican worship. Although Wesley refused to acknowledge it, by the time of his death
Methodism was clearly becoming a separate church.

The success of Methodism in England was partly due to the degree to
which it responded to new needs resulting from the Industrial Revolution.

During the latter half of the eighteenth century, England was undergoing a process of rapid industrialization. This created a mass movement of the population to the industrial centers. Such people, uprooted by economic circumstances, tended to lose their connections with the church, whose parish structure was unable to respond to the needs of the new urban masses. It was among those masses that Methodism filled a need and found most of its members.

In North America, a completely different process—the westward movement of settlers—gave rise to an uprooted population lacking traditional ecclesiastic links, and whom the older churches seldom reached. It was among these people that Methodism achieved its greatest success. Officially, North American Methodists became a separate church before their British counterpart. In 1771, Wesley had sent lay preacher Francis Asbury to the colonies. Asbury was the driving force behind Methodism moving westward along with the frontier. When the thirteen colonies declared their independence, Wesley wrote against their rebellion. But American Methodist preachers were mostly colonials who supported the cause of independence, or at least remained neutral. As a result, Methodists in the United States, while still admiring Wesley, were no longer bound by his wishes. It was against those wishes, and in response to the lack of Anglican ministers, that the American movement organized itself into the Methodist Episcopal Church. The name *Episcopal* was the direct result of a conflict with Wesley, who called both himself and Coke superintendents, but was enraged when he learned that Coke and Asbury—by then also a superintendent—called themselves *bishops*. From that point on, American Methodists have had bishops, and English Methodists have not.

Wesley died in 1791. After his death, Methodism underwent a period of inner struggles, mostly revolving around the question of relations with Anglicanism. Eventually, in England as well as in other lands where Methodism had grown strong, Methodist churches were formed that were completely independent of Anglicanism.

25

The Thirteen Colonies

God requires not a uniformity of religion to be enacted and enforced
in any civil state, which enforced uniformity, sooner or later, is the
greatest occasion of civil war, ravishing of conscience, persecution of
Christ Jesus in his servants, and of the hypocrisy and destruction of
millions of souls.

ROGER WILLIAMS

The sixteenth century had seen the building of the Spanish and Portuguese empires—each on its agreed side of the Treaty of Tordesillas,
signed in 1494 and modified in 1506. In North America, the Spanish Empire
included New Spain (Mexico), which at the time extended well into what is
now the western half of the United States. In the seventeenth century, however, other powers began building their own empires. In North America,
the French settled in Quebec in 1609. But the most successful of the new
colonial powers was Great Britain, whose overseas expansion began in the
seventeenth century and reached its peak in the nineteenth. Among its first
overseas enterprises were the thirteen colonies in North America that would
later become the United States.

It is customary to contrast the origin of these colonies with the Spanish
ones, and to try to explain their divergent results by those different origins.
It is commonly said, for instance, that the Spanish came for gold whereas the
British came for religious motives; that the Spanish were cruel to the Indians,
but the British tried to live in peace with them; that the Spanish brought the
Inquisition, while the British brought religious freedom; and that the Spanish came as aristocrats, and became rich on the basis of Indian labor, and that
the English came to work the land. Although there is a measure of truth in
some of these assertions, historical facts are much more complex.

The economic motivations of the British colonial enterprise were just as strong as those of the Spanish. But the fact was that the Spanish had already conquered the richest empires, and there were no longer treasures to be had as great as those of the Aztecs and the Incas. Nor were there large populations that could be forced to work for the colonizers. Most of the natives of the thirteen colonies—and beyond—were organized in nomadic or semi-nomadic tribes, and therefore could simply flee into the interior to avoid becoming servants or slaves to the settlers. Therefore, British investors could not hope to become rich by sheer conquest, as Cortez and Pizarro had done, nor by exploiting Indian labor, as the Spanish settlers did, but instead were forced to set their store in commerce. When it became clear that trade with the Indians would not produce the necessary returns, the colonies turned to agriculture, still with a view to exporting the produce to Europe and thus making a profit for the owners of the colonies. This was done with British labor. Generally, these were not free colonists cultivating their own land, but indentured labor working the land owned by a colonial company. At first, colonials were not even allowed to own land. As to religious freedom, while it is true that Rhode Island and Pennsylvania led the world in that direction, it is also true that the Pilgrims of New England were no more tolerant than the Spanish inquisitors. Finally, on the matter of mistreatment of Indians, one must not forget that the destruction of the original population in what eventually became the United States was much more thorough than that perpetrated by the Spanish in their colonies—with the exception of the Caribbean. This had little to do with one nation or the other expressing greater compassion. Rather, it was a matter of diverse economic circumstances. What the Spanish wanted from the Indians was their labor, and therefore they had no interest in decimating them. The British wanted their land; therefore, most often, in both the colonial period and after independence, they followed a policy of extermination and confinement. In areas where the goal of the Spanish and Portuguese was also to obtain land, they followed similar policies.

It is true that new circumstances in Europe—particularly in Great Britain—led many to migrate to the New World for religious reasons. In speaking of the Puritan Revolution in England, we have seen the great variety of religious persuasions that appeared. Such variety had no place in the policies of governments whose goal was religious uniformity as a means to political stability. Laws demanding religious conformity were more difficult to apply overseas; therefore, religious dissidents hoped for an escape from oppression by migrating to the colonies, or by founding new ones. Some of these dissidents were no more tolerant than were the governments from which they were fleeing. But others came to the conclusion that religious tolerance was best, not only as a matter of convenience, but also because it was God's will.

VIRGINIA

The first British colonial ventures in North America failed. In 1584, Sir Walter Raleigh, Queen Elizabeth's favorite, was granted a royal charter for the colonization of North America. He named the area that he hoped to colonize *Virginia*, in honor of Elizabeth, the *Virgin Queen*. But his two ventures, one in 1585 and another in 1587, did not succeed. The first contingent of settlers returned to England, and the second simply disappeared.

It was in the spring of 1607 that the permanent colonization of Virginia began. In May of that year, 105 settlers landed near the mouth of a river that they named *James* after their new king—Elizabeth had died four years earlier—and founded Jamestown. There was a chaplain among them, for the Virginia Company, under whose auspices the enterprise was taking place, hoped to establish the Church of England in the new land, and to offer its services both to the settlers and to the Indians. It was also hoped that the new colony would put a stop to Spanish expansion to the north, feared both for nationalist reasons and for dread of "popery." The colony's main purpose, however, was not religious but economic—to the degree that the Church of England never had a settled bishop in Virginia or in the rest of the thirteen colonies. The stockholders of the Virginia Company simply hoped that trade with the Indians, and perhaps agriculture, would yield a handsome profit.

Since the founding of Virginia took place at the high point of Puritan influence in the Church of England, many of the stockholders and settlers believed that the colony should be ruled by Puritan principles. Its early laws required attendance at worship twice a day, the strict observance of the Lord's Day, and stern punishment for profanity and immodest dress. But dreams of a holy commonwealth would have to yield to political realities. King James detested Puritanism, and would not have it in his colony, Virginia. A war with the Indians in 1622 served as an excuse, and in 1624 he placed the colony under his direct rule. After that time Puritan influence waned. Later Charles I, following James's policy against the Virginia Puritans, took a vast portion of Virginia, created the colony of Maryland, and granted it to a Catholic proprietor. Meanwhile the colony, at first a marginal enterprise, had found economic success by growing and exporting tobacco. Since this required much labor, by 1619 the colony began importing slaves from Africa. Thus began the slave-holding economy that became characteristic of Virginia and other colonies.

The Puritan Revolution in England made little impact on Virginia. By then settlers were more interested in growing tobacco and opening new lands for cultivation than in the religious strife in England. Their former Puritan zeal had lost its vigor in the midst of economic prosperity. In particular, the Puritan valuation of labor had little meaning in a society based on slavery. Therefore, when the revolution broke out in England, and later when the Stuarts were restored, these events did not shake the colony. Most of the settlers were still members of the Church of England. This was no longer the Puritan Anglicanism of times past, but rather a facile and aristocratic Anglicanism, one easily adapted to the plantation owners, but with little influence on the slaves or on the lower classes of the white population.

The Church of England did little for the conversion of slaves. One of the reasons for this was that there were ancient principles prohibiting Christians from holding fellow believers in slavery, and some insisted that those principles were still valid. Therefore, to avoid difficulties, slave masters preferred that their slaves not be baptized. In 1667, a law was passed declaring that baptism did not change a slave's condition—another indication of the degree to which established religion was willing to bend to the interests of the powerful. But even then, little was done for the conversion of the slaves, since many owners felt that keeping them in ignorance was the best way to assure their service and submission.

The adaptation of the church to the interests of the powerful also had consequences among the white population. While the nascent aristocracy remained faithful to Anglicanism, many in the lower classes began turning to dissident movements. Severe measures were taken against them, and hundreds migrated to nearby Catholic Maryland, where there was greater religious freedom. The Quakers also made inroads in Virginia, in spite of laws against them. When George Fox visited the colony in 1762, he rejoiced in finding many Friends, and also noted that, although the movement had been most successful among the lower classes, some of the aristocracy regarded it with favor. Later, through the efforts of Asbury and his preachers,

Methodism made great strides—although at that time it still considered itself a part of Anglicanism.

Other colonies were founded to the south of Virginia. The Carolinas, granted by the crown to a group of aristocrats and stockholders in 1663, were slow in developing. In order to foster immigration, the proprietors decreed religious freedom, thus attracting many dissidents from Virginia. The society that developed in the Carolinas—particularly in South Carolina—was similar to that of Virginia in its stratification. Again, the higher classes belonged to the Church of England, while many in the lower classes became either Quaker or Baptist. But even among the white population, most people seem to have had very little contact with any church.

Georgia was founded with two basic purposes in mind. The first was to halt the Spanish, who were moving north from their base in St. Augustine. The second was to serve as an alternative for debtors' prisons. By the beginning of the eighteenth century, there were many religious-minded people in England who sought to better the lot of the disinherited. This movement turned its attention, among other things, to prisons, whose inhuman conditions were the object of repeated attacks in Parliament. One of the leaders of this campaign was military hero James Oglethorpe, who decided that a colony should be founded in North America that could serve as an alternative to the incarceration of debtors. Royal approval was granted in 1732, and the first convicts arrived the following year. To these were soon added others, as well as many religious refugees from other areas. Although Anglicanism was the official religion, it made little impact on the colony. The failure of the Wesleys as Anglican pastors was typical of many others. The Moravians had a measure of success, although their number was never large. Perhaps the most significant religious movement in the early years of the Georgia colony was the popular response to George Whitefield's preaching, similar to what was taking place in England. By the time of his death in 1770, he had left his stamp on much of Georgia's religious life. Later, Methodists, Baptists and others harvested what he had sown.

THE NORTHERN PURITAN COLONIES

It was much farther north that Puritanism made its greatest impact. There, in what came to be called New England, several colonies were founded whose basic original motivation was clearly religious. The first of these was the Plymouth Plantation, founded by a group of dissidents who had left

England for the Netherlands, and then developed the idea of founding in the New World a community based on their religious principles. They came to an agreement with the Virginia Company, which was in urgent need of settlers, and among whose members there was strong Puritan influence. Finally, 101 settlers boarded the *Mayflower* and left for the New World. They reached land much farther north than they had intended, well beyond the limits of Virginia. Therefore, before landing they decided to organize themselves into a political body under the king of England but with the power to govern themselves. In their *Mayflower Compact,* they committed themselves to obey the "just and equal laws" passed by their own government. Then, after a tentative landing on Cape Cod, they settled at Plymouth. The first months of the new colony were tragic. The population was swept by an epidemic and only fifty survived. In the spring, however, the Indians taught the settlers how to grow corn; and with that crop, as well as by fishing and hunting, they set by enough stores to see them through the following winter. Eventually, they were also able to trade fur for things they needed from Europe, and thus the colony managed to survive.

Shortly after that first settlement, a group of English Puritans, wishing to found in the New World a community more akin to their conscience, organized the Massachusetts Bay Company. They agreed that they would take the company with them to the New World and establish its headquarters in the colony, thus hoping to avoid undue interference from the English government. When all was ready, more than a thousand settlers began the new colony. Unlike the Pilgrims of Plymouth, they were not separatists, but simply Puritans who still belonged to the Church of England yet wished to follow more closely the practices of the New Testament. Since they saw little hope for this in England, they migrated to America, where they expected to bring their ideals to fruition. This project was rendered all the more necessary by Archbishop Laud's measures against the Puritans. During his persecution, some ten thousand Puritans fled to New England, thus strengthening the colony of Massachusetts Bay, and giving birth to the new colonies of Connecticut and New Haven.

Charles I was preparing to take measures against these growing centers of Puritanism when he found himself involved in the civil war that cost him his throne and his life. But the war itself, and the Puritan victory, halted the migratory wave, for there was now hope of establishing the holy commonwealth, no longer on the distant shores of an unexplored continent,

The Mayflower "pilgrims" eventually became a symbol of the flight from religious and political oppression into a land of promise.

but in England itself. Although their sympathies were clearly on the side of the Puritan rebels, the colonies remained neutral, and devoted their efforts to increasing their territories and developing their institutions. Therefore, the restoration of the Stuarts was not as severe a blow for them as it was for Puritanism in England. Somewhat later, James II attempted to consolidate several of the northern colonies into the *Dominion of New England*. But his fall put an end to this project, and the colonies recovered many of their old privileges, although under new structures of government. It was at this time that religious tolerance was granted, although by royal decision, and not at the request of the settlers.

The Puritan colonies of New England—by then consolidated under the names *Massachusetts* and *Connecticut*—saw a number of theological controversies. The main difficulty was that many of these Puritans, while preserving the custom of baptizing children, insisted on the need of a conversion experience in order to be truly Christian. What, then, was the meaning of baptism? Would it not be better to wait until a person had the experience of conversion, and then administer baptism, as the Baptists claimed? Some found that to be the best solution. But this clashed with the Puritan goal of founding a society that would be guided by biblical principles. A Christian commonwealth is conceivable only if, as in ancient Israel, one becomes a member of it by birth, so that the civil and the religious communities are coextensive. For that reason, it was necessary to baptize the "children of the covenant," just as in ancient Israel they had been circumcised during infancy. But, on the other hand, if all who were baptized were members of the covenant, how could purity of life and doctrine be safeguarded? Furthermore, if infants were baptized as "children of the covenant," what was to be done with infants born of baptized parents who never had the experience of conversion? Thus, many came to the conclusion that there was a "half-way covenant," embracing those who, having been baptized, had not been converted. The children of such people were to be baptized, for they were still members of the covenant. But only those who had experienced a conversion were granted full membership in the church, and were vested with the power to participate in the process of making decisions. In any case, this controversy gave rise to bitter animosities, and as a result the original optimism of the settlers waned. There was also some debate as to the manner of government of the churches, and the relations between them. Finally, the majority settled on what amounted to congregational rule, although limited by the need for all congregations to agree to a *Confession of Faith* that was a revision of that of Westminster, and which the civil authorities were empowered to safeguard.

One of the most famous episodes of those early years was the trial of the "witches" of Salem, Massachusetts. Before those events, there had been other trials for witchcraft in Massachusetts, and three people had been hanged as a result. But in 1692, on the basis of the idle accusations of some young girls, rumors began circulating that witchcraft was widely practiced in Salem, and the rumors eventually led to hysteria. In total, twenty people—fourteen women and six men—were hanged, and several others died in prison. Some confessed that they had practiced witchcraft, and accused others of having been their mentors, thus hoping to save their lives. Eventually, accusations were leveled against respected members of the clergy, wealthy merchants, and even the governor's wife. At that point, the authorities decided that it was time to stop the investigations. Twenty years later, the courts of Massachusetts decided that the entire episode had been a gross injustice, and ordered indemnifications to be paid to the families of the victims. During the affair, two of the most influential religious leaders in New England were Increase Mather and his son Cotton. Increase (1639–1723) who came to serve as president of Harvard College, believed in the existence and power of witchcraft, and has been blamed for much of the Salem episode. On the other hand, he severely criticized the actual proceedings and the nature of the evidence leading to the condemnation of the "witches." His son Cotton took a similar position, writing against witchcraft and then deploring the manner in which the trials were conducted. Many have seen a connection between the Mathers's stringent views on women and on sexuality, and their attitude regarding witchcraft. The work of these two theologians, however, went far beyond the question of witchcraft, so that they—particularly Cotton, who wrote more that four hundred books and pamphlets—set the tone of the ethos of Puritan New England. In particular, much of what the Mathers said about women left its mark on a society that already limited the role of women. Even so, from the early years of the colony, women began to find new roles and means of expression, as may be seen in the work of the first American poet, Anne Bradstreet (1612–1672).

Some of the settlers did show an interest in the evangelization of their Indian neighbors. Remarkable on that score was the Mayhew family, who settled on Martha's Vineyard and worked for the conversion and education of the Indians for five generations—from 1642 until the death of Zacharias Mayhew, in 1806. However, the work that John Eliot began among the Mohicans in 1646 was of greater consequence. He was convinced that the Indians were the lost tribes of Israel, and that their conversion would bring about the fulfillment of ancient prophecies. He therefore gathered his converts in villages that were ruled according to the law of Moses. There he taught them European agricultural methods and mechanical arts, so that the communities could sustain themselves. Great stress was also placed on the reading and study of the Bible, which Eliot translated into Mohican after having laboriously learned that language and devised a method for writing it. Eliot himself founded fourteen such villages, and those who followed his inspiration founded many more.

In 1675, some Indians, under the leadership of a chief whom they called "King Philip," decided to put an end to the outrages being committed against them, and to the progressive invasion of their lands. In the conflict that ensued, known as King Philip's War, many of the converted Indians either took the side of the settlers or refrained from fighting. In spite of this, hundreds of them were kidnapped from their villages and forced to live on an overcrowded island in Boston Bay. Many others were killed by whites who felt that all Indians were enemies. When the settlers finally won the war, the captive Indians and those who surrendered were distributed among the whites—women and children to be their servants, and men as slaves to be sold and shipped as far away as possible. Few traces of Eliot's work remained after these events.

RHODE ISLAND AND THE BAPTISTS

The intolerance that reigned in the Puritan colonies forced some to abandon them. Most famous among these was Roger Williams, who had arrived in Massachusetts in 1631. After refusing to serve as a pastor in Boston, he declared that the Puritans in the colony erred in granting the civil authorities power to enforce those commandments that had to do with an individual's relationship with God. He was convinced that magistrates should be granted authority to enforce only those commandments that had to do with the ordering of society. He also declared that the land the colonies occupied belonged to the Indians, and that the entire colonial enterprise was unjust and illegal. These and other ideas, which at the time seemed radical, made Williams unpopular in Boston, and he moved to Plymouth. He became a pastor in Salem. But when he attempted the secession of his church, the authorities of Massachusetts expelled him. He then settled with a group of friends, first in Plymouth, and then in Narragansett, on lands that he bought from the Indians. There he founded the colony of Providence on the principle of religious freedom.

According to Williams, such freedom was required as part of the very obligation to worship God. Worship must be sincere, and all efforts to force it actually weaken it. Therefore, in the new colony the rights of citizenship would not be abridged on the basis of one's religious opinions or practices, and there would be a clear separation between church and state. These views he expounded in a treatise published in 1644, *The Bloudy Tenent of Persecution for the Cause of Conscience Discussed,* to which one of the main pastors of Massachusetts responded with *The Bloudy Tenent Washed and Made White in the Bloud of the Lambe.*

Meanwhile, others had moved to nearby areas for similar reasons. Late in 1637, prophet Anne Hutchinson was expelled from Massachusetts for, among other reasons, claiming to have received personal revelations. She and eighteen others founded Portsmouth on an island near Providence, also on the basis of religious freedom. Shortly thereafter, a group from Portsmouth founded the community of Newport, at the other end of the same island. All these communities grew rapidly with the influx of Baptists, Quakers, and others from the Puritan colonies. But the only legal claim of these new settlements was based on having bought their lands from the Indians, and many in the nearby colonies spoke of wanting to destroy what they considered the *sewer of New England*. Therefore, Roger Williams traveled to England, and in 1644 obtained from the Long Parliament the legal recognition of the Colony of Rhode Island and Providence Plantations, to be governed as a democracy. After the restoration of the Stuarts, Charles II confirmed the colony's legal rights.

Williams's church in Providence became Baptist. One of its members baptized Williams, who in turn baptized the others. But Williams himself did not remain in that church for long, for his ideas were becoming increasingly radical. His contacts with the Indians, whom he deeply respected, led him to declare that perhaps their religion was as acceptable in the eyes of God as was Christianity, and that in any case they did not have to become Christians in order to be saved. This attracted further attacks, not only from the Puritans of Massachusetts, but also from many Baptists in Providence. But he continued moving toward a radical spiritualism that eventually led him to the conclusion that all churches were false, and that Scripture was to be understood in purely spiritual terms.

Meanwhile, the Baptists of Providence were involved in their own controversies. In speaking of the Puritan Revolution in England, we had occasion to speak of the Baptists as one of the many groups that appeared at that time. Although some of their teachings coincided with those of the Anabaptists on the Continent, most Baptists did not derive such ideas from the Anabaptists, but rather from their own study of the New Testament. While in exile in the Netherlands, a number of these Baptists were influenced by Arminianism, which they took with them on their return to England. Others remained in England, and continued sharing in the strict Calvinism that formed the backbone of the Puritan movement. Thus, two different groups appeared among the Baptists: the *general* and the *particular*. General Baptists were those who held, as did the Arminians, that Jesus had died for all humankind. *Particular Baptists*, on the other hand, held to orthodox

Calvinism, affirming that Jesus died only for those individuals who were predestined to be saved. In Providence, some followed the Arminianism of the General Baptists, and others the Calvinism of the Particular Baptists.

The Baptist movement spread throughout the colonies, even though its followers were persecuted in several of them. Entire congregations were expelled from Massachusetts. This did not suffice to stop the supposed contagion, which infected some of the most prestigious members of that society—including the president of Harvard. Slowly, as religious tolerance became more common, Baptist groups surfaced in every colony. At first, most of these were General Baptists. But at the time of the Great Awakening—to which we shall return—there was an upsurge of Calvinism, and in many areas the Particular Baptists far surpassed the others.

CATHOLICISM IN MARYLAND

The main center of Roman Catholicism in the North American British colonies was Maryland. In 1632, Charles I granted Cecil Calvert, Lord Baltimore, rights of property and colonization over a portion of the territories that had earlier been claimed by Virginia. Lord Baltimore was Catholic, and the grant was made to him as part of Charles's policy of seeking Catholic support. Many Catholics in England wished to have a colony where they could live without the restrictions and difficulties they constantly faced in their own country. Since at that time it would have been politically unwise to establish a purely Catholic colony, it was decided that in Maryland there would be religious freedom. Lord Baltimore followed that policy in his instructions to his representatives in Maryland, whom he directed to avoid giving Protestants any excuse to attack the Catholics in the colony.

The first group of settlers arrived in 1634, and its social composition predicted the prevailing social order in the colony. Approximately one-tenth of the settlers were Catholic aristocrats, and the rest were mostly their Protestant servants. Tobacco soon became the mainstay of the economy, giving rise to large and prosperous plantations. The colony was governed by the Catholic landowners, but the majority of its residents were Protestants. Repeatedly, whenever the shifting political winds in Britain gave them opportunity, the Protestants sought to take power from the landed Catholic aristocracy. They finally succeeded when James II was overthrown. Anglicanism then became the official religion of the colony, and the rights of Catholics were restricted.

Pennsylvania also had a significant number of Catholics, thanks to the tolerant policies advocated by William Penn. There, as well as in other colonies, Catholicism made significant gains after the Stuart restoration. After the fall of James II in 1688, however, its growth was limited; and throughout the colonial period Catholics remained a minority in each of the thirteen colonies.

THE MID-ATLANTIC COLONIES

The colonies founded between New England and Maryland—New York, New Jersey, Pennsylvania, and Delaware—did not initially serve as a refuge for any particular religious group. We have already spoken of Penn's "experiment" in Pennsylvania. Although the basic inspiration for founding the colony was Quaker, from the very beginning its people of varied confessions comprised its population. The same was true of Delaware, which Penn bought from the duke of York, and which was part of Pennsylvania until 1701.

The political and religious history of New Jersey is complex. In general, however, east New Jersey followed the pattern of the strict New England Puritans, while in the west it was the Quakers who set the tone for the emerging society, and there was religious tolerance. Eventually, however, many of the Quakers of New Jersey became a slaveholding aristocracy whose relations with other Quakers were increasingly strained.

What later became New York was colonized by the Dutch, whose East India Company established its local headquarters in Manhattan, and whose Reformed Church came with them. In 1655, they conquered a rival colony that the Swedes had founded on the Delaware River, then they were conquered by the British in 1664, and what had been New Netherland became New York, while the earlier Dutch inhabitants, who in any case were not entirely satisfied with the previous regime, became British subjects. The British brought with them the Church of England, whose only members were the governor and his household and troops. But with increased British immigration, the religious composition of the colony approached that of Great Britain.

In short, during the seventeenth and eighteenth centuries, Great Britain founded and expanded a chain of colonies in North America. (In 1759, the British also took the French lands north of the St. Lawrence, but the history of that colony followed a different course.) Religious motivations played an important role in the founding of several of these colonies. Although at first some of them were intolerant of religious diversity, with the passage of time all tended to follow the example of Rhode Island and Pennsylvania, where religious freedom had existed from the beginning and was shown to be a viable option to the religious tensions that had repeatedly bled Europe. At the same time, the practice of slavery, social inequity based on the existence of vast plantations, the exploitation of the Indians and the expropriation of their land, and many similar factors, had dimmed the religious fervor and the hopes for a holy commonwealth that had sparked many of the early settlers.

THE GREAT AWAKENING

The eighteenth century brought to North America the same Pietistic currents that it brought to Germany and England. Presbyterians, for instance, were divided by a controversy between those who insisted above all on strict adherence to the teachings of Westminster—the Old Side—and those of the New Side, whose emphasis was on the experience of redeeming grace. Although the two sides would eventually come together, for a time the controversy led to schism—a schism that was made more acute by the enormous Pietistic wave which became known as the *Great Awakening.*

From an early date, many among the North American colonists had felt that a personal religious experience was of great importance to Christian life. But that feeling became more generalized by a series of events that began in 1734, when the first signs of the Great Awakening appeared in Northampton, Massachusetts. The pastor there was Jonathan Edwards, a staunch Calvinist who had been trained at Yale and was convinced of the need for a personal experience of conversion. He had been preaching in Northampton for several years, with average results, when his preaching began evoking a response that surprised him. His sermons were not exceptionally emotive, although they did underscore the need for an experience of conviction of sin and of divine forgiveness. In that year of 1734, people began responding to his sermons, some with emotional outbursts, but many with a remarkable change in their lives, and with increased attention to devotional practices. In a few months, the movement swept the area and reached into Connecticut. Soon it subsided, and after three years the extraordinary signs had almost disappeared. But the memory remained, as well as the hope that it would be rekindled.

Shortly thereafter, George Whitefield visited New England, and his preaching led to many experiences of conversion as well as outward expressions of repentance and joy. Although Edwards was a Congregationalist, he invited the Anglican Whitefield to preach in his church, and it is said that while the visitor preached, the pastor wept. This gave the awakening renewed impetus. The Presbyterian ministers of the New Side, and others of similar inclinations, joined it. While some preachers followed Whitefield's example, traveling throughout the countryside, many local pastors of various traditions—Anglicans, Presbyterians, and Congregationalists—brought new zeal to their pulpits, and extraordinary responses were evoked in their churches as well. People wept in repentance for their sins, some shouted for joy at having been pardoned, and a few were so overwhelmed that they fainted.

Such reactions to preaching led the enemies of the Great Awakening to accuse its leaders of undermining the solemnity of worship, and of substituting emotion for study and devotion. It must be said, however, that many of the leaders of the movement were not particularly emotive, that many were scholars, and that in any case the goal of the movement was not worship services marked by continual shows of emotion, but rather a single experience that would lead each believer to greater devotion and more conscientious study of Scripture. This may be seen in Jonathan Edwards's sermons. They are not emotive harangues but careful expositions of profound theological matters. Edwards believed that emotion was important. But such emotion, including the high experience of conversion, should not eclipse the need for right doctrine and rational worship. The leaders of the Great Awakening were orthodox Calvinists. It was precisely his Calvinism that led Whitefield to break with Wesley. And Edwards wrote solid and profound defenses of the doctrine of predestination. Although the movement in its early stages was led by Congregationalists and Presbyterians, in the long run it was the Baptists and Methodists who most profited from it.

At first, the Baptists opposed the movement, calling it frivolous and superficial. But the Awakening led many people to conclusions that were favorable to the Baptists. Indeed, if an experience of conversion had such central importance in Christian life, this raised doubts regarding infant baptism. Therefore, many Congregationalists and Presbyterians, led by the Awakening's emphasis on personal experience, eventually rejected infant baptism and became Baptists. Entire congregations did so.

Jonathan Edwards was both the leading theologian in the colonies and one of the prominent figures in the Great Awakening.

The Great Awakening also led both Baptists and Methodists to the Western frontier. At this time, whites were continually appropriating Indian lands, and it was the Methodists and Baptists who, imbued with the spirit of the Great Awakening, took up the task of preaching to these Western settlers and organizing their religious life. For that reason, these two groups became the most numerous in the newly settled areas. And, as a consequence of that Great Awakening, and of later similar movements, the hope for an "awakening" became typical of a significant sector of North American Christianity.

Finally, the Great Awakening had political consequences. This was the first movement that embraced all of the thirteen colonies that would eventually become the United States. Thanks to it, a sense of commonality began developing among the various colonies. At the same time, new ideas were circulating regarding human rights and the nature of government. Those ideas, combined with the growing sense of commonality among the colonies, would foment momentous events.

Suggested Readings

Sydney E. Ahlstrom. *A Religious History of the American People.* Second edition, David D. Hall, ed. Hew Haven: Yale University Press, 2004.

Carl Bangs. *Arminius: A Study in the Dutch Reformation.* Nashville: Abingdon, 1971.

Robert Bireley. *The Jesuits and the Thirty Years' War.* Cambridge [Eng]: Cambridge University Press, 2003.

Francis J. Bremer. *Puritanism: A Very Short Introduction.* Oxford: Clarendon Press, 2009.

Frederick C. Copleston. *A History of Philosophy.* Vols. 4–6. London: Burns, Oates and Washburne, 1958–1960.

Rupert E. Davies. *Methodism.* Baltimore: Penguin, 1963.

Janet Glenn Gray. *The French Huguenots: Anatomy of Courage.* Grand Rapids: Baker Book House, 1981.

Herbert H. Henson. *Puritanism in England.* London: Hodder and Stoughton, 1912.

Richard P. Heitzenrater. *The People Called Methodists.* Nashville: Abingdon, 1994.

Randy L. Maddox and Jason E. Vickers. *The Cambridge Companion to John Wesley.* New York: Cambridge University Press, 2009.

Henry Petersen. *The Canons of Dort.* Grand Rapids: Baker, 1968.

Meic Pearse. *The Age of Reason: From the Wars of Religion to the French Revolution.* Grand Rapids: Baker Book House, 2006.

F. Ernest Stoeffler. *German Pietism during the Eighteenth Century.* Leiden: E.J. Brill, 1973.

N. M. Sutherland. *The Huguenot Struggle for Recognition.* New Haven: Yale University Press, 1980.

Henry Van Etten. *George Fox and the Quakers.* New York: Harper, 1959.

PART III

———

BEYOND CHRISTENDOM

Chronology

Popes	Events
Clement XIV (1769–1774)	Captain Cook's voyages (1775–1779)
Pius VI (1775–1799)	U. S. War of Independence (1775–1783)
	Steam engine (1776)
	Tupac Amaru Rebellion (1780–1782)
	Kant's *Critique of Pure Reason* (1781)
	Methodist Christmas Conference (1784)
	National Assembly, France (1789)
	Taking of the Bastille (1789)
	Civil Constitution of the Clergy (1790)
	Legislative Assembly, France (1791)
	National Convention, France (1792)
	Particular Baptist Society (1792)
	King Louis XVI executed (1793)
	Carey in India (1793)
	Terror in France (1793–1795)
	London Missionary Society (1795)
	British take Ceylon (1796)
	Second Great Awakening begins (1797)
	Pius VI prisoner of France (1798)
	Roman Republic (1798)
	Consulate, France (1799)
	Founding of Sierra Leone (1799)
	Church Missionary Society (1799)
	Schleiermacher's *Speeches* (1799)
Pius VII (1800–1823)	Cane Ridge revival (1801)
	Louisiana Purchase (1803)
	Napoleon emperor (1804)
	British and Foreign Bible Society (1804)
	Independence of Haiti (1804)
	British in Cape of Good Hope (1806)
	Hegel's *Phenomenology of the Spirit* (1807)
	French occupy Rome (1808)
	Joseph Bonaparte, King of Spain (1808)
	Independence of Mexico (1810)
	American Board of Commissioners (1810)
	Independence of Paraguay and Venezuela (1811)
	British-American War (1812–1814)
	Napoleon in Russia (1812)
	Reorganization of the Jesuits (1814)
	Waterloo (1815)

Popes	Events
	Independence of Río de la Plata (1816)
	American Bible Society (1816)
	Etsi longissimo (1816)
	Gospel of Matthew in Burmese (1817)
	Independence of Chile (1818)
	James Long in Texas (1819)
	Independence of Peru and Central America (1821)
	Schleiermacher's *Christian Faith* (1821–1822)
Leo XII (1823–1829)	Monroe Doctrine (1823)
	Etsi iam diu (1824)
	Independence of Bolivia (1825)
	American Society for the Promotion of Temperance (1826)
	Panama Congress (1826)
Pius VIII (1829–1830)	Abolition of slavery in Mexico (1829)
	Book of Mormon (1830)
	Comte's *Course of Positive Philosophy* (1830–1842)
Gregory XVI (1831–1846)	Boer migration (1835)
	Republic of Texas (1836)
	Abolition of slavery, British Caribbean (1838)
	Opium War (1839–1842)
	Brooke government in Sarawak (1841–1946)
	Livingstone in Africa (1841)
	Kierkegaard begins his work (1843)
	Manifest Destiny (1845)
	Methodists and Baptists split over slavery (1845)
Pius IX (1846–1878)	Mexican-American War (1846–1848)
	Independence of Liberia (1847)
	Famine in Ireland, migration to U.S. (1847)
	Second Republic in France (1848)
	Communist Manifesto (1848)
	Roman Republic (1849)
	Taiping Rebellion (1850–1864)
	Cavour's government in Italy (1852–1861)
	Napoleon III (1852–1870)
	Dogma of Immaculate Conception of Mary (1854)
	Commodore Perry in Japan (1854)
	Holly in Haiti (1855)
	Darwin's *Origin of the Species* (1859)
	Kingdom of Italy (1861)
	U.S. Civil War (1861–1865)
	Presbyterians divide over slavery (1861)
	Congregation of Eastern Rites (1862)
	Bismarck chancellor (1862)
	Salvation Army (1864)
	Syllabus of Errors (1864)
	Catholics persecuted in Korea (1865)
	China Inland Mission (1865)
	First Vatican Council (1869–1870)
	Dogma of Papal Infallibility (1870)

Popes	Events
	Franco-Prussian War (1870–1871)
	Third Republic in France (1870–1914)
	Moody begins preaching (1872)
	Mary Baker Eddy's *Science and Health* (1875)
Leo XIII (1878–1903)	
	Protestant missionaries in Korea (1884)
	Rerum novarum (1891)
	U.S. Supreme Court approves segregation (1892)
	Five Fundamentals (1895)
	Spanish-American War (1898)
	Boxer Rebellion in China (1899–1901)
	Freud's psychoanalysis (1900)
Pius X (1903–1914)	Azusa Street Revival (1906)
	Pascendi domini regis (1907)
	Independence of Belgian Congo (1908)
	U.S. Federal Council of Churches (1908)
	Scofield's Bible (1909)
	N.A.A.C.P. founded (1909)
	Japan annexes Korea (1910)
	Methodist Pentecostal Church, Chile (1910)
	World Missionary Conference, Edinburgh (1910)
	Fall of Chinese Empire (1912)
	Assemblies of God (1914)
Benedict XV (1914–1922)	World War I (1914–1918)
	Russian Revolution (1917)
	Barth's *Commentary on Romans* (1919)
	U.S. Prohibition (1919–1933)
	Women's suffrage (1920)
Pius XI (1922–1939)	Mussolini in Rome (1922)
	Founding of *Zwischen den Zeiten* (1922)
	Stockholm Conference (Life and Work) (1925)
	United Church of Canada (1925)
	First six Chinese Catholic bishops (1926)
	Lausanne Conference (Faith and Order) (1927)
	Church of Christ in China (1927)
	Mexico confiscates church property (1927)
	Jerusalem Assembly, IMC (1928)
	Stock Market Crash (1929)
	Depression (1929)
	H. R. Niebuhr's *Social Sources of Denominationalism* (1929)
	Aulén's *Christus Victor* (1930)
	Nygren's *Agape and Eros* (1930–1936)
	Spanish Republic (1931)
	Encyclical *Quadragesimo anno* (social teachings) (1931)
	Encyclical *Non abbiamo bisogno* (against Fascism) (1931)
	Barth's *Church Dogmatics* (1932–1967)
	Hitler comes to power (1933)
	Vatican concordat with Germany (1933)

Popes	Events
	Roosevelt U.S. president (1933)
	Barmen Declaration (1934)
	Civil War in Spain (1936)
	Encyclicals against Nazism and Communism (1937)
	Oxford Conference (Life and Work) (1937)
	Edinburgh Conference (Faith and Order) (1937)
	War between Japan and China (1937)
	Bonhoeffer's *The Cost of Discipleship* (1937)
	H. R. Niebuhr's *The Kingdom of God in America* (1937)
	Madras Assembly, IMC (1938)
Pius XII (1939–1958)	Franco's victory in Spain (1939)
	Bonhoeffer's *Life Together* (1939)
	World War II (1939–1945)
	Bultmann's *The New Testament and Mythology* (1940)
	Germany attacks Russia (1941)
	United Church of Christ in Japan (1941)
	Japan attacks Pearl Harbor (1941)
	Niebuhr's *The Nature and Destiny of Man* (1941–1943)
	Fall of Mussolini (1943)
	Encyclical *Divino afflante Spiritu* (1943)
	Perón comes to power in Argentina (1943)
	†Bonhoeffer (1945)
	Germany surrenders (1945)
	Nuclear attack on Hiroshima (1945)
	Independence of Philippines and Indonesia (1945)
	Fall of Vargas in Brazil (1945)
	Church of South India (1947)
	Whitby Assembly, IMC (1947)
	World Council of Churches (WCC) founded (1948)
	†Mohandas K. Ghandi (1948)
	People's Republic of China (1949)
	Dogma of Assumption of Mary (1950)
	Korean War (1950)
	Encyclical *Humani generis* (1950)
	Billy Graham's Evangelistic Association (1950)
	Independence of India (1950)
	Supreme Court bans segregation in public schools (1952)
	Willingen Assembly, IMC (1952)
	Worker priest movement suspended (1954)
	Evanston Assembly, WCC (1954)
	†Teilhard de Chardin (1955)
	Fall of Perón in Argentina (1955)
	Conference of Latin American Bishops founded (1955)
	Independence of Ghana (1957)
	Ghana Assembly, IMC (1957–1958)
John XXIII (1958–1963)	Cuban Revolution (1959)
	Pope announces intention to call a council (1959)
	Pope creates Secretariat for Christian Unity (1960)

Popes	Events
	Independence of Seventeen African nations (1960)
	Encyclical *Mater et Magistra* (1961)
	First manned space flight (1961)
	New Delhi Assembly, WCC; IMC joins WCC (1961)
	Chilean Pentecostals join WCC (1961)
	Independence of Algeria (1962)
	†H. Richard Niebuhr (1962)
	Robinson's *Honest to God* (1963)
	Second Vatican Council (1962–1965)
	Moltmann's *Theology of Hope* (1965)
Paul VI (1963–1978)	War in Southeast Asia escalates (1965)
	Encyclical *Humanae vitae* (1968)
	†Martin Luther King, Jr. (1968)
	Medellín Assembly of CELAM (1968)
	Uppsala Assembly, WCC (1968)
	†Karl Barth (1968)
	Astronauts land on the moon (1969)
	†Reinhold Niebuhr (1970)
	Gutiérrez's *Teología de la liberación* (1971)
	Chicago Declaration (1973)
	Coup in Chile (1973)
	Fall of Haile Selassie (1974)
	Lausanne Covenant (1974)
	Nairobi Assembly, WCC (1975)
John Paul I (1978)	Camp David Accords (1978)
John Paul II (1978–2005)	Puebla Assembly, CELAM (1978)
	Organization of African Instituted Churches (1978)
	U.S.S.R. invades Afghanistan (1979)
	Islamic Republic of Iran (1979)
	Rhodesia becomes Zimbabwe (1979)
	Consejo Latinoamericano de Iglesias (CLAI) (1982)
	Falkland-Malvinas War (1982)
	Vancouver Assembly, WCC (1983)
	†Karl Rahner (1984)
	AIDS emerges (1984)
	Collapse of the Soviet Union (1985–1991)
	Fall of the Berlin Wall (1989)
	Tiananmen Square protests in Beijing (1989)
	U.S. invades Iraq (1991)
	Canberra Assembly, WCC (1991)
	Ratzinger to head Congregation of the Doctrine of the Faith (1991)
	European Union (1993)
	Encyclical *Ut unum sint* (1995)
	†Mother Theresa (1997)
	Harare Assembly, WCC (1998)
	†Hélder Câmara (1999)
	Terrorist attacks on U.S. (2001)

Popes	Events
	War in Afghanistan (2001)
	U.S. invades Iraq (2003)
	Terrorist attack in Madrid (2004)
	European Union adds ten new members (2004)
Benedict XVI (2005–)	
	Porto Alegre Assembly, WCC (2006)
	China Patriotic Council bishops excommunicated (2006)
	Independence of Kosovo declared (2008)
	Third Congress on World Evangelization (2010)

26

An Age Beyond Christendom

Here ends the 18th Century. The 19th begins with a fine clear morning wind at S.W.; and the political horizon affords as fine a prospect . . . with the irresistible propagation of the Rights of Man, the eradication of hierarchy, superstition and tyranny over the world.

NATHANIEL AMES'S DIARY, DECEMBER 31, 1800

The last years of the eighteenth century, and the first of the nineteenth, brought a series of political changes that shook Europe and the Western hemisphere. In general, those changes were the result of the convergence of the new political ideas with the economic interests of the growing bourgeoisie. During the second half of the eighteenth century, in both Europe and the Western hemisphere, the economic power of a new class had increased. In France, this new class was the bourgeoisie, which had come into its own with the growth of cities, trade, and industry. In the Western hemisphere, riches were based on agriculture and the trade derived from it; and therefore the colonials who owned the land had become the new aristocracy of money. The interests of this aristocracy and of the European bourgeoisie conflicted with those of the older aristocracy of blood. In France, the lower classes were allied with the bourgeoisie in their hatred of the aristocracy, whom they viewed as parasites living off the products of their labor. In the New World, the lower classes were also allied with the new economic aristocracy against the aristocracy of blood, whom they saw as foreigners profiting from the colonies without understanding their dreams and problems. All this resulted in the independence of the United States, the French Revolution, and the independence of most of Latin America. These revolutions mark the beginning of a new period in history, and were followed by other revolutions throughout the nineteenth century and well into the twentieth—in Germany and other parts of Europe in 1848, in Mexico in 1910, in Russia in 1917, in Cuba in 1959, and in Kenya leading to independence in 1963. . . . While the success of such revolutions, and their long-term consequences, vary from case to case, together they jointly show that the nineteenth and twentieth centuries were a time of great political and social upheavals that would have a serious impact on Christianity as a whole.

Also, the nineteenth century was marked by a geographic expansion of Christianity comparable only to that of the sixteenth. While the sixteenth century was the great age of Catholic expansion, the nineteenth played a similar role for Protestantism. Although the consequences of that vast enterprise are still not clear, there is little doubt that, from the perspective of the history of Christianity, the most important event of the nineteenth century was the founding of a truly universal church in which peoples of all races and nations had a part. On the other hand, however, it is necessary to point out that this took place within the context of colonialism and economic imperialism—a framework that also left its stamp on the life of the church.

At the opening of the nineteenth century, one could well have thought that European colonialism had passed its zenith. This was particularly true in the Western hemisphere, where European expansion had been most remarkable in previous centuries. The independence of the United States left Britain with no American colonies other than Canada, several islands in the Caribbean, and relatively small holdings in Central and South America. The French lost Haiti, until then their most productive colony. And Spain had to relinquish all its American lands except Cuba and Puerto Rico—both of which Spain would also lose by the turn of the century. Furthermore, the bloodletting of the Napoleonic Wars seemed likely to put an end to European hegemony in the world.

But what happened was exactly the opposite. The Napoleonic Wars turned Britain's attention toward the colonies held by its enemies. When Napoleon became master of the European continent, Britain was able to survive thanks to its naval superiority. Its most powerful squadrons protected it from invasion, while others sought to intercept trade between Napoleon's Europe—France, Spain, Portugal, and the Netherlands—and its colonies. British citizens learned to expect bad news from the armies that opposed Napoleon on land, and good from the ships that harassed him on the sea. When the wars ended, Britain found itself in possession of several former French and Dutch colonies.

These events coincided with the main reason for colonial expansion in the nineteenth century: the Industrial Revolution. As technological advances were applied to industrial production, greater capital and wider markets became necessary. For a time, those areas of Europe that had not been industrialized provided the necessary markets. But soon the industrial powers began to look for other outlets, and found them in Latin America and Asia.

In Latin America, even after a period of national liberation, declarations of independence and the establishment of national governments, these circumstances led to *neocolonialism*—a system in which the colonizing powers, rather than ruling directly over the colonized, allowed them a measure of political independence while still exploiting them economically and perpetuating their dependency. The former Spanish colonies had scarcely won their independence when Britain, France, and the United States began competing for control of the new markets. At first, foreign investors were interested mainly in urban markets. But by 1870 there was a race for control of the agricultural products of the interior. With new industrial and technological developments, what were needed now were not so much new markets as raw materials for industry. Greed then turned its eye to lands that it had scarcely noticed before, and much foreign capital was invested in railroads, harbors, and processing plants. These investments were made with the consent and support of the ruling *criollos,* whose holdings in land increased enormously in both size and value. Foreign and national capital thus formed an alliance whose interests were best served by the oligarchical governments that it usually supported. Given the power of such an alliance, radical changes in social and political structures were rare.

In Asia, the European Industrial Revolution had similar consequences, although colonialism usually took its more traditional form of military conquest and overt political domination. At first, the Western economic powers remained content with opening new markets. But again and again Western economic interests, feeling threatened by political developments in the area, by the weakness of the local government, or by another industrial power, forced their nations to intervene militarily and take over the governments of the region—or at least to hold them with a firm grip. By the middle of the twentieth century and into the twenty-first, however, there would be a reaction against all of this, and after war in the Pacific and revolution in China, nations such as Japan, China, India, and Korea would emerge as political and economic powers.

The colonization of black Africa, until then relatively slow, accelerated in the last decades of the nineteenth century, when Europe burned with imperialistic fever, and when what was sought was not new markets but rather sources for raw materials. Many in Europe became convinced that in order to be a power of the first order a nation had to rule an overseas empire. By then Britain, France, and the Netherlands had such empires, and now Belgium, Italy, and Germany joined in the mad scramble to claim every corner of the world. Here again, there were nationalistic reactions in the twentieth and twenty-first centuries, leading to a series of independent nations.

The colonial expansion of the nineteenth century was made possible thanks to another consequence of modern industrial development: military might. Western powers had weapons with which they could defeat even vastly larger armies. Even such proud and populous nations as China and Japan had to bow before what would otherwise have been second-rate powers. Only a handful of nations in Africa and Asia were able to retain their political independence, and even these were forced to surrender their economic independence. China and Japan, for instance, although never fully conquered by the Western powers, were literally forced to open trade with the West. For the first time in history, the world became a vast economic network.

Behind this new order stood an even deeper intellectual revolution—one that had begun with the Renaissance, but came to fruition in the nineteenth and twentieth centuries. Western civilization turned to observation and experimentation as the primary means of gaining knowledge, and then began applying such knowledge to the transformation of the world. The first major application of this new form of knowledge was closely connected with the Industrial Revolution, and with the energy it required. For centuries, the main sources of energy had been water and wind. They powered mills and moved ships. Now new forms of energy were developed. The modern piston steam engine, first developed in the late sixteenth and early seventeenth centuries, was now applied both to industrial production and to transportation, on land as well as on sea—the first commercially practical steamboat being built in 1802. Journeys that had previously taken months were now reduced to weeks and even days. Then came the internal combustion engine and its application to transportation, which led to the automobile and the trucking industry, to the building of wider roads, to new patterns of family life, to the colonization of the oil-rich lands of the Middle East, and to a myriad changes in the entire process of industrial production and marketing. The internal combustion engine, applied to aviation, made the world even smaller than the steam engine and the railroad had. Now journeys that had previously taken days could be completed in a matter of hours. By the second half of the twentieth century it was apparent that new forms and sources of energy had to be found and developed. Large hydroelectric plants were built not only in the industrialized world, but also in a number of poorer nations seeking to attain a level of development similar to that in Western Europe and the United States. It seemed that the world had become as small as it could ever be. Even the moon had been reached, and there was talk of building cities in outer space. Nuclear power had appeared on the scene, leading to debates between those who extolled its efficiency and those who feared its dangers. While oil was still the most commonly used source of energy, there were experiments and pilot projects seeking to develop alternative sources of energy—wind, solar, geothermal, and tidal.

If the rapid development in transportation surprised those who lived in the first half of the twentieth century, they were in for even bigger surprises still to come. The world that seemed to have shrunk through new methods of transportation was shrinking even faster through new methods of communication. Samuel Morse invented the electric telegraph in 1837 and by 1844 it had become a viable mode of communication; the first telephone was demonstrated in 1877. By the 1950s, television had become a common household feature in most of the industrialized world. People living in New York in 1950 marveled that they could call an operator who could connect them via telephone with someone in Cairo—sometimes in under an hour. But by 2010 it was possible, not only to speak with someone in Cairo, but also to send entire books and pictures in a matter of seconds. In 1975, the use of computers was limited to a relatively small number of people working mostly on technical matters. By 2010, pre-school children were using computers, people were able to get in touch with virtually anyone anywhere in the world instantly, and the Internet contained more information—both true and false—than any library could ever hold.

In a way, this was the culmination of developments that began in the nineteenth century and even earlier. Throughout the nineteenth century, Western civilization had considered itself destined to lead the world into an age of happiness and abundance. The Industrial Revolution had created wealth and comfort that two centuries earlier would have been considered unattainable. In Asia, Africa, and Latin America, the native populations appeared eager to absorb the ways and wisdom of industrial Europe and the United States. The cause of missions prospered in spite of such setbacks as the Boxer Rebellion in China (see Chapter 36), and there were hopes that in the very near future most of the world's population would be Christian. For almost a century, with minor exceptions, the European powers had lived in peace with each other.

Destructive currents existed beneath the surface, however, and they would eventually plunge the world into the most devastating war it had ever known—a war to be followed by revolution, economic upheavals, and an even more destructive conflagration. The relative peace of the nineteenth century in Europe was possible in part because competition among European powers took the form of colonial expansion. While Europe was at peace, war by proxy overseas became a common feature of international policies. By 1914, however, most of the territories of Asia, Africa, and Latin America had been colonized—if not politically, at least economically. Europe then turned its attention to its own southeastern region, the Balkans, where the progressive breakup of the Turkish Empire had created a number of states with unstable boundaries and governments. These lands became the bone of contention among European powers, and it was out of that contention that World War I would emerge. The very technological and industrial progress of which the West boasted would then be seen in all of its destructive power, for this war provided the occasion for the military use of technology in submarine, aerial, and chemical warfare. The control that the industrial powers had over distant lands meant that most of the planet was directly or indirectly involved in the conflict. The war, which lasted four years, involved thirty nations and a total armed force of sixty-five million, of whom almost one-seventh died and more than one-third were wounded in battle. The civilian casualties of the war, although more difficult to assess, numbered at least as many as the military.

Meanwhile, chaos in Russia had led to revolution. Russia was the one great European power where the liberal ideas of the nineteenth century had made practically no headway. Its autocratic government and landed aristocracy continued ruling the nation as they had centuries earlier. Karl Marx would never have expected Russia, where industrialization had been slow, to become the first country where the revolution he announced would succeed. His expectation was rather that the development of industry and capital would eventually lead to a revolution of industrial workers, and that peasants would not view such a revolution with sympathy. But the war upset his predictions. In Russia, nationalist bitterness against a government that appeared unable to win a battle was soon combined with protests in the cities over lack of bread and in the countryside over lack of land. In March, 1917, Czar Nicholas II was forced to abdicate in favor of his brother, who in turn abdicated a few days later. For a short time, the government was in the hands of moderates who hoped for a liberal capitalist republic. But this government's failures in both war and economic policies, and the agitation of V. I. Lenin and his Bolsheviks, lead to the November Revolution of 1917. Lenin immediately moved to set in motion his vast program of social reorganization, nationalizing the land and all banks, and placing factories in the hands of government-controlled trade unions. As part of this program, all church property was also confiscated. Thus, the Russian Church, which had considered itself the Third Rome after the fall of Byzantium, now found itself living under conditions similar to those of the Byzantine church after the Turkish invasion. The new government also withdrew from the war, but soon found itself immersed in its own civil war against counterrevolutionaries who had both international and ecclesiastical support. By the time the Red Army had won the war, the Soviet government was more convinced than ever that the church was its mortal enemy.

In the Western hemisphere, the consequences of the World War I were not as acutely felt. The United States did not enter the war until April 1917 and, although its armed forces suffered heavy casualties, other issues soon demanded national attention. The nation turned inwards, seeking to solve its own problems in isolation from the rest of the world and refusing to join the League of Nations. Two issues with roots in the nineteenth century came to occupy the center of the American stage: prohibition and women's suffrage. Prohibition of alcoholic beverages became the law of the land in 1919, less than a year after the end of the war. Women's right to vote was finally granted by the Nineteenth Amendment to the Constitution, in 1920. The 1920s were a decade of economic prosperity, particularly for the wealthy few (five percent of the population received one-third of all personal income). Then came the Great Depression, which led to the election of Franklin D. Roosevelt and to the New Deal. The recovery that took place during Roosevelt's presidency was seen as further proof that the nation was basically sound, and that the Depression had been but a passing phase that had been overcome through hard work and organization. Thus, the first half of the twentieth century in the United States was not marked by the self-doubt and pessimism that was beginning to sweep Europe.

In the rest of the hemisphere, the most notable event was the Mexican Revolution, a drawn-out affair, at times quite radical and at other times fairly moderate, which began in 1910 and went on for decades. Here again, there were constant conflicts between the Catholic Church and the revolution. In 1927, as earlier in Russia, church properties were confiscated. Eventually, without returning the confiscated property, the state relented in its most stringent policies against the church.

In Europe, it was hoped that the League of Nations would be able to prevent a repetition of the tragic events of World War I, but the growth of Fascism rendered such hopes futile. Fascism, which first gained prominence in Italy under the leadership of Benito Mussolini, exploited wounded national pride in order to glorify war and to turn the entire nation into a totalitarian military machine. Its social doctrines were confused; at first it sided with radical revolutionaries, but eventually it exploited the fear of Communism and joined forces with industrialists in order to create a new aristocracy of power and production. In any case, the dream of national grandeur, and hatred of democracy and political liberalism as the creation of an effeminate bourgeoisie, were characteristic of Fascism in all its stages. As Mussolini put it, "What maternity is to women, that is war to man." Soon the movement spread to other countries. Its German counterpart, the Nazi party, came to power in 1933, and eventually overshadowed Italian Fascism. Through Nazi influence, anti-Semitism became part of the established dogma of international Fascism—and led to the death of millions of Jews in Germany and elsewhere. By 1936, Fascism had attained at least a measure of power, not only in Italy and Germany, but also in Japan, Poland, Austria, Hungary, Greece, Rumania, and Bulgaria. In 1939, with the victory of Spanish dictator Francisco Franco in the Spanish Civil War, it became firmly established in Spain. Fascist attitudes toward Christianity varied. In Spain, Franco considered the Catholic Church one of his closest allies, and always declared himself its faithful son. Mussolini's attitudes wavered according to various circumstances. Hitler felt that Christianity, with its teachings of universal love and turning the other cheek, was antagonistic to his ultimate goals of conquest and domination—but he sought to use the church to support those goals.

Part of the allure of Fascism was in reviving dreams of ancient glories. Mussolini promised to restore the Roman Empire. Greek Fascists spoke of a rebirth of Spartan militarism and Byzantine power. Spanish *falangistas* sought a return to the *golden century* of the Spanish Empire. Obviously, these various dreams were mutually contradictory. But what stood behind them—the glorification of war, dread of the free exchange of ideas, a to-talitarian nationalism, and opposition to all forms of egalitarianism—united the various Fascist movements in opposition to all that sounded like democracy, liberalism, or pacifism. Italy and Germany joined forces in an Axis to which Japan was later added. Through a Soviet-German agreement, Russian neutrality was assured. A month later, in September 1939, Europe was at war.

Once again, for the second time in three decades, the entire world was swept into the conflict. At first, the Fascist powers—the *Axis*—ensured that Russia stayed out of the conflict. In fact, Russia took advantage of its friendly relations with the Axis to split Poland with Germany in a partition agreement and to extend its holdings in the Baltic. Soon most of Western Europe was in the hands of the Fascists, while their Japanese allies extended their holdings in the Orient. By 1941, with the German invasion of Russia and the Japanese attack on Pearl Harbor, no major power was allowed to remain neutral. Since the Axis had conquered most of Europe, the main fronts of battle were now the Pacific, North Africa, the Russian-German line, and the English Channel. But battles were also being waged in African colonies, in the Near East, and as far as the Río de la Plata (today Uruguay and Argentina). The names of Pacific islands until then unknown in the West became household words. Tribal peoples who lived in relative isolation from the rest of the world now saw their skies crisscrossed by military aircraft, and their lands disputed by nations until then unknown to them. In all, fifty-seven nations declared war, defending one side or the other.

By the time the smoke cleared and losses were calculated, it was clear that the cost of the war had been enormous. In the most belligerent nations, the number of military dead and missing was devastatingly high: one out of every four hundred and fifty people in the United States, one out of every one hundred and fifty in the United Kingdom and in Italy, one out of every two hundred in France and in China, one out of every twenty-two in the Soviet Union, one of every twenty-five for Germany, and one out of every forty-six people in Japan. The total number of military personnel killed or missing was more than fifteen million. To this must be added the larger number of direct civilian casualties, the millions of Jews killed by the Nazis and their allies, and the incalculable number of those who died of famine or disease as an indirect result of the war.

An uncounted casualty of the war was the optimistic view of the future of Western civilization that had prevailed during the nineteenth century. This was the civilization that, through an enlightened combination of Christian values and technical expertise, had been expected to bring about a new age for humankind. This was the civilization that it was the *white man's burden* to share with less fortunate people. And now, through the two most devastating wars the world had ever seen, this civilization had spread death and destruction throughout the world. Its technological prowess had been used to invent destructive machines that could not have been imagined a generation earlier, culminating in the explosion of the first atomic weapon at Hiroshima on August 6, 1945. Germany, once the epitome of European civilization, the nation that boasted of its intellectual leadership of the Western world, had fallen prey to a demonic fanaticism theretofore unknown among the most primitive tribes of the world.

The birth of the "atomic age" for the first time presented humankind with the ability to destroy itself.

A direct consequence of all this was a worldwide revolt against colonialism in all its forms. First, the colonial empires of the defeated nations were dismantled. But it soon became clear that even the victors had lost a great deal of prestige as a result of the war. Nationalist movements that had begun decades earlier suddenly took on new life, and in a span of two decades every colonial empire was dismembered. Political independence did not always lead to economic independence, for in many cases an economic neocolonial system of economic exploitation was developed to take the place of the old order. But twenty years after the end of the war, it was clear that there were strong movements against economic imperialism in the poorer nations. At times, nationalism took the form of a resurgence of ancient non-Christian religions. Some movements sought to change not only the international economic order, but also the social order of the nation itself, often following a socialist model. The first and largest example of this trend was China, where, partly as a result of the war, the Nationalist government was overthrown by the Communists. Although for some time China was faithful to Russian Communism, it eventually drifted away from links that still smacked of the older tutelage of the European nations over the rest of the world, and would eventually develop what amounted to its own form of capitalism. Japan followed the opposite tack: committing itself to capitalism and industrialization, it sought to compete with the older industrial nations of Europe and North America. Almost all of Africa and the Muslim world became independent of Western political rule. In the Muslim world, where traditional ways were often threatened by influences from abroad, radical, and violent forms of Islam came to the foreground, and by the twenty-first century these were causing grave concern not only among Western nations, but also in the Muslim world itself. Israel, seen by many as a Western enclave in a non-Western area, was hard pressed by its neighbors, who felt that this new state had been created at their expense. Regimes of white supremacy in Rhodesia and in South Africa collapsed. Many in the new nations all over the world, as well as in the older nations of Latin America, felt that the central agenda for the twenty-first century was the construction of an economic order less unfavorable to the poorer nations, the restructuring of foreign relations on that basis, and the redistribution of wealth within their own boundaries.

In the midst of all these changes, the industrialized nations of Europe, as well as the United States, often found themselves at a loss. Many in those countries had been taught that the entire colonial and neocolonial enterprise was the result of altruistic motivations and high ideals. From that perspective, the anticolonial reaction was nothing short of bewildering. It could only be explained by the presence of an evil conspiracy leading the so-called natives astray, away from their own best interests. This understanding of the anticolonial movement was encouraged by the mentality of the Cold War—the name given to the ongoing but bloodless conflict between capitalist and Communist nations that began immediately after World War II and continued with different degrees of intensity for several decades. As a result of World War II, the Soviet Union ruled most of Eastern Europe, and Germany was divided between the Federal Republic—West Germany—and the Democratic Republic—East Germany. This region of the world was the scene for much of the activity of the Cold War, including the blockade of Berlin by the Communists, and the building of a wall to prevent citizens of East Berlin from defecting to the West. In some areas, such as in Korea and Vietnam, the Cold War erupted into open hostilities—although the major powers, fearful of each other's nuclear capabilities, avoided direct military confrontation. Many in the West interpreted the entire anticolonial movement in terms of the Cold War. Since Communists were indeed at work in many revolutionary movements—although not always leading them—it was possible to see the entire anticolonial trend as a vast Communist conspiracy. This interpretation, more popular in the United States than in Europe, had the advantage of explaining how the altruism of the *white man's burden* had led to the virulent anticolonialism of the late twentieth century. But this easy explanation was achieved at the expense of a gross and dangerous oversimplification—one that threatened to alienate the West from the vast majority of humankind, for it saw Communist conspiracies in every struggle for justice and freedom. From the point of view of the Cold War, the great struggle was between East and West—between capitalism and communism.

The last decade of the twentieth century brought about the unexpected fall of communism in Eastern Europe and the dismemberment of the Soviet Empire, at which point it became clear that the struggle was not so much between East and West as between North and South, between rich and poor, between developed and underdeveloped. The breakdown of repressive regimes often led to the breakdown of countries until then held together by those regimes. Not only the Soviet Empire, but also Czechoslovakia, Yugoslavia, and others soon divided along ethnic, cultural, and religious lines, in several cases leading to war and even genocide.

Important changes were also taking place in the West. Since industrial production and communications technology were often cheaper in the poorer countries, many industrial plants and jobs moved to those countries, thus creating a sense of betrayal among many industrial laborers who witnessed their livelihood being exported. But at the same time that this was the impression in the industrialized nations, wealth was still flowing from the former colonies to their former metropolises, and people from colonial and neocolonial areas were moving to those metropolises in search of better lives, resulting in vast numbers of African, Asian, and Caribbean immigrating to Great Britain; Latin Americans to the United States; Africans and Arabs to countries throughout Western Europe; and Indonesians to the Netherlands. Thus, one could say that the earlier expectation that the entire world would be Westernized had to be corrected by the reality that those who had previously been Westernized were now exerting their influence on the West, and changing it in unexpected ways—from language to diet, and from family life to religion.

Another revolutionary change was also sweeping through the world late in the twentieth century and early in the twenty-first. People who until recently had seemed content to play a secondary role—particularly blacks and other minorities in white-dominated lands, and women everywhere—suddenly began claiming a share in the process whereby decisions were made. In Latin America, there was a strong reaffirmation of ancient Amerindian culture, often with political connotations. This was not entirely unrelated to the tragedy of two world wars and the clear threat of a third. Indeed, if those in leadership had plunged the world into such debacles, it seemed high time that others be given an opportunity at leadership. During World War II, blacks and women in the United States, and women in Great Britain, had been called to give their best for their country. After the war, they proved unwilling to return to their previous status. Both the civil rights movement and the feminist movement were at the same time an attempt to gain greater power for blacks and women, and a criticism of the manner in which white males were running the world.

In all of these situations, the church was present. More than any international organization, corporation, or political movement, the church cut across national boundaries, class distinctions, and political allegiances.

Indeed, the great legacy of the nineteenth century was that, for the first time in history, a truly universal church had been born. Although some in the twentieth century would see the missionaries of earlier generations as unrealistic dreamers, the truth is that they succeeded, for after their passing they left behind a vast network of Christians of every culture, color, and nationality. To such an international church, the issues of the twenty-first century were not simple. Especially in the poorer countries of the world, there were many who were convinced that their Christian faith required that they be involved in liberating the people from economic and social oppression; there were also many who insisted that this was not the task of the church. Threatened by the difficulty and complexity of the times, many turned to fundamentalism. Quite often such fundamentalism was allied to political and economic conservatism, particularly in the former colonial and neo-colonial centers. But there were also many—again, primarily in the poorer regions of the world—for whom Christianity became a means of individual and communal survival, promoting food production and distribution, education, health, and land reform, sometimes in fairly radical ways. All this took place in a context in which war and racial and class strife divided the church—often along lines that had little to do with earlier theological differences. At times it was persecuted; at other times it was used by people with ulterior motives. Amid the perplexities of the time, its members were often divided, bewildered, and even fearful. And yet, through war, persecution, and civil strife, they sought to give witness to the One whose rule of peace and justice shall have no end.

In the West, the church lost much of the political power and cultural prestige it had once held. This was seen in a series of revolutions that marked the end of the eighteenth century and the beginning of the nineteenth century, first in what would become the United States (see Chapter 27), then in France (see Chapter 28), and finally in Latin America (see Chapter 29). These revolutions—and the Russian Revolution in 1917 (see Chapter 35) —made it possible to speak of the post-Constantinian era, a time when the church no longer had the support of the state and its institutions. And this loss of power and prestige would go far beyond political matters, extending also to the cultural and the social. By the beginning of the twenty-first century, it was clear that the impact of the church and its teaching on the daily life of Western Europeans and North Americans was waning. Not only was attendance at church services declining, Christianity was virtually absent

Even high in the Andes Mountains, one finds indications of the interest in the occult that characterizes much of the twenty-first century.

or ignored by most forms of mass media and in much of social and family life. Although the main factor contributing to this decline was secularism, there were also throughout the world—but particularly in the West—many people who sought in ancient religions and practices a spiritual solace that they felt the organized church could not give them. There was a revival of Gnosticism, which the church had thought a matter of the distant past. Others turned to astrology, or to spiritism, or to magic practices; and many would simply gather bits from a variety of sources, and construct their own personalized religion.

The intellectual challenges were no less daunting. Modernity had drastically changed the world view of most people in traditional Christendom. Ancient authorities—including the Bible—were questioned as never before. New democratic ideals conflicted with the hierarchical structure of some churches—particularly the Roman Catholic Church. Darwin and his theory of evolution became a symbol of the intellectual and doctrinal challenges of the time. How were Christians to respond to these and other challenges of modernity? As we shall see, on this score Roman Catholicism (see Chapter 31) followed a path diametrically opposed to that of most Protestant theology (see Chapter 30)—with the immediate consequence that the rift between these two branches of Western Christianity widened in the nineteenth century more than ever before. But here again the twentieth and twenty-first centuries were also marked by unexpected developments. The failures of modernity were such that people began speaking of a post-modern period. In the field of theology, there was a pendulum swing in which both Protestant and Catholic theologians moved away from their former extremes—Protestants becoming generally more skeptical about the achievements and promise of modernity, and Catholics acknowledging some of its values and contributions. But all now had to deal with a new intellectual order in which many of the axioms of modernity were being questioned.

While all of this was occupying the attention of most theologians and church leaders, other momentous changes were taking place in the life of the church. It is to these events that the title of this final part of our story refers: *Beyond Christendom*. In this context, *Christendom* is understood in both spatial and political terms. Until this time, and for much of the history of Christianity, there were regions of the world that considered themselves Christian, as distinct from others that did not, and in these areas the church in its various expressions generally held significant political and social power. (Since this has happened at various times and places, some prefer to speak of Christendoms, in the plural.) But the word *beyond* also has two meanings in the title of this section, both equally important if we are to understand the state of Christianity in the early decades of the twenty-first century. First of all, *beyond* has a spatial meaning. It is used here to indicate that the most momentous events taking place in the nineteenth and twentieth centuries were probably not the theological debates in Western Europe that have traditionally occupied much of our attention. Nor were they the edicts of the Roman Church opposing the *evils* of modernity. They were not even the political and social revolutions that took place in Europe and North America. While all of these are important and must be given due consideration, from the perspective of the twenty-first century it would appear that the most important event in the history of Christianity in the nineteenth and twentieth century was that it moved beyond its traditional confines within Western civilization and became a truly universal faith. As we shall see (in Chapter 36) this was originally connected with the colonial expansion of the West. But when the tide of that expansion began to ebb, in many of the former colonial lands Christianity continued to grow, to put down roots, and to find new forms and expressions better adapted to the cultural and social landscape of each region. Thus, during the nineteenth and early twentieth centuries Christianity moved beyond Christendom in the spatial sense.

But the result of all this is that we can now speak of Christianity moving beyond Christendom also in a temporal sense. In the twenty-first century, it is clear that the time of Christendom has passed. It has passed in the West, with the end of the Constantinian fusion between church and state, and between Christian faith and cultural and social practices. But it has also passed in the sense that we have entered a new period of history in which the North Atlantic is no longer the center of Christian vitality and creativity.

Statistics confirm this. In 1900, 94.5 percent of Europeans and 96.6 percent of North Americans were Christian; by 2000, those numbers had declined to 76.8 percent and 84.2 percent respectively. In Africa, 9.2 percent of the population was Christian in 1900, and by 2000 the figure was 45.9 percent. In Asia, the most populous region in the world and the seat of several world religions, there was a Christian population of 2.3 percent in 1900, and of 8.5 percent in 2000.[12] Thus, numeric decline in the old centers of Christendom was more than balanced by explosive growth in areas where a hundred years earlier the presence of Christianity was minimal.

It is to these sometimes frightening, but certainly exhilarating, developments that we must now turn.

27

A Shifting Landscape: The United States

The God who gave us life gave us liberty at the same time; the hand of force may destroy, but cannot disjoin them.

THOMAS JEFFERSON

THE INDEPENDENCE OF THE THIRTEEN COLONIES

Since their foundation, the British colonies in North America had enjoyed a measure of autonomy. This was aided by the political and religious convulsions that shook England during the seventeenth century, making it more difficult for the British government to exercise authority overseas. Given these circumstances, many of the colonies had organized their government and their trade as best suited them, and not as best suited the interests of England. In the second half of the eighteenth century, however, the British government began seeking more direct rule in the colonies, and the latter reacted vigorously against this encroachment by royal authorities. Three main factors precipitated the open conflict. First, the British quartered seventeen regiments in the colonies. Since their defense did not require such military strength, the colonials viewed the army as an instrument of repression. Second, taxes were a constant point of friction. The crown decided that the colonies should pay the expenses of their governance—including the cost of keeping the much-resented regiments on the field—and to that end levied a series of taxes. In England there was a principle of long standing that the levy of taxes needed to be approved by a representative assembly. The colonials felt that they possessed the same right and that this right was being violated. Third, there were conflicts over Indian lands. For both political and moral reasons, British authorities decreed that there would be no more white occupation of areas beyond the Appalachian Mountains. This law was unpopular in the colonies, where poor whites hoped to establish a homestead in lands now forbidden, and speculators of the landed aristocracy had formed companies with the express objective of colonizing Indian lands.

For these reasons, tension grew between the colonies and the metropolis. Stricter laws evoked greater defiance. In 1770, British troops fired on a crowd in Boston, and five people were killed. Faced with the threat of these troops—now considered foreign—the colonial militia became more active and built up its arsenals. In 1775, when British forces threatened to destroy one of those arsenals, the militia offered resistance, and thus began the American War of Independence. On July 4, 1776, more than a year later, delegates from each of the thirteen colonies, calling themselves the Continental Congress, gathered in Philadelphia to proclaim their independence from Britain. France and Spain then became allies of the new nation, while England counted on the support of many Indian tribes who feared that the independence of the colonies would result in their own destruction—as did indeed happen. Finally, in 1782, a provisional agreement was reached, confirmed a year later by the Treaty of Paris.

These events profoundly affected North American religion. Many combined the struggle for independence with a rationalist ideology that spoke of Providence above all as a principle of progress. The new nation itself was living proof of human progress. Part of such progress was leaving behind the dogmatic attitude of traditional Christianity, and espousing only *natural religion*, or, at best, *essential Christianity*. The traditional teachings and practice of Christian churches, except what could be understood in terms of natural reason or common morality, were considered relics of a bygone age, unnecessary ballast on the ship of progress.

Such ideas became institutionalized in two originally independent movements that were soon entwined: Unitarianism and Universalism. The first was practically contemporary with independence, and made headway mostly in Anglican and Congregationalist circles that were no longer willing to subscribe to traditional orthodoxy. Although the churches that resulted from this movement were called *Unitarian* because they rejected the doctrine of the Trinity, in truth they disagreed with orthodoxy on many other points. They were rationalists, stressing human freedom and intellectual capabilities in contrast to the orthodox emphasis on divine mystery and human sin.

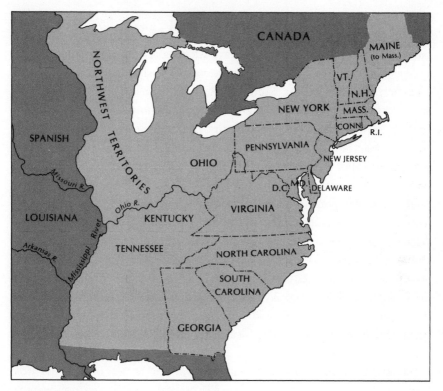

The United States (1800)

This movement became most influential among the merchant class in New England. *Universalism*—that is, the doctrine that in the end all will be saved—was introduced in the colonies by British Methodists shortly before the push for independence. These Methodists argued that the doctrine of eternal damnation was a denial of God's love. Some Universalist churches were organized in New England after independence. Soon the movement merged with the Unitarians. It was also in these circles that Transcendentalism found most of its adherents. This movement, whose most famous representative was Ralph Waldo Emerson (1803–1882), combined rationalism with Romanticism. It stressed self-knowledge as a means to understand the universe and its purpose, and held that there is a bit of the divine in every human being—what some called *the Oversoul*. Like Unitarianism, Transcendentalism gained most of its adepts from among the higher classes, although many of its ideas eventually infiltrated the rest of the nation.

In any case, the most immediate challenge facing the churches in the new nation was the question of their relations with Great Britain. As was to be expected, this issue was most grave for Anglicanism. Since long before independence, many had looked upon bishops as agents of the crown, and had therefore opposed the naming of bishops for the colonies. During the struggle for independence, a high proportion of loyalists were among the members of the Church of England, and eventually many of these emigrated to England, the Caribbean, or Canada. Finally, in 1783, those Anglicans who remained in the United States formed the Protestant Episcopal Church, which was strongest among the aristocracy.

At first, Methodism suffered similar reverses, for the same reasons. Wesley was a staunch supporter of the crown, and called on colonial Methodists to obey the royal edicts. He also criticized the rebellious colonists for claiming freedom for themselves at the same time that they denied it to their slaves. After the Declaration of Independence, all English Methodist preachers in the colonies, except Asbury, returned to Great Britain. This did not contribute to Methodist popularity among the patriots. But, thanks to the untiring efforts of Asbury, American Methodism began taking its distinct shape, and new preachers were recruited. Finally, in 1784, at the Christmas Conference, American Methodism was organized as a church, apart from both Anglicanism and from British Methodism. It was also decided that American Methodism would be led by bishops.

Other churches followed different courses. The Baptist Church grew rapidly, particularly in Virginia and other southern colonies, and from there penetrated the new territories of Tennessee and Kentucky. The Congregationalists, in spite of having gained prestige by their support of independence, made significant gains in membership only in the areas colonized from New England. In general, all denominations spent their best efforts in reorganizing themselves in view of the new situation, and in repairing the damage done by war.

In fact, the very word *denomination* points to one of the main characteristics of the Protestant Christianity resulting from the North American experience. The word itself indicates that the various *churches* are seen as *denominations*, that is, as different names given to Christians. In a religiously pluralistic society where tolerance was necessary for political survival, and in view of the bloodshed that dogmatism had caused elsewhere, North American Protestants tended to think of the church as an invisible reality consisting of all true believers, and of the visible churches or *denominations* as voluntary organizations that believers create and join according to their convictions and preferences.

A practical consequence of this distinction between the church and the *denominations* is that the great debates that have divided North American Protestantism have not been confined to a particular church, but have crossed denominational barriers. Thus, for instance, questions such as slavery, evolution, fundamentalism, liberalism, and racial policies have simultaneously divided several denominations, and the partisans of one position or another have joined across denominational lines.

The Disciples of Christ were born as a response to the denominationalism of American Christianity. The founders of this movement, Thomas Campbell (1763–1854) and his son Alexander (1788–1866), had no desire to found a new church or denomination. Their purpose was to call all Protestant Christians to unity through the proclamation of the gospel in its original purity. Alexander Campbell, who soon became the leader of the movement, combined some of the rationalism common to his age with a profound respect for the authority of the New Testament. Therefore, much of his interpretation of the New Testament was influenced by rationalist views, although his zeal in obeying what he took to be God's commands was unparalleled by the rationalists. With the firm conviction that Christian unity could be achieved by a common return to primitive Christianity as he understood it, Campbell launched a program of reformation that eventually (though much against his original designs) led to the formation of a new denomination, the Christian Church (or Disciples of Christ). Given the tensions in Campbell's own vision, as well as in various later influences, throughout their history the Disciples have included both a rationalist and a conservative wing. But all have been characterized by their interest in Christian unity.

EARLY IMMIGRATION

The thirteen colonies that later became the United States had been peopled by immigrants, mostly from Great Britain, but also from Germany and other parts of Europe. But late in the eighteenth century, and throughout the nineteenth, there were unprecedented waves of migration from Europe to the United States. This was due partly to conditions in Europe—the Napoleonic Wars, social upheaval caused by industrialization, the tyranny of various regimes, famine, and so forth—and partly to the vast expanse of land seemingly available in the West of the new nation. At the same time, the slave traffic also brought to the United States vast numbers of unwilling immigrants.

Such massive immigration had far-reaching consequences for the shape of Christianity in the United States. By the middle of the nineteenth century, the Catholic Church (which at the time of independence was a small minority) had become the largest religious body in the nation. At first, most Catholics were of English descent. Later came French and Germans. But around 1846 a great famine began in Ireland that lasted several decades, and soon Irish immigrants and their descendants made up the largest contingent of American Catholics. This created tensions within the Catholic Church, both locally and nationally. At the parish level, each group of immigrants saw the church as a means to preserve its culture and tradition; therefore, each wanted a separate parish. At the national level, there were power struggles between various groups, each wishing to be governed by a hierarchy that understood and represented it. Such tensions would continue well into the twentieth century, and would become more complex as other groups were added to North American Catholicism—Italians, Poles, and others by immigration; the French of Louisiana by purchase (1803); and the Hispanics of Mexico (1848); and Puerto Rico (1898) first by military conquest and then by immigration. Eventually, Catholicism in the United States would be characterized by its cultural diversity and by the degree to which that diversity and the pressure of the surrounding culture questioned and limited the traditional power of the hierarchy.

The growth of Catholicism provoked a strong reaction on the part of some Protestants. In the very early years of the new nation, there was already opposition to unlimited Catholic immigration, on the grounds that democracy was not compatible with the hierarchical understanding of authority of Roman Catholics, and that their growing numbers were therefore a threat to the nation. Later, the Ku Klux Klan would unleash its xenophobic fanaticism, not only against blacks, but also against Catholics and Jews, on the premise that the United States was called to be a white, Protestant, and democratic nation, and that these three characteristics were inseparable. When, in 1864, Pope Pius IX condemned a list of eighty "errors" that included several of the fundamental theses of American democracy, there were many in the United States, both conservative and liberal, who saw this as a confirmation of their worst fears regarding the political goals of the Catholic Church (see Chapter 32). It would take almost another century for the nation to be willing to trust its highest political offices to Roman Catholics.

Lutheranism also grew rapidly through immigration. At first, most Lutheran immigrants were German, but later there were also many Scandinavians. Each of these groups brought with it its own traditions, and for a long time the main goal of American Lutheranism was the eventual union of the various Lutheran bodies. Other religious groups that grew through immigration were the Mennonites, Moravians, Greek and Russian Orthodox, and Jews. The rich variety of such groups further necessitated the tradition of religious tolerance that had begun centuries earlier in Rhode Island and Pennsylvania.

Many immigrants also brought with them the ideal of life in a religious community governed by gospel principles and distinct—sometimes even withdrawn—from the rest of society. Thus the American countryside was dotted with small experiments in communal living. From very early times, one of the goals leading Europeans to the colonies of North America was the founding of a new society in a new land. The *Mayflower* Pilgrims were only the first of thousands with similar dreams. Both European immigrants and natives of the United States moved west, seeking places to found ideal communities. The Moravians founded settlements in Pennsylvania that still exist today, and similar experiments were undertaken by Mennonites and other Anabaptists in search of a place where they could freely practice their pacifist beliefs. German Pietists founded the community of Ephrata, also in Pennsylvania, and several others nearby and in Ohio. The commonality of goods was a characteristic of many of these settlements. In 1846, the Oneida community went so far as to practice *complex matrimony*, an arrangement in which all adults were married to all others of the opposite sex.

One of the most remarkable of these movements was that of the Shakers, led by Ann Lee Stanley—Mother Ann Lee. For a time they sought to live out their faith in their native England, but social pressure was such that they eventually decided to emigrate to America. In their new homeland, probably in imitation of neighboring groups, they opted for communal living. Mother Ann Lee claimed that she was the Second Coming of Christ (hence the official name of the Shaker church: The United Society of Believers in Christ's Second Appearing), who had now appeared in feminine form as he had appeared earlier in masculine form. Eventually, all would be saved, and the present community of belief was only the beachhead of that final salvation.

Meanwhile, believers must abstain from sex, which is the root of all evil. One of the characteristics of Shaker worship was the important role played by dance. For a few decades, the movement flourished, and several Shaker communities were founded. As experiments in communal living, they were quite successful, for conditions in Shaker communities were usually better than in neighboring areas. But eventually the movement dwindled, lacking in both converts and in new generations and today there are only a few surviving members.

THE SECOND GREAT AWAKENING

Toward the end of the eighteenth century, a Second Great Awakening began in New England. At first, it did not include great emotional outbursts, but was marked rather by a sudden earnestness in Christian devotion and living. Attendance at worship increased markedly, and many spoke of having had an experience of conversion. Nor did this awakening have at first the anti-intellectual overtones of other similar movements. On the contrary, it made headway among some of the most distinguished theologians of New England. One of its foremost advocates was Timothy Dwight, president of Yale University and a grandson of Jonathan Edwards.

That first phase of the awakening resulted in the founding of several societies whose purpose was to make the gospel known. Most important among these were the American Bible Society, founded in 1816, and the American Board of Commissioners for Foreign Missions, founded six years earlier. The latter was the result of a covenant made by a group of students meeting on a haystack, who vowed to devote themselves to foreign missions. When Adoniram Judson, one of the first missionaries sent by the American Board, became a Baptist, many Baptists in the United States set aside some of their extreme congregationalism in order to organize a General Convention the purpose of which was to support Baptist missionaries throughout the world. In local churches, women's missionary societies appeared, and some of these would later develop into various feminine organizations. Other societies born during the Second Awakening took up various social causes, such as the abolition of slavery—the American Colonization Society, to which we shall return—and the war against alcohol—the American Society for the Promotion of Temperance, founded in 1826. Women became leaders in the latter cause, to the extent that, in the second half of the century, under the leadership of Frances Willard, the Women's Christian Temperance Union became the foremost defender of women's rights. Thus, some of the roots of American feminism can be traced to the Second Great Awakening.

Meanwhile, the awakening had moved beyond the limits of New England and of the educated elite, and had made great headway among people of less education and lesser means. Many of these people were moving west, for one of the results of the War of Independence was that the European powers agreed to the expansion of the United States as far as the Mississippi River. Many of those who traveled west carried with them the vibrant faith kindled by the Second Awakening. But, since conditions on the frontier were different, the awakening now became more emotional and less intellectual, to the point that it eventually became anti-intellectual.

The Cane Ridge Revival of 1801, in Cane Ridge, Kentucky, marked a significant step in that process. It was originally organized by the local Presbyterian pastor, who announced a great assembly or camp meeting for the promotion of a deeper faith. Being in an area where there were few opportunities to gather and celebrate, the pastor's announcement had a resounding success. On the appointed date, thousands gathered. Many went to Cane Ridge for religious reasons. Others took the opportunity to gamble and carouse. Besides the pastor who had issued the original invitation, there were also several Baptist and Methodist preachers in attendance. While some played and others drank, the pastors preached. A critic of the awakening later declared that at Cane Ridge as many souls were conceived as were saved. In any case, the response to the call to repentance was surprising and overwhelming. While some wept and others laughed uncontrollably, still others trembled, some ran about, and some even barked. The meeting lasted a week, and since then many were convinced that such gatherings were the best way to proclaim the gospel. After that time, when the words evangelism and revival were used, they evoked images of Cane Ridge.

Although the gathering at Cane Ridge had been organized by a Presbyterian, that denomination did not favor the unbridled emotional response that was becoming part of the movement. Soon Presbyterians began taking action against ministers who participated in events such as Cane Ridge. But Methodists and Baptists took up the idea of celebrating camp meetings, and these eventually developed into periodic revivals. Since such revivals became an important part of social life on the frontier, both Methodist and Baptist groups achieved rapid growth. Another reason for their growth was that they were willing to present the message as simply as possible, and to use preachers with little or no education. While other denominations lacked personnel because they had no facilities within which to educate them on the frontier, Methodists and Baptists were willing to use whomever felt called by the Lord. The Methodist vanguard were lay preachers, many of them serving an entire area they called a *circuit*, always under the supervision of the connection and its bishops. The Baptists made use of farmers or others who made a living from their trade, and who also served as pastors of the local church. When a new area was opened for settlement, there usually was among the settlers a devout Baptist willing to take up the ministry of preaching. Thus, both Methodists and Baptists were strongly represented in the new territories, and by the middle of the century they were the largest Protestant denominations in the country.

Another important consequence of the Second Great Awakening was that it helped break down the strict correspondence between ethnic origin and religious affiliation. Among the new Baptists and Methodists there were German ex-Lutherans, Scottish ex-Presbyterians, and Irish ex-Catholics. Although it was still generally true that denominational allegiance coincided with ethnic origin, after the Second Great Awakening, and especially on the frontier, such correspondence could no longer be taken for granted.

During the Second Great Awakening, camp meetings such as this Methodist one were typical of frontier American Christianity.

MANIFEST DESTINY AND THE WAR WITH MEXICO

Since the first landing of the *Mayflower* Pilgrims, the notion that the British colonies in the New World had been founded with divine assistance, in order to fulfill a providential mission, was commonly accepted. Leaders in the struggle for independence spoke of a new experiment that would lead humankind along paths of progress and liberty. Later immigrants regarded the United States as a veritable promised land of freedom and abundance. Such ideas often went hand in hand with the conviction that Protestantism was superior to Catholicism, and that the latter was a hindrance to both freedom and progress. Very early on, England felt that its colonies were threatened by Spanish Catholics from the south, and by French Catholics from the north; therefore, such colonies were seen as a Protestant bulwark in the New World. All this was linked to a racist attitude; European immigrants often took for granted that whites were superior, and were therefore justified in taking lands away from Indians and freedom away from blacks.

In 1823, President James Monroe proclaimed his famous doctrine, that the United States would not countenance new European ventures in the Western hemisphere, and the destiny of the new nation seemed particularly manifest in connection with that hemisphere. At about the same time, Mexico's ambassador to the United States noted that many people with whom he spoke in his host country were convinced that the eventual result of the wars of independence in Spanish America would be that most of the continent would belong to the United States. When coined in 1845, the phrase Manifest Destiny referred specifically to U.S. expansion continuing west all the way to the Pacific by means of occupying Oregon—the possession of which was currently disputed by Great Britain—and by occupying all Mexican land that lay directly west of what was then the U.S. border. Once negotiations resolved the Oregon question, the matter of Mexico's territory standing between the United States and the Pacific remained to be settled.

American expansionism had previously played an important role in Texas. That area, a neglected part of the Mexican state of Coahuila, was invaded in 1819 by James Long, an adventurer who was defeated by the Mexican army. In order to dissuade others from similar adventures, Mexico began allowing people from the United States to settle in Texas, as long as they were Catholic and they swore allegiance to Mexico. The net result was a wave of immigration by people who were willing to deny their religion in order to become landowners and who, while nominally Mexican, believed that their race made them naturally superior to the *mestizos* (people of mixed Indian and European blood) who governed the area in the name of Mexico. One of these immigrants, Stephen Austin, would later declare: "for fifteen years, I have been laboring like a slave to Americanize Texas." He would add that his enemies were "a population of Indians, Mexicans and renegades, all mixed together, and all the natural enemies of white men and civilization."[13]

The question of slavery made matters more difficult. Mexico abolished slavery in 1829, and immigrants to Texas (who often depended on slavery for their wealth) responded by conspiring to secede from Mexico to join the United States. Such conspiracies were aided by those in the United States who had begun to fear the abolitionist movement, and who saw Texas as a possible ally. Others who supported the movement hoped to become rich by speculating on lands Mexicans would be forced to abandon. At one point, the U.S. ambassador to Mexico tried to bribe a Mexican official by offering him two hundred thousand dollars in exchange for his support for a proposed purchase of Texas.

Finally, war broke out. The Mexican army had far greater numbers, but the Texan rebels—both immigrants from the United States and discontented Mexicans—were better armed, and possessed more artillery as well as rifles with three times the range of Mexican muskets. At the mission of El Alamo, in San Antonio, some two hundred rebels resisted an entire Mexican army. After fierce struggle, the last survivors surrendered, and were executed by the Mexicans. "Remember the Alamo" then became the battle cry of the rebels, used in the United States to raise funds and recruit volunteers. The rebels were repeatedly defeated by the larger Mexican army; but, in 1836, Sam Houston took the Mexican headquarters by surprise and captured Mexican General (and dictator) Antonio López de Santa Anna, who bought his freedom by agreeing to the independence of the Republic of Texas. The government of Mexico consented to this, on the condition that Texas would remain an independent nation, and not be annexed by the United States—a stipulation to which the latter agreed.

The expansion of the United States to the West, however, could not be stopped by a piece of paper. James K. Polk was elected president in 1844, thus bringing to power those who felt that the nation should continue its westward thrust. Even before the new president was sworn in, Texas was made a state of the Union by a joint resolution of Congress. The next year the phrase Manifest Destiny was used for the first time. That destiny—and the powerful economic interests hiding behind it—required the conquest of Mexico's northern lands. But there were still many in the United States who opposed such expansion, agreeing with John Quincy Adams who said before the House of Representatives, that in a war with Mexico "the banners of freedom will be the banners of Mexico; and your banners, I blush to speak the word, will be the banners of slavery."[14] Therefore, it was necessary to make Mexico fire the first shot, and Polk ordered General Zachary Taylor into territory that the U.S. disputed with Mexico. Years later, Ulysses S. Grant, who as a young lieutenant had been part of that expedition, declared: "We were sent to provoke a fight, but it was essential that Mexico should commence it."[15] When the Mexican army refused to open hostilities, Taylor was ordered to continue advancing until he drew fire. When Mexico finally offered resistance, Polk obtained from Congress a declaration of war. Grant was convinced that behind all these events lurked a conspiracy to increase the number of slaveholding states.

The brief war was concluded by the Treaty of Guadalupe-Hidalgo in 1848, whereby Mexico ceded to the United States, in exchange for fifteen million dollars, more than three million square kilometers—the present states of New Mexico, Arizona, California, Utah, Nevada, and part of Colorado—and agreed to the annexation of Texas by the United States, with the Rio Grande as the border between the two nations. The treaty also guaranteed the rights of Mexicans who decided to remain in the conquered territory. But such rights were soon violated as new settlers moved onto the land as if it had no owners, and discrimination against Mexicans as an inferior race became common practice in the American Southwest.

Before 1848, churches in the United States had been divided in their opinions regarding the war and the notion of Manifest Destiny. Valiant voices of protest rose against what was seen as naked aggression and as an attempt to reinstitute slavery in lands where it had been banned. But after the war, as settlers rushed to quench their thirst for land, churches joined the westward movement, and soon several denominations were speaking of the *door* that God had opened for the evangelization of Mexicans.

The conquest of these lands had different consequences for Roman Catholicism. The most important was the sudden addition to its membership of a large flock belonging to an entirely different culture from that of the rest of North American Catholics. For several decades, American Catholicism refused to accept that difference, and worked toward the Americanization of its new constituency. In 1850, the Catholic Church in the Southwest was put in the hands of a hierarchy drawn from the East, and the number of Hispanic priests declined rapidly. Mexican-American historians have documented a marked contrast between the older Mexican priests, who lived among the people and served the poor, and the new ones brought from the East, who moved mostly among the English-speaking settlers and were content with saying mass for the deprived Mexicans. An example of this was the conflict between Father Antonio José Martínez—known among the native population as *el cura de Taos*—and the vicar general for New Mexico, Jean Baptiste Lamy. Although of French background, Lamy served under the diocese of Baltimore, and was a close friend of many of the new citizens of the area—Kit Carson among them. Since 1824, Martínez had headed a seminary in Taos, and most of the older clergy of the area had been trained by him. Although he openly rejected celibacy, many in the area called him a saint, for he devoted his entire life to the care of the poor. When Lamy ordered Martínez and the other Mexican clergy to be more assiduous in collecting the tithes of their flock and sending them to his office, they responded that it was immoral and unchristian to take money from the poor to give to the rich. Lamy excommunicated the refractory priest and his followers, but they continued in their ministry among the Mexicans, serving them as priests and administering the sacraments in open schism with the hierarchy of the church. The movement continued for some years after the death of Martínez, in 1867. As it waned, so did the number of Mexicans offering themselves for the priesthood. It was not until well into the twentieth century that there was in the Southwest a Catholic bishop of Hispanic origin.

SLAVERY AND CIVIL WAR

From colonial times, the issue of slavery had troubled the conscience of many. As independence approached, there were those who voiced the opinion that the new nation should be born free of such an evil institution. However, in order to present a common front against Great Britain, such voices were silenced, and the United States, while calling itself the *land of the free*, continued allowing the practice of slavery, though several denominations took a clear stance against it. In 1776, the Quakers expelled from their midst all who insisted on holding slaves. The Christmas Conference in 1784 that organized American Methodists as a separate church also banned slaveholding among its members. And many Baptists, although lacking a national organization that could take similar measures, nevertheless took a stance against slavery.

Those early stances, however, were modified with the passage of time. Only the Friends—who in any case were not numerous in the South—remained firm. Methodists as well as Baptists sought to attract the slave-holding whites of the South by moderating their opposition to slavery. By 1843, over a thousand Methodist ministers and preachers owned slaves. Other denominations were equally ambivalent. For instance, in 1818 the General Assembly of the Presbyterian Church, while declaring slavery to be against the law of God, also went on record as opposing its abolition, and deposed a minister for advocating abolition.

At first, antislavery sentiments were equally strong in both the North and the South. In 1817, the American Colonization Society was founded with the purpose of buying slaves, freeing them, and returning them to Africa. The founding of the Republic of Liberia was largely the result of the Society's work. But such efforts had little impact on slavery in general. Meanwhile, the abolitionist movement was gaining strength in the North, where slavery was of less economic importance, while the South, whose economic and social system was based on slave labor, took the opposite tack. Soon, many in the South were preaching that slavery was an institution sanctioned by God, and that even blacks profited from it, for by it they had been snatched out of pagan and uncivilized Africa and given the advantages of the gospel. In the North, the abolitionist movement was equally vehement in its conviction that God did not will slavery. Many in the Methodist Church began demanding that the old position of the church against slavery be reasserted. When, in 1844, the Methodist General Conference condemned the bishop of Georgia for holding slaves, the church split, and the following year witnessed the birth of the Methodist Episcopal Church, South. Something similar happened among Baptists, for when their missionary agency refused to commission a candidate who had been recommended by the Georgia Baptist Convention on the grounds that he owned slaves, the Southern Baptist Convention was born. In 1861, reflecting the nation's division, the Southern presbyteries withdrew from the Presbyterian Church and founded their own denomination. These divisions persisted into the twentieth century, when some of them were healed, and others were not. The only major denomination that was able to weather the storm without schism was the Catholic Church. The Episcopal Church, although divided during the war, was reunited almost immediately after the end of the conflict.

In 1861, the nation was split, first by the secession of the Confederate States of America, and then by civil war. During the armed conflict, pulpits on both sides defended the justice of their cause. After the war, hatred and prejudice were fostered because—after the period of Reconstruction, which essentially meant Northern military occupation—the South became an economic colony of the North. Southern whites were permitted to manage political and social matters as long as they did not interfere with Northern economic interests and their investments in the area. Southern whites, unable to vent their anger on the North, turned it toward the black population. Fear of blacks was fostered from many Southern pulpits, and when that fear led to the founding of the Ku Klux Klan there were preachers who openly supported its activities. The same hatred and fear of the North also led to anti-intellectualism and conservatism in the Southern churches, for most of the great educational centers were in the North, and any ideas coming from them were suspect.

Since southern whites could vent their anger and frustration on blacks, they did so. During Reconstruction, blacks were given positions of responsibility by the Northern invaders. But this served only to exacerbate the prejudice of Southern whites against them, and as soon as Reconstruction came to an end Southern whites moved to restrict the rights and power of blacks. In 1892, the U.S. Supreme Court approved segregation, which allowed for the enactment of local laws that mandated public services and facilities be separated along racial lines. Though these so-called *Jim Crow laws* required "separate but equal" rights for all races, they effectively excluded blacks from public places, from the right to vote, from a good public education, and so forth. Meanwhile, Southern white churches continued their racist teachings and practices. Blacks who had formerly attended such churches as slaves were now encouraged to leave them, and this in turn gave rise to various black denominations. Black Baptists formed their own congregations, that later joined in the National Baptist Convention. Black Methodists founded the Colored Methodist Episcopal Church—the C.M.E. Church, later to become the Christian Methodist Episcopal Church. Meanwhile, Northern churches—particularly Presbyterian and Methodist churches—began work among blacks in the South.

Blacks were encouraged to leave white churches and form their own, such as this one in Washington.

But the North was not exempt from prejudice and segregation. Even before the Civil War such attitudes had led to the formation of two black denominations that would later play an important role among freed blacks in the South: the African Methodist Episcopal Church, and the African Methodist Episcopal Zion Church. The former was founded by Richard Allen, who lived as a free man and became the first black ordained a deacon in the North American Methodist Church. Allen organized a local church for blacks in Philadelphia, but repeated conflicts with the white hierarchy of his denomination eventually led to its separation from the white church and the birth of a new denomination. Five years later, in 1821, similar events in New York led to the creation of the African Methodist Episcopal Zion Church. Both of these denominations played an important role among Northern blacks and, after the Civil War, also in the South. They also have done important missionary work in Africa.

Black churches soon grew to be one of the principal institutions of black society. Since the only prestigious position to which blacks had relatively free

Richard Allen, a free man who became the first black ordained a deacon in the North American Methodist Church.

access was the ministry, for a century most black leaders were also pastors. Some black churches advocated submission to present injustice while awaiting a heavenly reward. In others, more radical words of justice and black dignity were heard. But all contributed to the sense of identity and cohesion among blacks that would be the backbone of the struggle for civil rights a hundred years later.

FROM THE CIVIL WAR TO WORLD WAR I

The social and economic tensions of earlier decades increased after the end of the Civil War. The South became even more racist and anti-intellectual. In the North, immigration brought about rapid urban growth, and ecclesiastical structures proved unequal to the challenges of that growth and of the increasing number of blacks who moved to the North seeking a better life. In the West, relentless pressure continued to be applied on Indian lands, and Hispanics were the object of discrimination.

In the midst of such diversity, one element contributing to the unity of the nation was the notion that it would play a providential role in the progress of humankind. Usually that role was understood in terms of racial, religious, and institutional superiority—that is, the superiority of the white race, the Protestant faith, and democratic government based on free enterprise. Thus, late in the century the general secretary of the Evangelical Alliance, Josiah Strong, declared that God was preparing the Anglo-Saxon race, for a great moment, "the final competition of races" at which point that race, representing "the largest liberty, the purest Christianity, the highest civilization,"[16] would fulfill its God-given destiny of dispossessing the weaker ones, assimilating others, and molding the rest, so as to "Anglo-Saxonize" humankind. And such sentiments, expressed by one of the leaders of the conservative wing of American Protestantism, were similar to those of the liberal wing, who held that Protestantism and freedom of thought and opinion were the great contribution of the Nordic races against the tyranny and Catholicism of southern European races, and that therefore people of Nordic origin had the responsibility of civilizing the "backward" races of the rest of the world.

Such notions, however, contrasted with the urban reality of the United States itself, where recent immigrants were being exploited and living in overcrowded conditions, lacking all contact with organized Christianity—particularly in its Protestant form. Protestantism sought to respond to this challenge in various ways. One was the establishment of several organizations whose goal was to serve the urban masses. Most successful among these were the Young Men's Christian Association (YMCA) and the Young Women's Christian Association (YWCA), both imported from England in the mid-nineteenth century. Another Protestant response to the challenge of the new population was the creation of Sunday schools. At a time when the study of the Bible at home was falling by the wayside, and the knowledge of Scripture among the masses was waning, Sunday schools played a very important role. Eventually, there were churches where Sunday school surpassed Sunday worship in importance. In 1872, several large denominations began the practice—which continued into the twenty-first century—of agreeing on the Scriptural texts to be used in Sunday school, and this in turn was a significant step toward greater understanding and collaboration across denominational lines.

Protestantism also responded to the urban challenge by adapting the old camp meetings to the new situation, and revivals became an important element of the urban religious scene. The main figure in the early stages of this development was Dwight L. Moody. Moody was a Chicago shoe salesman who was moved to act by the lack of religious life among the masses of that great city. He began bringing people to the Congregationalist church he attended, but he soon founded an independent church. He also became involved in the work of the YMCA, where he was noted for his zeal in communicating the gospel to others. It was in 1872, while visiting London in connection with his YMCA responsibilities, that he was first invited to preach. The result was so encouraging that Moody then felt called to preach to the urban masses, first in England, and then in the United States. His method consisted of simple and emotive preaching, calling people to repentance and to accept salvation offered in Jesus Christ. He was convinced that the conversion of the masses would lead to better living conditions in the cities, and therefore he had little to say regarding the conditions and social structures that led to so much human misery. But there is no doubt that his message and style were singularly well adapted to the felt needs of the urban masses. Soon he had many imitators, some more successful than others and the revival became part of the American urban landscape.

New denominations arose in response to the urban challenge as well. Within the Methodist tradition, in both England and in the United States, there were many who felt that their church had abandoned some basic elements of Wesley's teachings. It was clear that Methodists had been progressively moving toward the middle classes, and paying less attention to the poor, especially the urban poor. Since it was precisely among such people that the movement had achieved its early success, there were many who sought to return to that earlier emphasis. In England, this gave rise to the Salvation Army, founded by Methodist preacher William Booth and his wife Catherine Munford—who was also a preacher, for one of the characteristic notes of the Salvation Army was the equality of the sexes within it. It was also concerned with both the spiritual and the physical well-being of people living in urban centers, and soon became known for its relief work among the poor, providing food, shelter, work, and so forth. Given the conditions of urban life in the United States, when the Salvation Army was brought over from England it found a fertile soil for its work.

Out of the Methodists' dissatisfaction with the direction their church had taken, several new ecclesiastical bodies were born in the United States. These groups wished to return both to the earlier concern for the masses, and to Wesley's teachings on sanctification. Because of this latter emphasis, these churches became collectively known as *holiness churches*. At first there were many such groups, though they were unconnected to one another. But slowly they crystallized into several new denominations. The most numerous in attendance was the Church of the Nazarene, organized in 1908 through the union of several holiness churches. But still, the main strength of the holiness movement was in the hundreds of independent churches, and

Phoebe Palmer was an outstanding leader in the holiness movement.

in others belonging to very small denominations, scattered throughout the country.

One of the leading voices in the holiness movement was Phoebe Palmer (1807–1874), a Methodist who, in 1835, began leading women's prayer meetings in her home. Four years later, men began joining her meetings. Her movement and her influence grew as she began speaking in public, to the point that by the middle of the century she was traveling extensively in the United States as well as in Canada, Great Britain, and continental Europe; there she conducted and spoke at "holiness revivals." Palmer was convinced that perfect holiness—the second blessing after conversion—must be the goal and the outcome of the Christian life. For this, she drew severe criticism from many of the leaders of her own Methodist Episcopal Church, who claimed that her views turned sanctification into an almost mechanical process. But she persisted in her views, while also emphasizing the social dimensions of holiness, which does not consist merely of personal purity and devotion but also in actions of love. On this basis she founded the Methodist Ladies' Home Missionary Society, which established work in some of the most deprived urban areas of the nation. Her work—and the work of many other women of similar persuasions—contributed to what would later become the American Feminist movement.

Worship in many holiness churches was marked by the outpouring of the gifts of the Spirit—speaking in tongues, miracles of healing, and prophetic utterances. Such practices, eventually abandoned by many holiness churches, reappeared with great vigor in 1906, in the Azusa Street Mission of Los Angeles. The movement began among a small group of believers meeting at a private home on Bonnie Brae Street. They were led by pastor William J. Seymour, a former slave who had been profoundly influenced by Pentecostal preacher Charles Parham, and whose preaching on the gift of tongues had led to his being banned from the pulpit. In the house on Bonnie Brae there were sudden manifestations of the power of the Spirit, particularly speaking in tongues. Inspired by those events, Seymour's followers moved to a larger location on Azusa Street. From that point on, Pentecostal fire, starting from that Azusa Street revival, spread throughout the nation. Since there were both black and white members on Azusa Street, the movement spread among both races—although eventually much of it resulted in churches reflecting the racial lines that divided the nation. It then moved beyond the limits of the Wesleyan tradition, and was taken up by many Baptists and others. By 1914, the director of a Pentecostal publication called for a great gathering of "believers in the baptism of the Holy Spirit," and out of that gathering emerged the Assemblies of God, the main Pentecostal denomination in the United States. The Assemblies and other Pentecostal denominations made significant inroads among the urban masses, and soon moved both to the rural areas and to distant countries, where they sent numerous missionaries. In the following century, this movement begun at Azusa Street would be a dominant element in the global Christian landscape.

Although it had gone through a long process of formation, another denomination that took its definitive form after the Civil War was the Seventh Day Adventists. Early in the nineteenth century, Vermont Baptist William Miller, by combining data taken from Daniel with other elements from Genesis and the rest of Scripture, had come to the conclusion that the Lord would return in 1843. When that date arrived and passed, most of Miller's followers left him. But a small remnant continued anxiously awaiting the Lord's return. The movement then led a precarious existence until the appearance of Prophet Ellen Harmon White. By then, through contacts with Seventh Day Baptists, they had begun keeping the Sabbath on Saturdays, and holding their major worship services on that day instead of Sunday. White was a superb organizer whose published visions attracted the rem-

The house on Bonnie Brae Street where the Azusa Street revival began is now a museum of early Pentecostal history.

nants of Miller's followers and many others, and these finally organized into a single body in 1868. Under White's leadership, the Adventists took great interest in medicine, dietetics, and missions. By the time she died in 1915, the movement had thousands of adherents both in the United States and several other nations. On this last score, this particular denomination led the way by ceasing to be a strict North American denomination with branches or missions overseas, and reorganizing itself in truly international fashion.

Protestantism in the United States had other challenges to face besides urban growth, and of these the most important was intellectual in character. Europe was constantly sending across the Atlantic, not only immigrants, but also ideas that questioned much that had earlier been taken for granted. Darwin's theory of evolution seemed to contradict the stories of creation in Genesis, and therefore produced quite a stir among the masses. But among theologians a greater challenge was posed by the historical and critical studies that were taking place in Europe. Such studies raised doubts about the historical authenticity of several—if not most—books of the Bible. As a methodological presupposition, all that seemed extraordinary or miraculous was to be rejected. In the same academic circles, great optimism prevailed regarding the human creature and its capabilities. Thanks to evolution and progress, the day was at hand when humans would be able to solve problems until then insoluble, thus bringing in a new age of joy, freedom, justice, peace, and abundance.

Protestant Liberalism was an attempt to couch Christianity in the mold of those ideas, and gained wide acceptance among the intellectual elite in the United States. It was by no means a monolithic movement, for the very idea of liberalism implied freedom to think as one saw fit—as long as one did not fall into what liberals called superstition. But it was a vast wave of thought that many saw as a denial of the Christian faith. In that wave there was a relatively small number of radicals—sometimes called *modernists*—for whom Christianity and the Bible were little more than another religion and one great book among many. But most liberals were committed Christians whose very commitment drove them to respond to the intellectual challenges of their time in the hope of making the faith credible for modern people. In any case, liberalism in the United States was limited almost entirely to the Northeast, and to the middle and upper classes, for whom the intellectual issues of the day seemed more pressing than the social conditions of urban laborers. In the South and the West, liberalism had little impact.

The reaction was not slow in coming, for many saw liberalism as a threat to the very core of the Christian faith. At the popular level, probably the issue most discussed was the theory of evolution, and there were even attempts to have courts of law decide on the matter. As late as the early decades of the twenty-first century, debate continued in some areas as to whether public schools should be allowed to teach the theory of evolution, and as to how this should be done so as not to contradict Scripture. But conservative theologians clearly saw that the question of evolution was only one instance of the threat the new ideas posed to the fundamentals of Christianity. Soon the term fundamentals became characteristic of the anti-liberal reaction that came to be called *fundamentalism*. In 1846, when that movement was beginning to crystallize, the Evangelical Alliance was formed, seeking to join all those who saw liberalism as a denial of the faith. But it was in 1895, at a meeting in Niagara Falls, New York, that the movement listed the five fundamentals that could not be denied without falling into the error of liberalism. These were the inerrancy of Scripture, the divinity of Jesus, the Virgin birth, Jesus' death on the cross as a substitute for our sins, and his physical resurrection and impending return. Shortly thereafter, the General Assembly of the Presbyterian Church adopted similar principles. From that point on, and for several decades, the majority of Protestants, particularly in the South, were fundamentalists.

On the other hand, it is significant to note that, while fundamentalism declared itself a defender of traditional orthodoxy, it gave rise to new interpretations of the Bible. Its emphasis on biblical inerrancy and its rejection of many of the conclusions of biblical scholars made it possible to juxtapose texts from different books of Scripture, and thus to develop a number of schemes outlining and explaining God's actions, past, present, and future. The most successful of these schemes were those of the dispensationalists—of which there were several. The most popular dispensationalist scheme was developed by Cyrus Scofield, who divided human history into seven dispensations—the present one being the sixth. In 1909, the Scofield Bible was published, outlining this interpretation of history, and it soon became widely used in fundamentalist circles. Thus, fundamentalism became closely tied with dispensationalism—although many fundamentalists differed from Scofield in matters of detail.

Meanwhile, liberalism was making its most significant contribution in what came to be called the *Social Gospel*. This was not the belief of most liberals, who belonged to the urban middle classes, and were scarcely interested in the plight of the poor. But a small core of liberals did devote their efforts to exploring and showing the relationship between the demands of the gospel and the misery in which the urban masses lived. Their leader was Walter Rauschenbush, who was a professor of church history at a Baptist seminary from 1897 until his death in 1918. He insisted that the social and economic life of the nation should conform to the requirements of the gospel, and showed that economic liberalism—the theory that the law of supply and demand suffices to regulate the marketplace—results in great inequity and social injustice. The task of Christians in that context is to seek to limit the unbridled power of runaway capital, and to advocate the enactment of laws that will aid the poor and promote greater justice. The point of contact between the Social Gospel and the rest of liberalism was their common optimism regarding human capabilities and the progress of society. But while other liberals simply trusted the natural progress of humanity and of capitalist society, the proponents of the Social Gospel feared that so-called progress would take place at the expense of the poor.

Both fundamentalism and liberalism reached their apex at a time when the political and economic future of the United States seemed assured. The war with Mexico, the abolition of slavery, and the war with Spain in 1898 seemed to promise that the United States—and the white race that ruled the nation—were destined to lead the world into an era of progress and prosperity. Then World War I broke out, followed by a period of economic distress. How this affected Christianity in the United States is a subject to which we shall return later in this chapter.

NEW RELIGIONS

One of the most remarkable phenomena in the religious life of the United States during the nineteenth century was the birth of several movements that so differed from traditional Christianity that they could well be called new religions. The largest of these were the Mormon faith, Jehovah's Witnesses, and Christian Science.

During his early years, Joseph Smith, the founder of Mormonism, seemed to be a failure. His parents were poor rural folk who had moved to New York from Vermont seeking, and failing to find, better economic conditions. Young Joseph was not inclined to labor in the fields, preferring to seek hidden treasures and to claim that he had visions telling him where such treasures could be found. He then declared that an angel named Moroni had appeared to him and had given him a collection of golden tablets written in ancient Egyptian hieroglyphs, as well as two seer's stones with which it was possible to read the tablets. Smith hid behind a curtain and dictated his translation of the sacred tablets to scribes on the other side of the curtain. The result was the *Book of Mormon,* published in 1830. The book also included the testimony of several witnesses who affirmed that they had seen the tablets before Moroni took them back.

Soon after publishing his book Smith had many followers. They were joined by an entire group who had already been practicing communal living, and the Mormons adopted a similar structure. According to them, their new religion was to Christianity what Christianity was to Judaism: its culmination. Meanwhile, Smith continued having new visions that led him further away from orthodox Christianity. After settling for a time in Ohio, he and his followers moved to Illinois, where they founded an autonomous community, with its own militia, and where Smith was eventually called King of the Kingdom of God. But tensions with surrounding society grew,

Brigham Young succeeded Joseph Smith, and under his leadership the Mormons reached Utah, where they settled.

especially when Smith declared himself a candidate for the presidency of the United States. Eventually, an unruly mob lynched the prophet and one of his followers.

The leadership of the movement fell to Brigham Young, who led the Mormons—more precisely, the Church of Jesus Christ of the Latter Day Saints—to Utah. They founded a state that remained autonomous, until the United States took possession of the area in 1850, as part of its westward expansion. This produced new conflicts. Two years later Young declared that Smith had had a vision, until then kept secret, reinstituting polygamy. In 1857, war broke out between the Mormons and the United States. Eventually and progressively, the Mormons allowed themselves to be shaped by the rest of society, leaving behind their emphasis on visions and community living, and finally, in 1890, officially abandoning polygamy—although it continued to be practiced in secret among some. Their political influence in Utah was substantial, and their missionaries soon spread their faith to several other nations.

The faith of Jehovah's Witnesses was a result of the manner in which many were reading Scripture, as a book where hidden clues could be found regarding future events and the end of the world. In its early stages, the movement also crystallized some of the resentment of the lower classes against the religious, political, and social establishment. Thus, Charles T. Russell, the founder of the new faith, declared that the three great instruments of Satan were government, business, and the church. He also rejected the doctrine of the Trinity and the divinity of Jesus, and declared that the Second Coming had taken place in 1872, and that the end would be in 1914.

The year 1914 brought World War I, but not the Armaggedon predicted by Russell, who died two years later. He was then succeeded by Joseph F. Rutherford, better known as *Judge Rutherford*. It was he who, in 1931, named the movement *Jehovah's Witnesses*, and who also organized it into a vast missionary machine, while reinterpreting Russell's teachings after the fiasco of 1914.

Christian Science was the main expression in the United States of a long religious tradition that we have repeatedly encountered in our narrative, when dealing with Gnosticism, Manicheism, Spiritualism, and so forth. In general, that tradition holds that the material world is either imaginary or of secondary importance, that the purpose of human life is to live in harmony with the Universal Spirit, and that Scripture is to be interpreted by means of a spiritual clue, which is usually unknown to the majority of Christians. The founder of Christian Science, Mary Baker Eddy, suffered repeated illnesses during her youth. Twice married and widowed, poor and sick, suffering from acute pain that extensive use of morphine could not assuage, she finally went to P. P. Quimby, who claimed that illness was error, and that the knowledge of truth sufficed to cure it. Having been healed by Quimby, she became his disciple and apostle. Several years after Quimby's death, in 1875, she published *Science and Health, with a Key to Scripture*. During her lifetime, this book was reprinted 381 times. In it, Eddy used traditional terms of Christian orthodoxy, such as God, Christ, Salvation, Trinity, and so forth, in a spiritual sense that differed from the traditional one—a practice reminiscent of the ancient Gnostic interpretations of Scripture, where words such as truth and life took a unique meaning. She held that illness was a mental error, the result of a mistaken perspective, and that to heal it one should not make use of physicians or drugs, but rather of the spiritual science that Jesus employed, and that she now had rediscovered. Likewise, the knowledge of such science would produce happiness and prosperity—as the middle class of the United States understood those terms.

The Church of Christ, Scientist, was officially founded in 1879, and it soon had followers throughout the nation. Two years later, Mary Baker Eddy founded in Boston a Metaphysical College, where practitioners—not pastors—of Christian Science were trained. She then developed a very centralized organization, completely under her control. The church in Boston was declared the Mother Church, to which all who wished to be members of the Church of Christ, Scientist, had to belong. She also took steps to ensure that no doctrinal deviation would ever find a place in her movement. She declared that the Second Coming of Christ had taken place in the divine inspiration with which her book was written. In order to avoid any variant doctrine, she banned preaching in her churches, placing in its stead prescribed readings of selected texts from the Bible and from her book. These texts, selected and prescribed by Mary Baker Eddy, are still read in worship by her followers, alternately by a man and a woman—for women have always held an important place in the movement.

In spite of the happiness and health that her doctrines promised, the last years of Mary Baker Eddy were filled with pain and anguish. Her physical pain could only be alleviated through increasing doses of morphine, and her spiritual anguish was such that she felt the need to be constantly surrounded by her followers, and thus protected from the waves of animal magnetism of her enemies.

As one now looks back at the shape and course of Christianity in the United State during the first century after independence, one is struck by the seemingly endless series of new denominations and movements that divided Christians, and by the impact of the social and economic order of the United States on the religion of the nation. Some denominations arose out of the diversity of religious traditions that immigrants from various countries brought with them, and others out of an attempt to purify the church by creating a new body, purer than the rest in doctrine, worship, and morals. Others arose out of political and social disagreements, particularly on the issue of slavery and its abolition. And still others arose out of literalistic interpretations of a few particular texts in Scripture in which someone claimed to have found the key to all of Scripture and all of history. Since the decades that followed marked the great age of American expansion, political as well as economic and religious, the events and currents we have just discussed have left their mark on Christian communities throughout the world—particularly in Latin America, Asia, and Africa, as we shall see in an upcoming chapter.

28

A Shifting Landscape:
Western Europe

There is no religious system or superstition that is not based on ignorance of the laws of nature. The creators and defenders of such folly did not foresee the progress of the human intellect. Being convinced that in their age all was known that would ever be known . . . they based their dreams on the opinions of their time.

ANTOINE-NICOLAS DE CONDORCET

The last years of the eighteenth century saw far-reaching political and cultural upheavals in Europe. Although such events took place in various countries, the most important were those connected with the French Revolution.

THE FRENCH REVOLUTION

Louis XVI—the king whom we have already mentioned as having decreed tolerance for French Protestants—was neither a good ruler nor a wise politician. During his reign, economic conditions in France grew steadily worse, particularly for the poor, while the expenditures of the king and his court soared. The crown sought funds from the nobility and the clergy, two groups that had traditionally been free of taxes. When they resisted, the king and his ministers called the Estates General, the French equivalent of parliament, composed of three *estates* or *orders*: the clergy, the nobility, and the bourgeoisie. Since the king's purpose was to use the Estates General to overcome the resistance of the clergy and the nobility, his ministers suggested that things be arranged so that the Third Estate—the bourgeoisie—would have more representatives than the other two. Steps were also taken so that the clergy would be represented, not only by bishops and other members of the hierarchy, but also by parish priests whose sympathies would run against the interests of the nobility and the hierarchy. When the assembly finally gathered on May 4, 1789, the Third Estate had more members than the other two together; and among the clergy less than a third were prelates. When the time came to open the sessions, the Third Estate insisted that the assembly should function as a single chamber, with decisions to be made by a simple majority. The clergy and the nobility preferred meeting as three chambers, which would give them two votes against the one of the Third Estate. But the bourgeoisie remained firm. Some priests, resenting the aristocratic leanings of the prelates, joined the Third Estate, and finally these two groups declared themselves a National Assembly, arguing that they represented the majority of the nation. Two days later the clergy voted to join the National Assembly.

While all these maneuvers were taking place, the economy continued to worsen, and hunger became even more widespread. Fearing the actions that the National Assembly might take, the government closed its meeting hall and ordered it disbanded. But its members refused to obey and solemnly swore to continue their sessions until France had a constitution. The king and his advisors responded by moving troops to the outskirts of Paris, and deposing Jacques Necker, a Protestant banker and government minister who was very popular among the bourgeoisie and the Paris populace. The people of Paris then expressed their anger in a series of riots that culminated on July 14, 1789, when they took the Bastille, an old fortress that served as a prison for the king's enemies.

From that point on, momentous events followed in rapid sequence. The king capitulated before the Third Estate, ordering the other two to join the National Assembly in a new body, the National Constituent Assembly. This group then issued the Declaration of the Rights of Man and the Citizen, which was to become one of the fundamental documents of democratic movements both in France and in other nations. When the king refused to accept this and other decisions of the Assembly, the populace of Paris rioted, and from that point on the king and his family were virtual prisoners in the capital city.

Following the principles of its own Declaration, and of the philosophers whose political ideas were discussed in Chapter 22, the Assembly reorganized the government of the nation, not only in its civil and economic aspects, but also in terms of its religious life. The most important step in this latter direction was the promulgation of the Civil Constitution of the Clergy, in 1790. For centuries the French church had boasted of its Gallican liberties which protected it from excessive interference by Rome, and placed it under the jurisdiction of French bishops and the French crown. Therefore, the National Constituent Assembly, which thought of itself as the depository of national sovereignty, felt that it had the authority to regulate the life and organization of the Catholic Church in France. Furthermore, some sort of reorganization was necessary, for there were many abuses. The highest positions in the hierarchy, occupied almost exclusively by members of the aristocracy, were not used for shepherding the flock but rather for the personal benefit of their occupants. Several ancient monasteries and abbeys had become centers of leisurely and luxurious living, and some abbots were known for their courtly and political intrigues. All this was in need of reformation. But there were also many members of the Assembly who were convinced that the church and its faith were remainders of superstitious times now past, and should therefore be destroyed. At the time of the Civil Constitution, those who hoped to see the church disappear remained few, and played only a minor role. But as events unfolded and the revolution became more extreme they came to the foreground.

Most of the measures included in the Civil Constitution were intended to reform the church. But what was at issue was the very question of whether the Assembly had the authority to issue such a decree "without consulting the church"—as some put it. However, the exact identity of the "church" that was to be consulted was not clear. Some suggested that a council of all the French bishops be called. But the Assembly knew that such a council would be in the hands of the ecclesiastical aristocracy. Others suggested that the pope be consulted—and indeed, this was the option chosen by the king before sanctioning the Assembly's decree. But this in itself would violate the national sovereignty, and would be a denial of the Gallican liberties. Pope Pius VI sent word to King Louis XVI that the Civil Constitution was a schismatic document that he would never accept. The king, fearing the Assembly's reaction, kept this decision secret, and continued trying to convince the pope to change his stance. Under pressure from the Assembly, the king agreed to the Civil Constitution, declaring that his approval was tentative, and depended on the pope's agreement. Finally, the Assembly simply decreed that all who held ecclesiastical office must swear allegiance to the Civil Constitution and that those who refused would be deposed.

The net result was that the church was divided. In theory, those who refused to swear would suffer no other punishment besides loss of their offices. On the basis of the Assembly's own declaration on human rights, they could not be deprived of their freedom of thought, and any who wished to continue having them as priests were free to do so—with the significant difference that those priests who had sworn would be supported by the state, while those who refused would have to be supported by their own followers. In fact, however, those who refused to swear soon became the object of persecution, purportedly not on the basis of their religious opinions but on suspicion of counterrevolutionary activities.

Meanwhile, revolutionary movements were gaining strength in other parts of Europe. Earlier revolutionary attempts in the Low Countries and Switzerland had failed, but monarchs and the high nobility feared that the French movement would spread to other lands. This in turn inspired the French revolutionaries to more extreme measures. In 1791, the National Constituent Assembly was succeeded by the Legislative Assembly, in which there were far fewer voices of moderation. Half a year later, France was at war with Austria and Prussia—thus beginning a long series of armed conflicts that would continue almost without interruption until the end of the Napoleonic Wars in 1815. When the fortunes of war turned against France, the Assembly directed its wrath against the king, who clearly sympathized with the foreign monarchs and aristocrats. At the Battle of Valmy, the French were finally able to halt the enemy's advance. The next day, the National Convention took the place of the Legislative Assembly, and on its first session the Convention abolished the monarchy and proclaimed the Republic. Four months later, under accusation of high treason, the king was tried, convicted, and executed. This, however, did not put an end to the nation's problems. Under the direction of the bourgeoisie, and with the added burden of war and inner disorder, the national economy was able to do little for the urban poor, and conditions were no better in the countryside. The peasants in the region of La Vendée revolted. Fear of foreign invasion mounted. All this led to a wave of terror where everybody was suspected of counterrevolutionary sentiments, and most of the major figures of the revolution were put to death one after another at the guillotine.

Combined with this was a strong reaction against Christianity, both Catholic and Protestant. The new leaders of the revolution were convinced that they were the harbingers of a new era in which science and reason would overcome all superstition and religion—which, after all, were nothing but the result of human ignorance. As the new age was being born, the time had come to leave aside the unfounded beliefs of old. It was on this basis that the French Revolution created its own religion, called first the *Cult of Reason*, and later the Cult *of the Supreme Being*. By then the Civil Constitution of the Clergy was forgotten, for the revolution wished to have nothing to do with the church. Even the calendar was changed, giving way to a more "reasonable" one in which weeks had ten days and months were named after conditions of nature in each season—"Thermidor," "Germinal," "Fructidor," and so forth. Great ceremonies were also developed to take the place of religious festivals—beginning with the solemn procession taking Voltaire's remains to the Pantheon of the Republic. Then temples to Reason were built, and an official list of saints was issued—which included Jesus, Socrates, Marcus Aurelius, and Rousseau. Other rites were prescribed for weddings, the dedication of children to Freedom, and funerals.

All this would have been merely ridiculous, were it not for its cost in suffering and bloodshed. The promoters of the new religion made use of the guillotine with cruel liberality. Christian worship was supposedly permitted; but any priest who refused to swear before the altar of Freedom could be accused of counterrevolutionary activity and sent to the guillotine. Thus, between two thousand and five thousand priests were executed, as well as several dozen nuns and countless lay people. Many others died in prison. In the end, no distinction was made between those who had sworn allegiance to the Civil Constitution, those who had refused to do so, and Protestants. In fact, French Protestantism—the old church of the desert—proved unready for the challenge, and was unable to respond with the same measure of heroism as the Catholics. Although the reign of terror abated in 1795, official government policy continued opposing Christianity. The military victories of the French in Switzerland, Italy, and the Low Countries extended a similar policy to those areas. In 1798, the French invaded the papal lands and captured Pope Pius VI, whom they took to France as a prisoner.

Napoleon Bonaparte, who had been gaining power in the army for some time, became master of France in November 1799. Pius VI had died a few months earlier, still a prisoner of the French. But Napoleon was convinced that the best policy was to seek a measure of reconciliation with the Catholic Church, and therefore opened negotiations with the new pope, Pius VII. It is said—probably with little basis in fact—that Napoleon sent a message to the pope to the effect that he wished to "make him a present of forty million French citizens." Finally, in 1801, the papacy and the French government agreed to a Concordat that provided for the naming of bishops and other prelates in such a way that the interests of both church and state would be safeguarded. Three years later, Napoleon decided that the title of First Consul, which he held, was not enough, and took that of emperor in a coronation ceremony presided by Pius VII. By then he had also decreed religious freedom for Protestants. Oddly enough, all these difficulties served to increase the authority of the pope over the French church. Until then, French kings and bishops had insisted on the Gallican liberties, precluding popes from direct intervention in the affairs of the French church. Now the emperor allowed the pope a greater measure of authority on the internal affairs of the French church—as long as papal actions did not interfere with the emperor's policies.

That agreement, however, did not last long, for the ambition of the emperor clashed with the firmness of the pope. As a result, Pius VII saw his lands invaded once again by the French, who made him a prisoner. But even

Napoleon was crowned emperor in a ceremony over which Pope Pius VII presided. When Napoleon saw this painting by David, he ordered the painter to alter the pope's gesture, so as to make it more favorable to the emperor.

in his captivity the pope remained firm, refusing to countenance Napoleon's actions, and particularly condemning his divorce from Josephine. Pius remained a prisoner until the fall of Napoleon, when he was restored to Rome. There he proclaimed a general amnesty for all his enemies, and interceded for Napoleon before the British victors.

THE NEW EUROPE

The Napoleonic Wars had created chaos throughout Europe. Reigning houses had been overthrown in Spain, Portugal, Italy, the Low Countries, and Scandinavia. After Napoleon's defeat, the main powers that had opposed him—Britain, Austria, Prussia, and Russia—determined the future shape of Europe's political map. The borders of France were set where they had been before the Revolution, and the house of Bourbon was restored in the person of Louis XVIII, a brother of Louis XVI. Most of the monarchs whom Napoleon had deposed were restored to their thrones. João VI of Portugal, who had fled to Brazil, did not immediately return to Lisbon, and when he did he left the government of Brazil in the hands of his son Pedro. The Netherlands and Belgium were placed under a single monarch. In Sweden, the crown was allowed to remain on the brow of Bernadotte, one of Napoleon's former marshals who had proven to be a wise and popular ruler. It was hoped that these arrangements would bring peace to a continent tired of war. Such hopes were not ill-founded, for—with the exceptions of the Crimean War in 1854–1856 and the Franco-Prussian war in 1870–1871—the rest of the century was a period of relative peace.

But under the surface of that international peace, social and political tensions led to conspiracies, revolts, and upheavals. One of the main sources of unrest was the quest for national unity among Italians and among Germans. Neither Italy nor Germany had yet achieved political unity, and in each of these countries there was a growing sentiment that the time had come for such unity. Those goals were opposed by the rulers of Austria, whose domains lacked cultural unity and included vast areas of Germany and Italy. Under the direction of the chancellor of Austria, C.L. Metternich, a vast network of international spies and saboteurs developed, with the clear goal of preventing German and Italian unity, and of undermining the various liberal and socialist movements in Europe.

Economic liberalism—not to be confused with theological liberalism—was enthusiastically espoused by the growing mercantile and capitalist bourgeoisie. At the heart of this economic liberalism was the doctrine of *laissez faire*—or *let do*—economics, which held that the law of supply and demand sufficed to regulate the marketplace and the entire economic order; and therefore no government regulations or restraints were necessary. According to this theory—in the twentieth and twenty-first centuries espoused by many who would today be called *conservatives*—governments should not intervene by regulating trade or the use of capital. Since at that time the Industrial Revolution was having the greatest impact on the continent of Europe, it was also a time when capital grew enormously—a growth that the theory of *laissez faire* did nothing to impede. The theory was that as capital grew and industry developed, the economic status of the poor would also improve. Such economic liberalism often went hand-in-hand with political liberalism, a stance that set great store by universal suffrage (although usually only for males) and constitutional monarchy modeled after the example of the United Kingdom.

The struggle between these ideas and earlier absolutism had different results in various countries. In Spain, Ferdinand VII restored prerevolutionary absolutism. In France, Louis XVIII showed greater prudence by establishing a parliamentary system. In Germany, Prussia became the champion of national unity, while Austria supported the old order. In Italy, some sought national unity under the kingdoms of Piedmont and Sardinia, others hoped to establish a republic, and still others saw the papacy as the center around which national unity should be built. In 1830, Belgium became independent from the Netherlands—a move in which religious sentiments played an important role, for Belgium was Catholic and the Netherlands Protestant. That same year, republican elements tried to overthrow the French monarchy. Although they did not achieve their goal, they did bring about the downfall of Charles X—a conservative ruler who had succeeded his brother Louis XVIII—and the crowning of Louis Philippe d'Orleans, a ruler of fairly liberal inclinations.

The year 1848 brought new revolutions. There were riots and revolts in Germany, Italy, Belgium, Great Britain, Switzerland, and France. Switzerland gained a new constitution. In France, Louis Philippe was overthrown and the Second Republic was proclaimed. This lasted until 1851, when Louis Napoleon, a nephew of the now-deceased emperor, took power and proclaimed himself emperor under the name Napoleon III. That same year marked the fall of Metternich in Austria; and the publication by Karl Marx

The year 1848 saw many revolts and revolutions, including this riot in Lyons, where workers barricaded themselves against the army.

and Friedrich Engels of their *Communist Manifesto*—an event that went practically unnoticed at the time.

The map of Italy began changing shortly after Camillo di Cavour became premier of the kingdom of Piedmont in 1852. With the help of Napoleon III, Cavour began the vast enterprise of Italian unity. At the time of his death in 1861, the new kingdom of Italy included the entire peninsula, excluding the territories of Venice and Rome. The first was annexed in 1866, when Prussia intervened against Austria's continued efforts to keep Italy divided. The story of Rome and the Papal States is more complex. In 1849, the revolutionary wave that was sweeping Europe led to the creation of the Roman Republic, and Pope Pius IX had to appeal to Napoleon III to restore him to his papal throne. Under French protection, the Papal States were then able to retain independence, though it was constantly threatened. Finally, at the time of the war between France and Germany in 1870, King Victor Emmanuel of Italy took Rome, and thus completed the unification of the peninsula. Besides a guaranteed annual income, the king also granted the pope three palaces that would be considered an independent territory: the Vatican, the Lateran, and Castel Gandolfo. But Pius IX refused, and the following years brought continued tension between the Vatican and the Italian government. It was only in 1929 that the papacy finally agreed to the loss of its extensive holdings and to an arrangement similar to what Victor Emmanuel had suggested.

While these events were taking place in Italy, the dominant figure in Germany was Otto von Bismarck, who had become chancellor of Prussia in 1862. His great achievement consisted of excluding Austria from the German Confederation, and then molding that Confederation into a single nation. After ten years of skilled diplomacy and military conquests, culminating in the war with France of 1870–1871, Germany was united under Wilhelm of Prussia. Bismarck's religious policy was directed against Roman Catholicism. That was the religion of the majority in Austria, and therefore the Prussian chancellor feared that Catholics in his own territories would sympathize with the Austrians. Also, his international policy required that he support the unification of Italy—which Austria opposed—and he therefore was greatly inconvenienced by Catholics under his rule who insisted that Prussia should intervene to restore the papal lands to the pope. But, above all, he was convinced that Catholicism was obscurantist, and that liberal Protestantism was better suited to the great historical mission that Germany would soon fulfill. For these and other reasons, Bismarck took several measures against Catholicism. Germany broke diplomatic relations with the papacy, several monastic orders were expelled from the country, and the traditional subsidies given to the church were cut. In 1880, for reasons of political expediency, Bismarck changed some of these policies and reestablished relations with the papacy. But the preceding conflicts were among the factors that convinced Pius IX—who served from 1846 to 1878—that there was an unavoidable opposition between the Catholic Church and the modern idea of the state—an issue we shall explore in Chapter 32.

Besides the theological developments and the missionary enterprise that we shall discuss in Chapters 31 and 33, the most significant developments in European Protestantism during the nineteenth century were those derived from the growing separation between church and state. After the Reformation of the sixteenth century, in those countries where Protestantism gained the upper hand, the new church continued relating to the state in the same manner as had the Catholic Church. After the French Revolution, however, this state of affairs began to change. In the Netherlands, for instance, the union between the state and the Reformed Church was broken when the French conquered the land and created the Batavian Republic, and after the Restoration the links between church and state never returned to their previous strength. In Germany, the quest for national unity led to the abrogation of many old laws that sought to enforce religious uniformity. Throughout Europe, political and economic liberalism had similar consequences. This in turn contributed to the growth of what were called *free churches*—that is, those to which one belongs by choice and supports by means of offerings, in contrast to the state churches, supported by state funds. The Methodists and Baptists spread throughout Germany and northern Europe. And, even in the government-related Lutheran and Reformed churches, Pietism made headway. Pietism led to the formation of several missionary societies, and of others whose purpose was to address the ills of Europe itself. In Germany and other northern lands, deaconesses and their organizations did much for the well being of the sick, the elderly, and the poor. In Denmark, Lutheran leader N.F.S. Grundtvig sought to respond to the plight of the rural poor by advocating cooperativism. In general, the lack of state support renewed the zeal of many Protestants in Europe, drawing great numbers to the various aspects of the churches' work.

DEVELOPMENTS IN GREAT BRITAIN

Throughout the nineteenth century, Great Britain followed a course parallel to that of continental Europe. The Industrial Revolution also had an impact there, but much earlier and to an even greater degree than elsewhere. That revolution benefitted the middle class and the capitalists, while undermining both the ancient aristocracy and the poor. The rapid growth of cities that resulted from industry and increased trade gave rise to overcrowded slums, and the poor found themselves living and working in conditions of misery and exploitation. Meanwhile, economic and political liberalism made great strides, thus increasing the power of the House of Commons at the expense of the House of Lords. One result of these conditions was a vast wave of migration to the United States, Canada, Australia, New Zealand, and South Africa. Another was the labor movement, which made enormous progress between the beginning of the century (when unions were forbidden by law) and the end of the century (when the Labor Party was a political power). It was also in England that Karl Marx developed many of his economic theories.

All this also influenced the church. At the beginning of the French Revolution, in the Church of England there were many of the evils that had once characterized the worst times of the medieval church: absenteeism, pluralism, and the use of ecclesiastical office as a means to further personal and dynastic ambitions. But during the nineteenth century there was a significant renewal in the Church of England. Aided by a number of reform decrees issued by the government, those who sought a more faithful church came to the foreground. Some of these people of reforming zeal belonged to the Evangelical wing of Anglicanism, a group that was profoundly influenced by the Pietism of the Continent and wished to see the Church of England more closely aligned with the rest of Protestantism. Others, particularly those of the *Oxford movement*, took the opposite tack and came to be known as *Anglo-Catholics*. In many ways influenced by Romanticism, and often looking to Eastern Orthodoxy for inspiration, the Oxford movement emphasized the authority of tradition, apostolic succession, and communion as the center of Christian worship. One of its leaders, John Henry Newman, was converted to Catholicism, and eventually was made a cardinal—although conservative Catholics never quite trusted him. But most of the members of the movement remained within the Church of England, and gave that church a renewed devotional life. Another result of the movement was the rebirth of monasticism within the Church of England, and soon Anglican monks and nuns were trying to meet the needs of the poor and the ill.

However, it was among dissident churches where the most vitality was found during the nineteenth century. The growth of the middle class brought about an upsurge in the membership of dissident churches. Methodists, Baptists, and Congregationalists showed many signs of vigor, not only in their numerical growth, but also in the many societies that they founded to help the needy, to remedy some of the more blatant social ills, and to take the gospel to the rest of the world. In order to reach the poor and uneducated masses, dissident churches founded Sunday Schools, and these eventually became a common practice among Protestants. Others organized the Young Men's Christian Association (YMCA) and the Young Women's Christian Association (YWCA). Also, a number of new denominations were born—particularly the Salvation Army, founded in 1864 as a means to reach the impoverished and unchurched urban masses.

All these groups, as well as the evangelical wing of Anglicanism, showed great concern for the social ills of the time. The support and inspiration of

Protestants in England began several new forms of ministry, including these centers where the homeless received both shelter and Christian instruction.

Methodists, Quakers, and others were important factors in the birth of labor unions, in prison reform, and in legislation regarding child labor. But the most significant accomplishment of British Christians during the nineteenth century was the abolition of slavery in most of the Western world. Years earlier, both Quakers and Methodists had condemned slavery. But it was in the nineteenth century, thanks to the effort of William Wilberforce and other committed Christians, that the British government took measures against slavery. In 1806 and 1811, Parliament issued laws forbidding the slave trade. In 1833, freedom was decreed for all slaves in the British Caribbean, and similar laws were later issued for other British colonies. At the same time, treaties were sought with other nations, agreeing to end the slave trade. When such treaties were signed, the British navy was given orders to enforce them. Within a short period of time, most Western nations had abolished slavery.

In summary, the nineteenth century brought about great political and economic changes in Europe. In general, Catholicism suffered more severe blows from those changes than did Protestantism. Therefore, the nineteenth century was for Catholicism a period of reaction against modern ideas, which were usually seen as threats. For Protestantism, on the other hand, the nineteenth century brought new opportunities. Protestant powers such as Great Britain and Germany increased their influence in the world. Political and economic liberalism were closely allied with Protestantism, and were seen by their adherents as the wave of the future against an outdated and authoritarian Catholicism. Protestants did take a leading role in the struggle against social ills, most notably against slavery. The result was that, while Roman Catholicism looked upon the new times with extreme caution (see Chapter 32), many Protestants looked upon them with unwarranted optimism (as we shall see in Chapter 31).

29

A Shifting Landscape:
Latin America

The successors of St. Peter have always been our fathers, but war had
left us orphans, as a lamb calling in vain for its lost mother. Now the
tender mother has sought him and returned him to the fold, and we
are given shepherds worthy of the church and of the Republic.

SIMÓN BOLÍVAR

A PANOPLY OF NEW NATIONS

The political upheavals that had taken place in Europe and in the British colonies of North America were also felt in Latin America early in the
nineteenth century. In the Spanish and Portuguese colonies there had long
been a tension between those recently arrived from Europe—the *peninsulares*—and the native descendants of earlier immigrants—the *criollos*. Through
the exploitation of Indian and slave labor, the *criollos* had become a relatively
wealthy class who felt it understood the affairs of the colonies better than the
peninsulares, and that they therefore ought to have a hand in running them.
But appointments to all significant offices—both civil and ecclesiastic—were
made in Europe, and therefore such positions were usually held by *peninsulares,* many of whom had never seen the lands of the New World before
they were appointed to rule them. The *criollos*—conveniently setting aside
the toil of Indians and black slaves—were convinced that the wealth of
the colonies was due to their efforts, and thus resented the authority of the
peninsulares. Although still faithful subjects of the crown, they deplored the
many laws that favored the metropolis at the expense of the colonies. Since
many of them had the necessary means, they often traveled to Europe, from

whence they returned imbued with the republican ideas that were sweeping that continent. Thus, the *criollos* played a role in Latin America similar to that of the bourgeoisie in France.

In 1808, Napoleon deposed King Ferdinand VII of Spain, and in his place crowned his own brother Joseph Bonaparte—whom the Spanish dubbed *Pepe Botella*, or Joe Bottle. Spanish resistance to the usurper had its headquarters at Cadiz, where a "junta" or board ruled in the name of the deposed king. Napoleon declared that all Spanish colonies should now obey King Joseph; but he did not have the power to enforce his authority, and local juntas were organized in the New World. While the *peninsulares* insisted that all such juntas should be under the Cadiz government, the *criollos* preferred independent juntas, and their opinion prevailed. Thus, the colonies began ruling themselves, although still in the name of the king. Ferdinand VII was restored in 1814, after Napoleon's defeat. But, instead of showing gratitude for those who had preserved his territories for him, he set out to undo all that the relatively liberal juntas had done. In Spain, he abolished the constitution that the Cadiz junta had issued, and the reaction was such that in 1820 he was forced to reinstate the constitution. Similar policies in the colonies exacerbated *criollo* resentment against Spanish policies, and soon those who had earlier proven faithful guardians of the king's inheritance rebelled against him. In the region often referred to as the Río de la Plata—what is today Argentina, Paraguay, and Uruguay—the junta simply continued governing the country, until independence was proclaimed in 1816. Three years later, Paraguay declared its independence from both Spain and the Río de la Plata. Uruguay broke away in 1828, becoming an independent nation. Meanwhile, José de San Martin had crossed the Andes and invaded Chile, whose independence was declared in 1818. While these events were taking place in the south, farther north Simón Bolívar organized an army that defeated the Spanish and proclaimed the independence of Greater Colombia—now Colombia, Venezuela, and Panama. Then Ecuador joined Greater Colombia, and Bolívar marched to the south, where Peru—which then included the territory that is now Peru and Bolivia—was also made independent.

Bolívar's dream had been to create a vast republic embracing most of the continent. But such dreams were soon shattered. Greater Colombia broke up into Venezuela, Colombia, and Ecuador. In Peru, the region of *Alto Perú—high Peru*—insisted on its independence, becoming the Republic

The nineteenth century brought the independence of most Spanish colonies in the New World, under the leadership of Bolívar and other members of the native aristocracy.

of Bolívar—now Bolivia. Bolívar's last hopes for a continental confederacy came to naught at the Panama Congress of 1826, where it became clear that regional interests—as well as those of the United States—precluded any close collaboration between the new nations. Five years later, a few days before his death, Bolívar expressed his disappointment: "America is ungovernable. Those who have served the revolution have plowed the sea."[17]

In Mexico, events followed a different course. The *criollos* were planning to grab power from the *peninsulares* when the conspiracy was discovered, and one of its leaders, Father Miguel Hidalgo y Costilla, decided to make a move before being arrested. On September 16, 1810, he proclaimed Mexican independence, and soon found himself at the head of an unorganized army of sixty thousand Indians and *mestizos*—persons of mixed Indian and Spanish blood. After his capture and execution, Hidalgo was succeeded by *mestizo* priest José María Morelos. Thus, from its very beginnings the new nation had the support and participation of Indians and *mestizos*. For a time, the *criollos* regained power; but later, under the leadership of Benito

Juárez, that situation was corrected. Therefore, the Indian and *mestizo* populations have played important roles in the political history of Mexico. Central America, originally part of Mexico, proclaimed its independence in 1821, and later broke up into Guatemala, El Salvador, Honduras, Nicaragua, and Costa Rica. (Panama was not originally part of Central America. It belonged to Colombia until 1903, when the United States fostered its independence in order to evade the conditions that Colombia required for the construction of the Panama Canal.)

Brazilian independence also resulted from the Napoleonic Wars. In 1807, fleeing from Napoleon's armies, the Portuguese court took refuge in Brazil. In 1816, João VI was restored to his throne in Lisbon but showed no inclination to return to Portugal until forced to do so by political circumstances in 1821. He left his son Pedro as regent of Brazil. Pedro later refused to return to Portugal, proclaimed Brazilian independence, and was crowned as Emperor Pedro I of Brazil. In 1825, Portugal recognized the independence of its former colony. Pedro I, however, was not allowed to rule as he wished, and was forced to agree to a parliamentary system of government. In 1889, after the abdication of Pedro's son Pedro II, the republic was proclaimed.

Haiti's independence was the direct result of the French Revolution. As soon as the French Revolution deprived the white population of military support, the blacks, who were the vast majority, rebelled. Independence was proclaimed in 1804, and it was acknowledged by France in 1825. The United States refused to do so until 1862, because until that time slave-holding states feared the example of a nation born out of a slave rebellion.

Looking at all these events as a whole, several common threads appear. Republican ideas from France and the United States provided the ideological framework for revolution and independence in Latin America. But those revolutions usually resulted in power residing in a *criollo* class—or, in the case of Haiti, in military leaders—that paid little attention to the needs of the masses. Vast tracts of land remained in the hands of just a few landowners, while the majority of the population had no land. Toward the middle of the nineteenth century, there was great economic development on the basis of foreign capital and the exporting of agricultural products. This in turn fostered even larger holdings of land, and created an alliance between *criollo* landowners and foreign capital. In the cities, there also appeared an urban middle class made up of merchants and government employees who had little power, but whose interests were closely tied to the sort of economic development that was taking place. What was hoped and repeatedly promised was that the development of trade, industry, and education would eventually benefit all social classes, for even the poorest would receive a share of the wealth that was being created. But economic progress required order, and thus dictatorships were often justified.

Throughout the nineteenth century, the great ideological debate in Latin America was between liberals and conservatives. In general, the leaders of both groups belonged to the higher classes. But, while conservative strength was based on the landed aristocracy, liberals found their support among the merchants and intellectuals in the cities. Conservatives feared such notions as freedom of thought and free enterprise. Liberals defended them, both because they were more modern and because they were better suited to the interests of the merchant class. While most conservatives looked to Spain for inspiration, liberals looked to Great Britain, France, and the United States. But neither group was willing to alter the social order so that the lower classes could share in the wealth of the country. The result was a long series of dictatorships (both liberal and conservative), of palace revolutions, and of violent excesses. By the turn of the century, many tended to agree with Bolívar: the continent was ungovernable. This view seemed to be warranted by the Mexican Revolution, which began in 1910 and resulted in a long period of violence and civil disorder that impoverished the country and led many to emigrate.

THE CHURCH IN THE NEW NATIONS

Throughout the colonial period, the church in Latin America had been under Royal Patronage—*Patronato Real.* This included the virtual naming of bishops by the governments of Spain and Portugal. Therefore, the tensions between *peninsulares* and *criollos* were also felt in the church, whose higher offices were in the hands of *peninsulares,* while *criollos* and *mestizos* formed the bulk of the lower clergy. Although a few bishops supported the cause of Spanish American Independence, most supported the crown, many by means of pastoral letters in which they condemned the rebellion. After independence, most of them had to return to Spain, thus leaving many dioceses vacant. It was impossible to name replacements, for Spain insisted on its ancient rights of Royal Patronage while the new republics could not accept bishops who were named by the crown, and even insisted on what they called a *Patronato Nacional,* claiming that, as heirs to the rights of the

Spanish crown, the new governments now had the right to nominate their own bishops. The popes wavered in their attitude, for Spain was still one of their main allies in Europe, but the new nations comprised a substantial part of the Catholic flock. Pius VII, in his encyclical *Etsi longissimo* (1816), spoke of the "grave evils of rebellion," and of "our most beloved son in Jesus Christ, Ferdinand, your Catholic king." Eventually, however, political reality forced him to take a neutral stance. In 1824, Leo XI, in the encyclical *Etsi iam diu,* spoke of the movement for independence as "tares," and of Ferdinand as "our very beloved son Ferdinand, Catholic king of the Spains." In Europe, France, Austria, and Russia joined Spain in opposing the acknowledgment of the new nations that would be implied in naming bishops for them without consulting with Spain. Finally, in 1827, Leo XII decided to name the first bishops for Colombia—which at the time included what are now Colombia, Venezuela, Ecuador, and Panama. This was the occasion for Bolívar's words quoted at the beginning of this chapter. But this did not put an end to the matter, for Ferdinand broke off relations with Rome, and the pope had to undo much of what he had done. It was only in the next decade that Gregory XVI officially acknowledged the existence of the new republics, and named bishops for them. Given the sacramental nature of Catholicism, the lack of bishops meant much more than the mere lack of leaders. Without bishops there could be no ordinations; and without sufficient ordained clergy, much of the sacramental life of the church was interrupted.

The attitude of the lower clergy, mostly *criollos* and *mestizos,* contrasted with that of the bishops. In Mexico, three out of four priests supported the rebellion. Sixteen out of the twenty-nine signatories of the Declaration of Independence in Argentina were priests. Also, at the beginning of the rebellion there was little popular support for independence, and parish priests did much to gain that support. This ambivalent attitude of the church was in many ways the continuation of the two faces that the church in Latin America had shown from the earliest colonial period. While there were those—particularly in the higher echelons of the hierarchy—who supported generally conservative policies, there were also many who supported political, economic, and social change.

To complicate matters, it became increasingly evident that, regardless of what the church taught officially, the people actually understood and practiced their faith in a wide variety of ways. The lack of priests led to less emphasis on the sacraments and more on religious observances and celebrations

Latin America after Independence

that did not require the presence of a priest, such as saints' days, the rosary, promises to the saints, written prayers with supposedly magical powers, and so on. And all of this was combined with the survival of many elements of the ancient religions of the original populations of the Americas and of the slaves brought from Africa—and later with an esoteric spiritism brought from Europe, which emphasized reincarnation and communication with the spirits of the dead. While most of this was often understood in purely religious terms, there is no doubt that much of it was an act of resistance against the powerful who held sway over the church.

For these reasons, the attitude of the new political leadership toward Catholicism was complex. All called themselves Catholic, and the various early constitutions affirmed that Roman Catholicism was the national religion. But tensions with Rome were such that some—particularly in Mexico—proposed breaking with Rome and creating national churches. Such projects reappeared again and again in later years, whenever the popes seemed inclined to oppose the political interests of a nation.

After independence, the conflict between liberals and conservatives was also reflected in their divergent religious policies. While conservatives wished to continue the ancient privileges of the clergy and the church, liberals opposed many of them. It was then that many native clergymen who had earlier supported independence joined the conservative ranks. The early liberals did not oppose Catholicism as such, but only what they took to be the narrow ideas and practices of a clergy that, while native born, still viewed Spain as the center of the universe. But the constant conflicts between liberals and the leadership of the church led to increased anti-Catholic feelings within the liberal ranks.

In the second half of the century, liberalism espoused the positivist philosophy of Auguste Comte and therefore became more anti-Catholic. Comte was a French philosopher, and one of the founders of modern sociology who was convinced that society could and should be reorganized following the dictates of reason. According to him, humanity has gone through three stages of development: the theological, the metaphysical, and the scientific or positive—for which reason his views were called *positivism*. Although there are still enclaves of the earlier two stages, Comte argued, we are now in the scientific age, and therefore society must be radically reorganized on the basis of scientific or positive principles. The resulting society will make a clear distinction between spiritual authority and temporal power. The latter must be placed in the hands of the capitalists and merchants, who best understand the needs of society. As to spiritual authority, this could well be placed on a new Catholic Church without a supernatural God, and devoted to the religion of humanity. Such ideas gained wide acceptance among the bourgeoisie in Latin America, especially in Brazil, but also in countries such as Argentina and Chile, where ideas from France had often been well

This Methodist Church in Mexico City shows some of the consequences of the Mexican Revolution, which took possession of all religious buildings and then determined and regulated their use. As a result, the Methodists now meet in the inner courtyard of a formerly Catholic convent.

received. The result was renewed conflict between liberals and the church, while states became increasingly secular.

In Mexico, these nineteenth-century trends culminated in the Mexican Revolution of 1910. After wars with Texas (1835–1836) and the United States (1846–1848), the liberal government headed by Benito Juárez put an end to many of the traditional privileges of the Church—eliminating the privileges of the clergy, who until then had been exempt from the jurisdiction of civil courts; ordering the church to divest itself of all property not directly related to its religious functions; and placing official records of births, marriages, and deaths in secular hands. All of this was then imbedded on the liberal Constitution of 1857. When the conservatives appealed for help to Napoleon III, the French invaded the country and set up Maximilian of Austria as its ruler (1864). This led to rebellion, and the capture and execution of Maximilian in 1867. After more civil unrest, and constant conflicts between liberals and democrats, Porfirio Díaz came to power. The *Porfiriato*, as his rule came to be known, was marked by thirty-four years of violent suppression of opposition, and of a rapprochement between the church and the government, which relaxed the provisions of the Constitution of 1857. By 1910, the repressive measures of the government, and the constant impoverishment of the rural population, led to revolution. Díaz was deposed in 1911, and the privileges of the church were once again abrogated. But the conflict continued unabated for years, with ever harsher anticlerical laws on the one hand, and more open political resistance by the leaders of the church on the other. By 1926 the supporters of the church led the Cristero revolution, in which more than thirty thousand rebels and almost twice as many federal troops died. When it became clear that neither party was able to suppress the other, a compromise was reached in 1929.

All over Latin America, the second half of the nineteenth century also brought new waves of immigrants—mostly European throughout the continent, but also Chinese to the Pacific coast. Such immigration was necessary for the sort of development that the ruling bourgeoisie envisioned for Latin America. Immigrants provided the labor necessary for industry and commerce, and also served as a balance against the masses of Indians and blacks. In any case, that wave of migration was of great importance for the religious life of the continent. Many of those who hoped to immigrate were Protestants, and therefore several countries felt obliged to grant religious freedom, at first only to such immigrants, but eventually to all. The most notable consequence of immigration, however, was the enormous growth in the numbers of baptized Catholics for whom the church could provide practically no ministry nor religious instruction. As a result, Latin American Catholicism became more superficial. In great cities such as Buenos Aires and São Paulo, most still called themselves Catholics but few participated in the life of the church.

For a long time, the Catholic hierarchy responded to all this with futile attempts to return to the past. The more widespread the new ideas became, the more vehemently the hierarchy condemned them. Eventually, many Latin American Catholics came to see faith as something to be held independently and even against the authority of the church. Therefore, when Protestantism made its appearance, it found the fields ripe for harvest.

30

A Shifting Landscape: Eastern Christianity

The time has come, when the duty of all Christians in the world is to unite their efforts to fulfill the words of the prophet Isaiah "to change swords into ploughs and spears into sickles," thus proving once more the viability and the permanent actuality of Christianity in the world.

RUMANIAN PATRIARCH JUSTINIAN, 1960

One of the main issues confronted by all Christians in the twenty-first century is how to live in the post-Constantinian era. What is meant by this phrase is that the church can no longer count on the political support that it enjoyed since the times of Constantine. As we have seen in the preceding chapters, in a process beginning with the American and French Revolutions, Western Christianity had to face the challenge of secular states that, although not always hostile, tended to ignore it. For Eastern Christianity, on the other hand, that process began when Constantinople fell to the Turks in 1453. It was at that point that we left our narrative on the course of Eastern Christianity, and to it we must now return.

BYZANTINE CHRISTIANITY

The support that Christianity had traditionally received from the Byzantine Empire was not an unmixed blessing. It is true that its relation to the empire gave the Greek Church great prestige, but it is also true that its freedom was greatly limited. While in the West popes were often more powerful than kings and even emperors, in the East the emperors ruled the church, and patriarchs who did not do their bidding were easily deposed and replaced. When the emperor decided that reunion with Rome was necessary in order to save his empire, that reunion was achieved even against the clear wishes of the vast majority of the Byzantine Church. A year later, in 1453, Constantinople fell to the Turks, and many Byzantine Christians interpreted this event as an act of liberation from a tyrannical emperor who had forced them into a union with heretical Rome.

At first, the Ottoman regime granted a measure of freedom to the church. Mohammed II, conqueror of Constantinople, invited the bishops to elect a new patriarch—the former one had fled to Rome—to whom he granted both civil and ecclesiastical authority over Christians in his territories. In Constantinople itself, half the churches were turned into mosques, but in the other half Christian worship continued with full tolerance from the state. In 1516, the Ottomans conquered Syria and Palestine, and Christians there were also placed under the government of the patriarch of Constantinople. A year later, when Egypt fell to the Turks, the patriarch of Alexandria was given special powers over Christians in Egypt. Although this policy made the patriarchs virtual rulers of a Christian state within the much larger Turkish state, it also meant that a patriarch who did not implement the sultan's policies was soon deposed.

For several centuries, theological activity in the Greek-speaking church was dominated by Western influences and reactions against it. The issues debated in the West during the Protestant Reformation were also discussed in the Greek-speaking church. In 1629, Cyril Lucaris, patriarch of Constantinople, published a *Confession of Faith* that was Protestant in many ways. Although Lucaris was deposed and murdered, his memory was venerated by many—some claiming that the *Confession of Faith* was spurious. Eventually, in 1672, a synod condemned him "if indeed he was a Calvinist heretic." By the next century, however, the issue was no longer Protestantism; rather, it was Western philosophy and science, and the impact they ought to have on Orthodox theology. In the nineteenth century, when Greece became independent of Turkey, this issue took on political overtones. In general, Greek nationalism sided with those who advocated the introduction of Western methods of research and scholarship—who also argued that the Greek Church, existing now in an independent nation, should be independent from the patriarch of Constantinople. The conservatives, on the other hand, held that commonly received tradition should guide scholarship, and that part of that tradition was subjection to the patriarch of Constantinople, even though he was subject to the Turkish sultan.

During the nineteenth and early twentieth centuries, the Ottoman Empire broke down, and national Orthodox churches were formed, not only in Greece but also in Serbia, Bulgaria, and Rumania. In each of these areas, the tension between nationalist sentiments and the transnational nature of Orthodoxy was a dominant issue. In the period between the two world wars, the patriarchate of Constantinople recognized the autonomy of the various Orthodox churches, not only in the former Turkish territories in the Balkans, but also in other parts of Europe, such as Estonia, Latvia, and Czechoslovakia. Since most of these territories fell under Russian hegemony after World War II, Soviet religious policies were generally applied in them.

Early in the twentieth century, the ancient patriarchates of Jerusalem, Alexandria, and Antioch found themselves under Arab rule. At first, these newly formed Arab states existed under the shadow of Western powers. At that time, significant numbers of Christians under those patriarchates became either Catholic or Protestant. Then growing Arab nationalism reacted against Western power and influence, and the growth of both Protestantism and Catholicism was curbed. By the second half of the twentieth century, the only nations where Orthodox Christianity could still count on something like the traditional union of church and state were Greece and Cyprus—the latter of which declared independence in 1960, and whose official religion is the Cypriot Orthodox Church.

In spite of the difficulties they suffered, the various Orthodox churches that had formerly been under the patriarchate of Constantinople and now found themselves under Soviet rule did show signs of vitality. For a time it was feared that the loss of church schools, and the pressure of government propaganda, would keep newer generations away from the church. But the experience of several decades seemed to indicate that the liturgy, traditionally the source of spiritual strength for Orthodox believers, was equal to the task of transmitting the Christian tradition even in the midst of hostile states—an indication that would prove true late into the twentieth century, after the fall of Russian Communism. Although the civil disabilities under which Christians were placed in several of these states at various times indeed resulted in a decline in active church participation on the part of those involved in the job market, it was significant that after retirement vast numbers returned to the church.

THE RUSSIAN CHURCH

The fall of Constantinople in 1453 was interpreted by many in Russia as God's punishment for its having agreed to reunion with heretical Rome. Eventually, the theory developed that just as Constantinople had replaced Rome as the "second Rome," now Moscow was the "third Rome," the new imperial city whose providential task was to uphold orthodoxy. In 1547, Ivan IV of Russia took the title of "czar" or emperor, by which he meant that he was the successor of the ancient caesars of Rome and Constantinople. Likewise, in 1598, the metropolitan of Moscow took the title of patriarch. To support this self-understanding, the Russian church produced an array of polemical writings against Greeks, Catholics, and Protestants. By the seventeenth century, these notions were so entrenched that an attempt at rapprochement with the Greeks led to schism in Russia.

Czar Alexis I Mikhailovich (1645–1676) saw this rapprochement with Greek Christians as a preliminary step to the conquest of Constantinople, and therefore encouraged Patriarch Nikon to revise the liturgy in order to bring it into agreement with Greek practices. But many in Russia, particularly among the lower classes, reacted violently. They were suspicious of everything foreign, particularly since it appeared that it was the aristocracy that was interested in promoting the new ideas. The result was the schism of the Old Believers, some of whom then joined the peasants in rebellion. This was crushed with great bloodshed, and the peasants' serfdom worsened. The Old Believers continued to exist, although they split over a number of issues—particularly whether to accept priests coming to them from the Orthodox Church, or not to have priests at all. Some were drawn to apocalyptic extremes, and thousands committed suicide as proof of their faith. Eventually, however, the more extreme groups disappeared, and the Old Believers lived on as a minority group within Russia at least until the twenty-first century.

Czar Peter the Great (1689–1725) took a different tack. He was not interested in a rapprochement with Greek Christians, but rather in opening his country to Western influences. In the life of the church, this led to increased interest in both Catholic and Protestant theology. Those who followed these conflicting schools of thought did not generally abandon their Orthodox faith. Rather, they sought to develop an Orthodox theology using either Catholic or Protestant methodologies. On matters that were open to debate, some followed the Catholic lead, while others took their cue from

Protestantism. The Kievan school, whose great figure was Peter Mogila, was associated with Catholic tendencies; while Theophanes Prokopovick and his followers felt that the Protestant critique of tradition ought to be heeded by Russian Orthodoxy. Early in the nineteenth century, the influence of the Enlightenment and of Romanticism gave the Prokopovickians the upper hand. But later in the century there was a nationalist reaction, with greater emphasis on the value of the traditionally Russian—the Slavophile movement. The principal figure of this movement was lay theologian Alexis Khomiakov (1804–1860), who applied Hegelian categories to show that the true Orthodox understanding of catholicity—*sobornost*—is a perfect synthesis of the Catholic thesis of the authority of the Church and the Protestant antithesis of the freedom of the gospel.

The Russian Revolution put an end to much of this debate. A different Western philosophy, Marxism, had gained the upper hand. In 1918, the church was officially separated from the state—and this was later ratified by the constitution of 1936, which guaranteed both "freedom for religious worship" and "freedom for anti-religious propaganda." In 1920, religious teaching in schools was outlawed. Two years earlier, all seminaries were closed. After the death of Patriarch Tikhon in 1925, the Russian Orthodox Church was not allowed to elect his successor until 1943. By then, partly as a result of the war with Germany, in which it needed all possible support, the government had decided to recognize the continued existence of the church. That very year, seminaries were reopened. Also, permission was granted for the printing of some books and periodicals, and for the manufacture of items necessary for worship.

As in the case of other Orthodox churches under communist rule, the Russian church found its liturgy capable of supporting the faithful and transmitting the traditions to new generations. Late in the twentieth century, after almost seventy years of communist rule, the Orthodox in the Soviet Union were still some 60 million strong.

OTHER EASTERN CHURCHES

Besides the churches discussed above, there are Orthodox bodies in various parts of the world. Some of these, such as the Orthodox Church of Japan, and those in China and Korea, were the result of the missionary work of the Russian Church. They are fully indigenous, with a membership and clergy that is mostly native, and they celebrate the liturgy in the native tongue of each land. Others are the result of what has been called the Orthodox Diaspora. For a number of reasons—political upheavals, persecution, the search for better living conditions—large numbers of Orthodox moved to areas distant from their ancestral homelands. Particularly in Western Europe and the New World, there were significant numbers of Russians, Greeks, and others for whom their faith and its liturgy were a means of keeping alive traditions and values that would otherwise be lost. Relations among these various bodies posed difficult problems for Orthodoxy, which has always held that there can be no more than one Orthodox church in a given place or area. On occasion, this put great stress on the bonds of unity within the Orthodox Communion. One example of these difficulties took place in the United States in the twentieth century, when the Russian Orthodox Church granted autocephaly—autonomy—to its American counterpart, raising protests from the patriarch of Constantinople and several leaders of various other Orthodox communities in the United States, and eventually giving rise to a number of conversations seeking to create a unified Orthodox Church in the United States.

But not all Eastern churches form part of the Orthodox Communion. Since the time of the Christological controversies in the fifth century, a number of Eastern churches that disagreed with the decisions of the councils had established an independent existence. In the former territories of the Persian Empire, the majority of Christians refused to call Mary Mother of God, and therefore they were dubbed *Nestorians*. These Christians—also known as *Assyrian*—have a long and checkered history. Although for a time in the Middle Ages this church had numerous members, and its missions extended into China, in more recent times it has suffered severe persecution, particularly from its Muslim neighbors. Early in the twentieth century, and again early in the twenty-first, such persecutions decimated its members. Many of the survivors fled to the Western hemisphere—including its head—*the catholicos*—who sought refuge first in Cyprus and then in Chicago, where his successor still resided in the twenty-first century. At that time, their total membership was approximately a hundred thousand believers, mostly in Iraq, Iran, Syria, and the United States.

Those churches that refused to accept the Chalcedonian *Definition of Faith* because it seemed to divide the humanity of Jesus from his divinity are usually called *Monophysites*, although such a name does not accurately describe their Christological understanding. The largest of these bodies were the Coptic Church of Egypt and its daughter church, the Church of Ethiopia. The latter was one of the last Eastern churches to receive the active support of the state; but such support ended with the overthrow of Emperor Haile Selassie in 1974. The ancient Syrian Monophysite Church, also known as *Jacobite*, continued to be strong in Syria and Iraq. Its head, the Jacobite patriarch of Antioch, resided in Damascus, the capital of Syria. Technically under this patriarch, but in reality autonomous, the Syrian Church in India, which claimed to have been founded by St. Thomas, was fully indigenous, and had about half a million members.

As noted earlier, the Armenian Church refused to accept the Chalcedonian *Definition of Faith*, mostly because it resented the lack of support from the Roman Empire when the Persians invaded Armenia. Their territory was conquered by the Turks, and their staunch refusal to abandon the faith of their ancestors was one of several causes of enmity between them and their Turkish masters. As the power of the Ottoman Empire waned, that enmity turned to violence. In 1895, and again in 1896 and 1914, thousands of Armenians living under Turkish rule were massacred. Approximately a million managed to escape and, as a result, by the twenty-first century there were significant numbers of Armenian Christians in Syria, Lebanon, Egypt, Iran, Iraq, Greece, France, and the Western hemisphere—many of these demanding that Turkey acknowledge a genocide that official Turkish history denied. In that portion of Armenia that was now under Soviet control, the church continued an existence similar to that of other churches under Soviet rule.

In the early decades of the twentieth century, the participation of the Eastern churches in the ecumenical movement was rather reserved. They feared that a willingness to discuss issues of "faith and order" would be construed as uncertainty as to their own beliefs, or as a willingness to compromise such beliefs. Therefore, although several of them collaborated with other Christians in practical matters, they refused any official participation in discussions that could be interpreted as attempting to settle matters of faith by negotiation. When the invitation was sent out for churches to attend the First Assembly of the World Council of Churches, to take place in Amsterdam in 1948 (see Chapter 33), most of the Orthodox churches conferred among themselves and decided to abstain. In 1950, the Central Committee of the World Council of Churches issued a statement that allayed most of the misgivings of the Orthodox. After that time, most of the Orthodox churches became full members of the World Council of Churches. Likewise, the participation of other Eastern bodies also increased. In this particular context, largely through the agency of the World Council of Churches, there were significant conversations between those churches that accepted the *Definition of Faith* of Chalcedon and those that rejected it—Nestorians and Monophysites. In these conversations, it was found that there was profound agreement among these various bodies, and that many of their disagreements were the result of misunderstandings. Thus, while opening the dialogue between Western and Eastern Christianity, the ecumenical movement also promoted a valuable dialogue among Eastern Christians.

FURTHER SHIFTS: THE FALL OF THE SOVIET UNION

The fall of the Soviet Union brought enormous changes to the Orthodox churches in the area. Mikhail Gorbachev's policy of *perestroika*, which was one of the first signs of a new era in the Soviet Union, included greater freedom for the church, and the world was surprised that, after more than eight decades in which the government sought to suppress it, Christianity still showed enormous force. In 1989 alone, more than a thousand new Orthodox communities emerged, a seminary opened in Siberia, and another in Belarus (White Russia), and several monasteries that had been closed by the government reopened. The next year Patriarch Pimen, noted for his conservatism and readiness to submit to the government, died. His successor, Patriarch Aleksey II (who, unlike his predecessors, was elected by secret ballot) proved to be a firm defender of democracy, and made a clear distinction between Christianity and Russian nationalism. In 1993, the Orthodox University of Moscow was founded. Similar events took place in several countries in Eastern Europe that now were no longer under Russian rule, such as the Ukraine, Estonia, and others. There was no doubt that Orthodox Christianity had emerged from Soviet rule with great signs of vitality.

But not all was rosy. In Russia the Orthodox Church now had to deal with the presence of other Christian communities, and protested vigorously when the pope named Roman Catholic bishops for Moscow and other Russian cities. Several Uniate bodies that had been generally suppressed under Communist rule, and even forced to be part of the official Orthodox Church, now came to the foreground, claiming the properties they had lost to official Orthodoxy. This was particularly true in the Ukraine, where conflicts became violent. In 1996, in Estonia, the government granted official and sole recognition to the Estonian Orthodox Apostolic Church, many of

Delegation from the Russian Orthodox church leaving Vigyan Bhaven (the Assembly Hall) for the opening procession of the Third Assembly of the World Council of Churches, New Delhi, India, 1961.

whose leaders had been in exile in Sweden during Soviet rule, and which the patriarch of Constantinople (Istanbul) decreed was an autonomous church under his authority. To this Aleksey II and the Russian Orthodox Church responded by temporarily suspending communion between its patriarchate in Moscow and its counterpart in Constantinople.

Similar events took place as various countries formerly held together by Communist rule now broke apart. This was particularly true in Yugoslavia, where civil war ensued and—even though Patriarch Pavle of Serbia called for an end to violence—religious conflicts among Muslims, Orthodox, and Catholics led to gross violations of human rights and crimes against humanity. In Albania and in some other areas formerly under Communist rule where the majority was Muslim, Orthodox leaders protested that the new governments placed undue restrictions on them and their followers.

Even outside the former Soviet Union, there were conflicts among the

St. Raphael of Brooklyn has become a symbol of Orthodox missionary efforts in the United States and elsewhere.

Orthodox, as that tradition sought to adapt to a new reality in which migration made it difficult to have national churches as it had in previous centuries. In the United States, Australia, Latin America, and other regions, Eastern Orthodox immigrants and their descendants carried their faith with them. Each particular group continued relating to the church of its ancestors, so that there were now different Orthodox churches in the same nation, each owing allegiance to a different patriarch or archbishop in its country of origin, and all resulting in confusion and conflict as different patriarchs and other prelates claimed authority over them.

As one looks at these various churches as a whole, two conclusions can be drawn. The first is that, although following a different chronology, these churches too had to find ways to live and serve in a radically shifting landscape, very different from the Christendom in which some of them—particularly the Russian Orthodox Church—had long existed. The other is that Western Christians—particularly Protestants—may have underestimated the power of liturgy and tradition, that allowed these churches to continue their life, and even to flourish, in the most adverse of circumstances. Thus, Eastern Orthodoxy would make an important contribution to the liturgical renewal of the twentieth and twenty-first centuries, and would prove attractive to Protestants seeking deeper roots in Christian tradition.

Both the shifting landscape and the vitality of the Orthodox liturgy and sense of tradition may be seen in movements that began in the twentieth century in regions of the world that were not traditionally Orthodox, to carry the message of Orthodoxy to new areas and ethnic groups. Although much of the geographic expansion of Eastern Orthodoxy was the result of the migration of Russians, Greeks, and others, early in the twentieth century among the Orthodox in the United States there were voices seeking to expand Eastern Orthodoxy beyond its traditional geographic and ethnic borders. A pioneer in these efforts was Lebanese-born Rafle Hawaweeny (1860–1915), now known as *St. Raphael of Brooklyn*. Through a ministry that included the founding of thirty parishes, St. Raphael began the systematic expansion of Orthodoxy in the United States. In 1988, his efforts bore noticeable fruit when the Evangelical Orthodox Church, which had been founded by Evangelical Protestants—many of them members of the Campus Crusade—joined the Antiochian Orthodox Christian Archdiocese of North America. It was also in that year that the Antiochian Church founded its Department of Missions and Evangelism, whose goal was "to make America Orthodox."

31

Protestant Theology

The historical foundation of Christianity as built by rationalistic, by liberal, and by modern theology no longer exists; but this does not mean that Christianity has lost its historical foundation. . . . We modern theologians are too proud of our historical method, too proud of our historical Jesus, too confident in our belief in the spiritual gains which our historical theology can bring to the world.

ALBERT SCHWEITZER

The nineteenth century posed great intellectual challenges for Christianity. While the response of Catholic authorities and theologians was usually to condemn and reject modern ideas (see Chapter 32), many Protestants sought ways to interpret their ancient faith in terms of the new frame of mind. Therefore, although the challenges were common to both branches of Western Christianity, we shall deal with the Protestant response in the present chapter and with Catholic reactions in the next.

NEW CURRENTS OF THOUGHT

By the beginning of the nineteenth century, the Industrial Revolution had reached most of Western Europe—and even some areas of the New World. Its impact went far beyond economic matters, extending to the whole of life. There were mass movements of people seeking employment in industrial centers, or simply leaving lands now taken over by crops to be used for industrial purposes. The traditional extended family—parents, uncles, aunts, cousins—was weakened by those movements, and the nuclear family had to bear a greater burden of responsibility in the transmission of values and traditions. More people came to see their lives as their private responsibility, and therefore individualism and preoccupation with the self became a common theme in both philosophy and literature.

The Industrial Revolution also contributed to the idea of progress. Throughout most of history, people had thought that the old and tried ideas and practices were better than most innovations. Even at the time of the Renaissance and the Reformation, when many new ideas were introduced, people sought to return to the ancient sources of religion, art, and knowledge. But now people were no longer looking to the past but to the future. Applied science had proven able to produce wealth and comfort that did not exist previously. Future possibilities seemed to have no limit. The leading classes of society viewed the problems created by the Industrial Revolution as passing clouds. Applied technology would soon solve them, and then all in society would benefit from the new order. Since most intellectuals belonged to those leading classes, these ideas were echoed in their teachings and writings. In a sense, even Darwin's theory of evolution was an expression of faith in progress, applied in this case to the natural sciences. Not only humankind but all of nature, is progressing. Progress is part of the structure of the universe. As is also the case with social progress, this is not an easy advance, but a harsh struggle in which the fittest survive and, in the very act of surviving, contribute to the progress of the entire species. This is expressed in the title of Darwin's book, published in 1859, *On the Origin of Species by Means of Natural Selection*, or *the Preservation of Favoured Races in the Struggle for Life.*

Since progress is such an important element in human life, and even in the entire universe, the same must be true of history, for what is history but the progress of the past? The nineteenth century became intensely aware of the radical changes that had taken place in society through the centuries—an awareness that was further prodded by increased contact with other cultures, especially in Africa and the Pacific. Thus, the conclusion was reached that humans had not always been as they are now, for their intellectual and religious views have also evolved. We have already mentioned Comte's theory of a progressive movement from "theology" to "metaphysics," and finally to "science." Such ideas were typical of the nineteenth century. The result was a series of historical studies that cast doubt on much of the traditional views of the past. These studies, applied to Scripture and to early Christianity, produced results that many found incompatible with faith.

Others witnessed the high social price of the progress brought about by the Industrial Revolution. Many Christians sought to respond to the needs of particular groups. The Sunday school movement was an attempt to reach those who no longer had much connection with the traditional means of religious instruction. The Salvation Army, the YMCA, and many similar movements sought to reach the urban masses and alleviate their misery. But the problems and their solutions went far beyond the level of what any charitable institution could do for the disinherited, and many began considering the need for a radical change in the social order. If it was true that there was progress, and that the structure of society had changed through the centuries, why not try to produce further changes in that structure? Comte, as mentioned earlier often considered one of the founders of modern sociology, proposed precisely such a change—one that placed society in the hands of capitalists and merchants. Such projects were frequently put forth in the nineteenth century. Socialism, in its varying hues, became a common theme of those preoccupied with existing social conditions, including vast numbers of Christians. The failed revolutions of 1848 were partly the result of such ideas and projects.

The socialist author who would eventually become most influential was Karl Marx, whose *Communist Manifesto* was published in 1848. His system went beyond the socialist utopias of the time, for it included an analysis of history and society on the basis of what he called "dialectical materialism." A basic element of that analysis was the notion that ideas, no matter how purely intellectual they might appear, have social and political functions. The dominant class develops an ideology that passes for a purely rational construct, but whose true function is to bolster the existing order. Religion itself is part of that structure of support for the powerful—hence, the oft-quoted dictum that religion is the "opiate of the people." But, Marx continued, history moves on, and its next step will be a vast revolution that will lead first to the "dictatorship of the proletariat," and eventually to a classless society in which even the state will be superfluous—the true Communist society. Although Marx's views would pose a serious challenge to Christians in the twentieth century, during the nineteenth they made relatively little impact.

Late in the nineteenth century, the work of Sigmund Freud posed new challenges. After many years of study in various disciplines, Freud became interested in the manner in which the human mind functions, especially at the subconscious level. On the basis of years of observation, he came to the conclusion that the psyche is moved, not only by that which it consciously knows, but also by other factors that never emerge from the level of the subconscious. This is particularly true of experiences and instincts that the mind suppresses due to social pressure or for some other reason, but never destroys. The instincts of sex and aggression, for instance, remain active no matter how deeply we repress them. This opened new horizons for psychology, but also for theology, which did not always know how to deal with Freud's insights.

Although they lived in the nineteenth century, both Marx and Freud made their greatest impact on the twentieth. But both serve as examples of what was taking place during their time, when scientific reasoning began to be applied beyond the natural sciences in an effort to understand both society and the human mind. It is for this reason that the nineteenth century gave birth to such disciplines as sociology, economics, anthropology, and psychology. It was in the context of those developing disciplines that theologians had to do their work.

SCHLEIERMACHER'S THEOLOGY

We have already seen that Kant's work put an end to the facile rationalism of the eighteenth century—or at least cast a shadow over it. If it is true that pure reason reaches an impasse when applied to questions such as the existence of God or life after death, what route can theology follow in dealing with these and other questions of similar importance for religion? If it is true that the structures of thought are in the mind, and do not necessarily correspond to reality, how are we to speak of ultimate realities? There were three possible ways to respond to such questions, and theologians explored all three, as we shall see in this and the following two sections of this chapter.

The first option was to seek a locus for religion other than pure or speculative reason. Kant himself did this in his *Critique of Practical Reason*. He argued that it is wrong to think that religion is basically an intellectual matter, for in fact religion is grounded, not in the intellect, but in the ethical sense. Human beings are by nature moral, and on the basis of that innate moral sense one can prove the existence of God, the soul, human freedom, and life after death. In a way, Kant thus attempted to salvage something of the Christian rationalism that his *Critique of Pure Reason* had undermined, and to do this by placing religion in a locus other than pure reason.

Early in the nineteenth century, Friedrich Schleiermacher proposed a similar solution, although he gave up the attempt to base religion on reason, be it pure or practical. He was born and raised in the home of a Reformed pastor of Moravian tendencies who placed his son's education in the hands of the Moravians. Although Schleiermacher was Reformed, Moravian Pietism did leave its mark on his theology. In any case, young Schleiermacher went through a period in which the pervading rationalism of his time made it difficult for him to continue juggling several of the traditional doctrines of Christianity. He was helped out of that situation by Romanticism. That movement held that there was more to human beings than cold reason, and gained many adepts among the younger generations who felt that rationalism was dehumanizing. Making use of the insights of the Romantics, Schleiermacher began to find his way out of the impasse and doubt in which rationalism had left him. His first major work, *Speeches on Religion to the Cultured among Its Despisers* (1799), was precisely an attempt to show to an audience steeped in Romanticism that religion must still occupy an important place in human life. His main argument was that religion is not a form of knowledge, as both the rationalists and the orthodox believed. Nor is it a system of morality, as Kant implied. Religion is grounded neither in pure nor in practical or moral reason, but rather in *Gefühl*—a German word that is best translated, although not quite accurately, as *feeling*.

The *Speeches* did not clarify the content of such *feeling*, and Schleiermacher undertook that task in his more mature work, *The Christian Faith*. There he clearly shows that this is not a sentimental *feeling*, nor a passing emotion or a sudden experience, but is rather the profound awareness of the existence of the One on whom all existence depends—both ours and that of the world around us. Thus, it is not an undefined or amorphous feeling, for its clear and specific content is our absolute dependence on God. Such *feeling* is not based on rational faculties or on moral sentiment, but it does have significant consequences in both rational exposition and in ethical responsibility.

This feeling of dependence takes a specific form in each religious community. The purpose of religious bodies is to communicate to others and to future generations their particular constitutive experiences, so that they may share in the same feeling. Schleiermacher himself is interested in the Protestant religious community, which is based on two fundamental historical moments: Jesus and the impact he made on his first disciples, and the Reformation of the sixteenth century.

The function of theology is to explore and expound on the implications of that feeling of dependence at three levels: the self, its relations with the world, and its relations with God. Anything that cannot be shown to be related to the feeling of dependence has no place in theology. Let us take, for instance, the doctrine of creation. That doctrine is of paramount importance to the feeling of absolute dependence, for it affirms that all existence depends on God. To deny this would be to deny the dependence that is central to Christian religious feeling. But this does not mean that we have to affirm a particular mode of creation. The creation as told in Genesis may or may not be historically accurate—Schleiermacher himself did not think it was—but in any case this is not a proper matter for theological inquiry, for it has nothing to do with the feeling of dependence. Even if the stories of Moses were true, and had been revealed in some supernatural way, "the particular pieces of information would never be articles of faith in our sense of the phrase, for our feeling of absolute dependence does not gain thereby a new content, a new form, or clearer definition."[18] And the same is to be said about other questions such as the existence of angels, of Satan, and so forth. For the same reason, the traditional distinction between the natural and the supernatural should be set aside, not because it opposes modern science, but rather because that distinction limits our feeling of dependence to those events or places in which the supernatural is made manifest. By thus insisting that religion is different from knowledge, Schleiermacher could interpret the central doctrines of Christianity in such a way that they did not contradict the findings of science.

Schleiermacher's influence was great. At a time when many believed religion to be a matter of the past, people flocked to church when he preached. But he had even more influence over later generations, which appropriately called him the father of liberalism.

HEGEL'S SYSTEM

Another route that remained open after Kant's critique was to agree with him that the mind stamps its seal on all knowledge, but then, instead of seeing this as proof of the limits of reason, to affirm that reason is reality itself. Reason is not something that exists in our minds, and which we then use in order to understand reality. Reason is reality, the only reality there is.

Such was the route followed by G.W.F. Hegel (1770–1831). Hegel began his intellectual career in the field of theology, but later decided that theol-

Hegel developed a philosophical system that soon had thousands of enthusiastic followers, including many who sought to interpret Christianity on the basis of Hegelianism.

ogy was too narrow a field of inquiry, for it was necessary to try to understand not only religion but the whole of reality. Reality must not be seen as a disconnected series of things and events, but as a whole. He proposed that this could be achieved by affirming the identity of reason and reality. It is not simply a matter of reason being able to understand reality, or of reality setting limits to reason. It is rather that reason is reality, and that the only reality is reason. As he said, "What is rational exists, and what exists is rational."

However, in speaking of *reason* Hegel does not refer to mere understanding, nor to the conclusions of reasoning but to the process of thinking itself. In thinking, we do not stand before a fixed idea in order to study it. On the contrary, we pose an idea, examine it so as to surpass it or deny it in favor of another, and finally reach a third idea that includes whatever there was of value in the two previous ones. This process of posing a *thesis*, questioning it by means of an *antithesis*, and finally reaching a *synthesis*, is what Hegel calls "reason." This is, therefore, a dynamic reason, a movement that is constantly advancing. This reason, however, does not exist exclusively in the human mind. The universal reason—*the Spirit*, as Hegel sometimes calls it—is the whole of reality. All that exists is that dialectic and dynamic thought of the Spirit.

On that basis, Hegel built an impressive system that included the entirety of history as the thought of the Spirit. The various religions, philosophical systems, and social and political orders are moments in the Spirit's thoughts. In that thought, the past is never lost but is always surpassed and included in a new synthesis. Thus, the present includes all the past, for it sums it up, and all the future, for the future is the rational development of the present.

Hegel was convinced that Christianity was the "absolute religion." This does not mean that Christianity denies other religions, but rather that it is their culmination—that it sums up the entire process of human religious development. The central theme of religion is the relationship between God and humanity. That relationship reaches its apex in the Christian doctrine of the incarnation, in which the divine and the human are fully united. The union of divine and human, which was implicit in earlier religions, is now made explicit in the incarnation. Likewise, the doctrine of the Trinity is the culmination of the idea of God, for it affirms the dynamic nature of ultimate reality. The dialectic of the Trinity includes three movements. First of all, God is the eternal idea, in itself and by itself, even apart from the development of that rational reality that we call creation. This is the Kingdom of the Father, which is simply God considered apart from any other being. The Kingdom of the Son is what we usually call *creation*, that is, the world as it exists in time and space, and its culmination is God's incarnation, which shows the ultimate identity between the divine and the human. The Kingdom of the Spirit follows this union of the divine and the human, and is made manifest in the presence of God in the community. All this taken together is the Kingdom of God, which comes to historical fruition in the moral life and in the order of the state—for Hegel had a lofty notion of the state. The result of this, as Hegel saw it, was a philosophy completely free of the narrowness of all dogmatic or partial systems.

This far-reaching scheme of reality found many admirers. It was said that finally humans were able to see reality as a whole. In order to bolster the system, Hegel's followers sought to show how various elements of reality fit in the vast Hegelian scheme. It was in protest against the popularity of Hegel's system that the Danish philosopher and theologian Søren Kierkegaard facetiously spoke of how all problems would be solved "now that the System is complete; or if not, will be complete by next Sunday." But even among many who did not accept it, Hegel's system forced philosophers and theologians to take history seriously. After Hegel, history would no longer be a secondary matter for those who were concerned with eternal realities, but would be seen rather as the locus in which eternal realities are known. This notion, which has helped later theologians recover much of the biblical perspective, is part of the legacy of Hegel and of the nineteenth century.

KIERKEGAARD'S WORK

Søren Aabye Kierkegaard (1813–1855) was one of the most interesting figures of the nineteenth century. Born in a strict Danish Lutheran home that left a deep imprint on him, Kierkegaard had an unhappy youth. His frail and slightly twisted frame made him the object of mockery that he suffered throughout his life. But he soon became convinced that his undeniable intellectual gifts meant that he was called to a special mission, and that before that call every other interest must give way. On that basis, he broke his engagement to a woman whom he deeply loved. Marriage, he thought, would have made him happy but would also have prevented him from being the solitary knight of faith that he was called to be. Years later, he would compare that painful decision with Abraham's willingness to sacrifice Isaac; and he would also declare that some of his books were written "because of her."

Kant's critique of rationalism left a third option, different from those followed by Schleiermacher and Hegel: although reason is unable to penetrate ultimate truth, faith can. Kant's *pure reason* can neither prove nor disprove the existence of God; but faith knows God directly. From this perspective, the basis for Christianity is not its reasonableness, nor its place of honor in a system such as Hegel's, nor even a feeling of absolute dependence. Christianity is a matter of faith—of faith in the God whose revelation comes to us in the Scriptures and in Jesus Christ.

But this is not all, for up to this point Kierkegaard has said no more than what has always been said by those who seek in faith a hiding place against the challenges of their time. That kind of "faith," Kierkegaard would say, is not really such; for true faith is never an easy matter, nor is it a means to a tranquil life. On the contrary, faith is always a risk, an adventure that requires the denial of oneself and of all the joys of the faithless. On that basis, Kierkegaard lambasted one of the most famous preachers of his time, declaring that it was ridiculous to speak of a person who had achieved worldly goods by preaching Christianity as a "witness to the truth." Along the same

Kierkegaard was both a philosopher who had little use for the Hegelianism then in vogue and a Christian of profound conviction who felt called to show the radical nature of Christian discipleship.

lines, he offered a radical critique of the Danish society of this time—although this is something that most students of Kierkegaard did not emphasize until the twenty-first century.

For Kierkegaard, the greatest enemy of Christianity was Christendom, the purpose of which is to simplify the matter of becoming a Christian. In Christendom, one is a Christian by simply being neither Jew nor Muslim. But in truth, those who understand Christianity in that fashion are mere pagans. Such *cheap* Christianity, with neither cost nor pain, is like war games, in which armies move and there is a great deal of noise, but no real risk nor pain—and therefore no real victory. What we call *Christianity* is simply playing at being Christians. And many preachers contribute to the mockery of that game when they seek to make Christianity an easy thing. This is the "crime of Christendom," which plays at Christianity and "takes God for a fool." And the tragedy is that few realize how ridiculous it is to speak of God in such terms.

In response to the travesty and tragedy of Christendom, Kierkegaard conceived his calling as "making Christianity difficult." This did not mean that he was to persuade people that Christian faith was wrong. Rather, it meant that he must tell them that what had been preached and taught to them was far from the true faith of Christianity. In other words, in order to be truly Christian, one must become aware of the cost of faith and pay the price. Without that, one may well be a member of Christendom but not a Christian.

True Christianity has to do with a person's very existence and not merely with the intellect. It is at this point that Kierkegaard feels compelled to reject the illusions of "the System"—his sarcastic name for Hegel's philosophy. What Hegel and his followers have done is to build an imposing edifice in which there is no place for true human existence—an existence that takes place in anguish, doubt, and despair. They have built a sumptuous mansion and decided to live in the barn, for their building is too good for them. Existence—actual, painful, human existence—is prior to essence, and much more important than it. This emphasis on existence made Kierkegaard the founder of existentialism, although many later existentialists pursued interests very different from his. Existence is a constant struggle, a struggle to become, to be born. In placing existence at the heart of matters, one is forced to abandon, not only Hegelianism, but also every other system, and even all hope for a consistent system. Although reality itself may be a system for God, it can never be seen as such from the perspective of one in the midst of existence.

Kierkegaard, however, was interested in a particular form of existence: Christian existence. It too cannot be reduced to a system. The tragedy of Christendom, of easy Christianity, is that existence has ceased to be an adventure and a constant risk in the presence of God, and has become a form of morality or a doctrinal system. Hence, Kierkegaard's great problem, which he sought to pose before all, was: how to become a true Christian when one has the disadvantage of living in the midst of Christendom.

CHRISTIANITY AND HISTORY

The interest in history that characterized the nineteenth century also left its mark on biblical and theological studies. In Tübingen, F.C. Baur (1792–1860) sought to expound on the development of theology in the New Testament following Hegel's scheme. Baur and his followers felt that at the very root of the New Testament one finds the conflict between Peter's Judaizing Christianity and the more universal perspective of Paul. The tension between that thesis and antithesis was then resolved in a synthesis that some said was the Fourth Gospel, and others said was second-century Christian-ity. Baur's basic scheme and its many variants, as well as the general inter-est in history that existed at the time, led to long and scholarly discussions regarding the date and authorship of each book of the Bible. Many looked upon such debates, and their startling conclusions, as a menace to faith. In any case, these debates led to increased refinement in the tools of historical research, and to a better understanding of the Bible and its times.

The study of church history followed a parallel course. The idea that Christian doctrines have in fact evolved through the centuries proved a stumbling block to many. Some insisted that such evolution was only the unfolding of what was already implicit in early Christianity. But others—among them the leading historian Adolph von Harnack (1851–1930)—saw the development of dogma as the progressive abandonment of the faith of the early church, moving away from the teachings *of* Jesus to teachings *about* Jesus. According to Harnack, Jesus taught the fatherhood of God, universal brotherhood, the infinite value of the human soul, and the commandment of love. It was later, through a process that took many years, that Jesus and faith in him became the center of the Christian message.

Many of these ideas were derived from one of the most influential theo-logians of the nineteenth century, Albrecht Ritschl (1822–1889), whom Harnack called "the last of the fathers of the church." Like Schleiermacher, Ritschl responded to Kant's challenge by placing religion in a sphere distinct from pure or cognitive reason. But he thought that Schleiermacher's "feeling of absolute dependence" was too subjective. For him, religion—and Chris-tianity in particular—was neither a matter of rational knowledge nor of sub-jective feeling but of practical life. Speculative rationalism he regarded as too cold, not requiring a commitment of faith. Mysticism, on the other hand, he rejected as being too subjective and individualistic. Christianity is practical in that it is lived out in the practical, moral life.

But Christianity is practical also in the sense that it must be based on a factual knowledge of events—particularly of the event of Jesus. What is of primary importance for the practical life is God's historical revelation in Jesus. When theology forgets this, it falls into either rationalism or mysti-cism. Against both errors, historical study shows that the center of the teachings of Jesus is the Kingdom of God and its ethics, "the organization of humanity through action based on love." Thus, the role of the community in Christianity must not be denied by an individualistic understanding of the faith. It was this aspect of Ritschl's theology that served as the basis for Rauschenbusch's *Social Gospel*.

The interest in history in the nineteenth century led to the "quest for the historical Jesus." In order to know the true essence of Christianity, it was thought, one must find the factual Jesus hidden behind the faith of the church and even behind the accounts of the gospels. The difficulty in such a quest, however, is that the historian's own values and image of reality are superimposed on any findings. Therefore, by the beginning of the twentieth century the famous theologian, musician, and missionary Albert Schweitzer concluded that the quest had looked for a man of the nineteenth century, and instead of finding Jesus had found its own image.

The theologians mentioned in this chapter are only a few of many worthy of study, for the nineteenth century was marked by a theological activity rivaled by few other periods. But the few mentioned suffice to give you an idea of the great variety of opinions and positions that appeared within Protestantism, and the intellectual vitality reflected in that very variety. Naturally, in that feverish intellectual activity, statements were made and positions taken that would soon require correction. But the undeniable fact is that the nineteenth century proved that there were in the Protestant ranks many who did not fear the intellectual challenges of their time.

32

Catholicism in the Face
of Modernity

We are horrified, venerable brethren, at seeing the monstrous
doctrines, or rather the enormous errors, that oppress us. They are
widely distributed by a multitude of books, pamphlets, and other
writings small in size, but great in their evil.

GREGORY XVI

While many Protestant theologians followed the route of liberalism, the
Catholic hierarchy tried to keep its theologians from following suit.
The main reason for this was the manner in which the new ideas had threat-
ened and damaged the authority of the church.

THE PAPACY AND THE FRENCH REVOLUTION

The pope at the outset of the French Revolution was Pius VI. Years earlier,
in 1775, he had begun his pontificate by issuing a bull in which he attacked
the ideas of those philosophers who advocated a new social and political
order. Therefore, from the very early days of the revolution, the pope did
all he could to impede its progress. By the time the new French government
issued the *Civil Constitution of the Clergy*, the tension with Rome was such
that negotiations were almost impossible. In retaliation for the pope's support of conservatism, the French republican government sought to weaken
the papacy, and this was one of the reasons for the birth of the cult of
Reason. In Rome itself, French agents undermined the pope's authority by
disseminating republican ideas. In 1798, the French army took Rome, proclaimed a republic, and declared that the pope was no longer the temporal

ruler of the city. Pius VI died a year later, while virtually a prisoner of the French.

The cardinals then gathered in Venice under the protection of Emperor Francis II of Austria, an enemy of the French Republic, and elected Pius VII. Napoleon's climb to power eased tensions between the new pope and France, and in 1801 an agreement was reached between the two parties. Although Napoleon was not particularly religious, he saw no need to spend his energies in conflicts with the papacy, and Pius VII, having been restored to his see, enjoyed a few years of relative peace. In 1804, he traveled to Paris in order to consecrate Napoleon as emperor—and Napoleon signaled his claim to absolute power by taking the crown from the pope's hand and crowning himself. The following year, the emperor's troops invaded Italy, and in 1808 took the city of Rome. The pope refused to flee, and excommunicated any who did violence to him or to the church. The French took him captive and he was not freed until the fall of Napoleon. He then returned to Rome, where his first official action was to forgive his enemies.

Pius VII died in 1823, two years after Napoleon, and was succeeded by Leo XII. Leo and his successors, Pius VIII and Gregory XVI, were able to reign in peace. But because of the memory of the French Revolution they were inclined toward political and theological conservatism, and they repeatedly blocked attempts by Catholics to lend their support to republican and democratic ideas. The most famous person thus condemned was the French theologian F.R. de Lamennais, who had staunchly resisted Napoleon in his attempts to use the church for his own ends. After a long spiritual pilgrimage, Lamennais came to the conclusion that absolute monarchs would always be tempted to use the church for their own ends, and that therefore Christians ought to foster movements to limit the power of monarchs. This should be done with the support and the direction of the papacy. As part of this vast political project, the pope should advocate the freedom of the press, for this would spearhead the new order. Lamennais was convinced that if the popes took the lead in such a project, the church would be able to claim its rightful place in the resultant order. Up to that point, Lamennais had been a champion of the church against absolutist governments that would not respect its prerogatives, and Leo XII had even considered making him a cardinal. But when Lamennais began arguing for an alliance between the popes and political liberalism, he lost all support in Rome, where the memory of the French Revolution was still fresh. He went to Rome, hoping to convince the pope of the wisdom of his plan. But Gregory XVI, then pope, condemned his ideas in two encyclicals. Lamennais then left the church, taking with him many others of similar ideas.

While this debate was taking place, nationalist sentiment was growing in Italy. A significant faction among Italian patriots hoped that the papacy would provide the center around which a new unified nation would be formed. But the papal fear of anything associated with sedition, and the popes' willingness to please the very monarchs who sought to keep Italy divided, soon lost the popes any support among Italian nationalists.

PIUS IX

The longest pontificate in history, that of Pius IX (1846–1878), was a paradoxical time for the papacy. The greatest of these paradoxes was that, at the same time that the popes were declared infallible, they lost their temporal power. The revolution of 1848 was felt in Rome, where the Republic of Rome was proclaimed in the following year. The pope, expelled from the city, was unable to return until the French intervened in his favor. After his restoration, instead of continuing some of the measures of reformation and liberalization introduced by the republicans, Pius IX tried to rule as an absolute monarch. He also clashed with Camillo Benso, conte di Cavour, the great statesman of the kingdom of Piedmont-Sardinia, whose goal was the unification of Italy. Eventually, on September 20, 1870, the troops of the new kingdom of Italy took the Papal States. Although for a long time the popes refused to accept the new reality, those events marked the end of their temporal power, for their sovereignty was now limited to a few palaces that Italy allowed them to keep, including the Vatican. At approximately the same time, Bismarck in Germany was taking measures against the power of the church, and other European powers were following his example. Therefore, the pontificate of Pius IX marks the end of the political power of the popes, which had reached its apex in the thirteenth century under Innocent III.

While losing his power, Pius IX insisted on reaffirming it, even if this could be done only in religious matters. Thus, in 1854, he proclaimed the dogma of the Immaculate Conception of Mary. According to that dogma, Mary herself, by virtue of her election to be the Mother of the Savior, was kept pure from all taint of sin, including original sin. This was a question that Catholic theologians had debated for centuries without reaching a consensus. But the most significant fact from a historical point of view was that, in proclaiming this dogma as the doctrine of the church, Pius IX was the first pope ever to define a dogma on his own, without the support of a council. In a way, the bull *Ineffabilis,* promulgating the dogma of the *Immaculate Conception of Mary,* tested the waters to see how the world would react. Since the bull did not meet much opposition, the stage was set for the promulgation of papal infallibility.

Meanwhile, the pope did not rest in his struggle against the new political ideas circulating in Europe and the Americas. In 1864, he issued the encyclical *Quanta cura,* accompanied by a *Syllabus of Errors* that listed eighty propositions that Catholics must reject. Some of the errors listed there show the mood of the papacy in the nineteenth century:

13. That the method and principles by which the ancient scholastic doctors developed their theology are not compatible with present needs or with scientific progress.

15. That each person is free to adopt and follow that religion which, guided by the light of reason, he shall consider true.

18. That Protestantism is simply another form of the same Christian religion, and that it is possible to please God in it as well as in the true Catholic Church.

21. That the church does not have the power of defining dogmatically that the religion of the Catholic Church is the only true religion.

24. That the church has no authority to make use of force, nor does it have temporal power. . . .

30. That the immunity of the church and of ecclesiastics is based on civil law.

37. That it is lawful to institute national churches, separate and completely independent of the Roman pontiff.

38. That the arbitrary behavior of the popes contributed to the break between the Eastern and Western churches.

45. That the entire management of the schools in which youth are educated in a Christian state, with the sole and partial exception of seminaries, can and should be in the hands of the civil power, in such a manner that no other authority be allowed to intervene in the management of schools, the direction of studies, the granting of degrees, or the selection and certification of teachers.

47. That the good order of civil society requires that public schools, open to children of all classes, and in general all public institutions devoted to the teaching of literature and science, and to the education of youth, be free of all authority on the part of the church, of all its moderating influence, and be subject only to civil and political authority, so that they may behave according to the opinions of civil magistrates and to the common opinion of the time.

55. That the church ought to be separate from the state, and the state from the church.

77. That in our time it is no longer convenient that the Catholic religion be the only religion of the state, or that every other religion be excluded.

78. That it is therefore praiseworthy that in some Catholic countries the law allows immigrants to practice publicly their own forms of worship.

79. That it is false that, if all religions are granted civil freedom, and all are allowed to express publicly their opinions and ideas, no matter what they may be, this will facilitate moral and mental corruption, and will spread the plague of indifferentism.

80. That the Roman pontiff can and should be reconciled with, and agree to, progress, liberalism, and modern civilization.

Thus, during the last decades of the nineteenth century, the papacy was openly opposed to such innovations as the separation of church and state, freedom of worship, freedom of the press, and public schools under state supervision. At the same time, the pope insisted on his authority, and on the evils that would follow if he was not obeyed. All this reached its high point in the First Vatican Council, still under the direction of Pius IX. In *Pastor aeternus,* the Council promulgated the dogma of papal infallibility:

Therefore faithfully adhering to the tradition received from the beginning of the Christian faith, for the glory of God our Saviour, the exaltation of the Christian religion, and the salvation of Christian people, the sacred Council approving, we teach and define that it is a dogma divinely revealed: that the Roman Pontiff, when he speaks *ex cathedra,* that is, when in discharge of the office of pastor and doctor of all Christians, by virtue of his supreme Apostolic authority, he defines a

The First Vatican Council, under the authoritarian leadership of Pius IX, marked the high point of tendencies begun at the time of the Council of Trent. Its most significant action was the declaration of papal infallibility.

doctrine regarding faith or morals to be held by the universal Church, by the divine assistance promised to him in blessed Peter, is possessed of that divine infallibility with which the divine Redeemer willed that his Church should be endowed for defining doctrine regarding faith or morals; and that therefore such definitions are irreformable of themselves, and not from the consent of the Church.[19]

This is the official statement of papal infallibility as the Catholic Church holds it. It is important to note that the text does not say that the pope is always infallible, but only when he speaks *ex cathedra*. These words were included in the declaration in order to respond to the objection that Pope Honorius, for instance, had been a heretic. The answer to that objection would then be that Honorius, in accepting erroneous doctrine, did not do so *ex cathedra*. In any case, of the more than six hundred bishops present, five hundred and twenty-two voted in favor, two against, and more than a hundred abstained. (Only once after this proclamation has a pope claimed to be making use of such authority. This was in 1950, when Pius XII promulgated the doctrine of the Assumption of Mary—that is, that at the end of her earthly life Mary was bodily assumed into heaven.)

The promulgation of papal infallibility did not cause the stir that might have been expected. In the Netherlands, Austria, and Germany, some withdrew from the Roman communion and founded the Old Catholic Church. But in general, protests and criticism were moderate—having lost its political power, the papacy was no longer as formidable as it had once been. In the old struggle between Gallicans and Ultramontanes (see Chapter 18), the latter had finally won. But that victory was possible because the papacy had lost much of the power that at an earlier time Gallicans had feared. Papal infallibility was promulgated on July 18, 1870, and on September 20 Rome surrendered before the armies of the kingdom of Italy. Pius IX declared himself a prisoner of King Victor Emmanuel, and refused to accept the new order. After all, Rome had been lost to the popes many times before, and always someone had intervened to restore it to the papacy. But this time no one intervened and, in 1929, Pope Pius XI finally accepted what had been a fact for more than half a century.

LEO XIII

Pius IX was succeeded by Leo XIII, whose tenure in office was also exceptionally long (1878–1903). Given political conditions in Italy, Leo XIII, who still insisted on his right to temporal authority over Rome and the surrounding area, declared that Catholics should not vote in Italian elections. That prohibition, which continued until well into the twentieth century, would in effect deny Catholics the opportunity to participate in the formative years of the Italian nation. But, while following that conservative policy in Italy, Leo saw the need to yield in other areas. Thus, he was able to reach a tacit agreement with Germany, with the result that some of the anti-Catholic policies begun by Bismarck were rescinded. In France, the Third Republic also took anticlerical measures, but the pope decided it was best to follow a policy of conciliation. In 1892, he even advised the French clergy to abandon their opposition to the republic—even though a few years earlier, in the bull *Immortale Dei,* he had declared democracy incompatible with the authority of the church. Thus, Leo XIII, while acknowledging the need to take into account the new realities and attitudes of modern times, understood papal

Leo XIII

authority in terms very similar to those of Pius IX, and still kept alive the dream of a Catholic society guided by principles formulated by the papacy.

This may be seen in the most important document of Leo's pontificate, his bull *Rerum novarum,* issued on May 15, 1891. The subject of that bull was one with which few popes had dealt before: the proper relations between laborers and their employers. In the bull, Leo shows that he is aware of the inequities that have resulted from the contrast between "the enormous fortunes of a few individuals, and the extreme poverty of the masses." Therefore, he writes, the time has come "to define the mutual rights and obligations of the rich and the poor, of capital and labor." Such relations have become all the more tragic since labor organizations have disappeared in recent times, and "a small group of very rich people have been able to throw upon the masses of poor laborers a yoke that is little better than slavery itself." Although it is an error to believe that between the rich and the poor there can only be class war, it is true that the defense of the poor merits special attention, for the rich have many ways to protect themselves, while the poor have no other recourse than the protection of the state. Therefore, laws should be such that the rights of the poor are guaranteed. In particular, this refers to the right of every laborer to a salary sufficient to sustain him and his family, without being forced to work beyond a fair limit. All this is to be done because "God seems to lean in favor of those who suffer misfortune."

On the other hand, this does not mean that the opinions of the socialists are correct, for private property is a right established by God, as is also the right of inheritance. Furthermore, the differences that exist in the social order are due, at least in part, to natural differences among human beings. What the pope then asks is, first of all, for the rich to practice charity. This means that no one is under obligation to give to the point of cutting into what is necessary for life, or even for maintaining one's stature in life. But, having met those needs, one is obliged to give the needy what is left. The poor, for their part, ought not to hate the rich, but are rather to remember that poverty is an honorable state, and that the practice of virtue leads to material prosperity.

Leo is well aware that charity and love will not suffice to produce justice, and therefore he calls on all Christians to defend the poor, and urges the formation of labor unions to defend the rights of laborers. Since those rights include fair wages, reasonable hours of work, and the right to practice the Catholic religion without interference, Leo calls for the formation of Catholic labor unions, arguing that in such unions there will not be the hatred and divisions that arise when poverty is unaccompanied by religion. In summarizing its position, the bull declares: "The urgent issue of today is the condition of the working classes. . . . But Christian laborers will easily solve it by forming associations, choosing wise leaders, and following the path that their ancestors have trod with so much profit to themselves and to society."

This encyclical renewed the motivation among the many Catholics who were already seeking solutions to the problems posed by the Industrial Revolution and growing capitalism. Some whom the bull prodded into action would later come to the conclusion that its solutions were too simplistic. Others would oppose the union movement by pointing out that Leo had encouraged Catholic unions, and not others. Therefore, while *Rerum novarum* marks the beginning of the modern Catholic trade-union movement, it is also an indication of Leo's ambivalence before the challenges and requirements of the modern world.

A similar ambivalence could be seen in his attitude toward modern scholarship. Leo did open the archives of the Vatican to historians, for he was convinced that the outcome of historical studies would strengthen the authority of the church. But his bull *Providentissimus Deus,* while admitting the value of historical study of the Bible, warned against its use to weaken the authority of either the Bible or the church. Therefore, both those who sought greater freedom in the critical study of Scripture and those who opposed them could point to sections in the encyclical that seemed to favor them. Likewise, Leo promoted a return to the theology of Thomas Aquinas, both creating a Leonine Commission to produce a critical edition of all the writings of Aquinas, and ordering that those writings—and not just commentaries on them—be the basis for theological instruction in seminaries. While there was certainly an element of conservatism in such measures, one should also note that Leo felt that Aquinas was particularly valuable because he too was forced to face the challenges of a changing age and new attitudes in the field of philosophy.

PIUS X

The pope who succeeded Leo, and who led the Catholic Church until the beginning of World War I, was Pius X (1903–1914). His policy was much more conservative than Leo's, and drew its inspiration from Pius IX. The result was a growing gulf between mainstream modern thought and society on the one hand and Catholicism on the other. Following the pope's instructions, the Holy Office—the old Inquisition—issued a decree condemning those who had dared apply the new methods of research to Scripture or to theological matters. These were the so-called Modernists, of whom the most famous were the Frenchman A.F. Loissy, the Englishman George Tyrrell, and the German Hermann Schell. Shortly thereafter, in the encyclical *Pascendi Dominici gregis,* Pius X confirmed the action of the Holy Office. The net result was that many of the Modernists left the church, while greater numbers of Catholics decided to remain in the church but pay little attention to pontifical directives.

BENEDICT XV TO PIUS XII

World War I had just broken out when Pius X died and was succeeded by Benedict XV (1914–1922). He had been made an archbishop by Pius X, whose policies he was determined to continue. Like the previous three popes, he insisted on his right to rule the papal states, which he claimed Italy had usurped from the Holy See. He directed most of his early efforts to the pursuit of peace; but he was repeatedly rebuffed by the belligerent powers. When peace finally came, and the League of Nations was established, he was not in a position to influence events in any decisive way. After the war he was able to sign concordats with several of the new states that resulted from the peace negotiations. In general, he was perceived as more open than his predecessor, but was not a very effective pope.

His successor, Pius XI (1922–1939), was a scholar and an able administrator. He was also acutely aware of the increasing importance of the non-European world, and therefore did all within his power to encourage missionary work and to help churches already established in former mission areas attain maturity. During his pontificate the number of Catholic missionaries doubled, and it was he who consecrated the first Chinese bishops. As we shall see, later in the century this emphasis on the development of Catholicism in other lands would bear significant and unexpected fruit. In contrast to most of the popes of this period, Pius XI was very interested in simple acts of piety and devotion, and therefore was a great admirer of Thérèse of Lisieux (1873–1897), whose devotion had been centered on the "little way" of obedience, and who had seen herself as an "apostle to the apostles," praying for priests and encouraging them in their ministry. Showing his admiration for Thérèse, and his conviction that her teachings were very much-needed by the church of his time, Pius XI beatified her in 1923, and then canonized her two years later. In a way, Thérèse was a symbol of Pius's interest in increasing the activity of the laity, although always under the supervision of the hierarchy. This he outlined in the first of his encyclicals, which set the goals and rules for Catholic Action, the most important Catholic lay organization of the first half of the century.

Although very concerned about the dangers of Communism and its avowed atheistic stance, Pius XI did not manifest the same concern over Fascism, particularly when it posed as Communism's chief enemy. Furthermore, Fascism appealed to the same principles that Pius IX had so strongly advocated in his *Syllabus of Errors:* a hierarchical understanding of society, a strong sense of authority, and a state dedicated to the enforcement of moral standards. Since Italian Fascism in the early stages of its development favored Catholicism, the pope was quite content to work with it. In 1929, his representative signed an agreement with Mussolini that finally resolved the issue of Italian sovereignty over Rome. Italy acknowledged the existence of a sovereign state, Vatican City, and granted the papacy sovereignty over it, as well as financial compensation for the loss of other territories. In return, Pius recognized the kingdom of Italy as a legitimate state, with Rome as its capital. Eventually, Pius clashed with Italian Fascism, and he repeatedly condemned Hitler and Nazism in the early stages of their rise to power. But later he weakened his stance against the Nazi regime, and he did support Franco's brand of Fascism in Spain. In Germany, fear of liberalism and Communism inclined many Catholics toward rising Nazism. In 1933, Catholic opposition to Hitler collapsed, and the political party led by prelate Ludwig Kaas gave Hitler the necessary majority to take full possession of the government. At about the same time, the bishops gathered at Fulda, and withdrew their earlier harsh words about the dangers of Nazism. In Rome, Pius XI and his secretary of state Cardinal Pacelli—who would later become Pius XII—felt that the time had come to reach an agreement with Hitler, and within a few months a concordat was signed that was seen in international circles as the Vatican's qualified approval of the Nazi regime. It took the pope several years to realize the dangers of Nazism; for a long time he had seen it as an acceptable alternative to Communism. Finally, in 1937, he issued two encyclicals, one against Nazism and the other against Communism. The first of these encyclicals, *Mit brennender Sorge,* declared that Nazism was a new form of paganism, and accused Hitler of disregarding the Concordat of 1933. Five days later, the parallel encyclical, *Divini Redemptoris,* condemned Communism, which now caused him grave concern because Russia had increased its antireligious propaganda. Communism was also making rapid progress in Asia, and the pope feared that the Mexican Revolution would lead to another Communist state. In this encyclical, he condemned the Marxist view that religion is a means of oppressing the lower classes, and declared that there could be no grounds for Christian collaboration with it. Meanwhile, the ties developing between Hitler and Mussolini, and repeated clashes with Italian Fascism, caused the pope to prepare a strong speech condemning some of the actions of the Fascist regime in Italy, but he did not yet break relations with it. He was still working on this speech when he died.

The conclave took only one day and three ballots to elect a successor. This was Cardinal Pacelli, who indicated his intention of continuing the policies of Pius XI by taking the name of Pius XII (1939–1958). A man experienced in diplomatic affairs, he had a slight penchant for nepotism, and a highly authoritarian and clerical view of the church. Pius XII was also a mystic who spent hours in prayer, an indefatigable worker whose aides often complained that he drove them too hard, and a man of personal magnetism who was much respected by friend and foe alike. The early years of his pontificate were dominated by World War II, which he had tried unsuccessfully to prevent. When war became inevitable, he directed his attention—again to no avail—to keeping Italy out of the conflict, and he also supported a conspiracy to overthrow Hitler. Once war broke out, Pius XII followed a policy of neutrality, hoping that by remaining above the fray he could serve as a mediator at the appropriate time. This neutrality, however, was achieved at the cost of silence in the face of Nazi atrocities against the Jews, a policy for which he has been severely criticized. On this point, even his apologists admit that he was aware of what was taking place in Germany, and defend his policy on the grounds that protests would have achieved little. But such considerations did not keep the pope from denouncing Nazi atrocities against Catholics in Poland—even though the Polish bishops reported that each protest over Vatican Radio was followed by further measures against their flock. On these issues, Pius XII seems to have been another exponent of what had been the basic mood of the papacy since the Council of Trent: to protect the church at all costs, seeking for it as much freedom and power as possible, subordinating all other issues to this overriding concern. It is also probable that, while he feared a Nazi victory, he was more concerned over the growth of Communism, and that in the war between the Axis and the USSR, his sympathies were with the former. In any case, he did repeatedly insist on the general principles by which nations and governments ought to be judged, although he refrained from making such judgments himself.

While the pope's reaction to the persecution of Jews in Germany and in the occupied areas of Europe left much to be desired, there were other Catholics who risked life and freedom for the sake of their Jewish brothers and sisters. Pius himself was aware of the clandestine networks that were helping Jews escape from Germany, France, and various countries in Eastern Europe. And among the "righteous Gentiles" whom the international Jewish community recognizes as having risen to the challenge of the hour, often to

The position of Pius XII with regard to Fascism was never clear. After the war he was accused of not having spoken out against the atrocities committed by Nazis against the Jews, while others affirmed that he had been quietly acting in defense of the Jews.

the point of heroism, there are a number of Catholics.

After the war, the pope's international policy was primarily directed at the threat of Communism. In 1949, he decreed automatic excommunication for any who supported the Communists in whatever country. It was the time of the great imperialistic expansion of Russia, whose orbit of influence soon included most of Eastern Europe. In Asia, China had also become Communist, and at the time it seemed that the Catholic Church in that vast country—as well as all other churches—had been completely crushed. Against this threat, and also hoping to avert future wars, Pius joined the voices calling for a unified Europe. In 1953, he signed a concordat with

Franco's regime in Spain—the main surviving bastion of Fascism after the war. His reasons for this were many. The influence of Communists in the government of Spain before the civil war had increased as tension mounted. Catholics who feared Communism saw Franco and his movement as the only alternative, which in turn gave rise to greater anticlericalism. Then the civil war unleashed violent passions, resulting in the deaths of thousands of priests, nuns, and monks. When the dust settled, Franco was in firm control of the nation, and his staunchest allies were the most conservative among the Catholic clergy. Therefore, in the midst of a world in which more and more governments seemed to be turning against the church, the Vatican welcomed Franco and his regime.

The pope's inclinations could also be seen in his understanding of the papacy and its teaching and administrative authority. He tended to centralize the government of the church, depriving the national episcopates of much of their initiative. While looking at the ecumenical movement with more favor than his predecessors, in 1950 he placed one more obstacle in that movement's progress by proclaiming the dogma of the Bodily Assumption of Mary into heaven. But, above all, he was extremely suspicious of innovations in the field of theology. In 1950, the bull *Humani generis* reiterated earlier warnings against innovations in theology. Some of the most creative Catholic theologians of the time were silenced, among them several whose writings laid the groundwork for the Second Vatican Council. One of the most creative Catholic thinkers of the twentieth century, Pierre Teilhard de Chardin, was forbidden by the Holy Office from publishing his theological works. They didn't appear until after his death in 1955. In France, some Catholic leaders had sought to penetrate the labor movement through worker priests, who took employment as common laborers, sometimes without even revealing their identity as priests until they were well-known and accepted by the group. Although the movement was criticized by the more conservative elements in French Catholicism, at first it had the support of the Vatican. But when several priests became leaders in the labor movement, and took a stance against capital, the pope withdrew his support. He ordered all worker priests to withdraw from the labor force, and he closed the seminary where most of them were being trained. It was the time of the Cold War, and the pope—who during World War II had hoped to be a mediator—now found himself drawn into the conflict, seemingly left with no alternative to Communism besides reactionary conservatism.

On the other hand, some of the policies of Pius XII did pave the way for the great changes that took place during the next pontificate. His encyclical of 1943, *Divino afflante Spiritu,* encouraged the use of modern methods of biblical study. Although he later insisted on the need for caution in that enterprise, the biblical studies that had been undertaken under the influence of *Divino afflante Spiritu* would later contribute to the renewal of the church. The reform of the liturgy, which was one of the earliest actions of the Second Vatican Council, had been encouraged by him, albeit with great caution. But, above all, he led the way to the internationalization of the church that eventually made possible the Second Vatican Council. He understood that the age of colonialism had come to an end, and therefore continued his predecessors' policy of strengthening churches outside of Europe. He also encouraged the emancipation of colonies, to the point that he was criticized as being an enemy of Europe—particularly of France, which for a time was very reluctant to grant independence to its colonies. While insisting on his universal jurisdiction and direct control of all churches, he encouraged the formation of indigenous churches under the leadership of native bishops. Very significant for later developments was the formation, under Vatican auspices, of the Conference of Latin American Bishops (C.E.L.A.M.), the first such official organization on an international and regional basis. He also brought non-Italians into the curia, and internationalized the college of cardinals, which at the time of his death was only one-third Italian. Thus, though he was a conservative pope after the fashion of the councils of Trent and Vatican I, he set in motion the machinery that would eventually lead to the Second Vatican Council and to the reformation it espoused.

In conclusion, after the American and French Revolutions, and in the midst of a radically changing context, all Christian churches had to face new political, economic, social, and intellectual circumstances. In general, Protestantism sought the means to take those new realities into account; but Catholicism took the opposite tack. Obviously, there were many exceptions to that generalization. One of the net results, however, was that by the time of World War I Protestants and Catholics were as far apart from each other as they had been at any previous time. Protestants looked upon the Catholic Church as a relic of bygone ages, while Catholics were convinced that Protestantism had confirmed its heretical character by capitulating before the challenges of the modern world. As long as such conditions prevailed, there was little hope for a rapprochement between the two branches of Western Christianity. Although, as we shall see (in Chapters 35 and 36), World War I forced much of Protestantism to reevaluate its facile acceptance of modernity, it would not be until the second half of the twentieth century, with the Second Vatican Council, that official Roman Catholicism would review its exceedingly negative view of modernity.

33

Geographic Expansion

Just as the development of improved means of communication has greatly facilitated the propagation of the Gospel and the sending forth of the pure and hopeful influences of western civilization, so the drawing together of the nations and races as a result of these improvements has made possible the more rapid spread of influences antagonistic to Christ's Kingdom.

WORLD MISSIONARY CONFERENCE, EDINBURGH, 1910

THE MISSIONARY ENTERPRISE IN
THE AGE OF COLONIALISM

In the Western world, the attitudes of Christians toward colonialism were widely divergent. Some opposed particular colonizing ventures on the grounds that they were contrary to the national interest. Many Christians of profound convictions protested against the treatment of people in some colonized areas. But in general the colonizers—including many devout Christians—were convinced that their enterprise was justified by the benefits the colonized would receive. As they saw matters, God had placed the benefits of Western civilization and Christian faith in the hands of white people—both Europeans and North American settlers—in order for them to share it with the rest of the world. That responsibility was the so-called *white man's burden*: to take to the rest of the world the benefits of industrialization, capitalism, democracy, and Christianity.

There were grounds for such visions. Medical science, for instance, reached many remote areas and saved countless lives. Trade and industrial development increased the wealth of many areas, and for that reason gained the support of certain classes among native populations. All over the world, there were people who benefitted from the improved conditions, and for whom modernity's promises of progress became a reality. But modernity also produced the dislocation of vast masses who now became landless, the destruction of many of the cultural patterns that had sustained societies for centuries, and growing disparities in living conditions between the rich and the poor throughout the world. In any case, the racial and cultural arrogance that formed the foundation of the entire enterprise could not fail to produce the anticolonial reaction that marked the middle of the twentieth century.

The church was deeply influenced by all these circumstances and ideas, but the relationship between colonialism and missions was very complex. Although the accusation is often made that missionaries were agents of colonialism, this was not always true, for there were missionaries who opposed colonialism, and many who criticized and condemned various aspects of it. Nor is it always true that missionary work entered through a door opened by colonialism; for, although in many cases missionaries worked in colonized areas, there were many other cases where missionaries reached regions that had never before been visited by white traders or colonizers. Also, many of the colonial authorities and commercial interests opposed missionary work, for they feared that religious conflict would interrupt trade. It is true that the colonial expansion of the West—particularly the Protestant West—coincided with its missionary expansion, so that the two at times aided and at times impeded each other.

One of the most remarkable characteristics of the missionary enterprise during the nineteenth century was the formation of missionary societies. Some of these drew their membership from a single denomination, while others broke confessional barriers. All were voluntary societies, for the churches as institutions did not usually support missions. Forerunners of the movement were the Society for Promoting Christian Knowledge (S.P.C.K.), founded in 1698, and the Society for the Propagation of the Gospel in Foreign Parts (S.P.G.), founded in 1701. Both were Anglican, and for some time most of their work was among British expatriates. Due to the impact of Pietists, Moravians, and Methodists, several similar societies were founded during the eighteenth century. But the heyday of missionary societies began late in the eighteenth century, and lasted through the nineteenth. In 1792, thanks to the perseverance of William Carey, the Particular Baptist Society for Propagating the Gospel amongst the Heathen was founded (its name was later shortened to Baptist Missionary Society). Three years later, partly

William Carey, often called "the father of modern missions," devoted a great deal of his time to learning the languages of India and translating the Scriptures into them.

through the example of the Baptists, a group of Methodists, Presbyterians, and Congregationalists founded the London Missionary Society (L.M.S.). The Church Missionary Society (C.M.S.), dating from 1799, drew its members from the evangelical wing of the Anglican Church. Other societies were also created with more specific goals, such as the British and Foreign Bible Society, founded in 1804. The movement then spread to other lands, and soon there were Protestant missionary societies in the Netherlands, Switzerland, Denmark, Germany, and several other countries. In France, there were both Protestant and Catholic societies. Congregationalists in the United States founded the American Board of Commissioners for Foreign Missions.

When one of its missionaries, Adoniram Judson, became a Baptist, a Baptist missionary society was organized to support him and others, and this society eventually gave birth to the American Baptist Convention.

The emergence of these societies points to another characteristic of the missionary movement of the nineteenth century: its widespread support. For centuries before that, most missionary work had taken place with the official support of the state. But in the nineteenth century, most Western governments had little or no official relationship with missionary enterprises. For years, the British East India Company tried to bar missionaries from the lands under its rule. Most European governments, as well as the United States, adopted a neutral—and sometimes slightly hostile—stance toward missionaries and their goals. In theory at least, missionaries could count on no other protection than that afforded to their fellow citizens engaged in other endeavors. But it was at the point of financial support that the contrast proved greatest between the modern missionary movement and its predecessors. Few governments—and few churches—contributed funds to the enterprise. Lacking such civil and ecclesiastical support, those interested in missions had to appeal to the public at large, and hence the growth and proliferation of missionary societies.

In consequence, for the first time in centuries the work of international missions captivated the interest of the general membership of churches. Naturally, even then there were many who showed no interest in the matter. But those who wished to do so, from the youngest to the oldest, could make a contribution to the preaching of the gospel in distant and even exotic lands. Missionary societies, for their part, brought news of what was taking place in the remotest areas of Asia or Africa, and thus became one of the main sources of public information and education regarding other lands and cultures.

Women played an important role in all this. In many denominations, both in the United States and in Europe, women organized their own missionary societies, and collected funds and supplies for work overseas. At first, all the missionaries themselves were men—although many were married and took their wives with them. But soon it was shown that women had a great contribution to make overseas. Some feminine missionary societies began sending their own missionaries. Among Catholics, such missionaries were usually nuns, and the work that they did in the mission field was similar to what they did in their homeland: teaching, nursing, caring for the aged, and so forth. Among Protestants, female missionaries began assuming responsibilities that were forbidden to them at home, such as preaching and organizing churches. (The underlying racism of the times made it acceptable for women to have over the natives an authority that sexism denied them in their own lands.) Eventually, the example of these women, and the news of their success, prompted women who remained at home in Europe and the United States to demand the opportunity to do the same. Thus, the missionary movement is one of the roots of the feminist movement among Western Protestants.

Finally, another important consequence of the missionary movement was the spirit of cooperation that began appearing between various denominations. Rivalries that seemed justifiable in Europe or the United States were a stumbling block to missionary work in India or China. Therefore, many missionaries, and soon their converts also, took steps to lower the barriers between denominations. Some missionary societies drew their members from more than one denomination. In the mission field, ways were constantly sought to present a common witness and avoid competition. Thus, the ecumenical movement, at least among Protestants, has one of its main roots in the missionary experience of the nineteenth and twentieth centuries.

ASIA AND OCEANIA

For centuries, the ancient civilizations of the Far East had fascinated Europeans. Medieval books included vague rumors of strange customs and incredible monsters. Then Marco Polo and other travelers brought news of fabulous riches in the courts of China and India. In the sixteenth century, the Portuguese established permanent trading posts there, and soon thereafter other European nations began seeking similar footholds. Commerce and its protection often led to military and political conquest, and by the time of World War I there were few countries in Asia and the Pacific that were not under colonial rule. Although not always in agreement with colonial policies, missionaries and the churches they founded played a role in the process of European expansion.

In Asia, the impact of the new wave of colonial expansion was first felt on the Indian subcontinent—now India, Pakistan, Bangladesh, and Sri Lanka. As we have seen, Christianity had existed there since ancient times (in Vol. I, Chapter 25), and Catholicism had been introduced in the sixteenth century (in Vol. I, Chapter 37). Early in the eighteenth century, the first Protestant missionaries had arrived under the auspices of a Danish king profoundly affected by Pietism. But it was in the nineteenth century, with the sudden growth of British influence, that the greatest Protestant missionary advance took place.

The British East India Company had begun its operations in India early in the eighteenth century. A hundred years later, it ruled almost the entire eastern coast of the subcontinent. A few years earlier, the British had taken Ceylon. By the middle of the nineteenth century, practically the entire area was under British rule, either direct or indirect. In 1858, through an act of Parliament, the government of India—then in the hands of the East India Company—was seized by the British government and placed directly under the rule of the crown.

During its first century in operation, the British East India Company opposed missionary work, for it feared that Christian preaching would cause tension and rioting that would hinder trade. This policy met little opposition in England, where interest in missions was scarce. It was partly as a result of the efforts of William Carey that these conditions changed, and therefore he has properly been called the founder of modern missions.

Although reared in an Anglican household, William Carey had become a Baptist. A teacher and cobbler by trade, he was fascinated by the news of new lands that Captain Cook was discovering in the Pacific. Combining his faith to his awareness of distant lands, he came to the conviction, unusual in his time, that Christians had the obligation to preach the gospel in distant countries to people who had not heard it. After much criticism, he was able to gather a number of like-minded people and create the Particular Baptist Society for Propagating the Gospel amongst the Heathen. When the Society proved unable to find someone to send as a missionary, Carey decided to go himself. In 1793, he finally landed in Calcutta with his family and a physician accompanying him in his labors. The difficulties were many—on one occasion he wrote to his supporters in England that there were obstacles all around, and, characteristically, that there was no alternative but to move ahead! His zeal, and particularly his reports to England, resulted in new interest in missions, and he was eventually joined by a second contingent of missionaries. Since the British East India Company would not allow the new arrivals to settle in Calcutta, Carey moved his residence to nearby Serampore, and this became the headquarters of the entire enterprise. He and his associates—one of whom was a printer—felt that one of their first

Carey baptizing his first convert.

tasks was to make the Bible available to the Indian population. Carey had an unusual gift for learning languages. Before he died, he had translated the Bible, in whole or in part, into thirty-five languages—translations later criticized for the errors resulting from his limited knowledge of many of these tongues. He also devoted his efforts to putting an end to the custom of burning widows on their husbands' funeral pyres. On both scores, he achieved remarkable success.

Carey's work, and the reports that reached both Britain and the United States, inspired many to emulate him. Many of the missionary societies founded early in the nineteenth century owed their existence to his influence. Increasing numbers of Christians, having heard of Carey's exploits, felt called to similar careers. In 1813, when the charter of the British East India Company came up for renewal, Parliament included in the new charter a clause granting missionaries free access to areas under company control.

In India itself, Carey's work did not at first produce many converts. But toward the end of his career, it was clear that a firm foundation for a church had been established in the land and that others would continue his work. In the next generation, the Scotsman Alexander Duff became famous for his work in education, for he was convinced that the best way for Christianity to enter India was through education. As a result of his work and that of others, by the time India gained its independence a century later, many of the leaders of the new nation were either Christian or people profoundly influenced by the Christian faith.

Meanwhile, there were mass conversions among the lower classes. Protestant missionaries insisted that the caste system that prevailed in India was wrong. In Indian tradition, the very breaking of bread that took place in communion was a breaking of caste if it took place among people of varying castes. Therefore, many of the people termed *untouchable*, and several tribes who had traditionally been excluded from mainstream society, found Protestantism liberating and joined it. Likewise, many women found freedom in Christianity, and responded by assuming positions of responsibility within it. Most remarkable among them was Pandita Ramabai, who traveled to England and the United States, and then returned to India to devote the rest of her life to the education of women. As a result of her work, many women were able to make significant contributions both to the church and to Indian society.

In Southeast Asia, zones of colonial influence were separated by the once-powerful kingdom of Siam (now Thailand). East of it, French colonies appeared—in what was then called French Indochina—while the British took charge of Burma (now Myanmar), the area west of Siam. In the French area, Catholic missionaries organized their converts into separate villages where they could live according to Catholic teachings. As a result, the area was divided between Catholic and Buddhist villages until well into the twentieth century. In Burma, the most famous missionary was Adoniram Judson, an American Congregationalist sent by the American Board of Commissioners for Foreign Missions who became a Baptist on his way to the mission field. Following Carey's example, he and his wife translated Scripture into Burmese, Thai, and other languages. They gained few converts, but one of these, Ko Tha Byu, later began a movement of mass conversion among his tribe, the Karen—many of whom later sought refuge in the United States in the twenty-first century to flee military repression. In Siam, the only land of Southeast Asia that managed to preserve its independence, there were both Catholic and Protestant missionaries. Although their work was hindered by brief periods of persecution, by the end of the century they had succeeded in founding fairly strong churches.

China remained the great empire of the Far East. Christianity had been introduced repeatedly, and repeatedly it had been quashed under severe persecution and isolation. Late in the sixteenth century and early in the seventeenth, Ricci and his Jesuit companions had managed to found a small church (see Vol. I, Chapter 27). But then another period of isolationism set in, and by the beginning of the nineteenth century the small Catholic community in China was leading a precarious existence. Protestant missionaries had long dreamed of entering China. One of Carey's companions had already begun the monumental task of translating the Bible into Chinese—a translation that, like most others, was done with substantial help and creativity on the part of native speakers. Then the Scotsman Robert Morrison settled in Canton and devoted his life to translating the Bible and other books into Chinese. It took him seven years to gain his first convert, and he never had many. But his example, and the existence of a Chinese translation of Scripture, kept alive the dream of penetrating that vast land with the message of Christianity. The great difficulty, however, was that the Chinese government did not favor the presence of foreigners within its borders. Only a small number of those whom the Chinese considered Western barbarians were allowed in certain restricted areas, and it was through these ports that all trade took place.

Then the Opium War broke out (1839–1842). This was one of the most shameful episodes in the history of Western colonialism, for the British found themselves going to war against China in defense of the alleged right of British merchants to import opium into China in direct violation of Chinese imperial decrees. The Treaty of Nanjing, ending hostilities, granted the British the island of Hong Kong and opened five Chinese ports important to British trade. After these events, other powers followed the British example, using their military might to force ever-greater concessions from the Chinese. Many of the treaties forcing such concessions also made provisions for the presence of missionaries in Chinese territory, some also granting them special protection. Eventually, even Chinese Christians were covered by a number of special provisions—leading to what many called rice Christians, people who apparently embraced Christianity in order to enjoy privileges such as food. Soon missionaries from various countries and denominations arrived in China, and their initial success was greatly encouraging.

One unexpected by-product of Christian preaching was the Rebellion of Taiping—*the Heavenly Kingdom*. This movement was begun by Hong

Hong Xiuquan, a school-teacher inspired by Christian writings, led a rebellion aimed at bringing about the Heavenly Kingdon—Taiping.

Xiuquan, a school teacher who read a number of Christian treatises and decided the time had come to establish the *Heavenly Kingdom of the Great Peace*, over which he would reign. In that kingdom, all things would be held in common, there would be equality between the sexes, and there would be laws against prostitution, adultery, slavery, binding of girls' feet, opium, tobacco, and alcohol. In 1850, the movement led to open rebellion, and the troops of the Heavenly Kingdom won several important victories. In 1853, they established the Heavenly Capital in Nanjing, and even threatened the imperial city of Beijing. Finally, with the help of the Western powers, the imperial armies crushed the rebellion. It had lasted fifteen years, and resulted in twenty million deaths. (It is interesting to note that many missionaries who celebrated the revolutions and military heroes of their native lands opposed the Taiping Rebellion on the grounds that its violence was incompatible with Christian faith.)

It was during the Taiping Rebellion that J. Hudson Taylor first arrived in China. Forced to return to England by ill health, he then devoted his efforts to founding and leading the China Inland Mission, under whose

The victorious Taiping established their capital in Nanjing, and gained control of a large portion of China.

auspices he returned to China. The purpose of this organization was to evangelize China without introducing the divisions that existed in European and American Protestantism. It accepted missionaries of all denominations, and resulted in hundreds of churches in various areas of the country. It also refused to make use of the supposed advantages to be obtained by foreign protection, being aware that the use of such privileges created resentment among the Chinese and would eventually prove costly.

Taylor's predictions came to pass. The Boxer Rebellion of 1899–1901 was the violent expression of Chinese resentment of foreign intervention. It is estimated that well over thirty thousand Chinese Christians were killed— some of them after being tortured, or after being forced to drink the blood of others killed before them. The foreign diplomats in Beijing, who had been bickering over the spoils of China, remained under siege until an army of combined Western forces came to their succor. Eventually, the Western powers crushed the rebellion, and the imperial government was forced to make even greater concessions—including the payment of a huge indemnification. Several missionary agencies, having learned the lesson of the rebellion, refused to accept any payments. Eventually, all these upheavals led to the fall of the empire. In 1911, rebellion broke out again, the emperor was forced to abdicate, and the way was cleared for the creation of the Republic of the United Chinese Provinces. By then, Protestant missionaries numbered in the tens of thousands, churches were flourishing in every province, and increasing numbers of Chinese were taking positions of leadership in the church. The future appeared so bright that some Western observers began speaking of a conversion of the entire nation similar to what had taken place in the Roman Empire during Constantine's reign.

During the first half of the nineteenth century, Japan was entirely closed to all Western contact or influence. In 1854, Commodore M.C. Perry of the U.S. Navy forced the Japanese to sign their first commercial treaty with a Western power. Then Britain, France, the Netherlands, and Russia followed suit. In 1864, a joint Western force put an end to all resistance to foreign

In the Boxer Rebellion much pent-up resentment against foreign intervention was expressed, resulting in the deaths of tens of thousands of missionaries and their converts, and in considerable damage to church properties.

influence. The Japanese response was to acknowledge Western technological superiority and to seek to learn as much as possible from the West. By the end of the century, Japan was an industrial and military power capable of defeating the Chinese and the Russians; in 1910, it annexed the ancient kingdom of Korea. This process of rapid Westernization aided the work of missionaries, who began arriving shortly after Commodore Perry's exploit. Soon there were churches in all the major cities of the nation, and native leadership emerged. It is also interesting to note that near Nagasaki Protestant missionaries found about a hundred thousand people who still retained vestiges of what their ancestors had learned centuries earlier from Francis Xavier and other Jesuit missionaries (see Vol. I, Chapter 37).

The Japanese had learned Commodore Perry's lesson well, and in 1876 they forced Korea to sign its first commercial treaty. Soon Korea found itself signing similar treaties with the United States (1882), Great Britain (1883), and Russia (1884). This opened the way for the first Protestant missionaries to Korea: Methodists and Presbyterians from the United States who arrived in 1884. Their strategy was to found churches that from the very beginning could be self-supporting, and to develop the native leadership necessary for such churches. The results were astounding. Although Japanese occupation in 1910 created difficulties for the churches, they continued to flourish, and soon Korea had more Christians per capita than any other Far East nation besides the Philippines.

The Philippines had been conquered and colonized much earlier by the Spanish, and therefore at the opening of the nineteenth century the population was mostly Catholic. The example of the Spanish-American colonies, however, led to increased hopes for independence, which was proclaimed in 1896, although not achieved until fifty years later. Two years later, as a result of the Spanish-American War, Spain ceded the Philippines to the United States. This did not stop the struggle for independence, which continued until the islands were finally made independent in 1946. During the struggle against Spain, the Catholic Church was an instrument in the hands of the colonial government, and this gave rise to the Filipino Independent Church—which later was influenced by Protestantism and departed even further from Catholicism. Protestants entered the islands during the period of American occupation, but by 1914 the number of churches they had founded remained small.

Indonesia, originally colonized by the Portuguese, was mostly in Dutch hands by the beginning of the nineteenth century. The Dutch East India

Reports of the voyages of Captain James Cook awakened interest in distant lands, and in missions to them.

Company, which until 1798 had been in charge of the colonial enterprise, had been inimical to missions. Therefore, it was mostly during the nineteenth century that substantial efforts were made to reach the Indonesian population. Corrupt governments and outright exploitation were strongly criticized by Christians in the Netherlands, and in 1870 a measure of reform was introduced. Meanwhile, English adventurer James Brooke had been named *rajah*—or king—of the state of Sarawak on the island of Borneo. He and his successors (first his son Sir Charles Anthony Brooke, then his grandson Sir Charles Vyner Brooke) invited missionaries into their territories, hoping that they would improve education and medical services. They also encouraged the immigration of Chinese Christians. By the end of the nineteenth century Christianity had made great numeric gains in Indonesia—although at present the region of Sarawak is part of Malasia.

To the east and south of these lands were other territories known only vaguely by Europeans since the sixteenth century, but which were brought to the attention of Britain by the explorations of Captain James Cook between 1768 and 1779. This was the case of William Carey, whose interest in foreign lands was awakened by Cook's voyages. The largest of these lands, Australia and New Zealand, were soon colonized by the British, who established in them churches similar to those in their homeland. Both the aboriginal inhabitants of Australia and the Maoris of New Zealand were decimated by European immigrants and the diseases they brought with them, and it fell to the churches to protest against the mistreatment and exploitation of these native people. In New Zealand, movements such as the *Hau Hau* and *Ringatu,* which combined ancient Maori traditions with Christian teachings and a desire for justice and vindication enjoyed a wide following among the Maoris into the twenty-first century. Smaller islands of the Pacific at first drew the interest of adventurers and dreamers, then of missionaries, and, finally, of imperial powers who entered the scene in their mad rush for colonies after 1870. By the end of the century, virtually every island had been claimed by a foreign power. By then, most of the population of Polynesia was Christian, and there were also churches in almost all the islands of Melanesia and Micronesia. Only in the remotest regions—the interior of New Guinea, for example—had the name of Christ not yet been proclaimed.

AFRICA AND THE MUSLIM WORLD

For centuries, Muslim power had blocked European expansion toward the south and the southeast. Beyond the Muslim lands on the north coast of Africa were barren lands, and beyond these were tropical areas deemed unhealthy for Europeans. Therefore, Europe came to see Africa and the Muslim world as obstacles to reaching the riches of the East. But during the course of the nineteenth century that perspective changed radically. At the beginning of the century, most of the Near East and the north coast of Africa belonged to the Ottoman Empire, whose capital was Constantinople—renamed *Istanbul* in 1930. By the opening of World War I, Great Britain, France, and Italy had control of the north coast of Africa, and the Ottoman Empire was about to disappear. This led many to consider the possibility of beginning missionary work in those areas and in other traditionally Muslim lands.

However, there were already other Christians in the region—it had, after all been the birthplace of Christianity. Therefore, the main issue for Western missionaries was how their work should relate to those older churches. In general, Roman Catholics sought to bring entire bodies of Eastern Christians into communion with Rome and obedience to the pope. Such groups, while keeping their rites and traditions, in fact became Roman

Catholics, known as *Uniates*. In order to deal with issues affecting them in a particular way, the Congregation of Eastern Rites was founded in Rome in 1862. Although Roman Catholics also sought to convert Muslims, they had relatively little success. Protestants, on the other hand, often sought to cooperate with the ancient Eastern churches, hoping that such cooperation would bring about a renewal in the life of those churches. This program did achieve a measure of success, but in the end it created tensions within the ancient churches, which then divided. While the conservative wing returned to its older practices, the more progressive simply became Protestant. It was from such schisms that Protestantism gained the majority of its earliest adherents, although eventually it also began making converts from the Muslim population. Such work was particularly successful in Egypt, Syria, and Lebanon.

There were few European enclaves in black Africa at the beginning of the nineteenth century. Portuguese rule in Angola and Mozambique did not extend far inland. In 1652, the Dutch had established a colony on the Cape of Good Hope. Shortly thereafter, the French opened a trading post in Senegal. In 1799, the British founded Sierra Leone as a land for freed slaves returning to Africa. That was the extent of European colonization in Africa at the beginning of the century. In sharp contrast, by 1914 the only independent states remaining in the entire continent were Ethiopia and Liberia—and the latter was a creation of the early abolitionist movement in the United States.

The process of colonization was fairly slow in the early nineteenth century. The British took the Cape from the Dutch, who moved north and founded new colonies. In 1820, the first American blacks arrived in Liberia, which became independent in 1847. Meanwhile, missionaries were penetrating into areas never before seen by Europeans, and reporting on the ravishes of the slave trade and the economic resources of the interior of Africa. In 1867, diamonds were found in South Africa. France sought to combine its holdings in Algeria with those in Senegal. Germany entered the contest in 1884 by taking possession of Namibia. Leopold II of Belgium, whose powers in his own kingdom were limited, took the colonization of the Congo as a personal enterprise, and in 1908 the area officially became the Belgian Congo. In 1885, the Spanish claimed Rio de Oro and Spanish Guinea. Then Italy took Eritrea. By then, the rest of the continent had been divided among the British, French, and German.

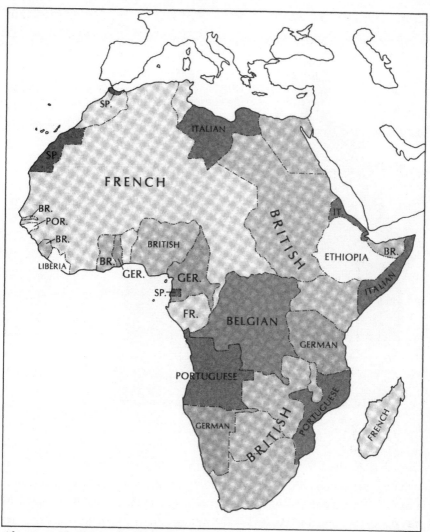

Africa 1914: The Height of Colonial Expansion

All these events aroused missionary interest in Europe and the United States. In general, Catholic missions were most successful in Catholic colonies, while Protestants gained more adherents in British and German colonies. Catholics were also hindered there by disputes over questions of jurisdiction—Portugal still claimed its ancient rights of patronage over the entire African church, while France and Belgium disputed the Congo valley.

*This statue in Cathedral Square in Edinburgh honors the memory of
David Livingstone.*

The most famous Protestant missionary to Africa was David Livingstone,
a native of Scotland who repeatedly traveled across southern Africa preaching the gospel, healing the sick—for he was also a physician—and taking
copious notes of all the marvels he saw. Livingstone's hope and purpose was
not only that people would be converted to Christianity, but also that the
horrors of the slave trade would be stopped by opening Africa to legitimate
trade. In pursuit of that end, he sometimes traveled as a missionary and
sometimes as a representative of the British government, always reporting
what he saw and gaining the trust and love of the many Africans who came
to know him. His writings did much to arouse interest in black Africa in
both his native Scotland and throughout the North Atlantic, and were important factors contributing to abolition of the slave trade.

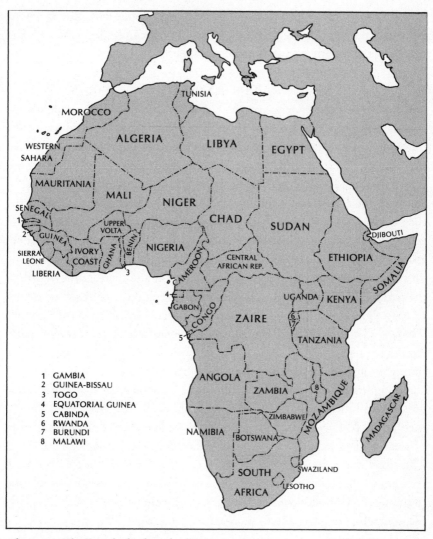

1 GAMBIA
2 GUINEA-BISSAU
3 TOGO
4 EQUATORIAL GUINEA
5 CABINDA
6 RWANDA
7 BURUNDI
8 MALAWI

Africa 1984: The Growth of Independent Nations

By 1914, not only was most of Africa in colonial hands, but in every one of those territories there were Christian churches. This was true both in the major cities and in many remote villages in the interior of the continent. By then, many of these churches were training their own leadership and extending their work to new areas. One of the first African-born missionaries, Samuel Crowther—ordained in 1843—enthusiastically related that the experience of worshiping and preaching in his native tongue was akin to having a dream. But a long struggle would follow, as African leaders emerged who sought equality with foreign-born missionaries.

LATIN AMERICA

The impact of independence on the Catholic Church of Latin America has already been noted in Chapter 29. Independence, however, also led to the founding of Protestant churches in every nation of Latin America. At first, this was the result of immigration. The new governments were convinced that they should encourage immigration for a number of reasons. First of all, since their goal was to imitate the industrial development of countries such as Great Britain, it was hoped that immigration from those areas would provide the experienced personnel necessary for such development. Second, there were still vast expanses of untilled, arable land. Immigrants settling on such lands would bring them into production and increase the wealth of the nation. Third, it was necessary to introduce and disseminate ideas contrary to those coming from Spain and still fostered by many in the Catholic Church. Therefore, throughout the entire nineteenth century, several Latin American governments—particularly the liberal governments—encouraged immigration from Europe and the United States.

To implement that policy, it was necessary to remember that many of the prospective immigrants were Protestants who were not willing to abandon their faith. To force them to renounce it would encourage the immigration of unprincipled hypocrites—a bitter lesson that Mexico learned in Texas. Therefore, many governments, even in countries that did not extend such freedom to their own citizens, issued laws guaranteeing freedom of religion to immigrants. Soon, however, they saw the incongruence of such laws, and felt compelled to grant their own citizens equal rights. Thus, the policy of encouraging foreign immigration eventually favored the spread of Protestantism among the native population.

Most of the early immigrants came from Europe. Very few came from the United States (if one discounts those who moved into territories taken from Mexico), for it was the time of North American expansion to the West, and there were ample lands to be had there without migrating to Latin America. Large numbers of Scots went to Argentina, Uruguay, and Chile, where they could find climates similar to their own, and in many cases better economic conditions than they had at home. Therefore, long before the first Latin

Americans were converted to Protestantism, Protestant services were held in English in the major cities of southern Latin America.

A particularly interesting case of mission-by-immigration was that of James Theodore Holly and his companions, one hundred and ten black Episcopalians who emigrated to Haiti from the United States hoping to find greater freedom and to preach the gospel to Haitians. After eighteen months, forty-three had died of various diseases. Most of the survivors decided to return to the United States or to move on to Jamaica. But Holly and a handful remained and founded a church. In 1876, Holly was consecrated by the Episcopal Church to be the first bishop of the Apostolic Orthodox Church of Haiti—later the Episcopal Church of Haiti.

Immigration eventually led to missions among native Latin Americans. The first missionary to arrive was probably the Scotsman James Thomson, a Baptist representative of the British and Foreign Bible Society who arrived in Buenos Aires in 1818. Over the next few years, he visited several countries— from Argentina and Chile to Cuba and Mexico—and then departed for other lands. In Colombia, with the aid of some liberal priests, he founded a Bible society. His work consisted mostly in the distribution of Spanish Bibles and in personal discussions with priests and others. It was during the second half of the century that permanent Protestant work began in most South American countries. The first record of a Protestant sermon given in Spanish in Buenos Aires is dated 1867. At approximately the same time, the Presbyterian Church was beginning work in Chile. In general, it was after 1870 that missionary agencies from the United States began taking an active interest in Latin America.

One of the factors inhibiting such interest, in Europe as well as in the United States, was the presence of Roman Catholicism in the area. To organize missions to Latin America was to imply that Catholics were not Christian—or that their Christianity was defective—a step that many Protestant agencies and churches were not willing to take. Particularly among Anglicans and Episcopalians, there was strong opposition to missions among Catholics. Therefore, the earliest Anglican missions in Latin America worked among Indians in Tierra del Fuego.

By the beginning of the twentieth century, however, Protestant missions had made great strides in Latin America. Most of the early missionaries were concerned not only with the salvation of souls, but also with both the physical health and the education of the populations they served. Therefore,

Protestants soon became known for their work in education and medicine. Also, as the prestige of the United States grew, so did the churches with ties to it. And, while most of the early missionaries had been representatives of the larger denominations, by the beginning of the twentieth century there was an increasing number of missionaries from small, conservative denominations.

Other new churches in Latin America were the result of schisms. In both Mexico and Puerto Rico, groups that broke away from the Catholic Church eventually became Episcopalians. In Chile, a small, charismatic group expelled from the Methodist Church in 1910 formed the Methodist Pentecostal Church, which soon outgrew its parent body (see Chapter 37). Thus, by the time World War I broke out in 1914, there were significant numbers of Protestants in every country in Latin America, both in churches that were the direct result of missions, and in others that had been born in Latin America itself.

THE ECUMENICAL MOVEMENT

In retrospect, it may well be that the most significant development in Christianity in the nineteenth century was the beginning of a truly universal church. Until then, Christianity had been almost entirely a Western religion. By 1914, there were churches in almost every nation on the globe, and these churches were beginning to develop their own leadership as well as their own understanding of what it meant to be Christian within their particular context. This was the birth of the ecumenical movement in two senses. First of all, the very word *ecumenical* means *pertaining to the entire inhabited earth*. Therefore, never before had Christianity been as *ecumenical* as it became in the nineteenth century. Second, if by ecumenical one means that which has to do with the unity of Christians, it is clear that one of the driving forces leading toward the modern Christian unity movement was the missionary movement.

In the United States, where people of different Christian confessions lived next to one another, ecumenical sentiments gained ground as the result of various causes that appealed to people across denominational lines: abolitionism, temperance, fundamentalism, liberalism, and so forth. But even there, since denominational allegiance usually posed no obstacle to the task at hand, divisions were seldom questioned. Perhaps the most serious such questioning was the founding of the Disciples of Christ (see Chapter 27)—

and in the end they became one more denomination.

In overseas missions, however, cooperation became mandatory. Bible translations prepared by missionaries of one denomination were used by others, and it soon became apparent that coordination in such efforts would be good stewardship of limited resources. Also, where such vast lands were waiting to hear the word of the gospel, it made sense to agree on which denomination or missionary agency would take responsibility for each area. Most important of all, however, was the importance of presenting a single interpretation of the gospel to people who had never heard of it rather than presenting a number of competing interpretations, each claiming to be true. Divisions that seemed perfectly natural in Europe or the United States made little sense in southern India or Japan. Therefore, those who were consumed with a burning zeal for the conversion of the world were soon convinced that Christians of different traditions must work together.

The great forerunner of the ecumenical movement was none other than William Carey, who suggested that an international missionary conference be convened at Cape Town, South Africa, in 1810. He hoped that such a conference would bring together missionaries and missionary agencies from all over the world in order to exchange information and coordinate their plans. At that time, many set great store by their particular traditions, thus, Carey's suggestion fell on deaf ears. It would be exactly a hundred years before his call would be heeded. Meanwhile, many conferences took place on a smaller scale, both in the sending countries and fewer people in the mission field.

Finally, in 1910, the first World Missionary Conference gathered in Edinburgh, Scotland. In contrast to earlier conferences, this one would be attended by official delegates of missionary societies, their numbers in proportion to each agency's financial contribution to the entire global missionary enterprise. It was also stipulated that the conference would deal exclusively with missions to non-Christians, and that therefore there would be no discussion of Protestant missions among Catholics in Latin America, or among the Eastern Orthodox in the Near East. It was also decided that questions of faith and order would not be discussed, for it was feared that such discussions could only lead to further alienation. In preparation for the conference, hundreds of people around the world participated in preliminary studies, keeping in contact with the entire picture through correspondence and regional or local conferences. When the conference finally convened, most representatives were British or North American. There was also a significant number of representatives from the rest of Europe. Only seventeen of the participants came from younger churches—three of them as special guests of the conference's executive committee.

The conference fully achieved its basic goal of exchanging information and plans, but its significance was far greater. For the first time, there had been an international conference of such magnitude whose participants were official representatives from missionary societies of various denominations. This in itself paved the way for similar meetings in which subjects other than missions would be discussed. Second, the conference appointed a Continuation Committee, thereby indicating that a movement had begun that was fully expected to continue. The work of that committee resulted in further studies, conferences, and eventually in the formation of the International Missionary Council. Third, the conference gave international stature to many who would become the leaders of the ecumenical movement in the early decades of the twentieth century—foremost among them Methodist layman John R. Mott. Finally, the conference of Edinburgh was important even in what it excluded—particularly issues of faith and order and of missions in Latin America—for out of such exclusions developed the Faith and Order movement and the Committee on Cooperation in Latin America. The former would be one of the strongest currents that led to the founding of the World Council of Churches in 1948. In short, the 1910 World Missionary Conference of Edinburgh was the most important forerunner of the modern ecumenical movement.

Meanwhile, international tensions were increasing, and Christians felt called to gather, not only to discuss ecclesiastical matters but also to seek ways to preserve international peace. On August 2, 1914, in the city of Constance, Germany, a world organization promoting peace through the churches was founded. That very day World War I exploded.

34

Roman Catholic Christianity

Let us be free of the scandal of having some nations, the majority of whose citizens call themselves Christian, enjoying great riches, while others do not have what is needful and suffer hunger, disease, and all sorts of misery.

SECOND VATICAN COUNCIL

When we last directed our attention to the Roman Catholic Church, in Chapter 32, we saw that its reaction to the modern world was mostly one of fear and condemnation. Among the reasons for such a reaction were the loss of the papal states to the new nation of Italy, the fear that the secular states would hinder the work of the Catholic Church, and the concern that minds would be led astray by modern ideas. In general, the history of the Catholic Church until the pontificate of John XXIII, in the second half of the twentieth century, was a continuation of the policies and attitudes set at the Council of Trent, mostly in reaction against Protestantism. At the same time, there were those within the Catholic Church who felt that an attitude of condemnation and wholesale rejection of modern trends was both a theological and a pastoral mistake. During the earlier part of the twentieth century, such loyal critics would repeatedly express their opinions and alternatives, only to be suppressed or ignored. Therefore, the history of Roman Catholicism during the first six decades of the twentieth century is to a large extent the history of the conflict between those who wished to continue in the direction set at Trent and at the First Vatican Council, and those who wished to see more openness in the Church and more creative encounters with the challenges of the modern world.

JOHN XXIII AND THE SECOND VATICAN COUNCIL

The election of the next pope was more difficult than the previous one had been. When the election of Cardinal Roncalli was announced, after the eleventh ballot, many commented that the seventy-seven-year-old cardinal had been elected as a transitional pope, to give the cardinals time to determine the course to follow in the future. The elderly pope took the name of John XXIII, and though his pontificate was brief (it lasted from 1958 to 1963), it was marked by momentous changes. His very decision to take the name of John, tainted by the bitter memories of the Avignon papacy and the Pisan antipope John XXIII, was an indication that the new pope was willing to break new ground. He soon distressed many in the curia, as well as his guards, by his unprecedented visits to the poorer neighborhoods of Rome. Some even voiced fears that he might be too simple a man for the heavy responsibilities that rested on his shoulders. But he was a man of wide experience and profound wisdom, who had shown in delicate posts in Bulgaria, Istanbul, and France that he understood the intricacies of negotiation and diplomacy. Also, by having lived both in Turkish Istanbul and in secularized Paris, he knew the degree to which the church had cut off communication with the world at large. His great task would be to restore that lost communication. It would be a task requiring all his diplomatic skills, for there were many in the curia and in other high positions in the church who did not share his perception of the situation.

An old man with a vast mission, John XXIII felt the need to move rapidly. Thus, three months after his election he announced his plan to call an ecumenical council. Many in the curia did not approve of the idea. In times past, most councils had been called in order to deal with a pressing issue—usually a heresy thought to be particularly dangerous. Furthermore, after the declaration of papal infallibility by the First Vatican Council, there were those who thought that the age of councils had come to an end, and that henceforth popes should rule the church as absolute monarchs. Indeed, from the time of Pius IX there had been a constant tendency toward further centralization. But Pope John saw matters otherwise. He insisted on calling other bishops "my brother bishops," and on asking their advice rather than commanding them. He was also convinced that the time had come for a total "updating"—in Italian, an *aggiornamento*—of the church, and that this could only be done through the combined wisdom and concerns of the bishops of the entire church. It is reported that when some among the curia questioned the need for a council, the pope simply opened the windows and said, "Let fresh air in."

The preparatory work for the council took more than two years. Meanwhile, the pope issued the encyclical *Mater et Magistra,* which was taken by many Catholic activists in the causes of justice as papal approval of their work. Finally, on October 11, 1962, Pope John formally opened the Second Vatican Council. Few expected that this assembly would mark a radical departure from the course the church had followed during the last four hundred years. The documents to be discussed and approved by the council had been prepared by the curia, and in general did little more than reaffirm traditional Catholic doctrine, warning against the dangers of the time. But the pope had also taken steps to lead the council in other directions. The previous year, he had created the Secretariat for the Promotion of Christian Unity, thus indicating his seriousness in the pursuit of a rapprochement with other Christians, and his intention to have the council pursue this concern. His opening speech also set a tone that was different from most of the preparatory documents, for he indicated that it was time for the church to respond to the concerns of the modern world with words of understanding and encouragement, rather than with blistering condemnations. These goals were further aided by the presence of non-Catholic observers—thirty-one at the outset, and ninety-three by the time the Council closed its last session—and especially by the composition of the assembly itself. Indeed, only 46 percent of the prelates present came from Western Europe, Canada, and the United States. Fully 42 percent represented Latin America, Asia, and black Africa. More than half of the bishops present came from churches of such limited resources that their living expenses while at the Council had to be covered with funds from the richer churches. Thus, the composition of the Council itself pointed to the shifts in the centers of world Christianity that marked the twentieth century—as we shall see in Chapter 37. Such bishops were deeply concerned with the need to address the plight of the poor, to speak to the non-Christian world, and in general to speak a word of compassion and understanding rather than of self-righteous condemnation. Therefore, the pope's call for the "medicine of mercy" in his opening speech did not fall on deaf ears.

Very soon, it became apparent that the majority of the assembly wished to see vast changes in the life of the church, and particularly in the manner in which it addressed the modern world. The first document to be discussed

*The Second Vatican Council turned a new page in the history of
Roman Catholicism.*

dealt with the liturgy. Of all the documents prepared beforehand, this was
the one that proposed most significant changes, for liturgical renewal had
been one of the concerns of the previous pope, and many in the curia had
come to accept the need for a renewal of the liturgy. Even so, the conservative minority sought to block the proposed changes; but those who supported an updating of the liturgy won the day. When the text was returned
to the commission that had drafted it, the instructions accompanying it
were a clear defeat for the conservatives. From that point on, the documents
written by the preparatory commissions were generally returned for rewrit-
ing, with instructions for drastic changes—and even with changes in the
composition of the commissions themselves.

Pope John did not live to see his council issue its first document, for he died in June 1963. The next pope took the name of Paul, usually associated with the Council of Trent, and some conservatives hoped that he would dissolve the Council, or at least take strong measures to hinder its deliberations. But Paul VI (1963–1978) almost immediately declared his intention that the Council would continue its work. While there is no doubt that he was more conservative than John XXIII, during the first session of the council he had seen the degree to which Catholic leaders throughout the world felt the need for significant new departures. When the second session opened, on September 29, 1963, he called those present to "build a bridge between the Church and the modern world."

Needing no further encouragement, the Council followed the pope's advice—probably sometimes with more alacrity than Paul VI would have wished. The document on the liturgy, which from the outset had been the most progressive, was approved by the assembly; but the rest were sent back to be redrafted along lines more consonant with the church's new openness to the modern world. The *Constitution on the Sacred Liturgy*, the most tangible result of this second session, soon made its impact felt among the faithful throughout the world, for it authorized the use of the vernacular languages to a degree not permitted before. It also declared that:

> As long as the essential unity of the Roman rite is preserved, in the revision of the liturgical books steps shall be taken for proper variations and adaptations according to the needs of various groups, regions, and peoples, particularly in mission territories.

The commissions that would then work on the redrafting of the various documents were reconstituted, with greater participation by members elected by the assembly. There were indications that the pope was not happy with the turn of events, and some even feared that he might declare an end to the Council. But Paul VI did not resort to such extreme measures, and the third session of the Council (September 14 to November 21, 1964) again proved that any documents presented before it that did not conform to its reformist spirit would be rejected and returned to commission. The Council issued documents on the church, the Eastern churches, and ecumenism. Many of its members were distressed to see the pope add an *explanatory note* to the document on the church, clarifying that episcopal collegiality was to be understood in terms of the primacy of the pope, and also add some interpolations to the decree on ecumenism—already approved by the assembly—that non-Catholics would find less acceptable than the original document. In addition, while many in the Council had emphasized the centrality of Christ, counteracting the extremes to which devotion to Mary could be taken, the pope on his own initiative declared the Virgin to be the "Mother of the Church."

Notwithstanding the implications of these papal actions, when the Council gathered for its fourth and last session (September 14 to December 8, 1965), its members were determined to see its work carried to fruition. There was bitter debate on the document on religious freedom, which was sternly opposed by conservatives from nations where Catholics were in the majority. But once that last attempt failed, the opposition collapsed, and for the rest of the session the more progressive in attendance maintained complete control of the deliberations. Therefore, with relative ease the Council issued fairly progressive documents on bishops, priests and their formation, the laity, the church and non-Christians, missionary activity, and so forth. The *Constitution on the Church*, (or *Lumen gentium)*, did not place its emphasis on the hierarchy and the clergy as the original document prepared before the Council had done, but instead emphasized the notion of the church as *the people of God*, of whom both laity and clergy are part. Equally significant in manifesting a spirit different from that which had prevailed in Catholicism for centuries were the documents on religious freedom, on Christianity and Judaism, and on the church in the modern world. The first of these declared that the religious freedom of individuals as well as of groups must be respected, and that all religious groups have the right to organize according to their own principles "as long as the just requirements of public order are not violated." On Christianity and Judaism, the Council expressly rejected much traditional prejudice against the Jews, and acknowledged the unique connection between the faith of the church and that of Israel. The *Pastoral Constitution on the Church in the Modern World* is the longest document ever issued by a council, and it sets a tone that is drastically different from the nineteenth century. While insisting on Catholic principles of faith and morality, it shows genuine openness to the positive aspects of modernity, and deals creatively with family life, economic and social issues, politics, technology and science, the significance and diversity of human cultures, and so forth. In general, its tone is set by its opening statement:

The joys and hopes, the griefs and anxieties of people of our time, particularly of those who are poor or in any way afflicted, are the joys and hopes, the griefs and anxieties of Christ's followers. Theirs is a community of people, people who, in union with Christ and with the guidance of the Holy Spirit, move forward toward the Kingdom of the Father and carry the message of salvation intended for all. For this reason this community knows that it is deeply united with humankind and its history.

By the time the Council adjourned, it was clear that the Catholic Church had entered a new epoch in its history. Many steps still needed to be taken in order to implement the decisions of the Council. In many areas there would be resistance; in others, changes would be rapid, and the Vatican would move to moderate them. After the adjournment of the Council, Paul VI moved slowly, perhaps fearing that changes that were too rapid could lead to schism or at least to the loss of some of the more conservative members of the Catholic Church. In 1968, he signaled his conservative inclination by issuing the encyclical *Humanae vitae,* in which he banned all artificial methods of birth control, overruling a papal commission that had recommended the admission of some such methods. The feared schism did occur, however, under the leadership of a conservative bishop. But it did not carry with itself many members, and twenty years after its first session it was clear that the Second Vatican Council had set in motion a process that could not be stopped. An example of this continuing influence was the American bishops' declaration on nuclear war and the arms race, a declaration that was much opposed by some as undue interference on the part of the church in political and military matters. In their declaration, the bishops were simply spelling out the declaration made earlier by the Second Vatican Council, that the arms race could produce no permanent or true peace. Later, in 1986, the American bishops issued *A Pastoral Letter on Catholic Social Teaching and the U.S. Economy*—an even more controversial statement on the social and economic order.

FROM PAUL VI TO BENEDICT XVI

Paul VI died in 1979 and, after the extremely brief pontificate of John Paul I, was succeeded by John Paul II, the first non-Italian pope since the sixteenth century. As a Pole, the new pope had known the struggle of the church under both Germans and Russians, and had no illusions about either Fascism or Communism. His pontificate was marked by growing tension in Poland between the Communist government and the Catholic Church, encouraged in its resistance by the election of one of its own to the see of Peter—and led by Catholic layman Lech Walesa. This eventually led to the fall of Communism in Poland, and to the nation's freedom from the Soviet Empire. In that struggle, the church in general, and the pope in particular, played a decisive role, widely acknowledged by the Polish population at large.

The events in Poland were soon followed elsewhere by others of equally cataclysmic import, ultimately leading to the dismemberment of the Soviet Empire, and in Russia itself Communism was overthrown. The impact of such changes would be felt most strongly in Eastern Europe, and therefore by Orthodox churches, but it was also felt within the Roman Catholic Church. Partly as a result of the new conditions among Eastern Orthodox, in 1995 John Paul II issued the encyclical *Ut unum sint*, calling for greater efforts to bridge the distance separating Catholics, Orthodox, and Protestants.

During the pontificate of John Paul II, several issues that had long been brewing came to the foreground. One of these was the accusation of rampant sexual abuse—particularly abuse of children—leveled at the clergy. Damages awarded by courts in cases of such abuse, particularly in North America and Europe, forced the Catholic Church to pay enormous sums to those who had suffered abuse, and the pope named a special commission to investigate such matters in the United States, and to set policy for dealing with sexual abusers. John Paul was also forced to face the issue of women's ordination, which had come to the foreground among Protestants in the second half of the twentieth century, and which now became a subject of debate among many Catholics. In 1995, half a million Catholics in Austria signed a petition for the ordination of women and against the requirement of celibacy for the priesthood. The pope staunchly opposed all of this. Also under his leadership, Roman Catholicism throughout the world reaffirmed its condemnation of abortion, at a time when several traditionally Catholic nations were legalizing it.

While conservative on issues having to do with the life of the clergy and those with monastic vows, and on matters of personal morality, John Paul II spoke strong words on the plight of the poor and the injustice of their oppression. He issued directives against priests holding political office—and made his feelings on the matter known in a visit to Nicaragua, where he was photographed wagging an accusatory finger at the Minister of Culture, Father Ernesto Cardenal—but also insisted that the Church be involved in issues of justice. Therefore, he was characterized both as conservative and as progressive, depending on the vantage point of the observer and the matter at issue. It should also be noted that it was probably during John Paul II's pontificate that the number of Roman Catholics in the world surpassed one billion.

John Paul II died in 2005 and was succeeded by German Cardinal Joseph Ratzinger, who took the name of Benedict XVI. (Significantly, the Catholic Church, which had not had a non-Italian pope since Adrian VI in 1522–1523, now elected two consecutive non-Italian popes. And at the time of Ratzinger's election, several prelates from outside the North Atlantic had been considered for the position.) In 1981, Ratzinger had been appointed by John Paul II to head the Congregation of the Doctrine of the Faith—a body created to guard Catholic orthodoxy in lieu of the Inquisition. In that role, he had become known for his conservative stance—particularly for his two directives against liberation theology (see Chapter 37). At the point of his election, some feared that his papacy would be dominated by his conservative stance; but the early years of his pontificate indicated that he was aware that new conditions in the world—and even resistance among many Catholics—required more moderate measures. Thus, in 2009, while insisting on celibacy as a requirement for the priesthood, he declared himself ready to accept into the priesthood married Anglican clergy who converted to Catholicism—an action that some saw as one of ecumenical openness, and others called "fishing in the troubled waters" of an Anglican communion deeply divided over the ordination of homosexuals. Three years earlier, in a similar vein, he had dropped the traditional title of patriarch of the West in what could be interpreted a gesture of openness to Eastern Orthodoxy, but the patriarch of Constantinople interpreted as expanding the claims of the papacy, pointing out that Benedict still retained the titles of *supreme pontiff* and *vicar of Christ*. Also once again, as during the reign of his predecessor, the issue of sexual abuse of children by priests, and of the hierarchy's attempts to cover up such practices, drew much criticism and demanded much of his attention.

THEOLOGICAL DEVELOPMENTS

The openness of the Second Vatican Council surprised the world, which was not acquainted with the undercurrents of thought that had long been moving within the Catholic Church. But the theological work that led to it had been taking place for half a century. Experiments such as the worker priests were the result of theological stirrings that Rome did not regard with pleasure. But, above all, there were a number of theologians whose Catholic faith was never in doubt but whose work was either rejected or ignored by the Vatican.

Probably the most original of these theologians was Pierre Teilhard de Chardin (1881–1955). The son of a family of the French aristocracy, at an early age Teilhard decided to join the Jesuits. He was ordained a priest in 1911. When World War I broke out, he refused the rank of captain—which he would have had as a chaplain—and served as a corporal, carrying the wounded in stretchers. When the war ended, he was admitted as a full member of the Society of Jesus, and in 1922 he completed his doctorate in paleontology. He had always been interested in the theory of evolution, not as a denial of creation, but rather as a scientific way of understanding the inner workings of God's creative power. His first writings on the relation between faith and evolution, however, brought swift condemnation from Rome. He was prohibited from publishing further works on theology, and was sent to serve in China, where it was expected that he could do little damage. As an obedient priest, he submitted. The ban prevented him from publishing his manuscripts, but did not prevent him from continuing to write. Therefore, while pursuing his paleontological work in China, he also continued his theological work, and gave his manuscripts to a few trusted friends. In 1929, he was instrumental in the identification of the Sinanthropus skull, which further confirmed the principle of evolution and brought him acclaim from within the international scientific community. Still Rome refused to allow him to publish his philosophical and theological works, now circulating among friends in France. Finally, in 1955, after his death, his friends published his works, which immediately won wide attention.

While accepting the general principles of the theory of evolution, Teilhard rejected the proposal that the survival of the fittest is the guiding force behind evolution. Instead, he proposed the "cosmic law of complexity and consciousness"—a pull in evolution toward the more complex and the more highly conscious. Thus, what we see at any given stage of evolution is a number of organisms that represent different stages or spheres in the evolutionary process. This evolution begins with the "stuff of the universe," which is then organized into the *geosphere*—matter organized into molecules, and molecules into bodies. The next stage is the *biosphere*, in which life appears. From this emerges the *noosphere*, in which life attains consciousness of itself. At this point, evolution does not end, but rather takes on a conscious dimension. Humans as we now know them are not yet the end of the evolutionary process. On the contrary, we are still part of ongoing evolution, leading to human *hominization*. What is characteristic of this new stage is that, as conscious beings, we are involved in our own evolution.

But we are not left without guidance on what human evolution should be. The evolutionary movement has an *omega point*, the converging point of maturation of the entire cosmic process. Indeed, to understand evolution one must not look at it from beginning to end, but rather from end to beginning. It is the end that makes the rest of the process meaningful. And that end, that—*omega point*—is Jesus Christ. In him a new stage of evolution— the final stage—has appeared: the *Christosphere*. Just as humanity and divinity are perfectly united without confusion in Christ, in the end each of us will be perfectly united with God, while also being perfectly ourselves. The church, the body of Christ, is the new historic reality centered in the omega point. Thus, Teilhard combined science with theology and even with a strong mystical inclination. But, in contrast to most mystical traditions, he was a world-affirming mystic.

Even among the many who did not accept Teilhard's grand cosmic scheme, his influence could be seen. His attempt to look at the evolutionary process "from end to beginning" encouraged modern theologians, both Catholic and Protestant, to look again at eschatology—that is, at the doctrine of the "last things." For very significant sectors of contemporary theology, eschatology proved a valuable starting point, rather than an appendix to the rest of theology. Second, Teilhard's emphasis on the continuing evolutionary process, and on our conscious participation in it, encouraged other theologians to explore the field of human participation in the divine purposes, and to look upon humanity as an active agent in the shaping of history. Finally, his this-worldly mysticism inspired many to relate their devotional life to their political activism.

Henri de Lubac (1896–1991), also a French Jesuit and a friend of Teilhard's, is another example of the theology that was developing within the

Roman Catholic Church, even against the wishes of the Vatican, during the first half of the twentieth century. Together with Jean Daniélou (1905–1974), de Lubac edited a voluminous series of ancient Christian writings. This sound, scholarly series was also intended for modern audiences, and thus reflected de Lubac's concern that the modern world and Christian tradition be combined in a dynamic and creative tension. He felt that in recent years the church had narrowed its understanding of tradition, and had therefore lost a great deal of the dynamism of the entire Christian tradition. When compared with the breadth and catholicity of the earlier tradition, the Catholic theology of his time appeared narrow and stale. Such views, however, were not well received in Rome, and by mid-century he too was silenced. After the ban was lifted, his fellow Jesuits asked him to write a critical study of the work and thought of Teilhard de Chardin, evaluating it in the light of Catholic tradition. He published the first volume of this project in French in 1962. Rome reacted against it immediately, stopping the project and forbidding the republication and translation of the volume already published.

De Lubac was not as inclined to grand cosmic views as was Teilhard; and this, together with his profound knowledge of early Christian tradition, resulted in his having greater impact on Catholic theology. But he too believed that all of humanity has a single goal, and that the whole of history can best be understood from the vantage point of this goal, which is none other than Jesus Christ. The church—not as a juridical organization but as the mystical body of Christ—is a sacrament in the midst of the world. Although silenced by Rome, de Lubac was much admired by many theologians and progressive bishops, and he was one of the *periti*—that is, *experts*—whose participation in the Second Vatican Council did much to influence the outcome of that assembly. His very notion of the church as a sacrament in the world stands at the root of the Council's concern that its documents reflect a church open to the world.

Yves Congar (1904–1995), another of the *periti* at the Second Vatican Council, represented a similar orientation. He had direct personal experience of the harshness of modern life, for in 1939 he had been drafted into the French army, and he was a prisoner of war in Germany from 1940 to 1945. A Dominican, he later became director of the Dominican monastery in Strasbourg. Like de Lubac, he was convinced that in response to controversy the church had narrowed its own tradition, and thus denied much of the richness of that tradition. He was particularly concerned with the church's self-understanding, and therefore felt the need to go beyond the juridical and hierarchical view of the church that prevailed at his time. For this he drew inspiration from earlier ecclesiologies, in which the image of "people of God" was dominant, and in which the laity were the focus of attention. From that perspective, he showed an openness to other Christians that was unusual among Catholics in the earlier part of the century. Like Teilhard and de Lubac, for a time he was silenced by Rome. But still his influence was widespread, and when the Second Vatican Council was convened he was appointed one of its theological mentors. His influence on that assembly can be seen particularly in the documents on the nature of the church, on ecumenism, and on the church in the modern world.

Probably the most influential Catholic theologian of the twentieth century was the Jesuit Karl Rahner (1904–1984), another of the periti at the Second Vatican Council. The son of a German high school teacher, and one of seven siblings—his brother Hugo was also a well-known Jesuit theologian—Rahner wrote more than three thousand books and articles. These deal with the most technical matters in theology as well as with everyday questions, such as "Why do we pray at night?" In all these cases, however, Rahner's method was similar: he affirmed both tradition and the modern world, and thus asked of tradition very different questions than were usually asked of it. His purpose was not to solve the mystery of the universe, but rather to clarify the mysterious nature of existence, to bring mystery back to the heart of everyday life. Philosophically, he drew both from Thomas Aquinas and from his professor Martin Heidegger, one of the foremost proponents of existentialism. But he was not particularly interested in philosophy except inasmuch as it helped to clarify Christian teaching. Also, he produced very little popular work, but was content to write mostly for theologians, calling them to a new openness and a renewed interpretation of tradition. He repeatedly offered interpretations of tradition that were at variance with commonly held views, but he was never silenced by Rome, as his French counterparts had been. Although his influence, both direct and indirect, can be seen in practically all the documents of the Second Vatican Council, it is probably in the understanding of the role of the episcopacy that he had the greatest impact. Indeed, for generations the tendency within Roman Catholicism had been toward greater centralization in Rome, after the model of a monarchical government. Rahner explored the notion of the episcopate and, without rejecting Roman primacy, underlined the collegial nature of the episcopacy. This in turn meant that the church could be truly catholic—adapting itself to each culture, and not necessarily taking Roman and Western European perspectives as the standards of truth. Such a view of catholicity and collegiality forms the foundation of the Council's decisions, not only with reference to the episcopacy itself, but also with reference to the use of the vernacular and the adaptation of the liturgy to various cultures and conditions. Rahner's judicious combination of sound theological scholarship. The retrieval and reinterpretation of tradition, and an openness to ask new questions of that tradition also served as a model for more radical theologies to which we shall return in another chapter—in particular, Latin American theologies of liberation.

After centuries of refusing to deal with the challenges of the modern world by any means besides confrontation and condemnation, during the latter half of the twentieth century, Roman Catholicism opened up to a dialogue with that world. As a result of that dialogue, Catholics as well as Protestants and even non-Christians were surprised to find in the Catholic Church an energy that few suspected it had. Long before the Second Vatican Council, theologians whom Rome viewed with mistrust were paving the way for this unexpected development.

Parallel to the theological renewal that first led to the Second Vatican Council, and then resulted from it, there was also a renewal of Roman Catholic piety. While this was true in various circles and many ways, two people were singular examples of this renewal taking place: Mother Teresa of Calcutta and Henri Nouwen. Mother Teresa (1910–1997), a native of Albania, devoted her life to serving the sick and the destitute in Calcutta, where she established the Missionaries of Charity. Her work won her praise and admiration throughout the world, and inspired many to follow a similar path. Henri Nouwen (1932–1996) was a Dutch priest who freely expressed the joy and the agonies of his inner life—both trusting God entirely, and hesitating to trust. After teaching at Harvard, Notre Dame, and Yale, he devoted the rest of his life to the service of people with disabilities, first in France and then in Canada. His writings, widely read by both Catholics and Protestants, were major factors in the emphasis on spirituality that marked the life of many believers late in the twentieth century and early in the twenty-first.

By the last decades of the twentieth century, it was clear that Roman Catholicism, while declining in the traditionally Catholic countries in Europe, was gaining strength elsewhere. Catholic vitality and theological leadership was no longer limited to North Atlantic or European men but also included women, minorities in the North Atlantic, and believers in Latin America, Asia, and Africa. In the latter regions, the number of Catholic believers continued to grow, with the result that, in spite of its numeric decline in Europe, by 2010 Catholicism had over a billion adherents. For Roman Catholicism—as was true for Christianity in general—a crisis occurring at its traditional centers was paralleled with unprecedented growth, creativity, and vitality at the periphery. Roman Catholicism, like Christianity as a whole, was moving beyond Christendom.

35

Crisis at the Center: Protestantism in Europe

> Our having grown up forces us to realize where we stand before God. God is teaching us to live as those who can manage without him.
>
> DIETRICH BONHOEFFER

WORLD WAR I AND ITS AFTERMATH

The upheavals of the first half of the twentieth century were felt most strongly in Europe. The continent had been the cradle of much of the optimistic philosophy and theology of the nineteenth century (see Chapter 31). It had dreamt that under its leadership humankind would see a new day. It had convinced itself that its colonial ventures were a vast altruistic enterprise for the good of the world. European Protestantism had been far more immersed in this illusion than its Catholic counterpart, for Catholicism during the nineteenth century had reacted to the modern world with wholesale condemnation (see Chapter 32), while Protestant liberalism had practically capitulated before the new age. Therefore, when the two world wars and the events surrounding them gave the lie to the false dreams of the nineteenth century, Protestant liberalism was shaken to its very foundations. During the nineteenth century, partially as a result of the failure of Catholicism to respond creatively to the challenges of the modern world, skepticism and secularism had become common in France. In the twentieth century, partially as a result of the failure of liberalism and its optimistic hopes, those areas where Protestantism had been traditionally strong—Germany, Scandinavia, and Great Britain—also witnessed a decided increase in skepticism and secularism. By the middle of the century, it was clear that northern Europe was no longer a stronghold of Protestantism and that other areas of the world had usurped its position of leadership in Protestantism. Thus, Europe, formerly the center of Christendom, was moving "beyond Christendom."

By the time war broke out in 1914, many Christian leaders were aware of the increasing tension in Europe, and had taken measures seeking to use the international connections of the churches in order to avert war. When this failed, some of these Christians refused to be carried by nationalist passions, and sought to make the church an instrument of reconciliation. A leader in these efforts was Nathan Söderblom (1866–1931), Lutheran archbishop of Uppsala since 1914, who used his contacts on both sides of the conflict to call for demonstrations of the universal and supranational character of the Christian communion. After the war, his efforts and contacts, as well as his unblemished record as a peacemaker, made him one of the leaders of the early ecumenical movement.

But Protestantism was sorely lacking in a theology that could help it understand the events of the times, and to respond to them. Liberalism, with its optimistic view of human nature and capabilities, had no word for the situation. Söderblom and others in Scandinavia began to deal with its deficiency through a revival of studies on Luther and his theology. During the previous century, German liberal scholarship had depicted Luther as both the forerunner of liberalism and the embodiment of the German soul. Now other scholars, first in Scandinavia and then also in Germany, took a second look at Luther's theology, and discovered there much that was not in agreement with the interpretations of the previous century. Significant landmarks in this movement were Gustav Aulén's *Christus Victor* and Anders Nygren's *Agape and Eros.* Both works are characterized by a sense of the power of evil and of the unmerited grace of God, which contradicted much of what had been said in the previous generation.

The most significant theological response to the challenges of the times, however, was the work of Karl Barth (1886–1968). The son of a Swiss Reformed pastor, Barth had been so intrigued by his confirmation classes in 1901 and 1902 that he decided to study theology. By the time he was ready to begin his theological studies, his father was a professor of church history and New Testament at Bern, and it was under his direction that young Barth planned his studies. After some time at Bern, and an uneventful semester at Tübingen, he went to Berlin, where he was fascinated by Adolf von Harnack and his grasp of the history of doctrine. Later, as a student in Marburg, he

Karl Barth was without doubt the most important Protestant theologian of the twentieth century.

was captivated by the writings of both Kant and Schleiermacher. It was also there that he met Eduard Thurneysen, a fellow student who would become his closest friend throughout his career. Finally, seemingly well equipped with the best liberal theology of his time, Barth became a pastor, first in Geneva—where he took the opportunity for a careful reading of Calvin's *Institutes*—and then in the Swiss village of Safenwil.

Safenwil in 1911 was a parish of peasants and laborers, and Barth became interested in their struggle for better living conditions. Soon he was so involved in the social issues of his parish that he read theology only when preparing sermons or lectures. He became a Social Democrat—a party he joined in 1915—and decided that this movement was, even unknowingly, God's instrument for the establishment of the Kingdom. After all, he felt, Jesus had not come to found a new religion, but to begin a new world, and the Social Democrats were closer to that purpose than a dormant church that was content with its preaching and worship. Then the war shattered both his political hopes and his theology. The new world that the Social Democrats had promised was not forthcoming—at least not in the near future—and the optimism of his liberal mentors seemed out of place in a

Europe torn by war. In a conversation with Thurneysen in 1916, the two friends decided that it was time to do theology on a different basis, and that the best way to do this was by returning to the text of Scripture. The next morning, Barth undertook a study of Romans that would shake the theological world.

Barth's *Commentary on Romans,* originally written for his own use and for a small circle of friends, was published in 1919. There, he insisted on the need to return to faithful exegesis rather than systematic constructions. The God of Scripture—he declared—is transcendent, never an object of human manipulation, and the Spirit that works in us is never something that we possess, but is always and repeatedly a gift of God. Barth also reacted against the religious subjectivism that he had learned from many of his teachers. In this regard, he declared that in order to be saved one must be free of such individual concern, and be a member of the body of Christ, the new humanity.

While readers in Germany and Switzerland poured a praise not always to his liking on his *Commentary on Romans,* Barth was pursuing further readings that convinced him that he had not gone far enough in that book. Particularly, he felt that he had not sufficiently underscored the otherness of God. He had spoken of transcendence; but now he feared that he had not yet escaped from the liberal and Romantic tendency to find God in the best of human nature. Also, he had not sufficiently stressed the contrast between the Kingdom of God and all human projects. He was now convinced that the Kingdom is an eschatological reality, one that arises from the Wholly Other, and is not of human construction. This led him to renounce the theology that had led him to join the Social Democrats. Although still a socialist, and still convinced that Christians ought to strive for justice and equality, he now insisted that none of these projects ought to be confused with the eschatological Kingdom of God.

Barth had just finished the second—and radically revised—edition of his *Commentary on Romans* when he left Safenwil in order to begin a teaching career in Göttingen—a career that he would later continue in Münster, Bonn, and finally in Basel. Kierkegaard's influence is clearly discernible in the second edition of Barth's *Commentary on Romans*—particularly in his insistence on the unsurmountable gap between time and eternity, between human achievement and divine action. It has also been said that Barth's second edition was his version of Kierkegaard's attack upon Christendom.

By the time he began his teaching career, Barth was being credited with having begun a new theological school that some would call *dialectical theology*, others *crisis theology*, and still others *neo-orthodoxy*. This was a theology of a God who is never ours, but always stands over against us; whose word is at the same time both *yes* and *no*; whose presence brings, not ease and inspiration to our efforts, but crisis. Around him gathered a number of theologians of stature: his fellow Reformed Emil Brunner, Lutheran pastor Friedrich Gogarten, and New Testament scholar Rudolf Bultmann. In 1922, Barth, Gogarten, Thurneysen, and others founded the theological journal *Zwischen den Zeiten (Between the Times)* to which Brunner and Bultmann also contributed. Soon, however, Bultmann and Gogarten drifted away from the group, which they considered too traditional in its approach to theology and not sufficiently engaged with the questions of modern doubt. Later, Brunner and Barth also parted company over the issue of the relationship between nature and grace—while Brunner felt that there must be in humans a "point of contact" for the action of grace, Barth insisted that this would lead to a reintroduction of natural theology, and that in any case it is grace that creates its own "point of contact."

Meanwhile, Barth had continued his theological pilgrimage. In 1927, he published the first volume of a projected *Christian Dogmatics,* wherein he declared that the object of theology is not the Christian faith, as Schleiermacher and others had made it appear, but the Word of God. The tone of his work had also changed, for in the *Commentary on Romans* he had been the prophet showing the error of old ways, and in *Christian Dogmatics* he was the scholar trying to offer an alternative systematic theology. The theology of crisis had thus become a theology of the Word of God.

But this entire project then became nothing more than a false start. Through a study of Anselm of Canterbury, and then of nineteenth-century Protestant theology, Barth became convinced that the *Christian Dogmatics* granted too much to philosophy. There, he had proposed that theology answers our deepest existential questions;, and had used existentialist philosophy as the framework on which theology was built. Now he declared that the Word of God provides not only the answers but also the questions. Sin, for instance, is not something we know by nature, and to which the gospel responds. What convicts us of sin is God's word of grace. Without knowing that word, we know neither grace nor sin. This new perspective led Barth to begin his great systematic work once again, this time stressing the ecclesiastical grounding of theology with the very title *Church Dogmatics*. The thirteen volumes of this work, which he never completed, were published between 1932 and 1967.

Church Dogmatics is unquestionably the great theological monument of the twentieth century. At a time when many felt that theological systems were a matter of the past, and that theology could at best consist of monographs, Barth wrote a work worthy of the best eras of theological scholarship. On reading it, one immediately notices his profound acquaintance with earlier theological traditions, which he constantly brings to bear. But one is also aware of the inner coherence of the entire work, which from beginning to end—and over a period of almost four decades of writing—is true to itself. There are shifting emphases in it, but no new starts. Most remarkable of all is Barth's own freedom and critical stance toward the entire task of theology, which he never confused with the Word of God. Indeed, he insisted, theology, no matter how true or correct, always remains a human endeavor, and therefore must always be seen with a combination of freedom, joy, and even humor.

RENEWED CONFLICTS

While Barth was preparing the first volume of his *Church Dogmatics,* ominous events were taking shape in Germany: Hitler and the Nazi party were rising to power. In 1933, the Vatican and the Third Reich signed a concordat. Protestant liberals had no theological tools with which to respond critically to this new challenge. Indeed, many of them had declared that they believed in the perfectibility of the human race, and this was precisely what Hitler proclaimed. They had also tended to confuse the gospel with German culture, and the Nazi claim that Germany was called to civilize the world was echoed at many Protestant pulpits and academic chairs. Hitler's own program included the unification of all Protestant churches in Germany, and then using them in order to preach his message of German racial superiority, and of a divinely given mission. Thus arose the *German Christians*, which combined traditional Christian beliefs, usually as they had been reinterpreted by liberalism, with notions of racial superiority and German nationalism. Part of their program was to reinterpret Christianity in terms of opposition to Judaism, thus contributing to the anti-Semitic policies of the Reich. In 1933, following the directions of the government, a united German Evangelical Church was formed. When its presiding bishop showed himself unwilling to obey the Reich in all matters, he was deposed and another named in his place. In 1934, several professors of theology, including Barth and Bultmann, signed a protest against the directions the united church was taking. Then, a few days later, both Lutheran and Reformed Christian leaders from all over Germany, gathered at Barmen for what they called a "witnessing synod," and issued the *Barmen Declaration*, which became the foundational document for the Confessing Church, a body that opposed Hitler's policies in the name of the gospel. The Barmen Declaration rejected "the false doctrine, that the church ought to accept as the basis for its message, besides and apart from the one Word of God, other events and powers, figures or truths, as if they were God's revelation." And it called all Christians in Germany to test its words against the Word of God, and to accept them only if they found it consistent with that Word.

The Third Reich's reaction was not slow in coming. Dr. Martin Niemöller, a pastor in Berlin and an outspoken critic of the government, was arrested and would remain in prison for eight years. Almost all pastors critical of the government were drafted into the army and sent to the battlefront. All professors in German universities were required to sign a statement of unconditional support of the Reich. Barth refused to sign and returned to Switzerland, where he taught in Basel until his retirement.

Most notable among those who suffered under Hitler's regime was young theologian Dietrich Bonhoeffer (1906–1945), who was a pastor in London when the Confessing Church invited him to return to Germany and head a clandestine seminary. His friends in England tried to dissuade him, but he felt that this was a call that he must accept, and he returned to Germany knowing that in doing so he was endangering his life. In 1937, he published *The Cost of Discipleship,* in which he attempted to show the significance of the Sermon on the Mount for contemporary living. That same year his seminary was disbanded by direct order of the Reich. In spite of this order, Bonheoeffer gathered two groups of students for continued theological instruction. The experiences of these years of shared community in obedience and danger are reflected in his book on *Life Together,* published in 1939. By then, war was about to explode. Bonhoeffer was on a brief visit to London when friends from England and the United States (where he had been a student years earlier) insisted that he not return to Germany. But return he did. Back in Germany, he decided to accept an invitation to spend a year in the United States. He had scarcely arrived, however, when he decided that he

Dietrich Bonhoeffer, hanged by the Nazis shortly before their surrender, left behind some tantalizing suggestions regarding the need for a "religionless Christianity."

had made a mistake, for his fellow Germans would soon be forced to choose between patriotism and truth, and he declared: "I know which of those alternatives I must choose; but I cannot make that choice in security."

Bonhoeffer's life back in Germany became increasingly difficult. In 1938, he was forbidden to live in Berlin. Two years later, his seminary was closed by order of the Gestapo, and he was forbidden from publishing anything or speaking in public. During the next three years, his involvement in the underground against Hitler increased. Until then, he had been a pacifist. But he came to the conclusion that such pacifism, leaving others to make the difficult political and practical decisions, was a way of escaping from his own responsibility. In a meeting with a friend in Sweden, Bonhoeffer said that he was part of a conspiracy to assassinate Hitler. This was not something he wanted to do, he said, but he felt that he had no other choice.

Bonhoeffer was arrested by the Gestapo in April 1943. While in prison, and later in a concentration camp, Bonhoeffer won the respect of both guards and fellow prisoners, whom he served as chaplain. He also carried on correspondence with those outside, some of it censored by the authorities and some smuggled out with the help of sympathetic guards. In that correspondence, and in other papers he left behind, he showed that he was grappling with new ideas, some of which have tantalized later generations. For instance, he spoke of the world "coming of age," and of God's presence in this world being much like that of a wise parent, who recedes into the background as a child grows. It was in this connection that he criticized Barth, whom he greatly admired, for having moved into what he called a "positivism of revelation," as if revelation let us know more than it actually does. But on other matters he took his cue from Barth, and tried to apply Barth's principles in daring fashion. For instance, Barth had declared that religion is a human effort by which we seek to hide from God, and on this basis Bonhoeffer spoke of a "religionless Christianity," while he groped for the future shape of such Christianity. Later generations would read these lines and feel compelled to follow Bonhoeffer's suggestions in a number of divergent ways.

As the Allied troops advanced, and defeat was unavoidable, the Third Reich moved to eliminate those it considered its worst enemies. Bonhoeffer was among them. After a hasty court martial, he was condemned to death. The prison doctor later told of seeing him kneeling in his cell, praying in preparation for his death. On April 9, 1945, two years and four days after his arrest, Dietrich Bonhoeffer was hanged. A few days later, Allied troops captured the prison where he had been executed.

AFTER THE WAR

One result of the war was that vast areas of Eastern and central Europe fell under Soviet rule. Most of these lands were predominantly Catholic, but in all of them there were significant Protestant minorities. The portion of Germany that fell under Soviet control was the cradle of Protestantism, where the population was overwhelmingly Protestant. This led both to difficulties between Protestants and Communist regimes, and to an increased dialogue between Marxists and Protestants. The nature of the relations between the state and the church varied from country to country, and from time to time. Orthodox Marxist doctrine certainly saw Christianity as an enemy, but some Communist leaders followed a policy of open opposition to the church, while others opted for benign neglect based on the conviction that religious

faith was a matter of the past and would simply disappear. In Czechoslovakia and Hungary, the state continued its traditional policy of supporting the
churches with public funds. In East Germany, on the other hand, Christians
were subject to serious civil restrictions that prevented them from pursuing
an education or holding positions of significant responsibility.

In Czechoslovakia, the Marxist-Christian dialogue was associated with
the name of Joseph Hromádka, dean of the Comenius Faculty of Theology
in Prague. In order to understand his attitude, and that of other Protestants in Czechoslovakia, one must remember that this is the land of Huss,
and also the land where the Thirty Years' War caused greatest devastation.
Ever since, Protestants in that land have seen Catholics as their oppressors.
Therefore, when the Communist regime declared that all churches would
have equal standing before the government, Czech Protestants saw in this
an act of liberation. The Vatican's opposition to the new regime in Czechoslovakia was seen as an attempt to regain the privileges that Catholics had
lost, and therefore as a move to oppress them again. Also, from the times of
the Hussite struggles against foreign invaders, Czechs had been convinced
that Christian faith must not be something private, but must also have an
impact on society, leading it to greater justice. For these reasons, Hromádka
and his followers responded positively to the Marxist regime, while not
abandoning their faith. Even before World War II, Hromádka had spoken of
the possibility that Russian Communism might be the beginning of a new
era in world history, one where issues of social justice would be paramount.
As early as 1933, he had also warned of the dangers of Nazism. After the
German invasion of his homeland, he fled to the United States, where he
taught at Princeton Theological Seminary for eight years. At that time, he
felt confirmed in his earlier belief that much of what passed for Christianity
in the United States was little more than the justification of liberal democracy and capitalism. Furthermore, he was convinced that Christians should
not be led astray by Marxist atheism, for the God whose existence the
Marxists deny is no more than a fiction. The true God of Scripture and of
Christian faith is not that God, but is One who is not touched by Marxism's
futile atheism. There is indeed a radical difference between Marxism and
Christianity. But the church must be careful not to confuse that difference
with the polarization of the world due to the Cold War. Christians must be
critical of the Marxist state; but they must not be critical in a fashion that
affirms the continuation of the injustices of the capitalist order—or of that

which existed in Czechoslovakia before the war.

Elsewhere in Europe, a lively dialogue was taking place between Christians and Marxists. Often, the Marxist participants in this dialogue were not orthodox Marxist-Leninists, but rather revisionists who, while agreeing with the fundamental elements in Marx's analysis of history and society, wished to pursue those insights their own way. A leader in this movement was Ernst Bloch, a Marxist philosopher who agreed with Marx that religion—and particularly Christianity in most of its history—has been used as an instrument of oppression. But, taking his cue from the young Marx himself, Bloch saw in early Christianity a movement of protest against oppression, and then went on to reinterpret Christian doctrines and biblical stories through that lens. For him, this value lies in the message of hope. The "principle of hope" was early Christianity's most significant contribution to human history. And this is of paramount importance, for—from the perspective of hope—humans are not determined by their past, but rather by their future. Such views, as well as those of other Marxist revisionists, paved the way for a dialogue that continued into the last decades of the twentieth century. This dialogue—and particularly Bloch's work—contributed to one of the main characteristics of Protestant theology in the late twentieth and early twenty-first centuries, namely, an emphasis on hope and on eschatology as a basic theme for Christian theology. A leader in this movement was Jürgen Moltmann, who was also influenced by a number of Third-World theologians, and whose books *Theology of Hope* and *The Crucified God* have been hailed as initiating a new era in European theology. Moltmann argues that hope is the central tenet of biblical faith. God is not yet finished with the world. Our God, Moltmann argues, meets us and calls us from the future. Hope for the "last things" ought not be the last chapter, but the first, of Christian theology. This is not a private, individualistic hope, but is the hope for a new order. Thus, a theology of hope must not lead the faithful to passive waiting for the future, but rather to join those struggles against poverty and oppression that signal God's future.

Meanwhile, in those areas of Western Europe that remained free of Soviet control, the process of secularization accelerated. Twenty years after the war, in traditionally Protestant areas such as Scandinavia, West Germany, and Great Britain, church attendance and participation had declined to the point that only a small minority—in some cases fewer than 10 percent—of the population had any significant contact with any form of organized

Christianity. In those areas, the issue that most concerned Christian leaders and theologians was the relationship between Christianity and the modern, highly secular view of the world—an issue Bonhoeffer had been grappling with in prison.

One of the most influential answers to this question—at least for a time (it was soon surpassed by other developments) was offered by Rudolf Bultmann in an essay published during World War II on *The New Testament and Mythology.* There, Bultmann argues that the message of the New Testament is couched in myth, and that for it to be heard today it must be "demythologized." This is important, not because without it faith would be impossible—people can force themselves to believe whatever they wish, no matter how irrational—but rather because without that demythologizing, faith is radically misunderstood. Faith is not an effort of the will to believe the unbelievable. The call of the New Testament to faith is not heard when one confuses it with the call to accept its myths. Myth is every attempt to express in images that which transcends this world. But in the New Testament, besides this basic myth, there is also a mythological worldview, one in which God and other supernatural forces intervene, and one in which the universe is seen as existing on three tiers, with heaven above and hell below. The modern world can no longer accept the notion of a world open to supernatural interventions, nor does it view earth as hanging between hell and heaven. All this, as well as the basic attempt to speak of God in human terms, must be demythologized.

Bultmann's method of understanding the New Testament drew its inspiration from existentialist philosopher Martin Heidegger. This aspect of his program, however, was not accepted as widely as his call for demythologization. Whatever the content of a new understanding of the New Testament may be, argue those who defend the program, it is clear that modern people no longer think in terms of a world open to supernatural intervention, and that therefore the stories of the New Testament, couched as they are in such terms, are an obstacle to faith. More than twenty years after the publication of Bultmann's essay, Anglican bishop John A.T. Robinson's *Honest to God,* which caused widespread debate and comment, was an attempt to popularize Bultmann's views—together with those of Bonhoeffer and Paul Tillich.

By the end of the century, however, a new dimension had been added to theological discussion, namely the conviction on the part of many that

In order to make the faith believable, Rudolph Bultmann proposed the demythologization of the New Testament.

modernity was coming to a close. For over two centuries, Christian theology had been dominated by the issue of modernity—the Roman Catholic Church at first reacting against it, then finally accepting it, and the majority of Protestant theologians claiming it or at least accepting its main tenets as given truth. Modernity had provided the basis for much of the colonial enterprise, for it was thanks to their modern armies and their modern machinery that the colonial powers were able to impose their will on the rest of the world. Now that colonialism seemed to be a matter of the past, the same was beginning to be true of modernity. In Europe and elsewhere, there was a growing conviction that notions such as objectivity and universality, and the view of the world as a closed entity guided by mechanistic principles—concepts that had marked much of modernity's claim in the human mind—were not as strong as they had once seemed. As we shall see, such views were also in the background of the contextual theologies that were developing throughout the world at the same time.

AT THE TURN OF THE CENTURY

The last decade of the twentieth century saw momentous changes in the political configuration of Europe. The decade began with the collapse of the Soviet Union and the dismemberment of its empire in Eastern Europe. Shortly thereafter, in November of 1993, the European Union was born; it would come to comprise most of the nations of Western Europe. While the latter event did not have the great impact on the life of the churches that the former did, the two together brought radical changes to European Protestantism. In Eastern Europe, although it was the Orthodox Churches that were most affected by the fall of Communism, the new order brought significant changes among Protestants, and impelled the churches to take on new roles. In Germany, for instance, the churches had been reduced to a defensive posture. To them, it was a great victory when, in 1978, the Communist government in East Germany reached an agreement with the churches, promising to put an end to discrimination against Christian children and youth, allowing regional and national mass gatherings of believers, and authorizing the building of a number of churches. In 1983, the government and the churches—including Roman Catholics—joined in an uneasy alliance for the celebration of the fifth centennial of Luther's birth. But this changed entirely with the fall of the Berlin wall and the reunification of Germany. In East Germany, much of the conspiracy to overthrow the regime and reunite the nation was led by Reformed and Lutheran pastors and lay leaders, several of whom came to occupy important positions in the effort to rebuild the nation after reunification.

Similar events occurred in other lands. In Hungary, Reformed pastor Laszlo Tokes played a role in resistance to the existing order, similar to the role of Lech Walesa in Poland. There, as well as in Poland and Romania, Reformed pastors and other leaders made important contributions in the framing of new constitutions. In all this process, the churches came to be seen as more relevant to the life of the people than they had been for decades. On the other hand, in Czechoslovakia a synod of the Silesian Lutheran Church deposed its bishop on the grounds of having collaborated with the regime that had now fallen. When Yugoslavia broke into pieces, so did the Reformed Christian Church in that nation.

In Western Europe, on the other hand, the process of secularization that had begun much earlier continued unabated, and even accelerated—perhaps fostered by an optimism about human abilities similar to that enjoyed in the nineteenth century. But this should not be interpreted to mean that the churches had lost all vitality, or that theological discussions on the meaning of secularism were their sole occupation. On the contrary, Western European Protestants, whose numbers had been drastically reduced, continued being an active leaven in their society, and took a place of leadership in the movement to stop the arms race, in issues of international justice, and in service to those disenfranchised or uprooted by industrial development and its consequences. In France, the Reformed Church of France was born in 1936 out of a union of two Reformed bodies with Methodists and Congregationalists. Throughout the twentieth century, and into the twenty-first, this church showed great interest and success in evangelistic work in heavily industrialized areas. Likewise, in West Germany Protestant churches employed a staff of a hundred and thirty thousand devoted to social assistance and relief, in both Germany itself and abroad. Behind that movement stood millions of committed Christians for whom the crucial question was not secularism, but obedience. When conditions changed and Germany was reunited after almost half a century in which the Communist regime had discouraged church attendance—particularly among children and youth— almost two-thirds of the population continued professing Christianity.

Thus, while shaken by the momentous and even disastrous events of the twentieth century, and in some places reduced to a minority of the population, European Protestantism had not lost its vitality. European churches continued serving the needy, calling for social justice, and supporting other churches in poorer countries.But they were no longer the dominant partners in such enterprises, for there were growing numbers who felt that secular agencies could respond to human needs at least as well as the churches. At the same time, large numbers of immigrants from former European colonies in Africa and Asia resulted in an unprecedented rate of growth of religions such as Islam, Buddhism, and Hinduism—to the extent that in some areas in any given week there were more people worshiping in mosques than in churches. Thus, by the second decade of the twenty-first century, there was no doubt that Europe was moving beyond Christendom, and becoming part of a much more complex world.

36

Crisis at the Center: Protestantism in the United States

We acknowledge our Christian responsibilities of citizenship.
Therefore, we must challenge the misplaced trust of the nation in
economic and military might. . . . We must resist the temptation to
make the nation and its institutions objects of near-religious loyalty.

CHICAGO DECLARATION

FROM WORLD WAR I TO THE GREAT DEPRESSION

Although the United States was involved in World War I, that conflict did
not have the far-reaching consequences there that it had in Europe. The
main reason was that the United States did not enter the war until its final
stages, and even then its own lands were never the scene of battle. By and
large, most Americans were spared experiencing destruction and bloodshed
first hand, and the sufferings of the civilian population did not compare to
those of its counterpart in Europe. Although for a long time public opinion
was in favor of keeping the nation out of what appeared to be a European
conflict, once the United States declared war the entire affair was seen as a
matter of glory and honor. The churches, which until 1916 had supported
the peace movement, now joined in the rhetoric of war. Liberals and fundamentalists spoke of the need to "save civilization," and some among the more
radical fundamentalists began interpreting the events of the time as the
fulfillment of the prophecies of Daniel and Revelation. Except for the traditionally pacifist denominations—such as the Mennonites and Quakers—
war fever and national chauvinism were the order of the day, to the point
that from some pulpits there was a call for the total extermination of the

German people in the name of God. Naturally, this created enormous difficulties for those Americans of German descent, including Walter Rauschenbusch, whose emphasis on the social dimensions of the faith, known as the Social Gospel, elicited much opposition among more conservative groups.

The lack of critical reflection on the war and its causes had serious consequences in the years following. First of all, President Woodrow Wilson's hope for a treaty in which the vanquished were treated fairly, in order to avoid bitterness and renewed conflict, was shattered by both the ambition of the victorious allies and the lack of support at home—thus paving the way for the World War II. Second, the nation was so blinded by the rhetoric of war that the United States never joined the League of Nations, a forum for the resolution of international conflicts that was the brainchild of the country's own president. By that time many church leaders were trying to undo the prejudice they had fostered during the war, but they found that their call for love and understanding was not as well received as their earlier message of hatred and prejudice.

Partly as a result of the war, the United States entered another period of isolationism, of fear of everything foreign, and of suppression of dissent. During the decade of the 1920s, the Ku Klux Klan enjoyed a revival and an unprecedented increase in its membership, in the North as well as in the South, by adding Catholics and Jews to blacks as the great enemies of American Christianity and democracy. In the Southwest, the Mexican Revolution led many to flee that country and migrate to the United States, as many had done earlier from Europe. But the race and religion of most of these newer immigrants were not always welcome, and discrimination against all persons of Mexican descent increased. Not a few religious leaders and churches contributed to these prejudices. This was the time of the "red scare," the first of a series of witch hunts for radicals, Communists, and subversives that swept the United States during the twentieth century. Adding fuel to the fire and benefitting from it, many churches presented themselves and the Christian faith as the main line of defense against the "red threat." Famous evangelist Billy Sunday declared that the deportation of "radicals" was too easy a punishment, and one that would be costly to the nation. Instead, he suggested, they should all be lined up and shot.

Some Christians, mostly in the mainline denominations, organized committees and campaigns to oppose such extremes. Often such committees gained the approval of denominational headquarters. Thus appeared a

Partly as a result of the war and of the fears aroused by the new conditions, the Ku Klux Klan enjoyed a period of unprecedented increase in its membership.

phenomenon that would characterize many mainline denominations for decades: the split, in theology as well as in politics, between a national leadership of liberal political and social tendencies, and a significant portion of the rank and file who felt that their own denominational leaders did not represent their views.

The conflict between liberals and fundamentalists was exacerbated in the post-war period. This was the time of the famous Scopes trial, which symbolized the high point of the effort on the part of fundamentalists to ban the teaching of the theory of evolution in public schools—an effort that in some quarters would continue into the twenty-first century. Almost all denominations were divided over the issue of fundamentalism—particularly the inerrancy of Scripture, which by then had become the hallmark of fundamentalist orthodoxy. In later years, these divisions would lead to open schism. Thus, for instance, the work of the great defender of fundamentalism among Northern Presbyterians, Princeton professor J. Gresham Machen, led to the founding of a rival seminary and eventually of the Orthodox Presbyterian Church (1936).

During the 1920s, however, most Protestants were united in one great cause: the prohibition of alcoholic beverages. Here was a cause that soon enlisted the support both of liberals for whom it was a practical application of the Social Gospel and of conservatives for whom it was an attempt to return to the earlier times when the country had supposedly been purer. Many linked drunkenness with all the evils they claimed had been brought about by the immigration of Jews and Catholics, thus appealing to the same

The Scopes trial was the high point of a campaign, lasting for several decades, against the theory of evolution.

prejudices against foreigners, Jews, and Catholics that fueled the growth of the Ku Klux Klan. The campaign first succeeded in a number of state legislatures, and then took on the federal Constitution. In 1919, by virtue of the Eighteenth Amendment, prohibition became the law of the land, and it remained so for more than a decade.

But it was easier to pass the law than to enforce it. Business interests, gangsters, and the drinking public in various ways collaborated to break the law. To the evils of drinking were then added those of corruption, encouraged by an illicit trade that had become inordinately profitable. By the time the law was repealed, the notion that "one can't legislate morality" had become commonplace in American folklore. This notion, popular at first among those liberals who had given up the ideal of prohibition, would later be used also by those conservatives who opposed legislation against racial segregation.

Through the end of World War I and the following decade, the basic American mood was one of high expectations. The war and its horrors were dim memories from a distant land. In the United States, progress was still the order of the day. In churches and pulpits, very little was heard of the new theology that was developing in Europe, a theology that left behind the optimism of earlier generations. What little was heard sounded alien, as referring to a world far removed from the cheerful expectations of "the land of the free and the home of the brave." Then came the crash.

THROUGH DEPRESSION AND WORLD WAR II

On October 24, 1929, panic gripped the New York Stock Exchange. With short periods of slight recovery, the stock market continued dropping until the middle of 1930. By then, most of the Western world was in the middle of a great economic depression. One-fourth of the labor force in the United States was unemployed. Britain and other nations had social security systems and unemployment insurance. In the United States, fear of socialism had prevented such measures, and therefore the unemployed found themselves entirely on their own, or forced to seek charity from relatives, friends, or churches. Soup kitchens and breadlines became common sights in all major cities and many smaller towns. Runs on banks, bankruptcies, and foreclosures reached a record high.

At first, the nation faced the Great Depression with the optimism that had characterized its handling of problems it had faced in earlier decades.

President Herbert Hoover and his cabinet continued to deny the existence of a depression for months after the market had crashed. When they finally admitted that there was a depression, they insisted that the American economy was sufficiently sound to rebound by itself, and that the free workings of the marketplace were the best way to ensure an economic recovery. Although the president himself was a compassionate man who suffered with the plight of the unemployed, there were around him those who rejoiced in the hope that the Depression would break the labor unions. Since their labor was no longer needed, thousands of Mexicans and Mexican-Americans—many of them American citizens—were deported to Mexico. When finally the government intervened to prevent further bankruptcies in industry and commerce, comedian Will Rogers quipped that money was being given to those at the top hoping that it would "trickle down to the needy."

All this put a halt to the optimism of the previous decade. Although historians have shown that the Depression that had hit the United States late in the nineteenth century was much worse, the American public was much less psychologically prepared for the Great Depression of the 1930s. An entire generation that had never known want, and had been promised that things would inevitably improve, suddenly saw its dreams shattered. At a time when survival was at stake, facile promises of a rosy future seemed shallow.

It was then that less optimistic theologies began making an impact on the United States. Karl Barth's *The Word of God and the Word of Man,* published in English just before the Crash, began to make sense to Americans who were affected by the Great Depression in much the same way that Barth and his generation had been affected by World War I (see Chapter 35). The theology of the two Niebuhr brothers, Reinhold (1892–1970) and H. Richard (1894–1962), came to the foreground. In 1929, H. Richard Niebuhr published *The Social Sources of Denominationalism,* in which he argued that denominationalism in the United States was an adaptation of the gospel to the various racial and socioeconomic strata of society, thus showing "the domination of class and self-preservative church ethics over the ethics of the gospel."[20] His conclusion, made all the more poignant because the world was approaching the worst war it had ever known, was that "a Christianity which surrenders its leadership to the social forces of national and economic life, offers no hope to the divided world."[21] In 1937, his book on *The Kingdom of God in America* further indicted this sort of religion by

Reinhold Niebuhr was one of the leading figures in a new theology—a theology that was not ready to accept the facile optimism of liberalism or to confuse American culture and traditions with the Christian faith.

declaring that in it "A God without wrath brought men without sin into a Kingdom without judgment through the ministrations of a Christ without a cross."[22]

Meanwhile, his brother Reinhold, who had been a parish minister in Detroit until 1928, came to the conclusion that unbridled capitalism was destructive, and in 1930 he and others joined in the Fellowship of Socialist Christians. He was convinced that, left to its own devices, any society is morally worse and more self-seeking than the sum of its members—a view that he forcefully expounded in a book entitled *Moral Man and Immoral Society.* In reaction against theological liberalism, he shared the doubts of the neo-orthodox concerning human capabilities, and soon commented that a more correct title for his book would have been "immoral man and even more immoral society." He meant that it was time Christians recovered a balanced view of human nature, including both a deeper understanding of sin and its ramifications, and a radical view of grace. This he attempted to do in 1941 and 1943, in two volumes on *The Nature and Destiny of Man*.

In 1934, thanks to the interest and support of Reinhold Niebuhr, German theologian Paul Tillich joined him on the faculty of Union Theological Seminary in New York. Hitler was rising to power in Germany, and Tillich, a moderate socialist, was among the first people forced to leave the country. He was not a neo-orthodox, but rather a theologian of culture who made use of existentialist philosophy in order to interpret the gospel and its relationship to the modern world. In contrast to Barth's emphasis on the Word of God as the starting point of theology, Tillich proposed what he called the "method of correlation," which consisted of examining the most profound existential questions of modern people—particularly what he called their "ultimate concern"—and then showing how the gospel responds to them. His *Systematic Theology* dealt with the central themes of Christian theology on the basis of this method. He was also a moderate socialist who did apply a revised form of Marxist analysis to try to understand the shortcomings of Western civilization. But after his move to the United States, this particular element of his thought was overshadowed by his interest in existentialism and in depth psychology.

The Depression produced a critique of *laissez faire* economics in more than just the theological faculties. The Federal Council of Churches (founded in 1908 by thirty-three denominations, it later became the National Council of Churches) went on record with the Methodist Church in supporting government participation in economic planning and in providing the means to safeguard the well being of the poor. This move, made in 1932, was considered radical socialism, and a reaction was not long in coming.

People responded with a combination of traditional fundamentalism with anti-socialist—and sometimes Fascist—political views. As the leadership of various mainstream denominations moved toward the conviction that a system of social security, unemployment insurance, and antitrust laws was necessary, many in the rank and file moved in the opposite direction, accusing that leadership of having been infiltrated by Communism. As the war approached, a significant sector of this movement allied itself with Fascism, and some of its leaders even declared that Christians ought to be thankful for Adolf Hitler because he was halting the advance of socialism in Europe. Seldom was any distinction made between Russian Communism and other forms of socialism, and all were often declared to be equally ungodly.

The advent of President Roosevelt's New Deal implemented many of the policies that the "socialists" in the leadership of the churches had been advocating. The very moderate steps taken at that time for providing relief to the poor and security to the labor force have been credited by some historians with saving the capitalist system in the United States. In any case, although the New Deal did improve conditions for the poor, the economy recovered slowly, and the last vestiges of the Depression disappeared only in 1939, as the nation was once again preparing for the eventuality of war. In a way, it was the war, and not the New Deal, that put an end to the Great Depression.

The nation was deeply divided over whether to enter the war which was already raging in Europe and the Far East. Those who opposed the war did so for a variety of reasons: some were Christians who still felt remorse for the unrestrained militarism and nationalism exhibited during the previous war; others were Fascists, or at least people whose fear of Communism overrode every other consideration; some Americans of German and Italian extraction felt spurred by a sense of allegiance to their ancestral lands; isolationists simply believed that the nation should leave the rest of the world to its own devices; and those who harbored racist and anti-Semitic attitudes felt that the United States should do nothing to hinder Hitler's plans.

In the end, however, the choice was made for them. That decision was made by the attack on Pearl Harbor, on December 7, 1941. After that, the national loyalty of any who opposed the war effort was questioned. Japanese-Americans—including many whose families had been in the United States for generations—were interned as potential spies. Sadly, the churches said little, while smooth operators took over the property and businesses of those interned. In general, perhaps chastised by their wholesale support of the previous war, the churches spoke with moderation during the conflict. They did support the war effort, provided chaplains for the armed forces, and declared their abhorrence for the crimes of the Nazis. But most leaders took care not to confuse Christianity with national pride. It is significant that at the same time there were in Germany those who insisted on a similar distinction, even at much higher cost. While the world was torn apart by war, Christians living on both sides of the conflict were seeking to build bridges. After the end of the conflict, such bridges would bear fruit in the ecumenical movement (see Chapters 33 and 37).

THE POSTWAR DECADES

The war ended with the horrors of Hiroshima and the dawn of the nuclear age. While at first there was much talk of the great promises of nuclear power, its destructive effect was also evident. For the first time in history, a generation grew up under the threat of the total annihilation of humankind through nuclear holocaust. This was also the largest generation in American history—the "baby boom" generation. In spite of the specter of nuclear war, the postwar years were a period of unprecedented prosperity both for the economy of the nation and for its churches. After long decades in which financial depression and war had limited the availability of material goods, there came a period of abundance. The industrial production of the nation had accelerated during the war in order to provide the materials necessary for the conflict. Now that production continued, resulting in the most affluent consumer society the world had ever seen. Through the "G.I. Bill," the government provided financial support for veterans who wished to obtain a college education or buy homes. There seemed to be opportunities for financial and social advancement for any who were willing to take them, although race did raise insurmountable barriers for many. Millions flocked to new areas in search of those opportunities and, having found them, settled in newly developed suburbia. Inner cities were progressively abandoned by the affluent, and became more exclusively the abode of the lower classes—particularly recent immigrants, poor blacks and other minorities. In the mobile society of suburbia, the churches came to function as an important source of both stability and social recognition.

It was also the time of the Cold War. Hardly had the Axis been defeated, when a new and more dangerous enemy appeared: Soviet Russia. This enemy seemed all the more insidious inasmuch as it had sympathizers in the Western world. In the United States, there was a renewed witch hunt for Communists and socialists of every stripe. During the heyday of the McCarthy Era (so-called because it was spear-headed by Senator Joseph McCarthy), lack of church membership was viewed as a possible indication of anti-American inclinations.

For all these reasons, churches in suburbia grew rapidly. The 1950s and early 1960s were the great age of U.S. church architecture, with affluent congregations financing the building of vast and beautiful sanctuaries, educational buildings, and other facilities. In 1950, the Billy Graham Evangelistic Association was incorporated. It did more than simply continue the old

American tradition of revivals. With abundant financial resources, it made use of the most advanced tools and techniques of communication. Although basically conservative in its outlook, the Billy Graham Association usually followed a policy of avoiding conflict with Christians of other persuasions. American revivalist tradition soon spread throughout the world, thus leaving its mark on every continent.

All, however, was not well. By and large, the mainline churches had abandoned the inner cities, now populated by the poor and by racial minorities. In spite of valiant efforts on the part of some, mainline Christianity had become so acculturated to the ethos of the newly affluent suburban areas, that it lost contact both with the masses in the cities and with its rural roots and constituencies. In rural areas, those who remained members of their traditional denominations were increasingly suspicious of the new leadership. In the cities, the Holiness churches sought to fill the gap, but vast numbers of people lost all contact with any form of organized Christianity. Twenty years after the great religious revival of the 1950s, the call repeatedly went out for a renewed mission to the cities; but few had a clear idea how to accomplish that mission. It was not until the 1980s that there were signs of renewed religious vitality in the inner cities—and even then, such signs were

The Billy Graham Evangelistic Association was both a continuation of the American tradition of revivals, and its adaptation to social conditions in the mid-twentieth century.

closely connected to either the arrival of new immigrants and their churches, or to the return to the area of moderately affluent churchgoers.

Another feature of the post-war revival was an understanding of the Christian faith as a path to inner peace and happiness. One of the most popular religious authors of the time was Norman Vincent Peale, who promoted faith and "positive thinking" as a route to mental health and happiness. Historian Sydney E. Ahlstrom correctly speaks of the religiosity of the times as "faith in faith," which promised "peace of mind and confident living."[23] This form of religiosity was well-suited to the times, for it provided peace in the midst of a confusing world, said little about social responsibilities, and did not risk conflict with those whose Cold War mentality had made them Grand Inquisitors of American political opinion. Ahlstrom's conclusion is a serious indictment:

> The churches by and large seem to have done little more than provide a means of social identification to a mobile people who were being rapidly cut loose from the comfort of old contexts.[24]

There were, however, other factors at work within American society. Although during the post-war years these new elements were not sufficient to undo the prevailing optimistic mood of the nation, the next decades would bring them to the foreground, and bring about radical changes in the nation's outlook.

One of these factors was the Civil Rights movement, which had been brewing for decades. The National Association for the Advancement of Colored People (NAACP), founded in 1909, had won a number of court battles long before the movement came to the foreground. Some in the African-American community persisted in finding refuge in an understanding of religion that promised otherworldly rewards, or gave them a sense of belonging to the small body of the faithful, without challenging the existing order. In some cases, this led to new religions with leaders who declared themselves to be incarnations of the divine. Most successful of these were *Father Divine* who was also known as Reverend M.J. Divine (1895–1965) and bishop Manuel Grace, or *Sweet Daddy Grace* (1881?–1960). Black soldiers and sailors returning from the war—where they had fought in military units that were separate from those of white soldiers—found that the freedom for which they had fought abroad was left wanting for them i.e., back in the U.S.

Most of the early leadership of the civil rights movement was drawn from the African-American clergy.

Government responded by desegregating the armed forces in 1949 and by the historic Supreme Court decision of 1952 that ordered the integration of public schools. A number of whites supported the movement for integration, and in the early years their aid and encouragement was valuable. The National Council of Churches (formerly the Federal Council of Churches), as well as most major denominations, also took a stance against segregation. But what made the movement irresistible was the participation and leadership of African-Americans themselves. Most of that leadership, until well into the 1960s, was drawn from black clergy—most notable among them Adam Clayton Powell, Jr., during the war and post-war years, and Dr. Martin Luther King, Jr., in the late 1950s and early 1960s. In an unprecedented manifestation of faith, courage, and perseverance, blacks by the thousands showed their determination to defy and unmask the oppressive laws and practices under which they lived. Through sit-ins, arrests, beatings, and even death, in places such as Montgomery and Selma, Alabama, they showed the world that they were at least the moral equals of those who had repeatedly accused them of being inferior. "We shall overcome" became both a cry of defiance and a confession of faith.

The Southern Christian Leadership Conference (SCLC), which Dr. King founded, along with a number of other Christian organizations that promoted nonviolence, did not suffice to channel all the frustration and anger that had accumulated in the black community. For several decades, more militant blacks had seen in Islam a religion not dominated by whites. Thus the Black Muslims and several similar movements were born. Others, particularly in the crowded ghettoes of cities such as New York and Los Angeles, vented their anger through riots—of which the most famous was the 1965 riot in the Watts area of Los Angeles. By the middle of the decade, blacks had come to the conclusion that they would not attain full rights until they had their just measure of power. Thus, the cry of "black power" arose—a cry often misinterpreted to mean that blacks intended to become masters over whites.

At the same time, due partly to its Christian inspiration, Dr. King's movement was branching out into other concerns that were not strictly racial. He and several other members of the SCLC became convinced that their struggle was against injustice of every sort. It was the time of the war in Southeast Asia, and Dr. King began criticizing the government's policies in the region, both because it was clear that the Selective Service System discriminated against blacks and other minorities as well as against the poor, and because he was convinced that the United States was perpetrating in Southeast Asia an injustice similar to what had been perpetrated against blacks at home. In the United States itself, Dr. King now felt that the struggle must involve all poor people of whatever race. He was leading a "poor people's march" when he was assassinated in 1968.

The entire movement found much of its inspiration in the Christian faith of the black community. The old "spirituals" gained new meaning—or rather, they were given once again the defiant meaning they had when first sung in the old plantations. Churches became gathering and training places for protesters. Preachers articulated the connection between the gospel and the movement. Finally, a "black theology" emerged. This was a theology that was both essentially orthodox and an affirmation of the black reality, hope, and struggle. Its main figure was Union Theological Seminary professor James Cone, who declared:

There can be no Christian theology which is not identified unreservedly with those who are humiliated and abused. In fact, theology ceases to be a theology of the gospel when it fails to arise out of the community of the oppressed. For it is impossible to speak of the God of Israelite history, who is the God who revealed himself in Jesus Christ, without recognizing that he is the God *of* and *for* those who labor and are heavy laden.[25]

At the same time, another movement, at first less publicized, was gaining momentum. This was the feminist movement. For over a century, women in the United States had been claiming their rights—often under the leadership of Evangelical women. They had showed and strengthened their political muscle in the abolitionist campaign, the Women's Christian Temperance Union, and their struggle for the right to vote—which they finally won in 1920. A few churches did ordain women during the nineteenth century. But as late as the middle of the twentieth century, most denominations still did not allow the ordination of women, and all were under the control of men. During the 1950s, in both the church and society at large, and as the result of vast changes in the fiber of society, the women's movement gained in strength, experience, and solidarity. In the churches, the battle was fought mainly on two fronts: women's right to have their call to ministry validated by ordination, and the critique of a theology that had traditionally been done and dominated by males. By the mid-1980s, most major Protestant denominations did ordain women; and in the Roman Catholic Church, which refused to do so, there were strong and vocal organizations campaigning against the ban on the ordination of women. In the field of theology, a number of women—notably Presbyterian Letty M. Russell and Roman Catholic Rosemary R. Reuther—proposed what were essentially orthodox corrections to traditional male theology. More radical were the views of Mary Daly, who declared herself a "graduate" from the male-dominated church and called on her sisters to await a "female incarnation of God."

While these movements were involving a significant number of blacks and women, other international and national events were also shaping the mind of the nation. Foremost among these was the war in Southeast Asia. What started as a relatively small military involvement, in 1965 began escalating into the longest war the United States had fought to date. It was a war in which, with the hope of halting Communist advance, the United States found itself supporting corrupt governments and unsuccessfully using its enormous firepower against a nation much smaller than itself. The media brought the atrocities of the war into every living room. Then it was discovered that the public—and Congress—had been purposefully misinformed on an incident in the Gulf of Tonkin which had precipitated the escalation of the war. Protests, bitterness, and patriotic disappointment swept the nation's campuses. Eventually, armed force was used against protesting students, resulting in fatalities at Kent State University and Jackson State College. In the end, the United States, for the first time in its history, lost a war. But more than that, it lost its innocence. The notion of "the land of the free and the home of the brave," exemplifying freedom and justice at home, and defending it abroad, was brought into question. The very prosperity that resulted from the war—followed as it was by a significant recession—led some to wonder if the economic system on which the nation was founded did not require the artificial stimulus of war. To this were added all the questions and doubts kindled by the scandal that finally led to the resignation of President Richard Nixon.

While all these events were taking place in society at large, the churches were also undergoing stress. The Protestant theological enterprise became fragmented, with theologians pursuing radically different avenues. Attempts to express the Christian message in secular terms led to the much-publicized "theology of the death of God" in the 1960s. Taking a different tack, Harvey Cox's *The Secular City* sought to reinterpret the Christian message in the light of an urban society, and to see the opportunities and challenges that such a society offers. John Cobb and others set about developing an understanding of the Christian faith on the basis of process philosophy. Moltmann's theology of hope found its counterparts on American soil. And many white male theologians began studying black, feminist, and Third World theologies for clues to a renewed understanding of the biblical message. In this vast array of different and even divergent theologies, there were three common themes: an orientation toward the future, an interest in sociopolitical realities, and an attempt to bring these two together. In other words, the dominant feature of these theologies taken as a whole was the recovery of eschatology as a future hope that is active in present-day social involvement. This was joined to a liturgical renewal that began with historical inquiry into early Christian worship, and eventually began emphasizing the eschatological dimension of worship and its social relevance.

This interest in social issues was further awakened by the international contacts of the churches. Questions of hunger, political freedom, and international justice became much more significant for those who were in almost constant contact with Christians in other nations suffering under those circumstances. Therefore, the National Council of Churches, the World Council of Churches, and the boards of missions of practically every major denomination were under attack by political conservatives who accused them of being infiltrated by Communists, or at least of being dupes for Communism.

Meanwhile, the charismatic movement that began early in the century on Azusa Street (see Chapter 27) had taken a new shape. During the first half of the century, it had made an impact mostly among the lower classes and the Holiness churches. Beginning in the late 1950s, it spread to suburbia and within mainline denominations—including the Catholic Church. Most of those involved in this new charismatic wave remained loyal members of their churches; but at the same time there was a feeling of kinship among charismatics of various denominations, thus giving rise to an ecumenical movement that had little or no connection with organized conciliar ecumenism. Although sometimes seen by critics as the religious counterpart of the escape to suburbia, in truth the charismatic movement was quite varied, including within its ranks both some who felt that their experience with the Spirit should lead them away from the world, and those who felt that it should lead them into daring social action.

Evangelicalism was similarly divided. In the late 1970s and early 1980s, its radio and television work grew enormously. Some television preachers created and headed vast corporations for the furtherance of their work which they organized into what many called their "ministries"—a widespread phenomenon dubbed by critics "the electronic church." A common theme of many of these evangelists was the loss of traditional values and the breakdown of society that they said would result from it—a theme that had been heard since the time of Prohibition and its repeal. Taking their cue from the earlier struggle against alcohol, some evangelical leaders organized the "Moral Majority" to defend moral values and to support conservative economic and social policies.

On the other hand, growing numbers of evangelicals began to feel that their faith led them to a commitment to critique the existing economic and social order, both at home and abroad. Christians, they believed, must strive against all forms of injustice, suffering, hunger, and oppression. In 1973, a group of leaders of similar convictions joined in the "Chicago Declaration," which articulated what seemed to be the growing conviction of many committed Christians in the United States:

As evangelical Christians committed to the Lord Jesus Christ and the full authority of the Word of God, we affirm that God lays total claim upon the lives of his people. We cannot, therefore, separate our lives in Christ from the situation in which God has placed us in the United States and the world. . . .

We acknowledge that God requires love. But we have not demonstrated the love of God to those suffering social abuses.

We acknowledge that God requires justice. But we have not proclaimed or demonstrated his justice to an unjust American society. . . . Further, we have failed to condemn the exploitation of racism at home and abroad by our economic system. . . .

We must attack the materialism of our culture and the maldistribution of the nation's wealth and services. We recognize that as a nation we play a crucial role in the imbalance and injustice of international trade and development. Before God and a billion hungry neighbors, we must rethink our values. . . .

We must resist the temptation to make the nation and its institutions objects of near-religious loyalty. . . .

By this declaration, we endorse no political ideology or party, but call our nation's leaders and people to that righteousness which exalts a nation.

We make this declaration in the biblical hope that Christ is coming to consummate the Kingdom and we accept his claim on our total discipleship till he comes.[26]

It is significant that this declaration was very similar to others being made by Christians in varied situations throughout the world, often coming out of entirely different theological backgrounds but reaching parallel conclusions. From a worldwide perspective, it seemed that the church in the United States was finally coming to grips with the challenges of a post-Constantinian and an ecumenical age. It was also a church responding to the new vision of the "space age"—an age when for the first time we viewed the earth from space, and saw it as a fragile "spaceship" in which all must either learn to live together or perish together.

A NEW CENTURY

In spite of dire apocalyptic predictions—including the soon forgotten scare over the possible failure of all computers as a new millennium opened—the twenty-first century opened on an optimistic note. The Cold War had ended, and so had the proxy wars that the United States and the Soviet Union had been waging in Central America and elsewhere. The demise of the Soviet Union left the nation as the only superpower on earth. The previous decade had seen years of unprecedented abundance.

Then, on September 11, 2001, terror and tragedy struck. Suddenly a nation that was still celebrating its victory over the Soviet Union found itself facing the more insidious and frightening enemy of terror, which had been espoused as the weapon of choice by small but fanatical groups within the Muslim community. Although the attack on the twin towers of the World Trade Center in New York City was in fact an attack on all of civilization, the American press and the government almost immediately turned it into an "attack on America," and vowed revenge. Such revenge came mostly in the form of the invasions first of Afghanistan, which was a haven for radical Islamic terrorists, and then of Iraq, which was not. While public sentiment rallied in opposition to terrorism, opinions were divided as to the policies the government was following in implementation of that opposition. The war in Iraq, which apparently had little to do with terrorism, gave grounds for doubt and debate. Also, that war had cost the United States the loss of much of the worldwide sympathy and support it had gained as the world responded in horror to the events of 2001.

In 2008, the country fell into its worst economic recession since the historic Great Depression seven decades earlier. Banks failed. Major corporations had to be salvaged by the government by means of large injections of capital. The housing industry was practically paralyzed. Unemployment and personal bankruptcies soared.

These two elements combined—fear of terrorism and economic recession—led to a renewed wave of nativism. By that time, the ethnic and cultural composition of the nation had changed drastically. There were in the United States millions of Muslim immigrants and their descendants, and many in the larger society feared that such Muslim communities would be hotbeds for terrorists. Economic crisis in Mexico, and the proxy wars that the United States had fought in Central America in the 1980s, had led to a wave of Latin American immigration. Others were immigrating from

Southeast Asia and Africa. In every major city, as well as in many smaller towns, mosques, Hindu temples, and other non-Christian religious buildings became a common sight. Clearly, the cultural and ethnic composition of the nation was changing, and many saw this as a threat to the nation and its values. Along the Mexican border, armed citizen groups took it upon themselves the task of hunting those seeking to enter the country in search of employment. In the media, some made a name for themselves by verbal attacks on immigrants. The earlier "red scares" had been surpassed with the demise of the Soviet Union, but now a new "brown scare" against all immigrants of darker skin came to take their place.

In the midst of all this, Christian churches sought to respond in both word and action. Practically every major denomination developed programs to reach the new immigrants. Some fostered a growing Christian-Muslim dialogue. Others provided shelters for the homeless, food for the hungry, legal advice for those who suffered injustice, support for immigrants risking their lives attempting to cross the desert, etc. But at the same time that all of this was a sign of vitality, it is significant to note that the voice of the churches calling for greater justice, toleration, and understanding was seldom heard. The media, and the public at large, did not show great interest in hearing what the churches had to say on these matters. In the last decades of the twentieth century, conservative Christians joined in a loose coalition to promote conservative social and political agendas, and conservative politicians sought their support. But by the end of the first decade of the new century it was clear that the time when churches spoke and society listened was passing—even though some religious leaders still insisted on claiming a political and social clout that they no longer had.

Statistics comparing the year 1900 with 2005 serve to summarize the radical changes that were taking place in the religious landscape of the United States. In 1900, 96 percent of the population declared themselves to be Christians. By 2005, that number had declined to 83 percent. While Roman Catholicism and Pentecostalism had grown—the former mostly by immigration, and the latter by both immigration and by conversion—most traditional "mainline" Protestant denominations had declined and continued to do so. Even though Pentecostalism had grown in the United States, that growth lagged far behind what was taking place in other parts of the world, so that even within the Pentecostal tradition the United States did not play the central role it had played fifty years earlier. The percentage of

Jews remained fairly stable, at about 2 percent. But this was not the case with other religions. In 1900, there were some ten thousand Muslims in the nation; and by 2005 there were almost five million. Other faiths with negligible numbers in 1900 had also made great inroads, with Buddhists approximating the three million mark, and Hindus surpassing a million. Although not at fast as Europe, the United States too was rapidly moving "beyond Christendom."

37

Vitality at the Periphery

Over the past century . . . the center of gravity of the Christian world has shifted inexorably southward, to Africa, Asia, and Latin America. . . . Christianity should enjoy a worldwide boom in the new century, but the vast majority of believers will be neither European nor Euro-American.

PHILIP JENKINS

While the nineteenth century was the time when Christianity finally became present in practically every corner of the world, the second half of the twentieth and the early decades of the twenty-first century marked the time when it ceased being mostly a Western religion. Those latter years marked a worldwide reaction against the colonialism of the nineteenth century, as well as against the neocolonialism that had taken its place in several areas—particularly Latin America. This reaction could be felt not only in the colonized regions, but also in the earlier colonial metropolises, where the shortcomings of notions such as *the white man's burden* and *Manifest Destiny* were laid bare. But the end of the heyday of Western colonialism did not mean that the churches founded in the midst of colonial expansion would cease to exist. On the contrary, at a time when, as we have seen, Christianity seemed to be in crisis in its traditional centers on the North Atlantic—Europe, Canada, and the United States—it was showing great vitality, growth, and creativity in the rest of the world. Thus, Christianity was moving "beyond Christendom," not only in the sense that the North Atlantic was no longer predominantly Christian, but also in the sense that new centers were emerging beyond the traditional centers of Christendom. In this, the last decades of the twentieth century, and the early decades of the twenty-first, would witness a geographical shift in Christianity such as those that had taken place in the second to the fourth centuries, when the early Jewish sect became an empire-wide religion, and then in the seventh and eighth centuries, when the ancient centers of Christianity in the Middle East and in North Africa were conquered by Islam, and Western Christianity found its center on an axis that ran from north to south—from the British Isles through the Carolingian lands, and then on to Rome.

By the second decade of the twenty-first century there were those in the North Atlantic who claimed that Christianity was receding, that its numbers were waning, that many churches were simply marking time and keeping old traditions. But this was only partially true, first of all, because even in the midst of its own crises Christianity in the North Atlantic showed significant vitality; and, secondly, because in the former mission territories of Asia, Africa, and Latin America, Christianity was more active and vibrant than it had ever been before. This was seen in each of these areas, not only in numeric growth—which in many cases was explosive—but also in evangelistic zeal, in ecumenical initiatives, and in cultural and theological creativity.

ASIA

India, the land where William Carey's work had inspired missionary efforts throughout the world, is a prime example of the changes that were taking place during the twentieth and twenty-first centuries. The years between the two world wars were marked by a struggle for independence whose most influential leader was Mohandas K. Ghandi (1869–1948), better known as Mahatma Ghandi. In 1946, after long years of struggle, the British government finally agreed to offer full independence to India. The ensuing years were a time of great unrest during which the subcontinent was divided—primarily on religious grounds—between Pakistan (later to be partitioned again, into Pakistan and Bangladesh) and India, and Ghandi was assassinated (1948). Finally, in 1950, the Republic of India was inaugurated.

India boasted some of the most ancient churches in the world, claiming to have been founded by none other than the Apostle Thomas. Anglican and other Protestant missions during the nineteenth century had sought to revitalize the ancient Indian church—which in many cases meant to make them more like Western Protestant churches. At the same time, Roman Catholics tried to draw those ancient churches into obedience to the pope. The eventual result was that the ancient Indian church was divided, with some retaining their earlier allegiance, some becoming Anglicans or Prot-estants of other denominations, others becoming Roman Catholic Uniates, and still others founding a Protestant body known as the Church of Mar Thoma, which early in the twenty-first century had approximately a million members.

One would expect such divisions, and the context of political unrest, to have sapped the strength of the church, or at least turn it into a series of iso-lated communities within Indian society. But this is not what happened. On the contrary, Christianity in India showed unusual creativity and evange-listic zeal. The mass conversions that had begun in the nineteenth century, particularly among the lower castes, now continued, often as a result of the charismatic movement, which reached India in the mid-twentieth century. New charismatic communities appeared throughout the nation, some simply repeating what they had learned from the West, but others founding schools in which traditional Indian culture was reaffirmed as a proper locus for the practice of the Christian faith. At the other extreme of the social scale, the "churchless Christians" were mostly people from the higher castes who sought to combine traditional Hindu contemplative practices with Chris-tianity without joining a church, and who were often accused of syncretism.

As for the Protestant churches that had been planted in that land earlier within a colonial context, they too showed great creativity in seeking new ways to express and live the faith within the context of Indian culture in an independent nation. They excelled in the development of an indigenous leadership capable of meeting these challenges. They played an important role in the educational system of the entire nation. And in general they gained the respect of the vast majority of the Indian population—even though late in the twentieth century and early in the twenty-first a revival of radical Hinduism led to occasional but significant clashes and even violence. They also provided ministry to the large numbers of Indians living abroad, particularly in Great Britain, in the United States, and in some of the former British colonies in Africa.

It was, however, in the field of ecumenism that the Indian churches showed their greatest creativity. As a result of his missionary experience in India, William Carey had called for a worldwide missionary conference to meet in Cape Town, South Africa, in 1810—a conference which finally met in Edinburgh a hundred years later, in 1910. Now India took the lead in pro-moting Christian unity. Even before the conference in Edinburgh, in 1901, several churches of the Reformed tradition had achieved organic union in India. By 1908, Reformed and Congregationalists joined to form the United Church of South India, and in 1947 this church, with the addition of Methodists and Anglicans, resulted in the Church of South India. At that time, this was an almost unique example of the degree to which, when mission becomes the central concern of the church, unity is one of the many results. This example was soon followed by many others, not only in North India, but also as far as Latin America, Africa, and the United States—where as late as 2010 a unity such as that achieved in South India six decades earlier still seemed an impossible dream. Furthermore, in part thanks to its early ecumenical stance, the Indian Christian community played an important role in the birth and leadership of the International Missionary Council, and later of the World Council of Churches.

Meanwhile, China was following a very different history. During the first half of the twentieth century, and in spite of the Boxer Rebellion at the beginning of the century, many Protestant missionary programs and endeavors focused their attention on China, to the extent that there were over six thousand missionaries in that land, and their success was such that some began to speak of a massive conversion that would dwarf the conversion of Constantine and of the Roman Empire. As part of that process, thousands of Chinese pastors and other church leaders were trained. At the same time, the Roman Catholic Church was also establishing deeper roots in China—a process marked by the consecration of the first six Chinese bishops in 1926. Catholics as well as Protestants spoke of the great success of their missions in China, and of the hope for even greater successes. Then came World War II and its aftermath, the establishment of the People's Republic of China and its communist regime, the Cold War, and finally the Cultural Revolution under the leadership of Mao Tse Dung. At the beginning of those turbulent years, practically all foreign missionaries left the country—some voluntarily and some by order of the government. And from that point conditions worsened. In 1950, the government forced the churches to adopt a "Christian manifesto" which many believed violated their conscience. Resistance led to persecution, mostly through a "denunciation campaign" in which people were encouraged to denounce those whose views did not entirely coincide with those of the government. Claiming that there were too many churches, the government began forcing the "consolidation" of churches—which effectively closed many churches and allowed church property to be confiscated. Then, in the 1960s the Cultural Revolution resulted in even further persecution and the closing of all churches. The point came where many, both inside China and outside, feared that the earlier history of Christianity in China, where the church had been repeatedly planted and then disappeared, would recur once again.

But, even while many Chinese Christians capitulated before pressure and persecution, many did not. In some major cities where churches were closed and worship gatherings were prohibited, believers would make it a point to walk in front of the church at the times formerly appointed for worship, nod at one another, and keep on walking. In private homes, and under great secrecy, small groups continued meeting.

Then, in the 1970s, when the failure of the Cultural Revolution, rising tension with the Soviet Union, and economic necessities led the government to allow more freedom to Christians, the world was surprised to find that Christianity had continued to grow in China. In a land were there were approximately five million Christians in 1900, there were now some fifty million. Even under the shadows of the Cultural Revolution the church had continued existing and growing. Many of the churches that had been

After the end of the Cultural Revolution, attendance at church was such that people had to gather outside the buildings, where they would listen and follow the readings in their Bibles.

closed for years now opened their doors and soon filled with worshipers. Communities that had met clandestinely either joined the recently reopened churches or simply became churches themselves—the "house churches." Seminaries were opened, and soon had hundreds of students. Christian and theological books—at first only a few, but then in increasing numbers—were published and translated into Chinese. By the end of the twentieth century, a limited number of foreign church workers were present in China, and Chinese Christian leaders were traveling to ecumenical gatherings abroad, telling their story, and contributing to the revitalization of churches in the older centers of Christianity.

The ecumenical movement in China followed a very different course than it did in India. Here it was the government that forced the churches to unite, mostly so that they could be controlled. As soon as such pressures were eased, a number of churches reasserted their differences from the rest, and reconstituted themselves as separate entities. But many did not.

Among Protestants, many began speaking of a "post-denominational" age into which China had been forced, but that pointed to the future shape of the church in other parts of the world.

However, divisions and tensions still remained. Among Roman Catholics, the most difficult question was whether to accept the authority of bishops who followed the policies of the government, and who often had been selected by the government. Thus, there was an "official" Catholic Church and also an "underground" Catholic Church, both claiming to be Catholic, and forcing authorities in Rome to walk fine diplomatic lines. In 2006, the Vatican excommunicated two bishops who had been consecrated by the Chinese Patriotic Catholic Association—a pro-government Catholic group—without papal approval. Similarly, among Protestants the church officially recognized by the government—known as the Chinese Christian Council—was accused by some of being too subservient to political authorities. Quite independently from it, many "house churches" continued meeting and affirming their faith, often with more charismatic overtones than the larger church. Such tensions, however, should not be exaggerated, for quite often the official church would intervene with the government on behalf of a house church, and there were people who belonged to both.

The story of Christianity in Japan during the twentieth century and early in the twenty-first is in some ways similar to that of China, and in other ways quite different. Here too, after American Commodore Perry and others

The church in China was noted for its services to the people. This outdoors counseling center was one of many such services.

after him forced Japan to open its markets to foreign products, and its lands to foreign missionaries, there were those who expected the entire nation to become Christian. Here too the Second Word War and its aftermath put an end to such dreams. Here too the government—although ideologically very different from the Chinese government—forced the churches to unite, forming the United Church of Christ in Japan (1941). And here too important segments withdrew from such forced unity as soon as new political conditions allowed it—although, as in the case of China, most Protestants remained in the united church or Kyodan. However, the growth of this church was not as spectacular as that of its counterpart in China. In Japan, most of the numeric growth of Christianity took place through the work of Pentecostal and Charismatic groups, whose presence in that nation can be documented as early as 1913.

Finally, since it would be impossible to survey here the story of Christianity in every nation in Asia, we must turn our attention to Korea, where Protestant Christianity would experience its most notable numeric growth. Late in the nineteenth century, missionaries in Korea had begun following the "Nevius missionary methods," named after their proponent John L. Nevius, who argued that missionary work should concentrate on the working and lower classes as well as women and girls, on the development of native leadership, and on the growth of the church toward self-support in terms of both finances and personnel. To this was added a great revival that swept many Korean churches—particularly Methodist and Presbyterian—in the early decades of the twentieth century. Therefore, although the Japanese invasion in 1910 brought great hardship to Christians—mostly Protestants—who refused to participate in the Shinto worship promoted by the Japanese, the Korean church continued its life and growth throughout World War II. By the time the Japanese were finally forced to withdraw from the peninsula, Korean Christians had shown that they were able to affirm both their faith and much of their culture. The partition of the peninsula into North and South Korea brought new hardships for Christians, who at the time were most numerous in the North, and now had to live under one of the most repressive communist regimes in the world. Even so, the growth of the churches continued unabated in both North and South Korea. To this were soon added Pentecostal missionaries, mostly from the United States, who settled in South Korea, founding new churches and reinforcing the experiences of the Korean revival several decades earlier. The result of all this was a vibrant church that was present in both the rural areas and the cities, where the membership of congregations often ran into the tens of thousands. Furthermore, the Korean church soon began sending missionaries overseas, including Japan and China—two nations that had repeatedly occupied and oppressed Korea itself—but also Africa, Latin America, and the United States. In this latter country, where there was significant Korean immigration, there was also rapid church growth among the Korean population—both because many of the immigrants were Christians, and because they evangelized their non-Christian Korean neighbors and friends.

Furthermore, in the decade of the 1960s the Korean church began producing its own brand of liberation theology, *Minjung* theology, which sought to affirm the struggles of those—Christians as well as not—who seek liberation from economic and social oppression.

Throughout Asia, the late twentieth century and the early decades of the twenty-first saw the growth of churches that were self-governing, self-propagating—even beyond the limits of their own nations—and largely self-supporting. Just as Korean Protestantism had grown sufficiently strong to send missionaries throughout the world, so were the Philippines sending Catholic priests and nuns to traditionally Catholic countries who now suffered a lack of priests and nuns. In all of this, the churches in Asia were fulfilling the dreams of earlier missionaries who hoped to plant such self-sufficient churches. But they were also going beyond such dreams by becoming, not only self-governing, self-supporting, and self-propagating, but also self-interpreting, proposing their own understanding of their mission as well as their own theological perspectives and readings of Scripture within their cultural, social, religious, and political contexts. Several of these churches were also showing the rest of Christianity the way into the future by uniting and collaborating in ways that were not common in the older centers of Christendom.

AFRICA

Africa too could boast of one of the most ancient churches in the world, the Ethiopian Orthodox Church, founded in the fourth century (see vol. I, Chapter 25), the largest of the churches that had refused to accept the decisions of the Council of Chalcedon, and thus dubbed *Monophysite*. This church was closely tied to Ethiopian tradition and national identity, and played an important role in the resistance to Italian imperialism during World War II. Later in the twentieth century it suffered significant difficulties, on the one hand, by the inroads of Islam from neighboring countries and, on the other, by the advent to power of a hostile regime in the 1970s. Yet it held its own, so that early in the twenty-first century it has approximately 35 million members. Although not intentionally, this church—as many others—spread to other areas during the second half of the twentieth century, as Ethiopians migrated to other lands—particularly Europe and the United States.

Roman Catholicism had long been present in Africa, first in the Portuguese colonies of Angola and Mozambique, and then in the vast French colonies in central and North Africa. The decisions of the Second Vatican Council, particularly regarding the liturgy in the vernacular languages and its adaptation to various cultures, produced some friction, for there was wide disagreement as to how far this should be taken. For instance, when Catholics in Zaire proposed their own liturgy, this was held back by the Vatican, which apparently considered it too radical a departure from its own standards, and finally approved it with significant modifications. Similar struggles took place in other areas, particularly as the colonial powers withdrew and nations began reaffirming their identity, culture, and traditions.

Even so, by the end of the twentieth century Roman Catholicism was grow-ing in practically every nation in sub-Saharan Africa, and African Catholics were making significant contributions to the church at large. This growth was particularly notable in that the Catholic Church in Africa produced large numbers of priestly vocations at a time when in traditional Catholic countries there was a crisis for lack of priests. Thus, by the early twenty-first century there were numerous African priests serving parishes in Ireland as well as in Portugal and France. This is one more example of how what had earlier been the periphery of the church was now becoming a new center of vitality and missionary activity.

It was, however, among Protestants that explosive growth took place. When the former British colonies became independent, most of the leaders of the new nations—not only in politics, but also in education, trade, and the professions—had been educated in Protestant schools, mostly spon-sored by the Church of England. At the same time, Protestant missionaries had long been working among the rural population and the poorer urban dwellers. Independence provided an opportunity for the growth of forms of Christianity that were connected with the ancient traditions of the people, and that often provided leadership in times of struggle. In places such as Uganda, Kenya and Tanganyika there were veritable mass conversions, so that in Kenya, for instance, where less than ten percent of the population was Christian before World War II, by the beginning of the twenty-first century that figure had risen to sixty percent. In other places in northern sub-Saharan Africa, such as Nigeria, southern Sudan, etc., there was also notable growth, but there was also a constant conflict with Islam—a conflict that often revolved around the conviction of many Muslims that Islamic law should be the law of the land, and the opposition of Christians and others to such measures.

In southern Africa, where the presence of Islam was not as strong, the great struggle was first against colonial rule, and then against systems of white supremacy. This was most notable in South Africa, where the struggle against apartheid was long and painful. In that struggle, black African Christians such as Anglican Desmond Tutu, Reformed Allan Boesak, and Methodist Nelson Mandela expressed the feelings of the black majority, connected them with their Christian faith, and sought resolutions that were both just and peaceful. Although less famous, there were similar leaders in Zimbabwe—which after its liberation found itself in the grips of a corrupt

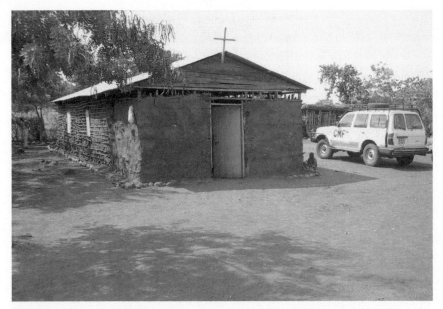

By the end of the twentieth century the countryside of sub-Saharan Africa was dotted by churches built and sustained by local believers, such as this one in Tanzania.

and oppressive regime—and Namibia.

Pentecostalism had arrived in Africa shortly after the Azusa Street revival, but it was in the latter half of the twentieth century that its growth was most impressive. Given its close connection with the United States, Liberia was the first country to feel the impact of the Pentecostal movement. But this movement soon spread throughout the continent, impacting the churches already there, planting new branches of the sending churches, and resulting in the birth of a number of independent autochthonous churches. A notable example of the latter was *The Church of Jesus Christ on Earth through the Prophet Kimbangu.* Samuel Kimbangu (1887–1951) was born in the Congo—now Zaire—when that land was under Belgian rule. Originally a Baptist, in 1921 he began preaching and practicing a charismatic form of Christianity, with emphasis on healing the sick and even raising the dead. His public ministry lasted only a few months, for the Belgian government had him arrested, accused of sedition, and condemned to death—a sentence that was then commuted to life imprisonment. But even while he was in prison his fame and the number of his followers grew—the latter coming to the conclusion that their prophet was a special envoy of Jesus. In 1959, eight years

The charismatic movement developed deep roots in African Christianity.

after his death, the Belgian government gave official permission for Kimbangu's followers to conduct public worship. Soon, under the leadership of the prophet's son, Joseph Diangienda, the church expanded to several other countries in sub-Saharan Africa. By the twenty-first century, partly through missionary work and partly through the migration of some of its members, its was to be found also in a number of countries beyond Africa—including the United Kingdom, the Caribbean, and the United States. At first quite independent of all other Christian groups, by the beginning of the twenty-first century the Kimbanguist church had begun to join councils of churches in various African nations.

While the Kimbanguist movement is probably the most numerous, there are many other autochthonous churches in Africa—more than ten thousand in southern Africa alone. By 2010, their total membership was estimated at between eighty and ninety million. Many of these churches followed a path similar to the Kimbanguist movement, eventually sending missionaries not only to other regions of Africa, but also to other areas of the world—particularly to Great Britain, the English-speaking Caribbean, and Haiti.

Since the presence of these churches, as well as the issue of the relationship between Christianity and the cultures of Africa, provoked much theological debate, by the twenty-first century Africa, which until recently had been the recipient of missions and had been learning its theology from overseas churches, had become a center sending missionaries to various parts of the world, and beginning to develop its own theologies. It has also become a center for its unique form of ecumenism with the creation in 1978 of the Organization of African Instituted Churches, which promoted cooperation in theological education by extension, the promotion of women's rights, and further attempts to incarnate Christianity in African cultures and traditions.

LATIN AMERICA

In Latin America, the early years of the twentieth century saw the continuation of the conflict between conservatives and liberals, and of the impact this conflict had on the life of the Catholic Church. The most notable among such conflicts was the Mexican Revolution of 1910—already discussed in Chapter 33—but similar struggles took place throughout the region. Eventually, during the course of the century, even the most conservative nations in the continent settled on constitutions granting freedom of thought and of religion, and most of the traditional privileges of the Church and its clergy were abolished. This process was complex, and need not be spelled out here. Two examples—one for Argentina and the other from Brazil—should suffice to show some of the issues at stake.

In Argentina, Juan Domingo Perón came to power in 1943 by means of a military coup. At that stage, he had the support of the Catholic hierarchy, who saw in his movement and in the military who supported him the best defense against Communism and secularism. As part of his program, Perón decreed obligatory religious instruction in schools. The Church, on its part, allied itself with the growing labor movement, which was Perón's base of popular support, and did not object to the slogan, "true Catholicism is Peronism." But then difficulties arose. Perón wanted to control the life of the church, giving it mostly a ceremonial role, and counting on it to give his government religious sanction. He even insisted on the canonization of his wife Eva—Evita. By 1954, the rebellion that finally overthrew him in 1955 had the support of many among the hierarchy, and the slogan of the rebels was "in the name of the Virgin, freedom, and the Catholic faith."

Eventually, as the dust settled, Argentina became a secular state in which the Church was reduced to an inspirational and ceremonial role.

In Brazil, during the dictatorship of Getulio Vargas in the 1930s, several laws were passed in support of the Catholic Church—divorce was outlawed, the Church was given authority to ban "indecent" movies, and church marriages were granted official recognition. All this was done mostly through the action of *Ação Integralista Brasileira*, a movement that did not have the official sanction of the hierarchy, but which the archbishop of Rio, Cardinal Sebastião Leme, secretly supported. However, eventually this movement went beyond the bounds of what the hierarchy deemed appropriate— offering its own rites for baptisms, marriages, and funerals, and even claiming that it was the road to eternal salvation—and began losing the support of the hierarchy. In 1937, using a supposed Communist conspiracy as an excuse, Vargas abolished the constitution and began governing by decree and seeking to limit the Church to a strictly spiritual role. In 1950, when, after being overthrown by a coup in 1945, Vargas returned to power through the electoral process. He refused to reestablish the privileges of the Church and its clergy. In this, he was expressing the sentiments of a growing number of Brazilians, who felt that the traditional privileges of the Church were unfounded and resulted in economic exploitation and lack of freedom. These new tendencies were seen in the growing prestige of the bishop of Recife, Hélder Câmara (1909–1999), a former member of the *Integralista* movement who now became a champion of the poor and the oppressed, and of revolution through peaceful means, and who was nominated four times for the Nobel Peace Prize. In 1967, he led an international group of bishops in formulating a *Declaration of Bishops of the Third World*, advocating for a more just social and economic order.

The watershed in the history of Latin American Catholicism in the twentieth century was the gathering of the *Consejo Episcopal Latinoamericano* (C.E.L.A.M.) in Medellín, Colombia, in 1968. By that time, Latin American liberation theology—to be discussed later in this chapter—had begun making inroads among the Catholic leadership, and therefore this conference was marked by a turning of the attention of the Church from its own inner issues and problems, to the needs of the people—particularly the oppressed and the poor. In his fairly mild opening statement, Pope Paul VI had encouraged the bishops to consider the plight of the poor, and to reaffirm the poverty of the Church. The conference took this encouragement to heart, as well as the declaration of Vatican II (in *Gaudium et spes*) that "the joys and hopes, the pains and anxieties, of people today, especially those who are poor or in any way afflicted, are the joys and hopes, the pains and anxieties of the followers of Christ." The very first document of the Medellín conference tackled the matter of the world economic order, declaring that both Communism and capitalism "militate against the dignity of the human person," and that "Latin America sees itself caught between these two options and remains dependent on one or the other of the centers of power which control its economy."

The changes in the life of the church that Medellín brought about were momentous. A church that had traditionally been preoccupied above all with its own privileges and power, and had often been employed by the powerful to sanction their privileges, now declared itself the champion of the poor and the oppressed. There were still many among the leadership of the church whose goals and perspectives remained largely unchanged. Soon C.E.L.A.M. itself sought to soften what had been declared at Medellín. But there were others who took these declarations as a call to explore new theologies and new ways of being the church. In these conflicts, the tensions that had existed in Latin American Catholicism from the very beginning— tensions between those whose main concern was the life of the Church, and those whose main concern was the life of the people—surfaced once again. To these we shall return later in this chapter.

As a result of both immigration and missionary work, Protestantism was well established in Latin America by the end of the nineteenth century. During the twentieth, most of the more traditional Protestant churches continued to grow—some of them quite rapidly. But it was the Pentecostal movement that resulted in explosive growth. The nation first noted for Pentecostal growth was Chile, where Methodist missionary Willis Hoover, who apparently had been influenced by the Azusa Street revival of 1906, led a movement in 1909. There was great rejoicing, speaking in tongues, faith healing, and other such phenomena, and the movement rapidly spread from Valparaíso—where Hoover served as pastor—to Santiago and other areas of the country. Eventually, Hoover—along with a tenth of his church's membership—left the Methodist Church to become pastor of a newly formed Methodist Pentecostal Church in Valparaíso. The new denomination, known as *Iglesia Metodista Pentecostal*, was the first such denomination in the Third World. From that moment, the movement grew by leaps and bounds. It soon became associated with nationalistic feelings and a desire to be freed from foreign missionary control, to the point that the names of several of its early churches include the word *nacional*. It also provided more room for leadership on the part of the common people and of women. As is often the case, the Iglesia Metodista Pentecostal divided repeatedly. As the movement became known in other traditional denominations—Presbyterians and Baptists among them—some left them to found their own Pentecostal churches. By 2005 there were more than five million Pentecostals in Chile, while the Methodist Church of Chile, from which the movement had emerged, had less than eighteen thousand members.

Similar events elsewhere in Latin America led to other Pentecostal churches, and to their unprecedented growth. In Brazil, the movement began among Presbyterians, but soon spread to other denominations. One of the larger groups, although not founded by missionaries from the Assemblies of God, eventually joined that denomination. In Mexico, people who had experienced the Azusa Street revival took the movement to the state of Chihuahua. Fleeing the chaos and dangers of the Mexican Revolution, a woman by the name of Romana Carbajal de Valenzuela and her husband moved to California, where they joined a church that had resulted from the Azusa Street revival, and which insisted that baptism should be only "in the name of Jesus," and not of the Trinity. In 1914, she returned to Mexico, and her testimony there resulted in the *Iglesia Apostólica de la Fe en Cristo Jesús*, which by the beginning of the twenty-first century had more than a million members, and missionaries and congregations throughout the Americas.

All of this resulted in such growth that some wondered whether Latin America would eventually become mostly Pentecostal. If one counts members and "adherents"—people connected to churches, but not officially part of them—by the second decade of the twenty-first century Pentecostals accounted for 47 percent of the population in Brazil, 36 percent in Chile, and 13 percent in Mexico. This challenged the traditional view of Christendom in a way that was different from what was taking place in Asia and Africa, for what was happening here was that a region that had long been counted as part of Christendom was now to a large degree changing its allegiance from one branch of Christianity to another—to the point that traditionally Roman Catholic Latin America was rapidly becoming one of the most Protestant regions of the world.

Such growth could not take place without repeated divisions as well as the birth of movements that departed from much of the traditional Christian faith. Most of these preached a "gospel of prosperity," promising economic and other success to their followers, while others turned their founders and leaders into objects of worship. Among the first, the most notable was the *Igreja Universal do Reinho de Deus*—Universal Church of the Reign of God—which was said to be the largest international economic enterprise in Brazil. In Mexico, the *Iglesia la Luz del Mundo—The Light of the World Church*—followed a similar path, although its success was not as great as that of its Brazilian counterpart. There were also "apostolic networks" whose members certified one another's "apostolicity," and often claimed that pastors who joined their networks would enjoy unprecedented success. One of these "apostles," for instance, invited others to join his network by announcing on the Internet that before becoming an apostle he would preach a fortnight for a bunch of bananas; but no more now that he had become an apostle and drove a luxury car! Another began his ministry as a "bishop," then became an "apostle," and finally claimed the title of "archangel." Among those who deified their leaders, there was one in Mexico whose leader entered the town in a large white convertible, while his followers shouted, "Blessed is he who comes in the name of the Lord!" In Puerto

Latin American Protestantism soon expanded to immigrant churches in the United States, such as this one in Providence, Rhode Island.

Rico—and later in Miami—a former heroin addict founded a movement based on the notion that he was the Lord incarnate.

While such radically heterodox movements draw much attention, it should be noted that the vast majority of Pentecostals remained firm in the traditional tenets of the Christian faith, that most did not preach a gospel of prosperity, and that in spite of many existing stereotypes many Pentecostal individuals and churches were deeply involved in social services and advocacy for the needy and the oppressed.

The ecumenical movement did not advance rapidly in Latin America for a number of reasons. First of all, most Protestant preaching and teaching had long been anti-Catholic and anti-Communist. As a result, there was among many the fear that the ecumenical movement was a papal ploy to reassert the pope's authority and force others into the Catholic fold, and there was among others the feeling that the social and political stances of the World Council of Churches were pro-Communist. Then, fundamentalism and power struggles caused many churches to divide repeatedly, resulting in relatively small groups that wished no connection with others. This was exacerbated by insistence on every minor point of doctrine, as if salvation depended on agreeing on each one of them. But even so, in Latin America too the quest for unity could be seen. In 1961, two large Chilean Pentecostal churches joined the World Council of Churches—the first Pentecostal churches ever to do so. In 1982, the *Consejo Latinoamericano de Iglesias*—CLAI, or Latin American Council of Churches—was founded with wide Pentecostal as well as Evangelical participation, and also with close ties to the World Council of Churches. In the same year, a more conservative counterpart, the *Confraternidad Evangélica Latinoamericana*—CONELA, Latin American Evangelical Confraternity—was founded, in clear competition with CLAI.

THE ECUMENICAL MOVEMENT

The nineteenth century had brought about the existence of a truly worldwide church. By the latter half of that century, there were movements seeking further collaboration among the various churches in each region. In 1910, the World Missionary Conference in Edinburgh gave further impulse to a movement that, although interrupted by two world wars, would eventually lead to the founding of the World Council of Churches and to other visible manifestations of Christian unity. Soon, however, it was discovered that such unity did not mean that Christians from other parts of the world would become one in an essentially Western church; rather, it meant that all Christians, whatever their race or nationality, would engage in a common search for the meaning of obedience to Christ in the modern world. Thus, the ecumenical movement had two facets. The first and most obvious was the quest for greater and more visible unity. The second, with perhaps even more drastic consequences, was the birth of a worldwide church to whose mission and self-understanding all would contribute.

The World Missionary Conference of 1910 appointed a Continuation Committee, which in turn led to the founding of the International Missionary Council in 1921. By that time, other regional and national organizations for missionary cooperation had appeared in Europe, the United States, Canada, and Australia, partly as a result of the work done at Edinburgh. These organizations provided the nucleus for the new body; but it was also decided that the "younger churches" that had resulted from missionary work would be directly represented. Again, the International Missionary Council did not intend to set guidelines or rules for missionary work, but rather to serve as a meeting place where strategies, experiences, and various resources could be shared. At the First Assembly of the International Missionary Council (which was appropriately held in Jerusalem in 1928), almost a fourth of the delegates belonged to the younger churches—a great advance from the seventeen who had been present at Edinburgh. Both in Jerusalem and in the Second Assembly, held in Madras, India, in 1938, the question of the nature of the church and the content of the Christian message came to the foreground, thus indicating that it was impossible to exclude theological discussion from a truly open encounter on the world mission of the church. Then the work of the Council was interrupted by World War II, and the Third Assembly, held in Whitby, Canada, in 1947, devoted most of its attention to reestablishing the links broken by the war, and to planning for the reconstruction of missionary work ravaged by the conflict. By then, however, there was a growing consciousness of the indissoluble union between church and mission, so that it seemed unwise to discuss missionary issues without also entering a dialogue on the nature of the church and other theological matters. This theme was increasingly heard in the next two assemblies of the International Missionary Council, held in Willingen, Germany, in 1952, and in Ghana, from 1957 to 1958. By then, it was decided that the International Missionary Council should join the World Council of Churches, which it did at the New Delhi assembly of the World Council, in 1961. At the time of this merger, steps were taken so that bodies that would not or could not join the World Council of Churches itself could still be fully represented in the division that fell heir to the work of the International Missionary Council.

Another major movement leading to the founding of the World Council of Churches was "Faith and Order." To allay suspicions, the convocation of the World Missionary Conference of 1910 had explicitly excluded matters of faith and order—meaning any discussion of the beliefs of churches, or of their understanding and practice of ordination, sacraments, and so forth. Although this was a necessary exclusion in order to make the conference as inclusive as possible, many were convinced that the time had come to open a forum for the discussion of those very issues. Foremost among these was a bishop of the Episcopal Church, Charles H. Brent. At his prodding, the Anglican communion took the first steps in calling for a meeting on faith and order. Others soon joined, and after the interruption of World War I, and prolonged negotiations thereafter, the First World Conference on Faith and Order gathered in 1927 in Lausanne, Switzerland. Its four hundred delegates represented 108 churches—Protestant, Orthodox, and Old Catholic (those who had left Roman Catholicism at the time of the promulgation of papal infallibility). Many of them had gained experience in international and ecumenical gatherings through their participation in the Student Christian Movement—which for decades provided most of the leadership for several branches of the ecumenical movement. At the conference, it was decided not to seek unanimity by either very broad and therefore meaningless statements, or by doctrinal definitions that would necessarily exclude some. On the contrary, the method followed was frank and open discussion of issues, with the drafting of a document that began by stressing those points on which agreement had been reached, and then clearly stating those other points on which differences still remained. Thus, the documents were characterized by phrases such as "we agree," or "we believe," followed by points of clarification introduced by phrases such as "there are among us divergent views," or "it is held by many churches represented in the Conference." By the end of the meeting, it was clear to all present that their agreements were much more significant than their disagreements, and that a number of the latter could probably be overcome by further dialogue and clarification. Before adjourning the conference, a Continuation Committee was appointed, under the leadership of William Temple, archbishop of York (and later of Canterbury). After Temple's death, Brent succeeded him, and the Second World Conference on Faith and Order finally gathered at Edinburgh in 1937. It followed the same method of Lausanne, again with valuable results. But its most significant decision was to agree with the call of the Second Conference on Life and Work, gathered at Oxford the previous month, for the founding of a "World Council of Churches."

The Life and Work movement was also the result of the missionary experiences of earlier generations, as well as of the conviction that the various churches must join in every practical endeavor in which such collaboration was possible. Its foremost leader was Nathan Söderblom, Lutheran archbishop of Uppsala in Sweden. World War I, while interrupting the plans for an international gathering, did give Söderblom and others the opportunity to work together in finding solutions to the enormous problems caused by the conflict. Finally, the first conference on "Practical Christianity"—the early name of the movement—gathered in Stockholm in 1925. Its agenda consisted in seeking common responses to contemporary problems on the basis of the gospel. Its delegates were divided into five sections, each discussing one of five main themes and its ramifications: economic and industrial matters, moral and social issues, international affairs, Christian education, and means by which churches could join in further collaboration. From the beginning, this movement took a firm stance against every form of exploitation or imperialism. Thus, at a time when mechanization was causing unemployment, weakening unions, and lowering wages, the Conference echoed "the aspirations of the working people toward an equitable and fraternal order, the only one compatible with the divine plan of redemption." Also, with a prophetic voice whose truthfulness would be confirmed decades later, it noted a "general resentment against white imperialism" that threatened to break into open conflict. This conference also appointed a Continuation Committee that organized the Second Conference on Life and Work. This gathered at Oxford in 1937, and its final documents included a strong word against every form of totalitarianism, and a condemnation of war as a method to solve international conflict. Also, as has been noted, it called for the combining of Life and Work with Faith and Order in a single World Council of Churches.

With that decision, and the concurrence of Faith and Order, the stage was set for the founding of such a council. The two movements appointed a joint committee, and work began toward the convocation of the council's first assembly. World War II, however, interrupted such plans. During the conflict, contacts made through the nascent ecumenical movement were instrumental in establishing networks of Christians on both sides of the battlefront, giving support to the Confessing Church in Germany, and saving Jews in various lands under Nazi rule. Finally, on August 22, 1948, the First Assembly of the World Council of Churches was called to order in Amsterdam. One hundred and seven churches from forty-four nations were part of it. The opening sermon was delivered by D. T. Niles, a Methodist from Ceylon who had ample experience as a leader of the Student Christian. Other speakers were Karl Barth, Joseph Hromádka, Martin Niemöller, Reinhold Niebuhr, and John Foster Dulles. The Council was organized so as to include the concerns previously related to Life and Work as well as those of Faith and Order—under its Division of Studies, there was a Commission on Faith and Order that continued meeting and organizing world conferences, while the more practical concerns of Life and Work were generally included under the Division of Ecumenical Action.

While rejoicing in the unity that the very existence of the Council mani-

Those who presided over the World Council of Churches in its early years were people who had long experience in various other ecumenical endeavors. American Methodist John R. Mott is second from the top.

fested, the delegates also looked at the world around them, and sought to deal with the issues confronting that world. Significantly, at a time when the Cold War was beginning, the Council called on all churches to reject both Communism and liberal capitalism, and to oppose the mistaken notion that these two systems exhaust all possible alternatives. As could be expected, this declaration, and similar later ones, were not always well received.

After 1948, the membership of the World Council of Churches continued growing. Most significant was the increased participation of the Orthodox, who had jointly decided not to attend the Amsterdam assembly. When it was clarified that the World Council was not and did not claim to be an "ecumenical council" after the fashion of Nicea, and that it had no intention of becoming a church, the Orthodox did join the Council. Since several Orthodox churches existed under Communist regimes, and their delegates could only attend World Council meetings with government approval, this increased the suspicion on the part of many that the World Council was becoming the instrument of an international Communist conspiracy. In any case, by the time of the Second Assembly, gathered in Evanston, Illinois, in 1954, 163 churches were present. The Council began to turn its attention to the church in its local concreteness, trying to avoid the dangers of forgetting that those who gathered in its assemblies were, after all, the representatives of millions living and worshiping in every corner of the globe. When the Third Assembly gathered in New Delhi, in 1961, the member churches numbered 197. The merging at New Delhi of the International Missionary Council with the World Council of Churches also gave the latter more direct contacts with the Third World and the younger churches. Such contacts were increased by the membership in the Council of two Pentecostal churches from Chile—the first such bodies to join. This assembly also continued the earlier emphasis on the church at the parish level by speaking of the unity of "all in each place." Later assemblies in Uppsala (1968), Nairobi (1975), and Vancouver (1983) continued these trends. Nairobi resulted in the much-discussed document on *Baptism, Eucharist, and Ministry*, that many saw as a breakthrough on these matters. At Vancouver, the delegates insisted on relating issues of peace and justice, speaking of the "dark shadow" of the most perilous arms race and the most destructive "systems of injustice" the world had ever known. By then, in response to the new openness of the Catholic Church connected with the work of John XXIII and the Second Vatican Council, the World Council had also established fruitful conversations with the Catholic Church, often leading to collaboration in various projects and studies.

At its seventh assembly, held in Canberra, Australia, in 1991, the World Council of Churches turned its attention to ecological matters and the care of creation and to the doctrine of the Holy Spirit, brought to the foreground by the far-reaching charismatic movement. The first of these concerns resulted on a programmatic emphasis on "Justice, Peace, and the Integrity of Creation." The second led to deep divisions, for some—led by the Orthodox—insisted on the role of the church and its tradition as channels of the Spirit, while others claimed that the Spirit was leading the church to unprecedented use and acceptance of the traditional religious views and practices of various ancient cultures.

By its eighth and ninth assemblies, held in Harare in 1998 and in Porto Alegre in 2006, it was clear that the World Council of Churches—and with it many similar organizations in countries such as the United States—was in crisis. While dwindling financial support was part of the crisis, this was only the tip of the iceberg, for many were questioning what they called "the Genevan model" of ecumenism, and sought other means to affirm and develop the unity of the church.

While these events were taking place at the global level, at the regional and national levels there was a similar movement toward Christian unity. This was manifested in regional, national, and local councils of churches, and in the organic unions that many churches sought. Most of these unions, particularly in Europe and the United States, comprised churches of very similar backgrounds and theology; but other areas took the leadership in more daring church unions. In 1925, the United Church of Canada was formed. Through a long series of unions—nineteen in all—that church comprised what had originally been forty different denominations. In 1922, the National Christian Council in China called on the missionaries and sending churches to "remove all obstacles" in the way of organic union. In 1927, the first synod of the Church of Christ in China was called to order. It included Christians of the Reformed tradition, Methodists, Baptists, Congregationalists, and others. During World War II, under pressure from the government, the Church of Christ in Japan—or Kyodan—was founded, with the participation of forty-two denominations. After the war, some of these groups withdrew; but most remained, convinced that obedience to the gospel demanded of them a common witness. In 1947, the Church of South India was founded. This merger was particularly significant, for this was the first time that such a union included Christians who insisted on bishops with apostolic succession—the Anglicans—and others who did not even have bishops. Since that time, there have been hundreds of union conversations throughout the world, and the mergers that have taken place are too numerous to mention. In the United States, the Consultation of Church Union (COCU) proposed to its participating denominations a plan for a "Church of Christ Uniting." Significantly, such unions have proceeded more rapidly in what used to be called "mission territories" than in the older centers of Christendom, thus showing once again that there is a connection between mission and unity.

While all this was taking place, other forms of Christian unity were being explored throughout the world. In some areas, more conservative churches that disagreed with the views and practices of the World Council of Churches and of regional or national councils created their own councils and associations of churches. Most of these followed the conciliar—or "Genevan"— model, although limiting it to those holding more conservative views. By the end of the twentieth century many of them were facing a crisis similar to that of the World Council of Churches and its affiliate ecumenical bodies.

There were many other efforts at expressing Christian unity during the twentieth century. In many cases, a measure of unity was brought about by common concerns cutting across denominational lines—concerns such as ecological responsibility, human sexuality, minority rights, etc. The most successful were those connected with a particular aspect of the traditional mission of the church—feeding the hungry, providing medical services for the poor, evangelism, etc. A good example of this form of ecumenism is the Lausanne Covenant. This resulted from the International Conference on World Evangelisation, which gathered in Lausanne in 1974 under the auspices of evangelicals such as the Billy Graham, of the United States, and John Stott, of the United Kingdom, and led to the founding of a Lausanne Committee for World Evangelization, and to affiliate regional bodies in various parts of the world. Significantly, the Lausanne Committee planned to celebrate the Third Congress on World Evangelisation in Cape Town in 2010—at the same place and in the same city where William Carey had hoped to gather a world missionary conference exactly two hundred years earlier—thus signaling once again the connection between unity and mission.

THIRD WORLD AND OTHER
"CONTEXTUAL" THEOLOGIES

While all this was happening, other momentous developments were taking place in the field of theology. Until well into the twentieth century, Christian theology had been dominated by people of white European stock, mostly male, at least middle class—or monastics living in relative ease—and generally residing in Europe or North America. But in the second half of that century, new theological tendencies emerged, and these would have an impact on the fields of theology and biblical hermeneutics throughout the world. The general name often given to these new forms of theology is "contextual theologies." This title is both correct and misleading. These are truly contextual theologies in that they take their own particular contexts very seriously, and seek both to address them and to use them as tools to develop their own understanding of Scripture and of theology. But the name itself is misleading in that it implies that the more traditional theologies are not themselves contextual—that they have somehow been given quite apart from the settings of various theologians, or of their culture, class, gender, and ethnicity. Thus, most "contextual theologians" would agree that their work is indeed contextual, but would insist that the same is true of every theological enterprise and of every interpretation of Scripture.

While agreeing on affirming their own contextuality, these new theologies vary widely according to the various contexts in which they develop and from which they speak. Also, most of these theologies agree that the gospel is a message of liberation—particularly, in each case, a message of liberation for those in their own particular context—and therefore are commonly called *theologies of liberation*. Thus, besides Black theology, which has been mentioned earlier, late in the twentieth century and early in the twenty-first many other theologies of liberation flourished—Latin American, Korean, South African, Feminist. There were also various combinations of these—for instance, black women would call theirs a "womanist theology," while some Latinas in the United States would call theirs *"mujerista theology."*

Since it is impossible to discuss these various theologies—and their complex interaction—in any detail, a quick overview of some of its main examples must suffice. It is in referring to Latin America that the term "liberation theology" is most often used, based on the publication in 1971 of the book *Teología de la liberación: Perspectivas*, by Peruvian Catholic theologian Gustavo Gutiérrez (1928–), followed by the work of others who seek to interpret the gospel as well as Scripture within the context of social and economic oppression—theologians such as Brazilians Ivonne Gebara (Augustinian) and Leonardo Boff (Franciscan), the Uruguayan Juan Luis Segundo (Jesuit), and the Argentinian José Míguez Bonino (Methodist). Many of these theologians make use of a Marxist—some would prefer to say "Marxian," in order to avoid the implication of Communism—analytical method in order to lay bare the degree to which traditional theological and biblical interpretations reflect the often unacknowledged interests of those who write theology and of their social class. Their theology is paralleled by the explosive growth of *Comunidades eclesiales de base*—C.E.B.s or basic ecclesial communities—that gather in small groups in order to discuss both the conditions in which they live and how the gospel and Scripture relate to those conditions. Their method is often characterized by three steps, *ver, juzgar,* and *actuar*—seeing, judging, and acting—which means to begin by describing a situation, then analyze its causes, connections, etc., and finally act on the matter on the basis of the gospel and Christian faith. Since there are tens of thousands of these C.E.B.s throughout the region, they are a source of renewed vitality within Latin American Catholicism. Since much of their leadership is lay, they also help provide some level of community and ministry for believers whose connection with the church has often been tenuous because of the extreme scarcity of priests that has plagued Latin American Catholicism for decades. As for liberation theology itself, twice then Cardinal Ratzinger—later Pope Benedict XVI—issued documents against it, and twice its leading voices declared that such condemnations did not describe them accurately, and therefore did not apply to them. Then, with the fall of the Soviet Union and the ensuing discredit of Marxist Communism, many predicted the decline of this sort of theology. But, more that twenty years after the demise of the Soviet Union, Latin American liberation theology is still strong and even spreading.

Similar theologies have developed elsewhere. In South Korea, under the leadership of Ahn Byungmu and others, *Minjung* theology developed as part of the *Minjung* movement—meaning the people's movement. In South Africa, Allan Boesak, president of the World Alliance of Reformed Churches from 1982 to 1991, developed a theology specifically addressing the issues of apartheid. Elsewhere in Africa, theologians such as Kwame Bediako sought to relate the Christian faith with traditional African culture, often suppressed by earlier preaching. In the United States, James Cone and others developed Black theology, based on the African-American experience of oppression and the hope of total liberation. Within that context, Jacqueline Grant and Delores Williams became known for their womanist theology—theology from the perspective of African-American women—and Ada María Isasi-Díaz for her proposal of a Mujerista theology, from the perspective of Latinas in the United States. Likewise, Virgilio Elizondo employed the image and experience of Galileans in first-century Palestine to interpret the Latino experience in the United States. While many theologians of European extraction, in both Europe and the United States, were extremely critical of such contextual theologies, others—notably German theologian Jürgen Moltmann—supported them and incorporated their insights into their own thought and writings.

MISSION FROM THE ENDS OF THE EARTH

The missionary enterprise has always declared that its purpose is to found indigenous and mature churches in various parts of the world. In Roman Catholic circles, this has traditionally meant the planting of a church with its own hierarchy—and eventually a native one. Among Protestants, the goal has often been expressed in terms of the "three selves": self-government, self-support, and self-propagation. In most of these early formulations, however, it was taken for granted—by both Catholics and Protestants—that Christian theology in general would have little to learn from the younger churches. At most, it was hoped that these various churches would express Western theology in terms of their own cultural setting. But the ecumenical movement, the end of colonialism, and a growing self-assurance on the part of the younger churches have produced unexpected results, for some of those churches are posing questions and offering answers that offer, not a mere adaptation, but a challenge to much of traditional theology. As we have seen when discussing the various contextual theologies that have recently emerged, what makes these theologies different is not only their cultural settings, but also that they take into account the social and economic struggles of the oppressed.

Among Catholics, the most surprising and far-reaching developments were taking place in Latin America. In El Salvador, Archbishop Oscar A. Romero was slain by those who considered him a threat to the established order. In Brazil, Hélder Câmara and Paulo Evaristo Arns led the bishops

Archbishop Oscar A. Romero became a symbol of Christian commitment and pastoral concern for the poor, and his tomb became a place of pilgrimage.

who called for a new order. In Nicaragua, there was a growing confrontation between the Sandinista regime and the episcopacy. In Guatemala and other countries, Catholic lay catechists by the hundreds were killed by those who considered them subversive. In the United States and Europe, some declared that the new theology was anathema, while many theologians and Christian leaders declared that its call for a new look at the radical implications of the gospel was justified.

While all this is taking place, it is also evident that the North is becoming increasingly de-Christianized, while the greatest numeric gains of the

Pope John Paul II's visit to Latin America symbolized the growing importance of that continent, and of other poor areas of the world, to the future of Christianity.

church are taking place in the South. Likewise, churches in the South that have long been considered dormant—including the Catholic Church in Latin America—are registering an unexpected vitality. Therefore, no matter how one reacts to the various emerging theologies of the Third World, it seems likely that the twenty-first century will be marked by a vast missionary enterprise from the South to the North. Thus, the lands that a century before were considered the "ends of the earth" will have an opportunity to witness to the descendants of those who earlier witnessed to them.

38

Epilogue: A Global History

But rereading history means remaking history. It means repairing it from the bottom up. And so it will be a subversive history. . . . What is criminal is not to be subversive . . . but to continue being superversive—bolstering and supporting the prevailing domination. It is in this subversive history that we can have a new faith experience, a new spirituality—a new proclamation of the gospel.

GUSTAVO GUTIÉRREZ

A NEW MAP BEYOND CHRISTENDOM

The vitality of Christianity in Africa, Asia, Latin America, and the islands of the Pacific, and its parallel crisis in the North Atlantic, meant that the map of Christendom which served as the stage for the history of Christianity until the mid-twentieth century is no longer operational in the first decades of the twenty-first. That earlier map was drawn in terms of Christendom, lands in Europe and the Western hemisphere that were traditionally and predominantly Christian, and were then the centers of mission to the rest of the world. By the end of the twentieth century, however, things had changed so radically that the former map had become obsolete. There were now new centers in every continent, resulting in a map of Christianity that, rather than seeing it as having its base in the West, and from there expanding outward, sees Christianity as a polycentric reality, where many areas that had earlier been peripheral have become new centers.

Such changes in the map of Christianity have occurred before. In the late first century, and for another two hundred and fifty years, Christianity, earlier centered in Jerusalem, spread throughout the Roman Empire creating new centers in Antioch, Alexandria, Ephesus, Carthage, and Rome.

At the same time, it was spreading eastward, developing centers in Edessa, Armenia, and India—even though most historians of the church, writing from a Western perspective, often paid little attention to those other areas. Then the Muslim invasions overran many of the older centers of Christianity—Antioch, Alexandria, Carthage—so that Western Europe now became the center of mission as well as of theological activity. In the sixteenth century, missionary activity centered in Spain and Portugal, while theological debate and innovation had their centers in northern Europe. In the nineteenth, with the growth of the British and other European empires, and of North American neocolonialism, the center shifted to the North Atlantic, so that most Protestant missionary work in the rest of the world came from London and New York, and its Catholic counterpart had its base in Paris and Brussels.

What is unprecedented in the changes that took place late in the twentieth century and early in the twenty-first is that the new map of Christianity does not have one center, but many. Financial resources are still concentrated in the North Atlantic, as are educational and other institutions. But theological creativity is no longer limited to that area. What is written in Korea, Peru, or the Philippines is read in the rest of the world, and often is as influential as what is published in New York, London, or San Francisco. The ecumenical movement is no longer limited to the World Council of Churches and its offices in Geneva, but has many counterparts in various regions of the world—some of them related to the World Council, and some not. The international missionary enterprise, which earlier radiated from New York and London, now is a complex network, with missionaries from Korea working in Argentina, the Dominican Republic, and the United States, Peruvians working in Japan, Puerto Ricans in New York, Africans in Ireland and in England, Indians in Sri Lanka and the United States, and so on. Thus, the new map of Christianity is truly a worldwide map, one far beyond the very notion of Christendom on which earlier maps were drawn.

Yet the challenge to our earlier maps is not only geographical and sociopolitical. It is also religious and intellectual. If it is true that there is no longer a Christendom because Christianity has expanded throughout the world, it is also true that there is no longer a Christendom because even in the traditionally Christian lands there are a variety of religions. Some of these are the result of the vast migrations that have characterized the most recent decades. Others are the result of a widespread interest in the occult,

Gnosticism, long presumed dead, is now being hailed as true knowledge, and the occult is often combined with it in a myriad ways that the ancient Gnostics would not have recognized.

and even in religious views—such as Gnosticism—that seemed long dead.

Intellectually, the challenge is equally serious. The demise of colonialism and the resurgence of a variety of cultures and views are among the many factors leading many to proclaim that modernity is a matter of the past, and we are now living in post-modernity. This may be a premature statement, for there are still many signs of the power of modernity. But there is no doubt that many of the certainties of modernity are passing, that for growing numbers of people the world is no longer the closed, mechanistic system of modernity, that we are becoming increasingly aware of the need to define and redefine terms, that various cultural and perspectives that modernity suppressed are once again coming to the surface. This will present Christianity with the opportunity to engage the post-modern world in a new way, but also with the challenge to do so in a way that is faithful to its own nature. In the coming post-modern world, being a Christian and proclaiming the gospel will be both a challenge and an adventure.

THE FUTURE OF SHAPE OF HISTORY

We thus come to the end of our narrative as far as we can carry it—to the present day. It is a complex narrative, with its ups and downs, its times of trial, and its times of glory. But, as every history, it is an unfinished narrative, for we too, with our own confusion, our ups and downs, our times of

This graffito on a wall in Puerto Rico illustrates the degree to which post-modernity challenges earlier definitions. Quite likely both the person who originally wrote "Christ is not religion," and the one who attempted to blot out the "not," are faithful Christians seeking to give witness to their faith.

trial and our times of glory, are now becoming part of the story. But it is not only as the most recent, still unwritten chapter, that we are part of the story. We are also part of it because we are its narrators. It is we who, from our own twenty-first century perspectives, shape and interpret the entire story even as we retell it. And therefore, as we come to the (temporary) end of our narrative, we must ask, what may be some of the ways in which the story as told in the twenty-first century will differ from the story as told earlier? What might emerge as the distinguishing marks of Christian history, when told from the perspective of the end of the twenty-first century?

To this question, my immediate answer is that a twenty-first history of Christianity must be global. We certainly need monographs on the history of specific denominations and movements, as well as on particular areas, and on Christian responses to various challenges and opportunities. But all of these must be part of a global perspective. We can no longer write the history of Christianity as if its culmination were our own particular expression of the faith. We must write in full recognition that our understandings and expressions of Christianity—whatever they may be—are but part of a varied kaleidoscope that includes many lands and cultures, many traditions, many forms of worship, and many theological expressions.

"Global," however, is more than a geographical matter. Our new global narrative must include those who have traditionally been excluded, no matter where they live. The new narrative must be global both in its horizontal, geographic dimension—covering all lands and peoples—and in a vertical, sociological dimension—acknowledging the faith, the lives, and the struggles of those whose story is too often excluded from the wider narrative. This includes women in most parts of the world—and certainly in most branches of the church—the poor, the uneducated, ethnic and cultural minorities, and any others who for whatever reason are considered less worthy of attention.

Finally, the new global narrative of the story of Christianity must be mission-centered. For decades, I have argued that the history of missions should not be a field apart from general church history but must be incorporated into it. There is no reason why the Protestant Reformation of the sixteenth century should be part of "church history," while the work that the Jesuits were performing in India at the same time is considered part of the "history of missions." I remain convinced that we need to combine these two traditionally separate fields; but now I have come to an even broader conclusion that it is time for historians of Christianity to explore the possibility of a narrative, so to speak, not from the center to the periphery but from the periphery to the center. After all, most likely not one book of the New Testament was written in Jerusalem! Christianity, like most living organisms, grows and relates to its environment at the edges, while the edges nurture the center and keep it alive.

This twenty-first century, this age "beyond Christendom," when Christianity no longer has clear centers, offers the opportunity to begin looking at the story of Christianity in a radically new way. How would that history look if we focused on those who heard the message for the first time at any given moment? What attracted or repelled them? How did this shape their own reception and interpretation of the faith? What did an average Roman hear when the gospel was first proclaimed to her? How did this affect the way the message was preached and interpreted? What did the Chinese hear when the Nestorians brought their witness to them? How did this affect the message? How is Muslim criticism of Christianity reflected in the iconoclastic controversy, or in Thomas Aquinas's *Summa contra gentiles*? How did the experience of exile shape Calvin's *Institutes*? What did the Aztec population understand when the first Franciscan missionaries spoke to them? How have women heard a gospel preached mostly by men? All of these are crucial questions that open new vistas to the entire field of church history.

The story is not finished. There is still much to do, much to learn, and much to write! Among the readers of this *Story of Christianity* will there be some who will take up this task? I hope and I pray to the God of all history that it may be so!

Suggested Readings

Sydney E. Ahlstrom. *A Religious History of the American People*. Second edition, David D. Hall, ed. Hew Haven: Yale University Press, 2004.

John Bagnell Bury. *History of the Papacy in the 19th Century: Liberty and Authority in the Roman Catholic Church*. New York: Schocken Books, 1964.

Carlos F. Cardoza-Orlandi and Justo L. González. *A History of the Christian Missionary Movement*. Nashville: Abingdon Press, 2011.

Justo L. González. *The Changing Shape of Church History*. St. Louis: Chalice Press, 2002.

Ondina W. González and Justo L. González. *Christianity in Latin America: A History*. Cambridge: Cambridge University Press, 2008.

August B. Hasler. *How the Pope Became Infallible: Pius IX and the Politics of Persuasion*. Garden City, NY: Doubleday, 1981.

Gerrie ten Har. *How God Became African: African Spirituality and Western Secular Thought*. Philadelphia: University of Pennsylvania Press, 2006.

Alasdair I. C. Heron. *A Century of Protestant Theology*. Philadelphia: Westminster, 1980.

Philip Jenkins. *The Next Christendom: The Coming of Global Christianity*. New York: Oxford University Press, 2002.

Kenneth Scott Latourette. *Christianity in a Revolutionary Age*, vols. 4–5. New York: Harper & Row, 1961–1962.

Stephen Neill, ed. *Twentieth Century Christianity*. London: Collins, 1961.

Mark Noll. *The New Shape of World Christianity: How American Experience Reflects Global Faith*. Downers Grove, IL: InterVarsity Press, 2009.

John O'Malley. *What Happened at Vatican Two*. Cambridge, MA: Harvard University Press, 2008.

Carla Gaudina Pestana. *Protestant Empire: Religion and the Making of the British Atlantic World*. Philadelphia: University of Pennsylvania Press, 2009.

Ruth Rouse and Stephen Neill, eds. *A History of the Ecumenical Movement, 1517–1948*. Philadelphia: Westminster, 1968.

Lamin Sanneh. *Translating the Message*. Maryknoll, NY: Orbis Books, 2008.

L. S. Stavrianos. *Global Rift: The Third World Comes of Age*. New York: William Morrow and Company, 1981.

Notes

CHAPTER 1
1. "Epistle to Laurinus," February 1, 1523.

CHAPTER 2
2. *Opera* 17:580.

CHAPTER 7
3. "Preface to the Commentary on the Psalms," *Opera* 31:22.
4. "Preface to the Commentary on the Psalms," *Opera* 31:26.

CHAPTER 12
5. *Autobiography* 1.10.
6. *Autobiography* 3.22–3.24.
7. *Autobiography* 3.27.

CHAPTER 23
8. *Apology to Tilken,* 2:298.

CHAPTER 24
9. *Selbstzeugnisse* ("Testimonies"), p. 25.
10. *Journal,* February 7, 1736.
11. *Journal,* May 24, 1738.

CHAPTER 26
12. Statistics taken from David K. Barrett et al., eds., *World Christian Encyclopedia* (Oxford: Oxford University Press, 2001), vol. 1, table 1-4.

CHAPTER 27
13. *The Austin Papers,* ed. Eugene C. Barker (Washington, D.C.: Government Printing Office, 1919), 3:345, 347.
14. *Speech of John Quincy Adams, May 25, 1836* (Washington, D.C.: Gales and Seaton, 1838), p. 119.

15. *Memoirs,* quoted in W. S. McFeely, *Grant: A Biography* (New York: Norton, 1981), p. 30.

16. Quoted in Sydney E. Ahlstrom, *A Religious History of the American People,* vol. 2 (Garden City, New York: Doubleday, 1975), p. 327.

CHAPTER 29

17. Simón Bolívar, *Obras completas.* vol. 3 (Havana: Lex, 1950), p. 501.

CHAPTER 31

18. Frederich Schleiermacher, *The Christian Faith* (Edinburgh: T. & T. Clark, 1928), p. 151.

CHAPTER 32

19. Tr. by H. E. Manning, 1871; quoted in Schaff, *The Creeds of Christendom.* vol. 2 (New York: Harper & Brothers, 1878), pp. 270–71.

CHAPTER 36

20. H. Richard Niebuhr, *The Social Sources of Denominationalism.* 1959 reprint (New York: Meridian), p. 21.

21. Niebuhr, *The Social Sources,* p. 275.

22. H. Richard Niebuhr, *The Kingdom of God in America.* (New York: Harper & Brothers, 1937), p. 193.

23. *A Religious History of the American People,* vol. 2 (New York: Doubleday, 1975), p. 451.

24. *A Religious History of the American People,* vol. 2 (New York: Doubleday, 1975), p. 460.

25. James Cone, *A Black Theology of Liberation* (Philadelphia: J. B. Lippincott, 1970), pp. 17–18.

26. Ronald J. Sider, ed. *The Chicago Declaration* (Carol Stream, Illinois: Creation House, 1974), cover and pp. 1–2.

Credits

Page 10 / Courtesy of the author

Page 11 / Courtesy the Museo de la Inquisición y del Congreso, Lima. Photograph by the author

Page 13 / Frontispiece of Galileo's *Dialogo;* Burndy Library

Page 15 / Erasmus, engraving by Dürer; Metropolitan Museum of Art (NY)

Page 20 / Martin Luther, by Lucas Cranach; Nationalmuseum, Stockholm (Sweden)

Page 28 / Courtesy of the JKM Library of the Lutheran School of Theology at Chicago and McCormick Theological Seminary. Photograph by the author

Page 29 / Bildarchiv Foto Marburg

Page 33 / Courtesy of the JKM Library of the Lutheran School of Theology at Chicago and McCormick Theological Seminary. Photograph by the author

Page 39 / Photo by the author

Page 45 / *Augsburg Confession*; Kunststammlungen

Page 46 / German National Tourist Agency, Foto Studio H. Muller

Page 49 / Courtesy of the JKM Library of the Lutheran School of Theology at Chicago and McCormick Theological Seminary. Photograph by the author

Page 56 / Courtesy of the JKM Library of the Lutheran School of Theology at Chicago and McCormick Theological Seminary. Photograph by the author

Page 59 / Ulrich Zwingli; Institut fur Kunstwissenschaft Zürich

Page 63 / Zentralbibliothek Zürich

Page 68 / Swiss National Tourist Office photo

Page 72 / Lancaster Mennonite Historical Society Archives, Lancaster, Pa.

Page 75 / Lancaster Mennonite Historical Society Archives, Lancaster, Pa.

Page 79 / John Calvin; Bibliothèque Publique et Universitaire de Genève

Page 83 / Geneva. Photograph by the author

Page 89 / Henry VIII, Leeds College; National Portrait Gallery

Page 91 / Sir Thomas More, after Holbein; National Portrait Gallery

Page 95 / Mary I, by Master John; National Portrait Gallery

Page 100 / Photograph by the author

Page 109 / Charles V, by Titian, Prado, Madrid; Alinari/Art Resource, NY

Page 118 / William of Orange, by A. Th. Key; Rijksmuseum-Stichting

Page 126 / Catherine de Medici; Bibliothèque Nationale

Page 130 / St. Bartholomew's Massacre 1572. Photograph by the author

Page 133 / Bibliothèque Publique et Universitaire de Genève

Page 136 / Coronation of Queen Isabella; Alcázar de Segovia. Photograph by the author

Page 138 / Courtesy of the JKM Library of the Lutheran School of Theology at Chicago and McCormick Theological Seminary. Photograph by the author

Page 139 / Photograph by the author

Page 141 / Photograph by the author

Page 142 / Photograph by the author

Page 143 / Photograph by the author

Page 145 / Polychromed and gilded wood. Museum Acquisition Fund, Meadows Museum, Meadows School of the Arts, Southern Methodist University. Accession number 87.15.

Page 148 / Council of Trent 1565; Bettmann Archives.

Page 149 / C. Benton Kline, Jr. Special Collections and Archives, John Bulow Campbell Library, Columbia Theological Seminary.

Page 149 / Courtesy of the JKM Library of the Lutheran School of Theology at Chicago and McCormick Theological Seminary. Photograph by the author

Page 152 / Photograph by the author

Page 153 / Courtesy of the Instituto Superior de Estudios Teológicos, Buenos Aires.

Page 164 / Bettmann Archives

Page 175 / Public domain

Page 179 / Defenestration of Prague 1618; Ullstein Bilderdienst

Page 181 / Count Wallenstein; Bettmann Archives

Page 186 / Richelieu; Giraudon/Art Resource, NY

Page 188 / Mazarin; Bettmann Archives

Page 197 / James I; Library of Congress (public domain)

Page 202 / Charles I; National Portrait Gallery

Page 205 / Oliver Cromwell, by R. Walker; National Portrait Gallery

Page 213 / Bibliothèque Nationale

Page 216 / Pascal; Photograph by the author

Page 222 / Melanchthon, by Lucas Cranach; Alinari/Art Resource, NY

Page 227 / Courtesy of the JKM Library of the Lutheran School of Theology at Chicago and McCormick Theological Seminary. Photograph by the author

Page 234 / Westminster Assembly; Photograph by the author

Page 243 / Hume; Photograph by the author

Page 252 / George Fox; Friends Historical Library, London

Page 255 / Library of Congress

Page 265 / John Wesley, by N. Hone; National Portrait Gallery

Page 267 / Reproduced with permission from the Methodist Collections at Drew University

Page 269 / Reproduced with permission from the Methodist Collections at Drew University

Page 270 / Reproduced with permission from the Methodist Collections at Drew University

Page 281 / Library of Congress

Page 290 / Jonathan Edwards; Library of Congress

Page 310 / Los Alamos National Laboratory

Page 315 / Photograph by the author

Page 328 / Library of Congress

Page 335 / Library of Congress (public domain)

Page 336 / Reproduced with permission from the Methodist Collections at Drew University

Page 339 / Reproduced with permission from the Methodist Collections at Drew University

Page 341 / Photograph by the author

Page 345 / Brigham Young; Brigham Young University

Page 354 / Coronation of Napoleon, by David; Cliché des Musées Nationaux—Paris

Page 357 / Bettmann Archive

Page 361 / Shelters for the poor. Engraving by Doré; The British Library

Page 365 / Simón Bolívar; Bettmann Archives

Page 371 / Photograph by the author

Page 381 / World Council of Churches

Page 382 / Courtesy of the Antiochian Orthodox Church of Atlanta; Photograph by the author

Page 391 / Hegel; Bettmann Archives

Page 394 / Kierkegaard; Det Nationalhistoriske Museum på Frederiksborg

Page 404 / Pope Pius IX at the First Vatican Council; Bettmann Archives

Page 406 / Pope Leo XIII; Bettmann Archives

Page 412 / Pius XII with Nazis; Popperfoto

Page 419 / William Carey; The Granger Collection

Page 423 / The Granger Collection

Page 426 / Photograph by Zhao Chengyi. Courtesy of Cheng Rongsheng, Dean, Taiping Heavenly Kingdom Palace, Nanjing

Page 427 / Photograph by Zhao Chengyi. Courtesy of Cheng Rongsheng, Dean, Taiping Heavenly Kingdom Palace, Nanjing

Page 428 / Courtesy of G. Thompson Brown

Page 430 / Monument in Vancouver, B.C. Photograph by the author.

Page 434 / Photograph by the author

Page 444 / Second Vatican Council 1962; Popperfoto

Page 459 / Karl Barth; Religious News Service

Page 464 / Dietrich Bonhoeffer; Religious News Service

Page 469 / Rudolph Bultmann; Religious News Service

Page 475 / United Press International

Page 476 / Brown Brothers

Page 479 / Reinhold Niebuhr; Religious News Service

Page 483 / Billy Graham, photographed by C. Capa; Magnum

Page 485 / Martin Luther King leading a march, U.S. Information Agency (public domain)

Page 499 / Photograph courtesy of G. Thompson Brown

Page 501 / Courtesy of the author

Page 505 / Photograph courtesy of Scott Price

Page 506 / Photograph courtesy of Scott Price

Page 511 / Photograph courtesy of Ida Nogueras Maldonado and Alfredo Maldonado II

Page 516 / World Council of Churches

Page 523 / Archbishop Romero; Wide World Photos

Page 524 / Pope John Paul II in Latin America; National Catholic News Service

Page 527 / Photograph by the author

Page 528 / Photograph by the author

Index

Page numbers of illustrations appear in italics.